ESSENTIALS OF EVANGELICAL THEOLOGY

Volume Two:
Life, Ministry, and Hope

DONALD G. BLOESCH

HarperSanFrancisco
A Division of HarperCollins*Publishers*

To
John R. W. Stott,
a defender of the faith

First HarperCollins paperback edition published 1982.

Library of Congress Cataloging in Publication Date

Bloesch, Donald G., 1928–
    LIFE, MINISTRY, AND HOPE.

(Essentials of evangelical theology ; v. 2)
    Includes bibliographical references and indexes.
    1. Theology, Doctrinal.   2. Evangelicalism.
I. Title.
BR1640.A25B57 vol. 2 [BT75.2] 230s [230] 78–3140
ISBN 0-06-060803-4

---

91 92 93 94 HAD 12 11 10 9 8 7

ACKNOWLEDGMENTS

I wish to acknowledge the substantial help and encouragement of my wife Brenda in the completion of this manuscript. I have also benefited from the helpful comments and criticisms of my colleagues, especially Joseph Mihelic, Virgil Cruz, Ralph Powell, and Thomas McGonigle. Thanks should also be extended to Arthur Holmes of Wheaton College for his valuable suggestions.

I am grateful to the Institute for Advanced Christian Studies for financial support, which has enabled me to visit various libraries and theologians. The views stated in this volume do not necessarily reflect the position of the IFACS board.

Again I wish to thank the Theological Seminary of the University of Dubuque for granting me a sabbatical leave, which has made it possible for me to complete my research and writing for this book.

Finally, I want to express my appreciation to *Spirituality Today* for granting permission for the republication of parts of Chapter V, which appeared in an article of mine in the September, 1978, issue. I also acknowledge the advance publication of Section 2 of Chapter XI in *Theology Today,* January, 1979.

ABBREVIATIONS

Scripture references are from the Revised Standard Version, unless otherwise indicated by the following abbreviations:

New International Version	NIV
King James Version	KJ
New English Bible	NEB
Today's English Version (Good News Bible)	TEV
Living Bible	LB

CONTENTS

PREFACE

While the first volume of *Essentials of Evangelical Theology* concerned the themes of God, authority, and salvation, this second volume focuses on life, ministry, and hope. At the same time in the discussion of evangelical distinctives and strategy in the last two chapters, I shall recapitulate and amplify some points that have been made earlier.

It is my intention in these volumes to reconceive evangelicalism so that it can become an effective force for renewal in the church. Too often in the past evangelicalism has been divisive and has drained needed energy and resources from the established churches. It would nevertheless be unfair to blame all these schisms on evangelicalism, since a protest had to be registered against the drift into a latitudinarianism and modernism that sundered the church from its biblical and historical roots. Moreover, reformers and prophets of an evangelical stripe were not tolerated in many denominations, and the dissidents had to withdraw if they were to maintain their integrity. In this task of reinterpretation I wish, by all means, to avoid a nebulous evangelicalism where the lines between true biblical faith and liberalism are blurred; instead, I seek an evangelicalism that is historically informed and theologically profound.

In a time when Christianity is being translated into social and psychotherapeutic commitment, evangelicalism, with its emphasis on the fundamentals of biblical religion, can help the wider church to recover the vertical dimension of the faith. It can remind the church that any lasting social change is based on interior spiritual transformation and that a new society ultimately rests upon a new humanity.

This book is addressed not only to evangelicals but to all Christians who are seeking to think through their faith in the light of new advances in biblical and theological scholarship as well as in the face of new challenges from a secularized culture. Its intent is to break down the walls that divide Christians from one another on significant doctrinal issues so that the church can give a unified witness to a world that sorely needs to hear and believe the good news of reconciliation and redemption through Jesus Christ.

I make no claim that this is an exhaustive systematic theology, a task that would entail several extensive volumes. My purpose is simply to spell out the core of the historic Christian faith from an evangelical and Reformed perspective. In the last two chapters I shall not only recapitulate previous themes but point directions for the church as it faces an uncertain future. Biblical authority and theological method will again receive attention as I seek to steer evangelicalism on a path that will insure its continuity with the historic church as well as confirm its fidelity to the Scriptures.

Then they said to him, "What must we do, to be doing the works of God?" Jesus answered them, "This is the work of God, that you believe in him whom he has sent."

JOHN 6:28, 29.

If we could have been saved by our works, it would not have been necessary for Christ to die.

ULRICH ZWINGLI

It is a hallmark of the true evangelical religion to emphasize that sin and morality are inward rather than outward . . . that a new birth is indispensable to a new life, and that therefore what pleases God is heart-religion and heart-morality.

JOHN R.W. STOTT

Evangelical theology is at war with all views which graft salvation on to natural goodness or revelation on to natural knowledge, on the grounds that such views fail to grasp both the sinfulness of sin and the graciousness of grace.

JAMES I. PACKER

To me the real distinction is not between high and low, but between religion with a real supernaturalism and salvationism on the one hand, and all watered-down and modernist versions on the other.

C.S. LEWIS

I.
INTRODUCTION

There is a pressing need today for evangelical unity as Christianity faces a world that is steadily becoming more secularized and therefore more hostile to traditional religious values. As we survey the current scene, however, we see a sorely fragmented evangelicalism. Carl Henry has sagaciously observed that we are now entering a new era of evangelical controversy, and this means that we can expect to see further division and polarization.

Evangelicalism, it should be remembered, is wider and deeper than nineteenth-century revivalism. It is even broader than the Reformation, though it was in that period that evangelical distinctives were rediscovered and proclaimed with power and authority. If evangelical fragmentation is to be overcome, we need to recover our historical roots not only in Pietism, Puritanism, and the Reformation but also in the biblical renewal movements prior to the Reformation. Evangelical unity can only be realized if we press for the unity of the whole church under the Word of God, and this means Evangelical-Catholic unity. If we are to break free from provincialism and sectarianism, we need to rediscover the evangelical motifs in the church fathers, including Irenaeus, Augustine, and Ambrose, and also in the doctors of the medieval church, such as Bernard of Clairvaux and Thomas Aquinas.

The present-day controversy in evangelicalism revolves around four issues: biblical authority, eschatology, election and reprobation, and the gifts of the Spirit. All these issues will be addressed in this volume, but particular emphasis will be given to the conflicts concerning baptism and the new birth, the gifts and ministries of the church, the millennial hope, and universal salvation.

Epistemology, too, figures in this controversy, since one's approach to biblical truth is integrally related to one's theory of knowledge. Those who see biblical revelation as basically, if not exclusively, propositional are inclined to be rationalists in their epistemology. Those who understand this revelation as predominantly historical are more likely to embrace an empirical methodology. On the other hand, those who view revelation as the living God in action disclosing himself and the truth of his Gospel through historical events as well as verbal concepts and imagery will stress the priority and supremacy of faith over reason.

The breakdown in biblical authority in the churches today creates both opportunities for evangelicalism and possibilities for new dissension. A critical method that a priori rules out supernatural intervention into human history has served to undermine confidence in the Bible as a document of revelation and must assuredly be rejected by evangelicals. At the same time we must not make the mistake of trying to turn the clock back to an earlier or precritical period in the history of the church, since we are living in a different age and must face the challenges that historical criticism presents to the church.

It is becoming customary in evangelical as well as ecumenical circles to speak of the culturally conditioned garment of faith, and I too occasionally use this language. Yet we must avoid the temptation to drive a wedge between the cultural expression of faith and the prophetic and apostolic witness to Jesus Christ, since we hear this witness only in its cultural form. There are some today, for example, who say that Paul was wrong in his conception of the man–woman relationship; but this kind of exegesis simply will not do, since what Paul says God also says, insofar as his Spirit reveals the full intent of Paul's affirmation. Yet we should also remember that what God says surpasses what Paul says, for Paul (as well as the other biblical authors) only partially grasped the import of the revelation given to him. The Holy Spirit made use of the patriarchal values and imagery of biblical times; but through his appointed witnesses, the prophets and apostles (including Paul), a patriarchal ideology was transcended, while the abiding truth in patriarchalism, the difference between an above and below, came to be seen as a sign of Christ's relationship to his church, a relationship in which Christ's authority is realized in the role of a servant (Eph. 5:21–33).

We need to see that revelation is incarnational, that is, it enters into the relativity and ambiguity of history and thereby has a this-worldly as well as a transcendent locus. We also need to consider that inspiration is organic in that the Holy Spirit makes use of culturally conditioned language and concepts in order to direct people to a supramundane truth and destiny. The Bible is not Spirit-dictated but Spirit-effected and Spirit-filled.

Evangelicals must firmly resist the tendency in neo-orthodoxy to equate revelation with an existential encounter. Revelation entails what God has definitively disclosed in the history of the past as well as what he wishes us to apprehend in the present. Barth's distinction between the event of revelation, which is always new, and the revealedness or inspiredness of the biblical record, which he disclaims, must be treated with a certain degree of reservation, since revelation in the biblical sense has a propositional and a historical pole as well as an experiential pole.

At the same time evangelicals should oppose the concept of verbal revelation, which denies the actual entrance of the Word of God into human history and rests the case for biblical authority on the errorlessness or faultlessness of the Bible's language or mode of expression. I agree with the orthodox theologian Gilbertus Voetius that it is necessary to distinguish between the material or content of Scripture and its external form or special mode of writing.[1] The inerrancy of Scripture pertains to its teaching authority, not to the impeccability of its text or language.[2]

Just as Christ was truly human but without sin, so Scripture is truly human but without error in its matter. But just as Christ entered into our limitations, so the Word of God also entered into the cultural limitations and history of the people of Israel. The analogy of the incarnation must not, of course, be pressed too far when we are dealing with Scriptural authority, since Jesus Christ is himself God, whereas Holy Scripture is the creation and instrument of God.

Likewise, we must oppose the view of faith as an irrational leap in the dark (an idea sometimes entertained in existentialist theology) and the view that identifies it primarily with intellectual assent (as in an orthodoxy gone to seed). Faith is a commitment of the whole person which entails rational understanding. At the same time the object of faith is not directly accessible to human reason, and this means that reason must rise above itself if it is to apprehend the mysteries of God (Calvin).

It can be shown that our position on faith and reason is inextricably tied to our view of biblical authority. If the object of our belief is the objective data recorded in Scripture, then the reason of unregenerated man is quite capable of coming to the truth of God on its own apart from any special illumination of the Spirit. On the other hand, if the focus of our belief is the living Christ and the abiding significance of his life, death, and resurrection, then reason must make way for faith as a special creation of God. The words and concepts in Scripture are the vehicles by which we apprehend the reality and goodness of the infinite God himself and by which we come to know his will and purpose for us. The Bible might be likened to a well that consists in a supply of water (the inner content) and a pump (the outer form).[3] We cannot see the inner content, but we can experience it when we go to the well to satisfy our thirst.

There is a need today for new statements that will bridge the barriers between the various parties in evangelical Christianity as well as the barriers between Evangelicalism and Catholicism. It is not only the doctrine of Scripture that has become a point of dispute but such themes as the new birth, the mission of the church, the immortality of the soul, the millennial hope, and the reality of hell. My intention is to open new ground in the discussion of these and related issues.

Certainly it is also imperative that we take seriously the call to the Christian life so that the boundaries between the church and the world will again become visible. Though our justification is to be attributed to the vicarious, imputed righteousness of Christ, apprehended by faith, our sanctification is inseparable from a life of love and obedience in the midst of the world's anguish. Only a life that is consonant with our doctrine will make the faith credible in the eyes of its cultured despisers. The social impotence of modern evangelicalism is to be traced partly to its overemphasis on polemics and apologetics and its neglect of ethics, particularly in the social or political dimension.

Eschatology could give a biblical rationale for a revolutionary style of life, but too often it is used to reinforce a reactionary social stance. The millennium has become a pretext for social apathy in many circles, whereas rightly conceived it could become a catalyst for social change. The Christian hope has been misunderstood to mean escape from the world (the Marxist opiate of the masses), whereas in its biblical context it should inspire the people of God to battle with the world and triumph over it. The church will regain its social relevance when it recovers an eschatology that gives meaning and direction to the ethical task of the Christian in today's world. Hope and vocation are integrally related, for only those who have hope can overcome and persevere.

At the same time, evangelicals must avoid the misunderstanding common in liberal social gospel circles that the dominion of Christ is extended by social engineering. Progress toward social justice must not be confused with the coming kingdom of God. The kingdom of God is present only where people enter into that higher righteousness, the fellowship of sacrificial love. A degree of social justice can be realized among all peoples because of God's common grace, but the higher righteousness of the kingdom is made possible only by the gift of redemption accomplished by Christ at Calvary and the outpouring of the

Holy Spirit. With the higher righteousness as our norm and goal, we can and should press for an ever greater measure of justice and freedom within our present world order. Yet penultimate hopes of peace, justice, and political emancipation must not be confused with the ultimate hope of the new heaven and new earth for which all creation is now groaning in travail (Rom. 8:22).

NOTES

1. See Heinrich Heppe, *Reformed Dogmatics,* ed. and rev. Ernst Bizer, trans. G.T. Thomson (London: Allen & Unwin, 1950), p. 15.

2. Despite my difficulties with Gerhard Maier, who completely equates the letter of Scripture and revelation, I find myself in agreement with him when he says that infallibility in Scripture "in the sense of authorization and fulfillment by God" must not be confused with "anthropological inerrancy." Gerhard Maier, *The End of the Historical-Critical Method,* trans. Edwin Leverenz and Rudolph Norden (St. Louis: Concordia, 1977), p. 72.

3. In this illustration the pump can also be said to be the external sign, and the supply of water the thing signified. The Bible, like the sacrament, consists in both an external sign and the matter or spiritual reality to which the sign points.

II.
THE NEW BIRTH

Do not marvel that I said to you, "You must be born anew." The wind blows where it wills, and you hear the sound of it, but you do not know whence it comes or whither it goes; so it is with every one who is born of the Spirit.

John 3:7,8

If any one is in Christ, he is a new creation; the old has passed away, behold, the new has come.

2 Corinthians 5:17

If there is one essential issue in our Christendom, it is surely that of the new birth . . . it is the well out of which all good has to come.

Philip Spener

There is a cost involved before one can come to peace with God. The new birth and its process does not happen without much pain.

Philip William Otterbein

In baptism Christianity gives him a name, and he is *de nomine* a Christian; but in the moment of decision he becomes a Christian and gives his name to Christianity.

Søren Kierkegaard

THE MEANING OF REGENERATION

The Scriptures speak not only of justification but also of regeneration. Regeneration is the creation of a new heart within man which entails new goals, new aspirations, new power for service. We read in Ezekiel: "A new heart I will give you, and a new spirit I will put within you; and I will take out of your flesh the heart of stone and give you a heart of flesh" (Ezek. 36:26; cf. Jer. 31:33; Ps. 51:10–12). Paul declares that when we were dead in our sins God made us alive with Christ (Col. 2:13). In his view the man in Christ "is a new creation; the old has passed away, behold, the new has come" (2 Cor. 5:17). In the Fourth Gospel those who become children of God are "born, not of blood nor of the will of the flesh nor of the will of man, but of God" (John 1:13). This same theme is also embodied in 1 Peter: "You have been born

6

anew, not of mortal parentage but of immortal, through the living and enduring word of God" (1:23 NEB).

While justification signifies the imputation of the righteousness of God, regeneration means to be engrafted into this righteousness. Whereas justification consists in the pardon for sin, regeneration refers to the taking away of sins, the interior cleansing of sin (cf. 1 John. 1:9). Salvation includes more than the declaration of pardon: it also involves being made righteous. In regeneration justification is made concrete. Regeneration can in one sense be regarded as the subjective pole of justification. It occurs simultaneously with justification, though the latter has logical priority. Yet while justification is complete, regeneration is incomplete. It must be continued through life, though its commencement signifies a radical and decisive break with the old pattern of life.

Regeneration is also integrally related to conversion. Indeed, conversion is the subjective response to God's decisive intervention in man's life. Conversion signifies man's turning to the way of the cross, but he could not turn unless he had already been inwardly liberated by divine grace. The initiative of God in the act of conversion is poignantly expressed by Isaiah: "I have swept away your transgressions like a cloud, and your sins like mist; return to me, for I have redeemed you" (44:22). In Ezekiel 37 the people of Israel are depicted as a valley of dry bones that cannot be brought to life until God causes his breath to enter them. Before man can obey in faith, he must have been breathed upon or baptized by the Holy Spirit. Even his repentance and obedience testify to the work of the Spirit within him, the grace that is drawing him irresistibly to Jesus Christ. The supernatural basis of conversion is made abundantly clear by Jonathan Edwards: "Conversion is a great and glorious work of God's power, at once changing the heart and infusing life into the dead soul; though that grace that is then implanted does more gradually display itself in some than in others."[1]

In the circles of radical mysticism conversion is understood as a turning from the manifold to the essential, from the world of the temporal to the Eternal. But in biblical faith and piety conversion means turning from the way of sin to the way of righteousness. It issues in service to the world, not in withdrawal from the world.

Conversion entails not only a turning to Christ (epistrephō) but also repentance (metanoeō). Repentance consists in the renunciation of sin and the commitment to lead a new and better life. It means not a certain discontent with oneself but brokenness of heart. It involves not merely feeling sorry for oneself but forsaking sin. It implies not simply coming to Jesus but casting oneself on the mercy of Christ.

Regeneration and conversion signify the coming to faith. Indeed, no one can be born again unless he believes, and if he believes, he is indisputably born again. As the apostle declares: "Everyone who believes that Jesus is the Christ is born of God. . . ." (1 John. 5:1 NIV; cf. John. 1:12, 13). Melanchthon and many who followed him separated the act of faith from regeneration by the Spirit. Against this view we contend that the new birth is simply another way of describing the awakening to faith. The new birth is not fulfilled apart from the decision of faith. This means that faith itself is instilled by the Holy Spirit, that faith itself is a manifestation of the work of the Spirit within. Calvin wisely observed: "Faith cannot apprehend Christ for righteousness without the Spirit of sanctification."[2]

It is perhaps allowable to distinguish between the Spirit as agent and as gift (as we find in some contemporary Lutheran theologians).[3] In this perspective faith becomes the means by which we receive the gift of the Spirit, though the Spirit is the agent by which faith is created. There is some biblical basis for this distinction (cf. Acts 2:38; 5:32; 11:17; Gal. 3:2–5),[4] but if pressed too far it can give rise to a serious misunderstanding. Faith is not simply the receptacle of the Spirit but a living union with Christ created by the Spirit (as Luther was fond of saying). The bestowal of the Spirit is equivalent to being united with Christ in faith. We do not first have faith and then the Spirit makes his abode within our hearts; the very entry of the Spirit into our lives gives rise to faith. Faith is the response created by the Spirit as well as a means by which the Spirit becomes resident in our lives. We were made alive while we were dead through our trespasses and sins (Eph. 2:1), and this means that the grace of regeneration is definitely prior to faith,[5] though this grace does not become a permanent indwelling reality in our lives except through our faith.

Regeneration does not consist in the alteration of the old nature but in the impartation of a new nature. In the traditional Catholic view grace builds upon nature, but in Evangelical Protestantism grace transforms nature. The new birth signifies not rehabilitation or reformation but a new being. As Luther phrased it: "The putting on of Christ according to the Gospel, consisteth not in imitation, but in a new birth and a new creation."[6] In the liberal view enunciated by Schleiermacher and Bushnell grace is an awakening and stimulation of our natural powers. In the Catholic perspective grace is an infusion of supernatural power. In the Reformation position grace is the invasion of the Holy Spirit. The key word in both neo-Catholicism and neo-Protestantism is *development.* In Evangelical Christianity the key word is *crisis.* The old man must die. He must be crucified and buried. He cannot evolve into the new.

The Evangelical understanding of regeneration is certainly present in the history of the Catholic church. Tertullian insisted: "A man becomes a Christian, he is not born one." Augustine and Pascal both testified to dramatic experiences of conversion by which their lives were completely altered. In their view conversion is upheaval, reversal, and reorientation.

For Luther and Calvin the new birth was certainly a fundamental doctrine, but it was given peculiar emphasis by the Anabaptists and Pietists. While the Anabaptists conceived of the new birth as a great obligation and task, a decisive commitment to the will and work of God, the Pietists (Spener, Francke, Zinzendorf) understood it more in terms of the peaceful possession and enjoyment of salvation. The Anabaptists stressed bearing the cross in lowly discipleship; the Pietists emphasized believing in the cross of Christ and upholding this cross in our preaching and life.

There was no general consensus among the Pietists on how the new birth comes to man. Spener spoke of a preparation of the heart prior to regeneration, though he allowed that the new birth sometimes occurs suddenly. Francke stressed the struggle for repentance *(Busskampf)* as necessarily preceding the new birth. For Zinzendorf the new birth is an instantaneous gift. They were all agreed, however, that the new birth signifies a radical alteration of man's being and not simply a reformation of his character. Oswald Chambers, a representative of later Pietism, put it this way: "The entrance into the Kingdom is through the panging pains of repentance crashing into a man's respectable goodness."[7]

In the contemporary period Karl Barth has stressed the incongruity between grace and nature and the radicality of the new birth. While maintaining that man's ontological change has already occurred in the life and death of Jesus Christ, he nevertheless affirms that a second ontological change happens in the event of conversion. "When a man becomes a Christian," he declares, "his natural origin in the procreative will of his human father is absolutely superseded and transcended."[8] Indeed, "the man involved in the act of conversion is no longer the old man. He is not even a corrected and revised edition of this man. He is a new man."[9]

On the British scene P. T. Forsyth has emphasized the radical nature of conversion and the new birth. While recognizing that not all

Christians will undergo a crisis experience like that of St. Paul, he nevertheless perceived that such an experience is the paradigm of Christian conversion.[10] Every Christian should be translated from the way of sin to the way of righteousness, though not every one will be conscious of the precise moment that this occurs. "The Kingdom of God," Forsyth contends, "can only come by the Cross, by crisis, by a breach with the natural life, though not a disruption of it."[11] For him regeneration signifies not simply the fulfillment of man's yearnings and strivings but their transformation. The state of grace and of faith is qualitatively different from the state of nature.

THE NEW BIRTH AND EXPERIENCE

The new birth is both an event and an experience, but it is primarily and essentially the former and only secondarily the latter. What is regenerative is the event of the new birth, even though it cannot happen apart from an upwelling of joy and an outpouring of love.

There can be no equivocation concerning the need for an experience of the love of Jesus Christ and the joy and power of his resurrection. Jesus held out this hope to his disciples: "You will be sorrowful, but your sorrow will turn into joy" (John 16:20). The disciples were not imbued with spiritual power and joy until after the resurrection of Christ, when he sent forth his Holy Spirit. St. Paul fully expected that the Christian would experience "joy in the faith" (Phil. 1:25). To belong to the kingdom of God is to experience "righteousness and peace and joy in the Holy Spirit" (Rom. 14:17). Calvin made his position quite clear: "The whole man must be born again if he wishes to enter into the kingdom of God, for in both mind and heart we are entirely alienated from the righteousness of God."[12] In this perspective the whole man includes his feelings as well as his mind and will. "It is not enough to know Christ as crucified and raised up from the dead, unless you experience, also, the fruit of this. . . . Christ therefore is rightly known, when we feel how powerful his death and resurrection are, and how efficacious they are in us."[13] Luther agreed: "No one can correctly understand God or His Word unless he has received such understanding immediately from the Holy Spirit. But no one can receive it from the Holy Spirit without experiencing, proving and feeling it."[14]

The emphasis on a personal experience of Christ's salvation was even more pronounced in the circles of Pietism, Puritanism, and Evangelicalism. Neither Spener nor Zinzendorf could point to the exact time when they were saved (here they differed from Francke and Wesley), but they both stressed the need to experience the joy and peace of Christian salvation, the fruits of the resurrection of Christ. For Zinzendorf faith was basically trust in God as revealed in Christ, but it must be authenticated in personal religious experience.

While one can expect to feel the love and joy of Christ, this feeling should not itself be identified with the new birth. It is a sign and fruit of the new birth, but it is not the event itself. We can and must experience the new birth, but the new birth itself is not the same as the experience. It is not realized apart from experience, but in itself it transcends experience. We here concur with Abraham Kuyper: "The union of believers with the Mediator, of all matters of faith the most tender, is invisible, imperceptible to the senses, and unfathomable; it escapes all inward vision; it refuses to be dissected or to be made objective by any representation. . . ."[15] Paul declared that our new life in Christ is hidden with Christ in God (Col. 3:3). Yet if the root and sap are hidden, the fruit is visible not to the one who himself is born again but to others who see the work of the Holy Spirit in his life.

The new birth is not accompanied by rational guarantees, but there are signs which are persuasive to the eyes of faith. Foremost among these are heartfelt repentance for sins, a sense of the love of God and the assurance of salvation which enables one to give praise and pray to God (Rom. 5:5; 8:14). The new birth is also attested by the exercise of a new power over temptation and a new love for one's neighbor (1 John 3:9–14; 4:7; 5:4). It is the fruits of the Spirit that prove that we have the Spirit (Gal. 5:22, 23; I John 3:7), and the crowning fruit is love.

One cannot be converted apart from conviction of sin and joy in the Spirit, and yet the essence of conversion is not feeling but the forsaking of sin and the practice of the new life. We should heed again these words of Dwight L. Moody: "Repentance is deeper than feeling. It is action. It is turning right about. And God commands all men everywhere to turn."[16] The new birth is not only a spiritual reality but a moral action that gives rise to deeds of loving service.

BAPTISM BY WATER AND THE SPIRIT

The baptism of the Spirit, or the new birth, is integrally related to water baptism, and yet the two are not identical. That there is a very close connection between the two is attested by our Lord: "Truly, truly, I say to you, unless one is born of water and the Spirit, he cannot enter the kingdom of God. That which is born of the flesh is flesh, and that which is born of the Spirit is spirit" (John 3:5,6). In Peter's Pentecost sermon the implication is that the cleansing work of the Spirit is accomplished through repentance and baptism, or at least in conjunction with them (Acts 2:38). Paul proclaimed: "As many of you as were baptized into Christ have put on Christ" (Gal. 3:27; cf. Rom. 6:3, 4; Eph. 5:26). This emphasis is also reflected in Titus 3:5: "He saved us, not because of deeds done by us in righteousness, but in virtue of his own mercy, by the washing of regeneration and renewal in the Holy Spirit." Biblical scholars generally agree that the washing of regeneration refers to the rite of baptism. Similarly, in Hebrews we are enjoined to "draw near with a true heart in full assurance of faith, with our hearts sprinkled clean from an evil conscience and our bodies washed with pure water" (10:22).

In the New Testament the gift of the Spirit does not always occur at the very same time as the rite of baptism. The disciples of Jesus had been baptized, but they did not receive the Spirit into their hearts until Pentecost. On the other hand, Paul's regeneration took place at the time of his baptism (Acts 22:16). The Samaritans in Acts 8 and the Ephesians in Acts 19 had both received baptism by water but had not yet received the Spirit. Apollos in Acts 18:24–25 was in the Spirit and yet had only received the baptism of John.

The overall witness of the New Testament seems to be that baptism by itself is not indispensable for salvation, but baptism joined with repentance and faith becomes the means by which people receive the gift of regeneration. The integral relation of baptism and faith is attested in Acts 2:38 and Colossians 2:12. To be effectual for salvation baptism must be accompanied by faith or else give rise to faith (cf. Heb. 10:22; Col. 2:12; Acts 2:38). Though they had been baptized, the Samaritans in Acts 8 and the Ephesians in Acts 19 had not yet received the Spirit because they still did not possess effectual faith *(pistis)*. They did not have the "full assurance of faith" which distinguishes the truly converted. The Spirit came to them as they were awakened to repentance and faith through the preaching of the Word. The Word of God alone is the indispensable means of salvation, while baptism is a spiritual aid.

In our view baptism is the sign and seal of the new birth. There is only one baptism, and the gift of the Spirit and immersion or sprinkling with water are its two sides. Water baptism is the outward sign; the Spirit is the inward reality. With John Nevin we affirm the reality of baptismal grace but not baptismal regeneration.[17] The Holy Spirit is indeed working upon a person at baptism, even upon an infant, but he does not make his abode within that person until the decision of faith. Our new birth can be said to be initiated at baptism (in the case of infants), but it is not fulfilled until conversion. In the case of adults who are already believers baptism is a confirmation of their conversion. We can say that baptism is not a condition of salvation but a preparation for it in some cases and a certification of it in others.

In the New Testament baptism was a public testimony of faith. It is also a means or instrument by which faith is strengthened and even fulfilled. The inward seal is the Spirit himself (Eph. 1:13; 4:30), which is attested by the rite of baptism, the outward seal.

This brings us to the enigma of infant baptism. Since infants cannot have faith, why then should they be baptized? The New Testament answer is that the promises given to the parents extend to the children (Acts 2:39), and our Lord expressly wished to receive the little children into his presence (Luke 18:16). Moreover, there are grounds for arguing that the practice of infant baptism goes back to the very first century; it is said that whole households were baptized (Acts 16:33; 18:8; 1 Cor. 1:16), though this in itself does not prove the case for infant baptism.[18]

It cannot be denied that infant baptism became a rite of cheap grace very early in the history of the Christian church, and the Reformation did little to correct this abuse. The Pietist movement did not discard the practice of infant baptism but sought to link it with the faith that, it was hoped, would follow. Philip Spener, who adhered to baptismal regeneration, nevertheless contended that, because many fall away from their regeneration, it is necessary that such persons be regenerated anew through personal repentance and faith. August Hermann Francke insisted that the promise of salvation is not connected with baptism alone but with baptism and faith. The Pietists advocated the rite of confirmation as a supplement to baptism to give people an opportunity to confess their faith before the congregation.

We affirm the validity of both infant and believer's baptism but insist that, in both cases, one must not presume that regeneration has indeed taken place. The new birth is an inward reality imperceptible to the senses, but it is not realized apart from personal faith in the living Christ. With Luther we can say that in the sacrament of baptism the treasure of Christ is given to us, but we still need to appropriate or receive it into our hearts. The sacrament may have objective validity, but its benefit extends only to those who repent and believe. In the case of infant baptism one is baptized *toward* faith rather than *into* faith. As John Calvin put it, "children are baptized for future repentance and faith."[19] Again we contend with Luther that baptism is not completed until that which it symbolizes takes place on the last day, namely, perfect regeneration or glorification.

Contrary to the traditional Catholic view we hold that there is no automatic development from baptism into conversion. Sometimes Catholic scholars use the illustration of the oak tree and acorn to clarify their understanding of the relation between baptism and conversion. Conversion is indeed a ripening process but only after the new birth has taken place. Infants cannot be said to be regenerated, for they lack conscious faith in Jesus Christ. At the same time, if they have been baptized, we can say that they are under the claim of divine election and are within the sphere of the kingdom of God.

Again in opposition to what has come to be the recognized Catholic position, we contend that baptism is efficacious not on the basis of the work of the priest or pastor nor on the basis of the rite itself (ex opere operato) but on the basis of its union with the promises of God in Scripture. It is not baptism by itself that results in salvation but baptism joined to the Word of God and to the faith of the recipient.

Our position by no means contradicts the whole of the Catholic tradition, since many of the fathers and doctors of the church stressed the necessity for faith and repentance if baptismal grace is to be effectual. St. Cyril of Jerusalem in his Catechetical Lectures warned that "if you persist in any evil purpose, the water will receive you, but not the Spirit."[20] Symeon held that a baptism without genuine conversion is a baptism only in water. In the view of Catherine of Siena some people have "the form of holy baptism, but none of the light, for they have been deprived of the light by a cloud of sin."[21] There are signs that current Catholic theology is seeking to give greater recognition to the decisive role of faith and repentance in the life of the believer without underrating sacramental objectivity.[22]

Baptism does not need to be repeated, since a person is born again only once. To be sure, the spiritual reality may still need to take place even though one is baptized, but the sign has permanent validity, since it has the blessing of both God and the church. When Catholic religious made their solemn vows this was regarded in Luther's day as a second baptism. Luther vehemently opposed such an understanding, since it detracted from the efficacy and sufficiency of the sacrament of baptism. This practice among Catholic religious was never given dogmatic formulation, but it pointed to the need for a personal profession of faith that would give substance to the rite of infant baptism.

Baptism is a sign of God's efficacious grace poured out for us in Jesus Christ and sealed in our hearts by the Holy Spirit. It is a sign that God elects us before we decide for him, that God's grace is the basis of our decision of faith. This is particularly evident in infant baptism, but believer's baptism too symbolizes this reality. Yet baptism is more than a sign: it is a means by which the Holy Spirit comes to us and works upon and within us. Baptism plays a prominent role in our conversion and is not just a symbol of our conversion. This is because the God of the Bible works in and through human instruments to accomplish his purposes among people.

CONTINUAL CONVERSION

While the new birth happens only once, conversion is a broader term which applies to the whole of the Christian life. Conversion is both an event and a process in that what has been begun must be carried forward and completed. The new birth itself is sometimes depicted in the New Testament as something begun but also continuing insofar as the renovation of human nature must continue (note that the perfect tense is used in 1 Pet. 1:3 and 1:23). Reformed theology has understandably identified the new birth with the first intrusion of God's grace into human life, but we must bear in mind that in the total biblical perspective regeneration indicates something much more than the initial change within man.

The old man was indeed crucified and buried in the decision of faith (Rom. 6), but he reappears like a corpse coming back to life. He was drowned at baptism, but he ever again bobs up to the surface (Luther). Sin is expelled from our lives in the moment of conversion, but it returns whenever we look to ourselves instead of to Christ. This means that our regeneration is both complete and incomplete. When the Holy Spirit comes into our lives, we are cleansed from all sin (1 John. 1:7), but an inclination to sin lingers on, and this is why sin can take root within us once again.

It was a man of God who declared: "Create in me a clean heart, O God, and put a new and right spirit within me. Cast me not away from thy presence, and take not thy holy Spirit from me" (Ps. 51:10–11). This must also be the prayer of the born-again Christian who, though united with Christ, nevertheless falls away from the ground of his being again and again and must therefore be restored to the state of grace.

It is true that Paul announced with confidence: "We know that our old self was crucified with him so that the sinful body might be destroyed, and we might no longer be enslaved to sin. . . . So you also must consider yourselves dead to sin and alive to God in Christ Jesus" (Rom. 6:6, 11). Yet he went on to say: "Let not sin . . . reign in your mortal bodies, to make you obey their passions. Do not yield your members to sin as instruments of wickedness, but yield yourselves to God as men who have been brought from death to life, and your members to God as instruments of righteousness" (Rom. 6:12, 13). Here he recognized that though the Christian is dead to sin in principle and should be in fact, he nevertheless remains vulnerable to temptation and can and does fall into sin ever again. Paul's perception that conversion must continue in the Christian life is even more evident in his admonition to the Christians at Ephesus: "Put off your old nature which belongs to your former manner of life and is corrupt through deceitful lusts, and be renewed in the spirit of your minds, and put on the new nature, created after the likeness of God in true righteousness and holiness" (Eph. 4:22–24; cf. Col. 3:5).

The Reformers were adamant that conversion and regeneration must continue throughout life. In Calvin's view, "It is not enough to have embraced only once the grace of God, unless during the whole course of your life you follow His call."[23] Luther considered the remission of sins a divine work continuing until death:

Forgiveness of sins is not a matter of a passing work or action, but of perpetual duration. For the forgiveness of sins begins in baptism and remains with us all the way to death, until we arise from the dead, and leads us into life eternal. So we live continually under the remission of sins. Christ is truly and constantly the liberator from our sins, is called our Savior, and saves us by taking away our sins. If, however, he saves us always and continually, then we are constantly sinners.[24]

In later evangelical revivalism the event of the new birth was perceived in terms of a climactic transformation, and the subsequent life of the Christian as simply basking in the glory of a past conversion. It was held by some that selfishness and sloth are all consumed and annihilated in the fiery baptism of the Holy Spirit so that a new man emerges without any stain of past sin.

Such naiveté, however, was not characteristic of Jonathan Edwards, who remained faithful to the Reformation in his keen awareness of the struggle and travail in the Christian life. Like the Reformers he acknowledged that we in ourselves are "utterly without any strength or power to help ourselves."[25] Yet when grace comes upon us, we are impelled to turn to a new way of life. But it is not enough to turn to Christ: we must remain in Christ, and this entails a lifelong struggle against sin, death, and the devil. Edwards spoke of a "continued conversion and renovation of nature" in the life of the Christian, but this view was eclipsed in the perfectionism that later came to dominate revivalism.

Kierkegaard too perceived the struggle involved in a life of conversion. Becoming a Christian is not an immediate transformation but a lifelong decision. He in no way denied the reality of the transforming grace that comes into one's life at the moment of conversion, but he recognized that, because evil in the human heart is not wholly extirpated, one must be engaged in a constant battle to subdue it. This gives the initial decision of faith more significance rather than less, since it means embarking on a pilgrimage in which one is arrayed against the forces of evil both within and without. It means breaking with the values of the world and facing perpetual opposition from the world. "Becoming a Christian," Kierkegaard declared, "is then the most fearful decision of a man's life, a struggle through to attain faith against despair and offense. . . ."[26] But then having made the decision, one must continue in trust and obedience. The gate is narrow and the way is hard by which one gets to heaven (Matt. 7:13, 14; cf. Luke 14:27–30). "Conversion is a slow process," he observed. "One has to go back along the same road where one previously went forward."[27]

It is possible to recognize several stages in regeneration. First there is the pre-Christian stage in which one is encountered by the grace of God and thereby awakened to seek for salvation. We are not here affirming a universal prevenient grace: it is redemptive grace itself that arouses man and quickens him, grace that comes to him only through the hearing of the Word. The disciples before Pentecost were in this stage. They had been converted to the way of the cross but not yet to the Gospel of the cross. They had embraced Christ as the Messiah of Israel but not yet as the Savior of the world. They were seeking for salvation, but they were not baptized by the Holy Spirit into the salvation of Christ. The Holy Spirit was with them but not yet in them (John 14:17). Their natural yearnings for God were appealed to and awakened by the Spirit as they heard the preaching of Christ.[28] It might be said that they had the faith of a servant, but not yet the faith of a son (Heb. 3:5,6). John Wesley, before his Aldersgate experience, described himself as "almost a Christian," though he had led a life of exemplary piety. As he confessed, he had repented in a legal sense but not in an evangelical sense. He was pursued by grace but not yet convicted by grace.

The second stage of regeneration is the new birth in the narrow sense. Here the Holy Spirit enters into our lives and makes his dwelling place within us. Now we are convicted of sin and awakened to faith. Now we repent of our sins and acknowledge Christ as Lord and Savior. Now we have the power of godliness and not just the form of godliness (2 Tim. 3:5). Now we taste and live in that forgiveness which is already ours by virtue of our election in Christ. Now we seek the glory of God and not simply the help of God.

On the road to Damascus Paul was confronted by the blinding light of grace, but the new birth did not take place until he received the Spirit at his baptism by Ananias (Acts 9:17, 18). Then he was not only blessed with true faith but empowered to confess his faith before the world.

Regeneration must continue into sanctification, where we take up the cross and follow Christ in costly discipleship. It will entail new decisions, new dedications which confirm and renew our baptismal decision. Having been baptized by the Spirit, we must go on to be filled with the Spirit, and having been filled, we must seek to be more deeply filled. Regeneration culminates in glorification, where we are completely transfigured in the image of Jesus Christ. But glorification does not occur until the resurrection at death, and final glorification does not occur until the final resurrection on the last day.

Both Lutheran and Reformed orthodoxy as well as Pietism and Puritanism affirmed a preparatory stage of conversion before the new birth itself, a period of gestation before the actual delivery. Lutheran orthodoxy was accustomed to speak of two acts of grace. The first act seeks to divert the unconverted man from his state of sin and instill within him a horror and detestation of his past sin. As Heinrich Schmid says:

The second act of divine grace is this, that it drives man, alarmed on account of his sins, to take refuge in the merit of Christ, which covers his sins and is accounted as his merit; so that *conversion,* which commences in *contrition,* is finished in *faith.* The former is produced by the preaching of the Law, the latter by the preaching of the Gospel.[29]

While this point of view has much to commend it, our interpretation is somewhat different. First, we contend that the man who is confronted by divine grace is no longer an unregenerate person but a person who has already tasted the grace of regeneration. He is already under grace, though grace has not yet fully possessed him. This position is in agreement with some of the representatives of Lutheran orthodoxy, but not with Hollazius, for example, who restricts the term *conversion* to the excitation of contrition and the term *regeneration* to the bestowal of faith. Moreover, we maintain that the conviction of sin is the result not of the Law alone but of the Law joined with the Gospel. Indeed, one cannot fully or truly repent of sin until one is awakened to the depth of Christ's love revealed in his suffering and death at Calvary. Both the Law and Gospel are a means of the redemptive grace of God by which he both convicts people of sin and awakens them to faith in Jesus Christ. This same redemptive grace creates within one a desire for salvation so that one is prompted to seek for the mercy of Christ. This very seeking is conditional on the divine calling (cf. Ps. 27:8), since the natural man in and of himself cannot seek for God (Rom. 3:11; Pss. 14:1–3; 53:1–3). The person who seeks for salvation is on the way to conversion, but he is not truly converted until his seeking culminates in repentance and faith. And faith itself is not fulfilled apart from obedience to the commandment of Christ (1 Pet. 1:5–7).

It is possible to speak of a type of faith that is already operative in the early stages of the sinner's salvation, but as Wesley says, it is "a low species of faith, i.e., a supernatural sense of an offended God."[30] It is not yet faith in Christ and his Gospel, which alone is saving faith. The Samaritans in Acts 8 and the Ephesians in Acts 19, it can be argued, had this preliminary or external faith but not yet "the full assurance of faith" which characterizes the truly converted, those whose hearts have been sprinkled clean from an evil conscience (Heb. 10:22). The same can be said for the disciples of Jesus, as has been indicated. True faith is the wellspring of true repentance, but there is no true faith apart from the gift of the indwelling Spirit.

ERRONEOUS INTERPRETATIONS

Erroneous interpretations of the new birth are surprisingly abundant, especially today. On the right there are the dangers of sacramentalism and predestinarianism and on the left, religious enthusiasm and perfectionism.

In the circles of enthusiasm the new birth is frequently reduced to a stereotyped experience, which is considered the hallmark if not the essence of the new birth. In the Halle brand of Pietism this experience was conceived as a struggle toward repentance *(Busskampf)*, in which people were inwardly stricken with sin. Upwelling joy and assurance were regarded as further distinctive signs of the new birth.

Many insist upon a datable, palpable experience of conversion, and it is a fact that a study of the lives of the great saints of the church nearly always reveals some special personal salvific experience. This is true of Paul, Anthony, Augustine, Francis of Assisi, Calvin, Luther, Edwards, Francke, Charles Finney, Moody, Wesley, John of the Cross, and Loyola. Yet not all these experiences necessarily coincided with the moment of translation from the kingdom of darkness to the kingdom of light. In some cases experiences after an initial conversion proved to have greater depth and intensity. Moreover, it can be shown that, in many cases, there was a preparation for the experience as well as a subsequent development of it. Conversion is both sudden and gradual, though the experience itself may often be cataclysmic.

It is also well to recognize that the great saints often warned against placing trust in one's feelings. Feelings can be deceptive, and one must persevere in faith even when there is an absence of joy or rapture in one's life. Hannah Whitall Smith advises:

Pay no regard to your feelings . . . in this matter of oneness with Christ, but see to it that you have the really vital fruits of a oneness in character and walk and mind. Your emotions may be very delightful, or they may be very depressing. In neither case are they any real indications of your spiritual state.[31]

Then there are those who interpret the experience of the new birth as so transforming that the Christian is no longer in the state of nature but wholly in the state of grace. They appeal to passages like 1 John. 3:9: "No one born of God commits sin; for God's nature abides in him, and he cannot sin because he is born of God" (cf. I John. 5:18). While it is true that no one can sin in union with Christ, the irrefutable fact is that time and again we fall away from this union and thereby into sin. We have the power not to sin, but we inevitably, though not necessarily, succumb to the temptation to sin. John himself gives this word of warning: "If we say we have not sinned, we make him a liar, and his word is not in us" (I John: 1:10).

Against the enthusiasm of his day Luther contended that the decisive mark of being a Christian is the consciousness of sin. "No saint," he declared, "regards and confesses himself to be righteous, but he always asks and waits to be justified."[32] This orientation is also reflected in the writings of Pascal, Kierkegaard, Barth, and many others. It is evident, too, in the Baptist missionary Oswald Chambers: "No man knows what sin is until he is born again. . . . The evidence that I am delivered from sin is that I know the real nature of sin in me."[33]

In the Holiness movement emerging in the middle nineteenth century, the doctrine of the second blessing was advanced: it was asserted that a second experience after conversion brings entire sanctification or perfection. The rudiments of this idea are to be found in John Wesley, who clearly distinguished between justification on the one hand, and on the other, perfection in love, which he associated with a second crisis experience. Among those representative of this movement were Charles Finney, Joseph H. Smith, Hannah Whitall Smith, Andrew Murray, Daniel Warner, and Samuel Brengle. Like most spiritual movements this one contains a solid core of truth, namely, that there are blessings of the Spirit beyond conversion and that a relative perfection is attainable in this life. Yet many of the people involved went further, speaking of sinless perfection whereby one was believed to be free from the very taint of sin though not from temptation. It was said that the sanctified Christian is still stained by faults and weaknesses in character, but he is free from actual sin. If sin is conceived as a conscious transgression of a known law of God, as Wesley defined it, then there is some substance to the Holiness allegation. But if sin is thought of as any inclination to evil within man, in the manner of the Reformation, then, of course, no one, not even a sanctified Christian, can be free from sin. Wesley himself never claimed to have achieved entire or total sanctification and maintained that even the perfected Christian is guilty of sins of omission and therefore must continue to pray the Lord's Prayer: "Forgive us our trespasses."

The experience of the second blessing was sometimes called the filling of the Holy Spirit and the baptism with the Holy Spirit, and the door was thereby opened to separating the new birth from the gift of the Spirit. This signified a clear divergence from Wesley, but the idea became ever more prevalent that the new birth is only a condition or preparation for the higher experience in the Christian life, perfection in love or the baptism of the Spirit.

In Pentecostalism, which grew out of the Holiness movement, the second experience was said to be accompanied by the sign of speaking in tongues. Some Pentecostals distinguished three aspects of the Spirit's activity: his regenerating, sanctifying, and energizing work. Beyond Christian perfection is the experience of empowering for public witness, and it is this which is considered the baptism of the Holy Spirit. Most Pentecostals, however, follow the position of the Assemblies of God in equating the second crisis experience with the baptism in the Spirit. Some conceive this experience as a baptism of love and associate it with Christian perfection (as in the Holiness churches);

others see it as one of empowering for service and regard sanctification as progressive (as in the Assemblies of God) rather than instantaneous.

None of these positions is without some biblical support, and it must be remembered that we, too, speak of stages in regeneration. Yet we insist that the baptism of the Spirit must not be distinguished from the new birth. There is one baptism—into the body of Christ (Gal. 3:27; 1 Cor. 12:13), and this baptism signifies the entrance of the Holy Spirit into our lives. To be "baptized with the Holy Spirit" is tantamount to "repentance unto life" (Acts 11:16–18). Yet Spirit-baptism has two sides: regeneration and empowering. The initiation into the Christian community may precede the consecration to his service, though ideally the two go together. Moreover, there is the promise of deeper empowering and further purification, which the New Testament calls being filled with the Spirit (Eph. 5:18). Again, there are anointings and visitations of the Spirit that equip the saints for special ministries. Peter, who had been baptized and filled with the Spirit at Pentecost, received a further visitation of the Spirit (a second blessing?), which enabled him to preach the Gospel to the Gentiles (Acts 10). In Ephesians 1:-16–19. Paul prays that God will grant those who already believe a "Spirit of wisdom and revelation" (cf. Rom. 12:2; 2 Tim. 1:6). This can take the form of a definite experience, though it is always an ongoing process as well.[34]

At the same time, we must not presume that faith needs to be superseded by love; rather, faith needs to be deepened. Faith itself is an empowering; indeed, it is the victory that overcomes the world (1 John 5:4). In the decision of faith we were "washed," "sanctified," and "justified in the name of the Lord Jesus Christ and in the Spirit of our God" (1 Cor. 6:11). Karl Adam has rightly observed: "If it be genuine divine faith, the faith of a Christian is in very truth a 'showing of the spirit and of the power' of the Holy Ghost."[35] We must not strive for a higher salvation beyond faith but seek the renewal of our faith. Indeed, we must return to the wellspring of our faith, our crucifixion and burial with Christ at Calvary, the outward sign of which is Holy Baptism (cf. Rom. 6:3–6; Col. 2:12).

It is a promising ecumenical sign that some Pentecostals and neo-Pentecostals today are reexamining their position and are now giving the new birth more prominence. The view held by some (Derek Prince, Harold Horton) that the Holy Spirit is only *with* the believer in conversion but comes to *abide* within him in Spirit-baptism is increasingly coming under criticism. Arnold Bittlinger sees the Pentecostal experience as a manifestation of the presence of the Spirit who already dwells within the born-again Christian. "We Christians," he declares, "do not look for a special act of receiving the Spirit in 'sealing' or 'Spirit-baptism,' but we know that the Holy Spirit dwells in each Christian and also in each Christian can, and wants to, become manifest."[36]

The tension between Reformation theology and Holiness- Pentecostal theology is similar to that which exists between the former and Christian mysticism. Whereas the Reformed faith stresses the theology of the cross *(theologia crucis)*, the mystics and enthusiasts put the accent on the theology of glory *(theologia gloriae)*. While one tradition concentrates on bearing the cross in lowly discipleship and waiting for the manifestation of glory on the last day, the other contends that we can enter into this glory already, that heaven can be experienced now.[37] There is truth in both sides, since the person of faith can have a foretaste of the glory that is to be revealed (1 Pet. 5:1; cf. 2 Cor. 1:22; 3:18). The Psalmist enjoins us to "taste and see that the Lord is good" (Ps. 34:8). At the same time the experience of glory is only partial, and the life of faith entails waiting and hoping, not a continual basking in this glory. Because the Christian is still a sinner, he must not claim too much and must always look forward to the second coming of Christ (Rom. 8:22, 23). The Holy Spirit indeed now abides within us, but he is not within our control or possession. He directs us to the eschatological day of redemption, which still lies ahead of us.

Karl Barth, who seeks to do justice to both dimensions of salvation —past reconciliation and future redemption, gives this timely warning: "To desire to receive redemption prematurely, to possess it, to feel it, to give it form and actuality in our own experience, leads not merely to unprofitable illusions but to disobedience and rebellion."[38] Barth does not deny that redemption and eternal life are already assured to the Christian: "Grace has already in itself redemption, the life eternal. . . . God *is* already, now and here, all in all to the sinner. But all in *faith*. . . . For redemption in its true, strict sense we *wait*."[39]

While the enthusiasts and mystics are prone to give undue weight to extraordinary experiences of conversion, neo-Protestantism and neo-Catholicism stress the continuity between nature and grace. In this perspective conversion is simply the unfolding of what is already present within the human soul. A universal prevenient grace is affirmed by which one can prepare himself to receive the gift of conversion. In liberal theology it is commonly asserted that one grows into grace or faith instead of making a decisive leap of faith.

According to Horace Bushnell "the child is to grow up a Christian, and never know himself as being otherwise."[40] Though he criticized the humanistic view that growth in Christian character is a "vegetable process," a mere "outward development," Bushnell averred that in families that are united in covenant with Christ, the child is already "regenerate when born."[41] He will grow up into Christianity naturally just as he grows up into citizenship. The child should be conscious of himself as already a Christian, though he will need to struggle against evil as he grows into a mature faith.[42]

In evangelical theology one is neither born a Christian nor grows into Christianity; instead he must be challenged to make a life and death decision. He needs to make a decisive break with the old pattern of living. He must be translated from the kingdom of darkness into the kingdom of light (Col. 1:13). One is not a Christian by nature, but he must be reborn as a Christian through the grace of God.[43]

The divine summons that comes to us is not simply to accept the fact that we have already been accepted into the family of God (as in some neo-Lutheran and Barthian theology). Rather, we are called to lay hold of the outstretched hand of Jesus Christ, to respond to his gracious invitation, and apart from our response we are not included in God's family. Faith is not simply an acknowledgement of God's saving work in Christ: it is the indispensable means by which this saving work is realized in our lives.

In secular-liberation theology, which is now in vogue, we find a blending of liberal and radical motifs. Conversion is seen as involving a decisive break not with man's inherent drive for power but with the conditions that hold people in economic and political bondage. The new birth signifies an initiation into the revolutionary struggle for a new world. Paulo Freire puts it this way: "The real Easter is not commemorative rhetoric. It is praxis; it is historical involvement. . . . I can only experience rebirth at the side of the oppressed by being born again, with them, in the process of liberation."[44] What is disturbing about this point of view is that it locates the misery of man in oppressive conditions in society rather than in the concupiscence within the heart of man and sees a revolution by violence as a way to salvation.

Finally, we need once more to consider the heresy of sacramentalism, where grace is believed to be given automatically even to those who cannot yet make a response in faith. Sacramentalism is to be found not only in Roman Catholicism but also in Eastern Orthodoxy, Anglo-Catholicism and high-church Lutheranism. It is also a conspicuous feature of Mormonism, which teaches that baptism and the laying on of hands are absolutely necessary for justification. The baptism of the dead is practiced in that communion, since even the departed cannot partake of glory unless their sins are cleansed through vicarious baptism.

In the medieval period the sacrament of confirmation received prominent attention. In some circles it was regarded as the fulfillment of baptism, whereby the child was given an opportunity to make a public profession of faith. Baptism was seen as the sacrament of the new birth and confirmation as the sacrament of growth and spiritual maturity. While the remission of sins is conveyed through baptism, the empowering of the Spirit is given through confirmation. In our time Dom Gregory Dix, Anglo-Catholic Benedictine, conceives of confirmation as the seal of the Spirit and baptism as the sign of the remission of sins.[45] Baptism in water is only a preliminary to the baptism of the Spirit given in confirmation. What is disconcerting in this theological tradition is that Calvary is separated from Pentecost, thereby pointing to an affinity with Pentecostalism. We endorse the rite of confirmation not as a sacrament whereby grace is necessarily imparted but as a commissioning service in which one confirms the vows made on his behalf at his baptism.[46] Baptism is the sacrament of both Calvary and Pentecost, though the reality of both these events will be experienced somewhat later in the case of those who are baptized as infants.

Our position is not very far from that of Evangelical Pietism in its earlier phase, where the reality of baptismal grace was affirmed without in any way minimizing the need for a personal profession of faith. Kierkegaard echoed the views of many sensitive souls within the state churches: "If people absolutely insist on infant baptism, then they ought all the more vigorously see to it that rebirth becomes a decisive determinant in becoming a Christian."[47] What Kierkegaard called "the Moment of decision" of course does not happen at confirmation but is presupposed by confirmation. This solitary decision of faith can only be made when the Holy Spirit is poured out on the sinner, and this is not within man's control. The sacrament of baptism proclaims the miracle of conversion, but it does not guarantee it. As our Lord declared: "The wind blows where it wills, and you hear the sound of it, but you do not know whence it comes or whither it goes; so it is with every one who is born of the Spirit" (John 3:8).

Evangelical revivalism protested against both the sacramentalist view, in which one is automatically baptized into the body of Christ, and the Reformed covenant view, in which one is regenerate by virtue of having been born in the covenant community. Yet, especially in its later phases, Evangelicalism also succumbed to the temptation of formalism in its invitational or altar-call, where decisions of faith were called for at the end of a revival service. In early nineteenth-century revivalism on the American frontier this decision involved considerable agonizing and sometimes days of deliberation. The place of decision, the mourner's bench, was regarded as an altar of repentance, and it frequently turned out to be so. When revivalism became more domesticated, the mourner's bench was replaced by a counseling room or simply by the act of going forward and bowing for a moment at the altar. The new birth was reduced to a packaged formula, and what David du Plessis calls "the sovereign unpredictability of the Holy Spirit" was disregarded. Some contemporary evangelists, including Billy Graham, have recognized the dangers of confusing decisions at the altar with the new birth itself. Graham now prefers to speak of public decisions as inquiries rather than conversions.

It is not within man's power, nor even within the power of the church, to bring about the new birth. The church can only proclaim the Word and hope and pray that the Spirit of God, who alone can penetrate the hearts of sinners, will act in his own time and way. Baptism by water is the sacramental sign of the new birth, but baptism itself does not effect the new birth. Like the Word of God itself baptism can be an instrument of the Spirit's redemptive action, but it is not a precondition for this action. The new birth will be accompanied by conviction of sin and assurance of salvation, but these are not absolute guarantees that the new birth has actually occurred, since feelings are not always trustworthy. The new birth may be followed by mystical phenomena, including speaking in tongues, but these, too, cannot be considered rational or even experiential proofs. Our certainty is based not on our feelings or experiences but on the promises of God in Scripture that whoever calls on the name of Christ will be saved (Acts 2:21; 16:31; Mark. 16:16), and whoever repents and believes will indeed receive the Holy Spirit (Acts 2:38). Yet repentance and the obedience of faith are not the presuppositions of the new birth but the evidence and consequence of it.

The new birth signifies the concrete realization of divine predestination in the lives of the saints. This does not mean that we should simply sit back and do nothing. We can earnestly hope and pray for the gift of the Spirit. We can go to the church where the Word is proclaimed, for we have been told that faith comes by hearing (Rom. 10:17). Our obedience before faith remains a dead work of the law unless it is fulfilled in faith (Bonhoeffer). If it is fulfilled in faith, then this is a sign that the Holy Spirit has already been working upon us, that we have already been made beneficiaries of God's special solicitude. God's efficacious grace does not render us powerless but instead empowers us for faith, service, and discipleship under the cross. The new birth means to enter into the full dispensation of Christian freedom, yet freedom, true freedom, needs to be constantly exercised if it is to serve the cause of the kingdom.

NOTES

1. C. C. Goen, ed., *The Works of Jonathan Edwards,* vol. 4 (New Haven: Yale University Press, 1972), p. 177.

2. John Calvin, "Reply to Sadoleto," in *The Protestant Reformation,* ed. Hans J. Hillerbrand (New York: Walker & Co., 1968), p. 163.

3. We here have in mind such respected scholars as Gerhard Krodel and Tormod Engelsviken. Similarly, Edmund Schlink makes the distinction between the Spirit creating faith and the gift of the Spirit in baptism (*The Doctrine of Baptism,* trans. Herbert J. A. Bouman (St. Louis: Concordia, 1969), pp. 71, 77). Also see K. F. Noesgen, *Geschichte der Lehre vom Heligen Geiste* (Gütersloh: Druck und Verlag von C. Bertelsmann, 1899). Noesgen contends that Luther distinguishes between the Spirit as sender or mediator and the gift of the Spirit to our hearts (pp. 137, 138).

4. It should be recognized that in Acts Luke generally sees the gift of the Spirit in terms of charismatic manifestations which accompany or follow faith. Even where the reference is to salvation, the charismatic dimension is very much apparent (as in Ac. 10:44; 8:14–24; 19:1–7).

5. We can affirm with Hollazius: "Regeneration is the action of the Holy Spirit, efficacious and sufficient to produce faith." In Heinrich Schmid, ed., *The Doctrinal Theology of the Evangelical Lutheran Church,* 3rd ed. (Minneapolis: Augsburg, 1961), p. 464.

6. Martin Luther, *A Commentary on St. Paul's Epistle to the Galatians,* ed. Philip Watson (Westwood, N.J.: Fleming H. Revell, 1953), p. 340.

7. Oswald Chambers, *My Utmost for His Highest* (London: Marshall, Morgan & Scott, 1967), p. 342.

8. Karl Barth, *Church Dogmatics,* IV, 4, ed. G. W. Bromiley and T. F. Torrance (Edinburgh: T & T Clark, 1969), p. 9.

9. Barth, *Church Dogmatics,* IV, 2, (Edinburgh: T & T Clark, 1958), p. 563.

10. "Our conversion may be sudden or slow, but its type and idea is given in the swift, sharp, decisive and permanent cases of it represented by St. Paul's." P. T. Forsyth, *The Principle of Authority,* 2nd ed. (London: Independent Press, 1952), p. 65.

11. P. T. Forsyth, *This Life and the Next* (London: Independent Press, 1918), p. 86.

12. Calvin, *The Epistles of Paul the Apostle to the Romans and to the Thessalonians,* 12, 2 ed. David W. Torrance and Thomas F. Torrance, trans. Ross Mackenzie. (Grand Rapids: Eerdmans, 1961), p. 265.

13. John Calvin, *Commentaries on the Epistles of Paul the Apostle to the*

Philippians, Colossians, and Thessalonians, trans. John Pringle (Edinburgh: Calvin Translation Society, 1851), p. 98.

14. Martin Luther, *Luther's Works,* vol. 21, ed. Jaroslav Pelikan (St. Louis: Concordia, 1956), p. 299.

15. Abraham Kuyper, *The Work of the Holy Spirit,* trans. Henri De Vries (Grand Rapids: Eerdmans, 1966), p. 327.

16. Cited in J. F. Findlay, Jr., *Dwight L. Moody: American Evangelist, 1837–1899* (Grand Rapids: Baker Book House Reprint, 1973), p. 240.

17. See James Hastings Nichols, *Romanticism in American Theology* (Chicago: University of Chicago Press, 1961), p. 245.

18. For the debate between Jeremias and Aland on whether infant baptism goes back to the apostolic church see Joachim Jeremias, *Infant Baptism in the First Centuries* (London: SCM Press, 1960); Jeremias, *Baptism: A Further Study in Reply to Kurt Aland,* trans. Dorothea M. Barton (Naperville, Ill.: A. R. Allenson, 1963); and Kurt Aland, *Did the Early Church Baptize Infants?* trans. G. R. Beasley-Murray (London: SCM Press, 1963). Aland argues that the practice of infant baptism emerged around A.D. 200.

19. John Calvin, *Institutes of the Christian Religion* trans, Henry Beveridge Vol. II (Grand Rapids: Eerdmans, 1957) IV, 16, 20, p. 543.

20. *Procatechesis* 4. Cited in Simon Tugwell, *Did You Receive the Spirit?* (New York: Paulist Press, 1973), p. 52.

21. Tugwell, *Did You Receive the Spirit?* p. 52.

22. See Paul C. Empie and William W. Baum, eds., *Lutherans and Catholics in Dialogue,* II (New York: National Lutheran Council, 1966); Hans Küng, *The Church,* trans. Ray Ockenden and Rosaleen Ockenden (N.Y.: Sheed & Ward, 1967), pp. 203–211; Tugwell, *Did You Receive the Spirit?,* pp. 50–58.

23. Calvin, *The Epistles of Paul the Apostle to the Romans and to the Thessalonians,* p. 252.

24. *Luther's Works,* vol. 34, p. 164. Cf.: "As often as a person comes into faith anew, so often Christ is born in him." Luther, *Martin Luthers Werke* (Weimarer Ausgabe, 1883 ff.) (Henceforth known as W.A.) 10, 1, 1, p. 387.

25. Sermon on Romans 5:6. Cited in Carl W. Bogue, *Jonathan Edwards and the Covenant of Grace* (Cherry Hill, N.J.: Mack Publishing Co., 1975), p. 219.

26. Søren Kierkegaard, *Concluding Unscientific Postscript,* trans. David F. Swenson and Walter Lowrie (Princeton, N.J.: Princeton University Press, 1944), p. 333.

27. Søren Kierkegaard, *The Journals of Soren Kierkegaard 1834–1854,* ed. and trans. Alexander Dru (London: Oxford University Press, 1951), p. 28.

28. We can say that the Holy Spirit in this stage assists the will without transforming the will. He augments what is already in nature but does not yet impart a new nature.

This may seem strikingly similar to Jonathan Edwards' position, since he, too, posits a seeking for God prior to the new birth. He, too, makes a place for preparatory grace before conversion. Yet in contradistinction to Edwards we maintain that the person who seeks for God is to be considered not spiritually lost but assuredly on the way to regeneration, even though the Holy Spirit does not yet dwell within him as the abiding principle of the new life. For Edwards our seeking is a recognition that we are now spiritually condemned but that we may be saved if we persist in our seeking. In our view our seeking is a sign that salvation is assured to us, indeed already extended to us. Edwards maintains that our seeking is a natural ability that is simply stimulated by the Spirit. We contend that our seeking for salvation is a potentiality aroused in nature by the special, miraculous work of the Spirit upon nature.

Edwards differentiates between the seeking made possible by common grace and the genuine seeking for Christ that is a product of regeneration. We too acknowledge that the preliminary seeking for the help of God is not yet the seeking of faith, since it is invariably mixed with unworthy motivations, including a desire for our own security and welfare rather than God's glory. At the same time, such seeking is not to be regarded as obnoxious in the eyes of God (as Edwards insinuates), since it is caused by the preliminary work of the Holy Spirit.

For a stimulating discussion of the two kinds of seeking in Edwards see Bogue, *Jonathan Edwards and the Covenant of Grace,* pp. 279–298.

29. Heinrich Schmid, *Doctrinal Theology of the Evangelical Lutheran Church,* p. 460.

30. Albert Outler, ed., *John Wesley* (New York: Oxford University Press, 1964), p. 137.

31. Hannah Whitall Smith, *The Christian's Secret of a Happy Life* (Westwood, N.J.: Fleming H. Revell, 1952), p. 222.

32. Wilhelm Pauck, ed. and trans., *Luther: Lectures on Romans* (Philadelphia: Westminster Press, 1961), p. 113.

33. Oswald Chambers, *My Utmost for His Highest* p. 361.

34. For an illuminating discussion of the work of the Spirit both in and after baptism see Tugwell, *Did You Receive the Spirit?*

35. Karl Adam, *Christ Our Brother,* trans. Dom Justin McCann (New York: Macmillan, 1931), p. 165.

36. Cited in J. Rodman Williams, *The Pentecostal Reality* (Plainfield, N.J.: Logos, 1973), p. 64.

37. A theology of glory is patently reflected in this statement of the nineteenth-century Carmelite mystic, Mary of Jesus: "Spiritual joy is the radiance of love, it is the flower of charity, it is the delight of him who loves and of him who is loved. . . . Joy gives wings to the soul, raising it above the earth, its trials and its sufferings, to soar to God alone." In her *A Carmelite of the Sacred Heart,* trans. M. E. Arendrug (New York: Benziger, 1923), pp. 126, 127.

38. Karl Barth, *Theology and Church,* trans. Louise Pettibone Smith (New York: Harper & Row, 1962), p. 348.

39. *Ibid.*

40. Horace Bushnell, *Christian Nurture,* reprinted. (New Haven: Yale University Press, 1960), p. 4.

41. *Ibid.,* p. 197.

42. This covenantal view is anticipated in Calvin, who regarded children within the covenant as "presumably regenerated." Yet Calvin also made a definite place for personal conversion in the plan of salvation.

43. Bultmann reflects the biblical view when he declares: "For rebirth means . . . something more than an improvement in man; it means that man receives a new *origin,* and this is manifestly something which he cannot give

himself." In Rudolf Bultmann, *The Gospel of John: A Commentary,* trans. G. R. Beasley-Murray, eds., R. W. N. Hoare and J. K. Riches (Philadelphia: Westminster Press, 1971), p. 137.

44. Paulo Freire, "Education, Liberation and the Church." In *A Reader in Political Theology,* ed. Alistair Kee (Philadelphia: Westminster Press, 1974), [pp. 100–106], pp. 101–102

45. Dom Gregory Dix, *The Theology of Confirmation in Relation to Baptism,* 3rd ed. (Plymouth, England: Bowering Press, 1953).

46. See Donald G. Bloesch, *The Reform of the Church* (Grand Rapids: Eerdmans, 1970), pp. 87–95.

47. Howard Hong and Edna H. Hong, eds. and trans., *Søren Kierkegaard's Journals and Papers,* vol. 1 (Bloomington, Ind.: Indiana University Press, 1967), p. 219.

III.
SCRIPTURAL HOLINESS

Strive . . . for the holiness without which no one will see the Lord.
Hebrews 12:14

For God did not call us to be impure, but to live a holy life.
I Thessalonians 4:7 (NIV)

Because they have been called to holiness, the entire life of all
Christians must be an exercise in piety.
John Calvin

Gospel holiness differs greatly from the holiness of man in innocency.
Man had the Holy Ghost then as the Spirit of God but now he must
have it as the Spirit of the Son of God, the Spirit of a Redeemer.
Jonathan Edwards

Repentance is the porch of religion, Faith is the door of religion,
Holiness is religion itself.
John Wesley

We need the work of the Holy Spirit as well as the work of Christ; we
need renewal of the heart as well as the atoning blood; we need to be
sanctified as well as justified.
Bishop J. C. Ryle

Holiness is the architectural plan on which God builds up His living
temple. God has set apart His people from before the foundation of the
world to be His chosen and peculiar inheritance.
Charles H. Spurgeon

THE CALL TO HOLINESS

The call to holiness resounds throughout the Scriptures, and in
every church and theology rooted in the Scriptures. According to the
Bible only God is holy in the full sense of this word. His holiness is his
power, majesty, righteousness, and love. Such holiness has the character of depth and mystery and elicits reverence, awe, and fascination.
While God's holiness is realized in its fullness on the plane of humanity
only in Jesus Christ, all believers participate to some degree in it.

Indeed, God declares his children righteous and holy through faith (Gen. 15:6). To be righteous means to stand in a right relationship with God; to be holy connotes separateness as well as ethical purity. We are made righteous in order to pursue holiness (Col. 1:21, 22). We receive travails and crosses from the hand of God so that we might share in his holiness (Heb. 12:10).

The Scriptures do not teach self-sanctification, but they do depict man as active in realizing the fruits of his sanctification in Christ. The righteousness of faith is based on the substitutionary work of Christ on the cross, but the righteousness of daily living is conditional upon our cooperation with the Holy Spirit.[1] The work of Christ is substitutionary, but the work of the Holy Spirit is not. He engrafts us into the body of Christ so that we might strive for the holiness which Christ exemplifies (Heb. 12:14). It is not enough to believe in the light; we must also walk in the light (1 John. 1:6,7; Eph. 5:8). We are not co-redeemers in procuring the light of salvation, but we are co-workers in manifesting this light. Christian practice is the proof and consequence of authentic discipleship (John 15:8). Though the grace of God is sufficient, it must be given maximum effect by the earnest endeavors of believers. A living faith will give rise to godliness and brotherly love (1 Pet. 1:5–7).

Yet the Scriptures also teach us that the basis of our acceptability before God is not our own holiness but the righteousness of faith in Jesus Christ. The gift of righteousness (Rom. 3:21, 22; 5:17), which is imputed, must not be confounded with the gift of sanctifying love (Rom. 5:5; 6:22; Heb. 6:4, 5), which is imparted. Moreover, it is not our own works in and of themselves that deserve a reward after faith. Our works count for nothing unless they are united with the regenerating and purifying work of the Holy Spirit within us. God equips us with all we need for doing his will, but it is he, working in us, who makes our work pleasing in his sight (Heb. 13:21).

The biblical meaning of piety is fear of the Lord. It is deemed one of the seven gifts of the Spirit in traditional Roman Catholic theology (Isa. 11:2). Piety is focusing attention upon God and his self-revelation in Jesus Christ, not upon our own spiritual status or experience. Moses was able to endure because he saw "him who is invisible" (Heb. 11:27). Piety is seeking to know Christ and the power of his resurrection in the hope of attaining the resurrection from the dead (Phil. 3:10–11).

Piety or godliness is a gift from God, but it is also a goal that we should strive to realize. The motivation and power come from the Holy Spirit, but it is up to us to cooperate with the Spirit in bringing this blessing to fruition. "Train yourself in godliness," the apostle advises, "for while bodily training is of some value, godliness is of value in every way, as it holds promise for the present life and also for the life to come. . . . For to this end we toil and strive, because we have our hope set on the living God. . . ." (1 Tim. 4:7–10).

In the patristic period the pursuit of holiness was held in high esteem, but biblical motifs were often subverted by too great an openness to Graeco-Roman philosophy. Christ came to be depicted as a teacher and law-giver, and the Christian faith was regarded in many circles as a new code of ethics. The emphasis of the apologists was on the imitation of Christ as an example and on obedience to Christ as teacher. Christianity was distinguished from pagan religions by its superior standard of moral conduct. For Clement of Alexandria Jesus Christ was a tutor whose aim was to improve the souls of his charges and to train them for a virtuous life. In this theology it is "by learning that people become noble and good." Harnack observed: "It is not Judaeo-Christianity that lies behind the . . . doctrines of the Apologists, but Greek philosophy . . . the Alexandrine-Jewish apologetics," and "the maxims of Jesus."[2]

This is not to discount those among the church fathers who placed the accent on the atoning sacrifice of Christ and salvation by grace (e.g., Athanasius, Irenaeus). Yet even with them the emphasis was not simply on the descent of God to man but on the ascent of man to God. This idea in itself has a biblical basis (cf. 2 Cor. 3:18; 2 Pt. 1:3, 4), but attention came to be focused on the holy life as a means to salvation. Moreover, through the influence of Gnosticism and Platonism it came to be believed that perfect, active holiness is attained by the renunciation of all earthly blessings, even of life itself. In the dualistic asceticism that eventually prevailed one sought to gain release from the body in order to return to the World Soul, or the ground of all being. After the age of the martyrs, anchorites and monks were seen as the new models of holiness. The Christian life was viewed as a preparation for death (Irenaeus). This world was depicted as a vale of tears which had to be endured through patience and resignation. The Platonic Eros came to overshadow the New Testament Agape (particularly in Dionysius). The goal in life was reunion with the Eternal, deification, the perfection and realization of the self in union with God. This was a far cry from the biblical understanding of the Christian life as one of outgoing service to one's neighbor, oblivious of any gain for the self.

In the medieval period a dual standard of morality came to prevail. A distinction was drawn between the active and the contemplative life; the former, oriented about corporeal works of mercy, was believed to be inferior to the latter, where attention was devoted exclusively to the love of God and the beatific vision. The religious life, which connoted separation from the world, was considered more worthy before God than the secular life, life in the world. Whereas the religious were under the counsels of perfection (poverty, celibacy, obedience), ordinary Christians were only under the commandments. Both ways, of course, lead to heaven, but the counsels give a practical assurance of eternal life. Holiness was seen as a higher happiness, and love *(Caritas)* was regarded as self-perfecting, under the influence of the Platonic Eros (see Nygren). While salvation was still thought to be anchored and grounded in the grace of God, the growing consensus was that it could at the same time be earned through works that proceed from faith. Little by little holiness came to be understood as a task rather than a gift. Although both these notions have roots in the Bible, the task of holy living is never regarded as the condition or prerequisite for salvation and justification (as in the later medieval period).

The Reformers of the sixteenth century sharply protested against the works-righteousness that had come to dominate the piety of the cloister. To counteract the view that costly discipleship is intended only for the religious elite, Luther and Calvin sounded the universal call to discipleship. Luther opposed not the pursuit of holiness but the idea that one's own efforts toward holiness merit eternal salvation. He also firmly rejected the notion that holiness is for those who embark on an ostensibly religious life and not for all Christians. He sought to extend rather than restrict the call to holiness: "I hope that by this time almost everybody knows that whoever prides himself on being a Christian must also take pride in being holy and righteous. Since Christendom is holy, a Christian must also be righteous and holy, or he is not a Christian."[3]

While the popular piety of his time understood holiness in quantitative terms, as a matter of greater or lesser degree, Luther viewed the Christian as sinful and righteous at the same time *(simul peccator ac iustus)*. The separation is not between those who are more holy and those who are less holy but between those who trust in Christ for their salvation and those whose confidence lies in their own works and experiences. The Christian is always a sinner because he is never freed from the contagion of sin, though he can withstand and subdue this through repentance and faith. At the same time the Christian is always righteous because he is covered by the righteousness of Christ through faith. Justification is an act whereby God declares the sinner righteous through faith in the perfect righteousness of Christ.

Luther did not deny the regenerating work of the Spirit but insisted that this interior work of purification is a life-long process, completed only at death. The righteousness which justifies us is not this inherent righteousness, which is incomplete, but the alien righteousness of Christ, which is perfect in the eyes of God. Luther expressed the paradox of the Christian's life this way: "He is perfectly whole in hope, while he is in fact a sinner, but he has already begun to be actually righteous, and he always seeks to become more so, always knowing himself to be unrighteous."[4] The Christian is righteous not in fact but in hope. He cannot boast of his own righteousness, since it is always accompanied by the inclination to sin. He is victorious over sin only when he ceases to rely on his own strength and trusts only in the might and power of Christ. "In this trial and struggle," Luther wrote, "the righteous man always resembles more a loser than a victor, for the Lord lets him be tested and assailed to his utmost limits as gold is tested in a furnace."[5]

While the medieval theologians were concerned with an active righteousness, in which man is an active collaborator with the grace of God, Luther's emphasis was on passive righteousness. It is not produced by us but provided for us. It is God-given, not man-made. This is why it is alien to our perception and to our being, though its effects take root within us through faith and hope.

Luther repudiated not good works but works-righteousness. If he emphasized the continuing sinfulness of the Christian, he also sought to hold out the note of victory over sin in the life of the Christian. "Christ did not so die for sinners that we might continue to live in sin. . . . Rather He came to redeem men from sin."[6] Thus "a Christian struggles with sin continually, and yet in his struggle he does not surrender but obtains the victory."[7] The Christian life should be characterized by works of love, but these good works are the sign and fruit of our salvation, not its basis. They show to the world that we are justified, but they do not earn divine justification.

In his later years, because of the controversy in which he was engaged, Luther placed the accent more and more upon extrinsic or forensic justification and sometimes lost sight of its mystical dimension. While he never separated justification and the life of regeneration, he often gave the impression that trust in the holiness of Christ is far more important than the pursuit of holiness in daily living.[8] Though in the biblical perspective this is true, it must not be supposed that the pursuit of holiness is of little importance. Luther sometimes suggested this, but some of his followers went further and actually denigrated the life of holiness.

It remained for Calvin to give due recognition to the pursuit of holiness. Whereas for Luther the dominant motif was the justification of the ungodly, for Calvin the pervading concern was the Christian life. Nonetheless, he too saw forensic justification as the foundation of the holy life, but the purpose and goal of justification is perfection in holiness. Our calling, he declared, "demands purity of life and nothing less; we have been freed from sin to this end, that we may obey righteousness."[9] While Luther frowned upon the cultivation of interior piety, Calvin believed that our entire lives must be an exercise in piety, which he defined as "that reverence joined with love of God which the knowledge of his benefits induces."[10] In addition to upholding Christ as the Savior from sin, Calvin also saw him as a model or example for righteous living.[11] Indeed, "only those can be called disciples of Christ who truly imitate him and are prepared to follow in His footsteps."[12] To follow Christ in discipleship entails self-denial and the willing bearing of the cross. To spurn the call to discipleship and holiness is to render the cross of Christ ineffectual: "Paul not only exhorts us to exhibit an example of Christ's death but declares that there inheres in it an efficacy which ought to be manifest in all Christians, unless they intend to render his death useless and unfruitful."[13]

At the same time, Calvin agreed with Luther that the presence of sin can never be entirely eradicated in the Christian while he is still in mortal flesh. The work of regeneration is effected not in one eventful experience but throughout the life of the Christian. "And indeed, this restoration does not take place in one moment or one day or one year; but through continual and sometimes even slow advances God wipes out in his elect the corruptions of the flesh. . . ."[14]

Even more than Calvin, the Anabaptists stressed the need for holy living, not simply as a fruit and sign of salvation but as a condition for continuing salvation.[15] They accepted justification by grace through faith, but this is not the whole of salvation. We must also go on to sanctification, which entails cross-bearing, mortification of the flesh, and separation from the world. They sought to combine the medieval stress on the holy life with the Reformation emphasis on faith and grace. According to Menno Simons we are not only accounted righteous by faith but "the righteous must live his faith."

In the polemics that followed the Reformation right doctrine came to be viewed as more important than right living, and the call to holiness, which was present in the original Reformation, receded more and more into the background. It remained for the movements of Pietism and Puritanism to recover this dimension of the Christian faith for the mainline churches within Protestantism. The Christian life was seen not simply as a by-product of salvation (as in later Protestant orthodoxy) but as the arena of salvation, the field in which salvation is recovered and renewed. Jonathan Edwards expressed it this way: "Those who fight as those that beat the air, never win the crown of victory . . . the kingdom of heaven is not to be taken but by violence."[16] The notion of the heart-prepared came to dominate in Puritanism, where the Christian was summoned to cooperate with preparatory grace so that he might be ready to receive the work of justification.[17] Yet for many of the Puritans our seeking for salvation is already a sign that we have tasted of the grace of justification, that we are already within the sphere of the kingdom.

In Pietism and Puritanism the holy life was regarded as the inevitable consequence of interior renewal. The Holy Spirit does not simply bring knowledge of what Christ has done but implements and actualizes the work of Christ in the personal history of his people. The revelation in the Bible is not completed in a theological or conceptual system (as in Protestant scholastic orthodoxy) but in the life history of the believer. As Philip Spener phrased it: "It is by no means enough to have knowledge of the Christian faith, for Christianity consists rather of practice."[18] Francke preached that an outwardly honorable walk of life is insufficient: the entire inner man must be renewed in holiness. Good works are not simply a testimony of our salvation but its goal and crown. "Though we are not saved by good works, as procuring causes," declared Walter Marshall, "yet we are saved to good works, as fruits and effects of saving grace."[19]

Whereas the Reformers focused their attention primarily on the glory of God and the advancement of his kingdom in the world, the Pietists were concerned with personal salvation and the demonstration of this salvation in daily living. This is not to deny that they, too, were devoted to the glory of God, but one's own salvation as well as the conversion of souls to Jesus Christ are precisely what gives glory to God. Spener sought to preserve a balance between the goals in life in this way: "Next to God's glory my great object is that God shall save my soul and those whom he has entrusted to me."[20]

An otherworldliness characterized Pietism; this was not, however, the world-denying spirituality of a certain kind of Catholic mysticism but an evangelical spirituality that sought to bring the heavenly vision to bear on practical activities in this world. Asceticism came to be seen not as a means to salvation (as in popular medieval piety) but as a method of service by which the Gospel is carried into the world in both words and deeds. The Puritans encouraged people to distrust the world and to look for true life in spiritual religion. Yet, armored in the righteousness of God, they could then sally forth against the world and bring it into submission to Jesus Christ. Included in the Puritan dream were holy commonwealths in which the Law of God would be brought to bear upon the political and economic life of nations.

Much more than the Reformers the Pietists emphasized the separated life.[21] They saw themselves as a leaven in a hostile and fallen world. The way the world would be changed was through the creation of a new humanity by the grace of the Gospel. The radical Pietists, unlike the Puritans, sought to build not holy commonwealths but eschatological communities, anticipatory signs of the coming kingdom of God.

Both Puritanism and Pietism signify a reaction against a purely external religion. The worship in the Anglican churches in England, as in the state churches of Protestant Europe, had become formalistic. Prayers were recited rather than spoken from the heart. Symbols and ceremonies gradually preempted the preaching of the Word. Creedalism came to be the badge of orthodoxy. Jonathan Edwards protested that outward ethics and mere profession of the creed save no one. Against a barren orthodoxy he stressed the necessity for a living experience of the Word of God. Spener believed that people would not come to a sufficient knowledge of Scripture by what they heard in church. This must be sustained by piety and the continuing study of the Bible in the home.

There was in Pietism, and also in Puritanism, a stress on the optimism of grace over the pessimism of nature (Gordon Rupp). This note finds poignant expression in John Preston: "With every godly man, in every regenerate heart there is a Spring of Grace which works out anything that fouls it."[22] The redeeming work of the Holy Spirit was given virtually as much weight as the reconciling work of Christ on the cross. Christ *in* us *(Christus in nobis)* came to be seen as a necessary complement of Christ *for* us *(Christus pro nobis)*. The focus was no longer on perseverance in faith under the cross but on victory over sin through power from on high. While Luther emphasized the continuing struggle against temptation and unbelief, the Pietists, though allowing for an initial period of struggle *(Busskampf)*, stressed the joys of life and the assurance of God's favor in service to the world.

This same emphasis on the holy life can be detected in the later Evangelicalism of John Wesley and George Whitefield. With the Reformers Wesley maintained that the righteousness of Christ—both his

active and passive righteousness—is the meritorious cause of our justification. Yet he insisted that though this alien righteousness entitles
us to heaven, personal holiness is necessary to qualify us for heaven.
"None shall live with God," he declared, "but he that now *lives to* God;
none shall enjoy the glory of God in heaven but he that bears the image
of God on earth."[23] In Wesley's view personal holiness signifies the
culmination and fruition of faith.

There is no doubt that the spiritual movements of purification subsequent to the Reformation (Pietism, Puritanism, Evangelicalism)
brought new life and vigor to the churches of the Reformation. In one
sense, they signaled the fulfillment of the Reformation, since a reform
in life is just as necessary as a reform in doctrine. At the same time,
the legalism of taboos reappeared in these movements, especially in
their later phases. The good news of God's free grace was frequently
overshadowed by an overriding concern with one's own salvation or
spiritual status.

The bane of legalism and moralism was particularly apparent in
radical Pietism, which stressed the evangelical counsels, that is, nonresistance, not going to law courts, the absolute prohibition of divorce,
and literally giving up the goods of life. Celibacy, too, came to be a
requirement among some of the radical Pietists: here can be mentioned
such religious communities as Ephrata, Bishop Hill, and Harmony.
Johann Beissel, founder of the Ephrata community, taught that marriage represented a fall from grace. In the Amana Society and the
Society of Separatists at Zoar, Ohio, celibacy was for a time deemed
evidence of a higher spiritual state. This code of moralism was not
present in the founders and guiding lights of the Pietist movement,
including Spener, Francke, Wesley, and even Zinzendorf. While recognizing the merit in some of these practices, none of these men saw them
as indicative of deeper sanctification nor as a prerequisite to full salvation.

On the modern scene two theologians who have reaffirmed the biblical call to holiness, but within the context of *sola gratia* are Karl Barth
and Dietrich Bonhoeffer. Bonhoeffer was heavily influenced by Barth,
and his *Nachfolge (The Cost of Discipleship)* was fully endorsed by
Barth. Both these men reflect concerns of German Pietism as well as
the Reformation. Barth has acknowledged his indebtedness to Johann
Christoph Blumhardt and Kierkegaard and has spoken highly of Bengel and Zinzendorf.

Barth vigorously opposed a theology which takes for its point of
departure man's religious experience (as in Schleiermacher), and this

is why he often appears highly critical of an overt concern for personal piety and holiness. At the same time he affirmed the reality of a true piety, a biblical piety that points beyond itself to Jesus Christ. While he was accustomed to speak of both justification and sanctification as realities that have happened to man in Jesus Christ, Barth nevertheless contended that these realities must make contact with the actual ongoing lives of people. Sanctification is something that has happened to man in the cross of Christ, but it must also take place within man by the power of His Spirit. Faith is not only cognitive but creative and regenerative, though the regeneration which the Spirit works within man is necessarily incomplete and partial. Nevertheless, it is possible for the believer to be faithful and obedient to Christ, since his life is now grounded in Christ and directed to him. According to Barth, "man is righteous and holy before God and on the way to eternal life to the degree that he lives *by* the grace of God and therefore *for* the grace of God, for its glorification in his creaturely existence."[24] In and of themselves these works fall dismally short of the perfection that is in Christ, and yet because these works are the product of a living trust in Christ, they are acceptable before God. Barth goes beyond the Reformation in his view that it is possible for the man in Christ to do works that are truly pleasing in the sight of God. He also diverges from Luther and Calvin in maintaining that sin is not a part of, but alien to, the nature of man, and this is especially true for the Christian who is indwelt by the Spirit of God.

Dietrich Bonhoeffer inveighed against what he termed *cheap grace,* which has been the ruin of more Christians than any commandment of works. Cheap grace is the grace that assures the pardon of God without demanding repentance and obedience. It is something guaranteed to man, either through the sacraments or preaching, without sounding the call to discipleship. It is the justification of sin without the justification of the sinner. Costly grace is the grace that cost God the life of his own Son, and it must also cost us our lives, our reputations, our time, as we seek to follow Christ. "When Christ calls a man," Bonhoeffer says, "he bids him come and die. It may be a death like that of the first disciples who had to leave home and work to follow him, or it may be a death like Luther's, who had to leave the monastery and go out into the world. But it is the same death every time—death in Jesus Christ, the death of the old man at his call."[25]

Bonhoeffer departs from the Reformation in maintaining that obedience must sometimes precede the gift of faith. He acknowledges, however, that such obedience is a dead work of the law unless it is fulfilled in a commitment of faith to Jesus Christ. Bonhoeffer sees the relation of faith and obedience in terms of a paradox: only he who is obedient can believe, and only he who believes can be obedient.

According to Bonhoeffer the Reformers were mistaken in viewing the salt in Matthew 5:13 as the Gospel.[26] The disciples themselves must be salt and light. They are called not only to uphold the Gospel before the world but to manifest the truth of the Gospel in their lives. The law of Christ must be not only taught but *done,* for "otherwise it is no better than the old law." The righteousness of Christ is not only a righteousness of faith; it must also be put into practice.

At the same time, Bonhoeffer is adamant that all the credit and glory for the practice of Christian righteousness must be given to God himself:

All our good works are the works of God himself, the works for which he has prepared us beforehand. Good works then are ordained for the sake of salvation, but they are in the end those which God himself works within us. They are his gift, but it is *our* task to walk in them at every moment of our lives, knowing all the time that any good works of our own could never help us to abide before the judgment of God.[27]

Even in his *Letters and Papers from Prison* Bonhoeffer maintains his intense concern for the practical demonstration of the Christian faith in daily life.[28] His preoccupation now, however, is not simply with individual holiness but with social holiness. The Christian is summoned to strive and suffer "for the sake of justice, truth, and humanity." The ground of our faith is the reconciliation that God has worked for us in Christ, but the goal of our faith is the humanization of a world that has been bedeviled by a cultural and religious heritage that has crippled rather than supported man.

JUSTIFICATION AND SANCTIFICATION

The call to holiness in the biblical sense cannot be adequately understood apart from an examination of the relation between justification and sanctification. *Justification (dikaiosune)* in the New Testament has primarily the forensic meaning of being accounted righteous before the divine tribunal. *Sanctification (hagiasmos)* means to be engrafted into the righteousness of God. Justification is imputed righteousness, whereas sanctification is imparted righteousness. In justification the guilt of sin is removed and in sanctification the stain of sin. Justification makes man acceptable to God; sanctification makes God desirable to man. Justification confers a new status whereas sanctification instills in man a new character. As justification is related to faith, so sanctification is related to love. Justification has logical priority over sanctification, since man is justified while he is still in his sins (Rom. 5:6–8). But sanctification is the invariable corollary of justification, just as love is the necessary concomitant of faith. He who is forgiven much (justification) will love much (sanctification) (Luke 7:40–47).

Paul Tillich is helpful in the distinctions that he makes between justification, regeneration, and sanctification.[29] Justification is acceptance of the New Being; regeneration is participation in the New Being; sanctification is transformation by the New Being. On the human plane regeneration has priority over justification, since no one can accept the message without participating in the power of the message. As a divine act, however, these two facets of salvation are one. Sanctification necessarily follows, and is dependent on, justification and regeneration. Tillich reminds us that the Lutheran emphasis was on justification, whereas the Pietist and Methodist stress has been on regeneration. It is the Spirit who works faith within us, and faith is a creative as well as a cognitive event.

In our view regeneration is, in one sense, the subjective pole of justification insofar as the Holy Spirit as well as the atoning death of Christ plays a role in justification. Regeneration can also properly be considered the beginning of sanctification, which is a lifelong process. Tillich's analysis has much to commend it, but we must insist (and Tillich would agree) that it is not the reality of justification that is dependent on regeneration but rather its efficacy in human life. God's will to justify us is based on the sacrificial life and death of Jesus Christ, not on the actual righteousness which the believer possesses.

The traditional controversy between Reformation Protestantism and Roman Catholicism has revolved about this issue: whether justification is based on an inherent righteousness which the Spirit bestows on man, or whether the latter is the consequence of the former. The Reformers were adamant that justification goes out to the undeserving and that any progress toward holiness is based on God's gratuitous favor toward man. In the Catholic view people are justified only to the degree that they are actually and morally renewed. Justification is virtually absorbed into sanctification so that its forensic dimension is obscured or ignored. The danger in the Reformation position is that justification can be conceived of as exclusively forensic, to the neglect of its mystical and eschatological dimensions. Hans Küng, in his celebrated work *Justification,* accepts the biblical and Reformed distinction between justification and sanctification, though he is emphatic that the two can never be separated.[30]

Both Luther and Calvin affirmed the priority of justification over regeneration and sanctification, but Luther much more than Calvin saw the Christian life as a continual returning to justification (the sign of which is baptism). For Luther sanctification is not so much an increase in empirical piety as a continual taking refuge in Christ's righteousness. Progress in sanctification is a constant repetition of the beginning of justification. For Calvin, on the other hand, sanctification is a steady but sure ascent to Christian perfection. Justification is the narrow gate, while sanctification is the straight way. The metaphor that most clearly describes Luther's position is the ship or ark which holds sinners, not righteous people, but which is destined for the city of righteousness. If one falls away from grace, he must return to the ark (baptism). Calvin is more to be associated with the Augustinian and later medieval metaphor of the pilgrim road which begins at a definite point but on which some individual believers can make much more progress than others.

The ascetic dimension of Christian spirituality is considerably more pronounced in Calvinism than in original Lutheranism. It is especially apparent in this remark of Jonathan Edwards: "Without earnestness there is no getting along in that narrow way that leads to life. . . . Without earnest labor, there is no ascending the steep and high hill of Zion. . . . Slothfulness in the service of God . . . is as damning as open rebellion."[31]

This ascetic dimension within Calvinism is again apparent in the way in which Calvin treated the Law of God. Whereas Luther saw the primary purpose of the Law as a mirror to show man his despair, Calvin saw it principally as a guide for Christian living. The Gospel does not so much abrogate the Law (as in Luther) but confirms and fulfills it. The Christian life consists not so much in freedom from the law as in keeping the commandments in the spirit of love.

Though Calvin regarded justification alone as the enduring basis of the Christian life, he strove to preserve a balance between justification and sanctification.[32] His successors were often less zealous in this endeavor, particularly where Pietism came to be dominant.[33] Yet the intent of the mainstream of Reformed theology was to regard both these facets of salvation as of prime importance, as can be seen in Heinrich Heppe's summary of the historic Reformed position:

Man needs this sanctification exactly as he does justification. The elect are called not only to redemption from the curse of sins, but also to the serious purpose of the sanctification of their hearts, since those who have found in Christ the atonement for the guilt of their sins ought also to rise with Christ to a new, holy life.[34]

Among many of the early Puritans humiliation was seen as chronologically prior to both justification and sanctification.[35] Through the preaching of the Law people were convicted of sin and then driven to the cross in repentance and faith. This signifies a partial return to the Catholic view that man's justification is contingent on his cooperation with preparatory grace. Yet the Puritans were adamant that legal repentance, which brings remorse over guilt, is clearly to be distinguished from evangelical repentance, which proceeds from faith, an unmerited gift of God. This view of the heart prepared by prevenient grace coexisted with the older Calvinist view that man is dead in sin until he is awakened and justified by redemptive grace.

In the piety of the Reformation, as well as in certain strands of early Pietism and Puritanism, the Christian life is depicted as a struggle toward righteousness rather than possession of it. While the Pietists and Puritans were generally inclined to stress the "already" over the "not yet," the Reformers placed the emphasis on the latter. Luther maintained that the Christian life is not a matter of being but of becoming. It is not righteousness but justification, not purity but purification, not health but healing. It consists "not in victory, but in the fight . . . not in comprehending, but in stretching forward."[36] Luther's view is reiterated by Bonhoeffer: "The life of faith is nothing if not an unending struggle of the spirit with every available weapon against the flesh."[37]

Calvin, more than Luther, underlined the need for personal sanctification, but he was convinced that sanctification always entails suffering, though the forgiveness of sins takes away its sting. Calvin reminds us that no matter how much the Christian is tormented by unbelief, it does not and cannot gain ascendancy: "Unbelief does not hold sway within believers' hearts, but assails them from without. It does not mortally wound them with its weapons, but merely harasses them, or at most so injures them that the wound is curable."[38]

Wesley reflected the emphasis in later Pietism by which sanctification was more and more distinguished and even separated from justification. In his interpretation of I John 1:9 he saw forgiveness as chronologically prior to being cleansed "from all unrighteousness."[39] Calvin, on the other hand, was adamant that justification can no more be separated from sanctification than the heat of the sun can be divorced from its light. Wesley acknowledged that in the moment of justification or conversion our sanctification begins, but then he posited a second work of grace, entire sanctification, which he described as "complete salvation" or "full salvation." This work of grace, like the first, is unmerited, conditional not upon good works but upon faith alone. Yet the Christian can make progress toward it through the power of the Spirit within him. There can be no doubt that Wesley tended to subordinate justification to perfect sanctification, since the latter was seen as a still higher salvation. At the same time he was aware of this peril, urging that when we are about to speak of entire sanctification, "let us first describe the blessings of a justified state as strongly as possible." While Luther placed sanctification under the umbrella of justification, Wesley set sanctification alongside justification. In later revivalism justification was virtually absorbed into sanctification.[40]

Reformed piety has constantly warned of the danger of losing sight of justification as the ground and goal of Christian life. Justification is not mere forgiveness of sins (as in the Arminian view) but the eradication of sin and guilt through faith in Jesus Christ. What has been removed de jure by Christ (justification) must be taken away de facto by the Holy Spirit (sanctification), but the latter is always dependent on the former. In Kuyper's words: "It wounds the very heart of the Reformed confession when the pulpit aims at sanctification without zeal for justification."[41] Berkouwer avers that the "heart of sanctification is the life which feeds on justification." Torrance sees sanctification as the continual unfolding and maintaining of our justification.[42]

Sanctification is to be deemed not a higher stage than justification (as in the Arminian view) but the concrete enactment of justification in our lives. Sanctification signifies the personal or interior appropriation of the fruits of justification. Paul declares: "Those whom he called he also justified; and those whom he justified he also glorified" (Rom. 8:30). Paul does not here expressly mention sanctification, though this concept is implied in verse 29 and also presumably included in glorification in verse 30. The point is that justification reaches all the way from calling and conversion to glorification. Daily we need forgiveness, justification, for a right standing before God. This must be affirmed against all kinds of perfectionism.

The danger on the other side is, of course, giving justification such primacy that sanctification is relegated to the background. This is more evident in the neo-Lutheranism of Nygren, Elert, Prenter, and Jensen than in the neo-Reformed theology of Karl Barth. Prenter sees the Christian life as a circular movement, whereby we begin and end in a state of faith and repentance, rather than as a steady progression toward perfection.[43] Empirical piety is not denied, but it is always subordinated to the alien righteousness of Christ, which alone justifies and sanctifies. He is certainly correct that empirical piety does not pardon or take away sin, but is it not the supreme sign and evidence of our pardon and purification?

There is also a tendency in neo-Lutheran theology to depict man as wholly passive not only in justification but also in sanctification. Jensen declares: "Holiness is either God's work in us or our work for God. It is one or the other."[44] To be sure, we are justified apart from our works (though not apart from the experience of faith), but we are sanctified always through works of love. Sanctification is by grace alone, but this grace moves man toward good works, and it is efficacious only in and through these works. Good works give shape and meaning to man's sanctification.[45] Jensen also insists that sanctification or holiness is alien to man's being. It is certainly alien to the perception of the man of faith, but it is not alien to his being, since it signifies a change or alteration in his being. Indeed, we can even speak of sanctification as an ontological change within man by which he is given new motivations, new hopes, and a new heart.[46]

Finally, it is important to remember that justification and sanctification have both an objective and a subjective pole. The objective pole is Jesus Christ, for he has been made our justification and sanctification (1 Cor. 1:30; cf. Heb. 10:10). The subjective pole is faith (for justification) and love (for sanctification). Karl Barth is noted for his emphasis on the objective reality of both justification and sanctification to the detriment of their subjective realization. He can even say: "Sanctification is entirely God's grace. It is not man's affair, but God's—the affair of the God who works for man in Jesus Christ."[47] This, of course, ignores the divine imperative that we should sanctify and purify ourselves (Lev. 11:44; James 4:8). At the same time, Barth corrects this kind of objectivism by recognizing that man is summoned to works of love which give shape and substance to his sanctification. Robert D. Brinsmead of *Present Truth* magazine also errs in the direction of objectivism when he says: "Justification is an act of God's grace that is wholly outside the experience of the one who believes."[48] This imbalance can be detected in a certain kind of Lutheran orthodoxy which depicts justification as wholly extrinsic and forensic. Justification and sanctification have happened objectively for all people, but they have not yet happened in them or to them. All people are claimed for justification and sanctification, but no one is justified or sanctified in fact until he believes.[49]

CHRISTIAN PERFECTION

Few doctrines have created more divisiveness throughout the history of the church than Christian perfection. Yet it is indisputable that the Scriptures call us not only to seek holiness in our walk of life but also to press on toward the goal of perfect holiness in Christ. The words of our Lord are unmistakably clear: "You, therefore, must be perfect, as your heavenly Father is perfect" (Matt. 5:48; cf. Lev. 20:7, 8). Paul advised that we should "cleanse ourselves from every defilement of body and spirit, and make holiness perfect in the fear of God" (2 Cor. 7:1). His prayer for the Thessalonians was: "May the Lord make you increase and abound in love to one another and to all men . . . so that he may establish your hearts unblamable in holiness before our God and Father, at the coming of our Lord Jesus with all his saints" (1 Thess. 3:12, 13; cf. Eph. 1:4; 1 Cor. 1:8; 2 Cor. 3:9 NIV).

To be sure, Jesus Christ is depicted as having perfected for all time "those who are sanctified" (Heb. 10:14), but it is incumbent on the believer to strive for this perfection in his own life (Heb. 12:14). Holiness is both a gift and a task. It has been accomplished by Christ in his sacrificial work on Calvary, the fruits of which are applied to our lives by the Holy Spirit. At the same time, it is realized through our striving and prayers. Empirical piety, works of love, are a sign and manifestation of holiness but not its essence. The essence of holiness is the love of God poured out upon our hearts. We do not earn or create holiness, but we can and must work toward it.

The righteousness of the Christian is the higher righteousness of self-sacrificing love to those who do us wrong. It means love toward enemies, doing good to those who hate us, blessing those who curse us, and praying for those who abuse us (Luke 6:27, 28). This is the righteousness that will exceed that of the Scribes and Pharisees (Matt. 5:20). It is a spiritual righteousness that supersedes all forms of civil righteousness.

In Catholic theology it was believed possible for Christians to attain this higher perfection, and consequently distinctions came to be drawn between Christians. The "perfect" were those who embraced and fulfilled the evangelical counsels, those who lived lives of exemplary dedication, those whose merits were superabundant. For Bonaventure the culmination of the ascent to perfection consists in "the enjoyment of eternal delights" through mystical rapture.[50] The author of *The Cloud of Unknowing* perceived four levels in the Christian life beginning with the "common" and culminating in the "perfect"; the perfect retire from the world and engage in contemplation. In heretical movements like Gnosticism and Montanism ordinary Christians were called *psychics,* those who still lived by animal standards, while the Spirit-filled, those whose lives were characterized by perfect dedication, were the *pneumatics.* The term *saints* came to denominate those who suffered publicly for the faith or those whose holiness became widely known through extraordinary feats of asceticism.

Happily, there remained within the church enough Christian realism to recognize that remnants of sin persist even in sanctified Christians and that the beatific vision of God cannot be fully realized while we are still in mortal flesh. For Augustine the saints are praiseworthy not because of their sinlessness but because of their poignant awareness of their continuing sin and their striving in hope for a perfection that will become a reality only after death. Bernard of Clairvaux, who sounded the call to sanctity throughout his life, said at his death: "Oh, I have lived damnably and passed my life shamefully."

Against the perfectionism endemic to Catholicism the Reformers contended that the sanctification attainable in this life is only partial and rudimentary. In Luther's words: "Paul also calls Christians righteous, holy, and free from sin, not because they are, but because they have begun to be and should become people of this kind by making constant progress."[51] He depicted the Christian as a convalescent who, if he is in too much of a hurry to get well, "runs the chance of suffering a serious relapse." The whole of the Christian life is a cure from sin; the church is a hospital or nursing home for those who are still sick. Calvin's contention was that Christians are "partly unbelievers," and must therefore constantly "fly to Christ for aid." It follows that "the highest perfection of the godly in this life is an earnest desire to make progress."[52] Nevertheless, Calvin, much more than Luther, upheld the goal of Christian perfection, a goal that could be approximated in the here and now. "Perfection must be the final mark at which we aim, and the goal for which we strive."[53]

Philip Spener did much to bring Christian perfection to the attention of the church once again. He distinguished between "having" and "committing" sin and "keeping" and "fulfilling" the law. We cannot be free from evil desires and thoughts, but we can be free from willful transgressions. For "even if we shall never in this life achieve such a degree of perfection that nothing could or should be added, we are nevertheless under obligation to achieve some degree of perfection."[54]

Francke followed Spener in stressing the need to strive for Christian perfection but at the same time recognizing that one can never be free from sin in this life.[55] For Francke the believer is both perfect and imperfect. He is perfect in Christ, since through faith he is covered by the imputed righteousness of Christ. Yet he remains imperfect in his manner of life constantly falling short of the ideal of perfection embodied in Christ, however much progress he may make toward it by the power of the Spirit.

In Puritanism the reality of the continuing sinfulness of the Christian was duly recognized, though this was counterbalanced by an acknowledgement of the very real work of inward sanctification accomplished by the Holy Spirit. John Bunyan was keenly aware that the saint "when he hath done what he can to bring forth good works by faith, yet he dares not shew these works before God but as they pass through the Mediator Christ, but as they are washed in the blood of the Lamb."[56] J. C. Ryle observed: "The holiest men have many a blemish and defect when weighed in the balance of the sanctuary. Their life is a continual warfare with sin, the world, and the devil; and sometimes you will see them not overcoming, but overcome."[57] Our very repentance, George Whitefield believed, "needeth to be repented of, and our very tears to be washed in the blood of Christ."[58] That nineteenth-century heir of Pietism, Kohlbrügge, agreed that even when we are obedient to God's commandment, we need the cleansing of the blood of Christ.[59] Perfection was held to be a lifelong process not completed until death. In the words of the Shorter Westminster Catechism: "The souls of believers are, at their death, made perfect in holiness, and do immediately pass into glory."[60]

Wesley went further in claiming that Christian perfection, understood as freedom from inward sin, can be attained by any believer through faith in Christ. This is not an absolute perfection, where people are spotless and faultless before the throne of God, but a relative perfection, which reflects the glory and radiant love of Christ and which admits of a greater degree. "Scriptural perfection," he wrote, "is pure love filling the heart and governing all the words and actions." Insofar as he is motivated by pure love, the Christian can be free from the impulsion to sin. Yet because of ignorance he can never be free from sins of omission and therefore must constantly depend upon God for forgiveness. Christian perfection means freedom from sin as a conscious transgression of a known norm but not escape from the error and frailty that are part of the human condition.[61]

The Holiness movement, which was inspired by Wesley, was inclined to minimize or ignore the presence of sin in the life of the sanctified Christian by conceiving of the second blessing as total purification. Some strands within this movement spoke of sinless perfection, though this idea was disputed by many.[62] It followed as a logical corollary from Wesley's contention that all inward sin is eradicated in the gift of entire sanctification. Moreover, Wesley's definition of sin as a conscious act of wrong-doing prepared the way for a surface view of sin which does not consider that sin is essentially a state of being out of which proceed wrong actions. Jonathan Edwards warned of this when he referred to "the labyrinthian depth of self-deception in the human heart." The Holiness movement nonetheless recovered the note of victory in the Christian life and, at its best, recognized that the life of sanctification entails conflict and struggle. The perfected Christian can never be free from trials and temptations, though he is promised the possibility of victory over actual sin. Hannah Whitall Smith reminds us that great temptations are a sign of great grace, not of little grace. J. Sidlow Baxter perceptively observes that the nearer we come to the ideal of perfection, "the less conscious of it we are, and the more humblingly conscious are we of our own *im*perfection."[63]

Kierkegaard, who was also intensely interested in the Christian life, presented a somewhat different picture in his Lutheran emphasis upon the continuing sinfulness of the Christian and the constant need for grace and forgiveness. Christ must be upheld as Model but only because, first of all, he is confessed as Savior: "The true imitation is not produced by preaching on the theme: Thou shalt imitate Christ; but as a result of preaching about how much Christ has done for me. If a man grasps and feels that truly and profoundly then the imitation will follow naturally."[64] As he saw it, "the forgiveness of sins . . . does not mean to become a new man under happier circumstances, but to become a new man in the consoling assurance that the guilt is forgiven, even though the consequences of sin remain."[65] He did not mean that the penalty for sin continues, but that after-effects of sin remain. The Christian is no longer afflicted by the curse of sin, but he continues to be bruised and weakend by sin.

Neo-orthodoxy reclaimed the Reformation emphasis on the helplessness and sinfulness of man, but the summons to Christian perfection was seldom heard. Reinhold Niebuhr referred to love as an "impossible possibility," a transcendent ideal that can only be approximated and partially realized in personal relationships. In affirming that one is "saved in principle, not in fact," he tended to underplay the reality of sanctification. His emphasis was on "a sober and watchful life," not a victorious life.

Karl Barth was much more open to the idea of sanctification and even allowed for the possibility of Christian perfection so long as one would remain totally in Christ. Yet he recognized that sin intrudes ever again into the life of the Christian and that therefore the man of faith, in whom the victory of Christ is only imperfectly reflected, must still struggle against sin. "Good works," Barth declared, "are always works of repentance, works in which our sin is recognized, works in which we pray for the divine mercy, works in which we are helped because they are not the works of self-help, but a sighing—and finally and inwardly a happy sighing—for the help of God."[66]

In presenting our own position we must first point out that there are two kinds of perfection—that of Jesus Christ, which is perfect, and that of the Christian, his own works of love, which is forever imperfect. Yet we can speak of a Christian perfection that is possible for the believer —not an ethical perfection (which Wesley referred to) but a perfection of faith. Christian perfection is an evangelical, not a legal, perfection. Its measure is faith, not any kind of work, and at every stage it remains dependent on the forgiveness of sins. It is a spiritual maturity reflected in increasing dependence on God and on the merits of Jesus Christ (cf. Heb. 5:14; 6:1). "It is," says Forsyth, "a perfection of attitude rather than of achievement, of relation more than of realization, of trust more than of behavior."[67] It is the perfection of a relationship with Christ, not a perfection of conduct or character. Christ will not leave us *to* our sin, but he leaves us *in* our sin so that we might ever more cleave to him in repentance and faith (Forsyth). We have the promise of victory over every particular sin but not of escape from the very presence of sin either outside us or within us. We must repent of our virtues as well as our vices, because sin accompanies every good work, and yet we have the full assurance that the perfect love of Christ covers the multitude of our sins (cf. James 5:20; 1 Pet. 4:8). The hallmark of maturity in Christ is a boldness of faith and a freedom of love which make our very lives a vibrant witness to the love of Jesus Christ. The fullness of perfection ever lies before us (as Wesley also recognized), but even now we can grow up and be mature in Jesus Christ.

As he moves toward an ever greater perfection, however, the Christian is ever more conscious of his imperfection. The fruits of his faith are visible to others but not to himself. In Calvin's view, "the more eminently that any one excels in holiness, the farther he feels himself from perfect righteousness, and the more clearly he perceives that he can trust in nothing but the mercy of God alone."[68] Luther realized that "it profiteth us very much to feel sometimes the wickedness of our nature and corruption of our flesh, that even by this means we may be waked and stirred up to faith and to call upon Christ."[69] Bonhoeffer agreed that "the saints are only conscious of the strife and distress, the weakness and sin in their lives; and the further they advance in holiness, the more they feel they are fighting a losing battle and dying in the flesh."[70] Our assurance is based not on our good works, which are hidden from us, but on the promise of the mercy of Christ.

The Christian life is a movement from faith to faith. Faith cannot be replaced by anything else, even love. Love is the flower of faith, but it is always dependent upon its foundation—trust and confidence in the mercy of Jesus Christ on the cross. The genuine Christian will forever focus his attention not on his own piety or works of love but on God's act of reconciliation and redemption in Jesus Christ. He will be oblivious to his own works even while assiduously serving his neighbor in love. In Luther's words: "He who believes in Christ empties himself and becomes disengaged from his own works, in order that Christ may live and work in him."[71] Pietism and Methodism rightly perceived that there is also a place for examining our lives to see whether we are really doing the will of God. Yet later in these movements attention began to be focused unduly on the self, and one became preoccupied with one's own salvation rather than with serving the glory of God and the cause of his kingdom. Our faith is deepened and strengthened not by continuous introspection but by outgoing service to God and neighbor.

A catholic evangelical theology will seek to learn from all the great spiritual movements of the past, including medieval Catholicism, without succumbing to their pitfalls. There is even a place for the doctrine of the saints in a true evangelical piety. We are thinking here not only of the company of the saints, which is the church triumphant and militant, but of individual saints whose lives noticeably reflect and bear witness to the passion and victory of Christ. Such persons are not necessarily paradigms of virtue but public signs and witnesses of the One who alone is perfectly holy—namely, Jesus Christ. While they are not conscious of their holiness, they may well be poignantly aware that God is working in them and through them to bring others to Christ.[72] They know in their hearts that ever again they fail to live up to God's expectations, but they also know that God will never fail them. They are potent testimonies to the reality of divine sanctification in the lives of his people. Their perfection is one of persevering faith in their Lord and Savior, Jesus Christ, manifested in a life of outgoing love to the poor and despised of this world. Such individuals can be held up in the church as models of holiness, though it must always be pointed out that their holiness is symbolic and derivative, that it has its source and goal in the perfect holiness of Jesus Christ that alone atones for sin.

HOLINESS IN THE WORLD

In contrast to an ethereal mystical spirituality evangelical piety emphasizes a holiness in the world. The world is deemed the theater of God's glory (Calvin), where Christians are to live out their vocations in vicarious identification with the needs of their neighbors. Discipleship is interpreted not in terms of withdrawal into a cloister but of wounded servanthood, bearing the cross in the midst of the agony of the world. Bonhoeffer put it this way:

The antithesis between the world and the Church must be borne out in the world. That was the purpose of the incarnation. That is why Christ died among his enemies. That is the reason and the only reason why the slave must remain a slave and the Christian remain subject to the powers that be.[73]

This evangelical strand was not absent in the tradition of Christian mysticism, but attention was focused more upon the vision of God than service to our neighbor. Gregory the Great contended that the contemplative should regret the necessity of action even when it becomes a matter of duty. Other mystics, however, spoke of a spiritual fecundity whereby one pours out the fruits of his contemplation in love to others. Yet even among these persons the cloister was seen as a surer road to salvation than the active life in the world. Some mystics, under the influence of Quietism, upheld a "holy indifference" over vicarious identification.

In the mysticism of the Eastern religions the call to detachment and withdrawal from the world is even more pronounced. The *Bhagavad Gita* speaks of the world as *maya* (illusion) and *lila* (the play of the gods). But in the Bible the world is real, not an illusion; it is solid, not a jest. It is not abrogated by God but instead is the arena of his action. People are saved not from the world of nature but in it.

Whereas mysticism placed the emphasis on the journey inward, Luther stressed the importance of breaking out of the self into service to others. For the Reformers the road to God is the road to our neighbor's needs. Works of piety must be supplemented by works of mercy, though the latter should always be grounded in the former. Worship without morality is indeed positively displeasing to God.

The need to identify oneself with the suffering and travail in the world is made dramatically clear by Calvin:

Christians certainly ought to display more than a smiling face, a cheerful mood, and polite language when they practise charity. . . . Christians ought to imagine themselves in the place of the person who needs their help, and they ought to sympathize with him as though they themselves were suffering; they ought to show real mercy and humaneness and offer their assistance as readily as if it were for themselves.[74]

Schleiermacher, in his earlier phase, reflects a mystical more than an evangelical spirituality, since he placed the accent on detachment and contemplation. In his *Speeches to the Cultured Despisers of Religion* he contended that a pious person does not theorize or perform but sits quietly in a corner experiencing life in receptive contemplation. The experience of piety is passive, not active. The essence of piety is neither knowing nor doing but feeling. Silence is valued over words and contemplation over action. God-consciousness is contrasted with world-consciousness, which is seen as an impediment to spiritual progress. This orientation is considerably qualified, however, in his *Dogmatics,* where he cautions against withdrawal from the world: "Still less is there room for an arbitrary flight from the sphere of temptation which would be at the same time a flight from the sphere of duty. . . . Fellowship with Him is always a fellowship with His mission to the world, and this such a withdrawal would contradict."[75]

The themes of contemplation, meditation, and silence became prominent again in Pietism and Puritanism. Yet a biblical perspective generally predominated over a Platonic one. Contemplation was reinterpreted to mean living one's whole life toward the love of God. All activities should be performed in a constant awareness of God. Silence was used not to get beyond the Word (as in neo-Platonism) but to prepare oneself for it.

Asceticism, too, came to be appreciated in these movements, but as Troeltsch and Weber have observed, it was an "inner-worldly asceticism." The emphasis was on expanding the kingdom of God in the world rather than calling people out of the world into a purely spiritualized kingdom. Detachment was prized but only for the purpose of greater involvement in the world. An urgency for action distinguished the Puritans. In this spirit John Preston warned: "Cowardliness may lose your souls," for just as "Christ takes notice" if you "suffer for him," so he does if you "decline the cross."[76] In order to lay hold of the assurance of his salvation, one must assent not only to the promise of the Gospel but also to its demands, which may very well entail persecution and imprisonment and even martyrdom. Patience in bearing the cross is not enough: one must cultivate courage and not lose opportunities for doing good through fear or cowardice. The saints can prepare the way for the kingdom of God and must not simply wait in blissful expectation.

Whereas Lutheranism sought to come to terms with the political order in such a way as to preserve freedom of worship, Calvinism laid the foundations for a new political order, one that would be shaped by the law of God revealed in the Bible. Troeltsch trenchantly observed that Calvinism, much more than Lutheranism, was politically creative and therefore also politically subversive. In Lutheranism the intramundane asceticism took the form of a metaphysical depreciation of the sinful world, whereas in Calvinism it took the form of the methodical disciplining of life. Calvinism endorses all legitimate worldly means to produce a holy community, but it reduces these to a means only, having no particular value in themselves. In early Calvinism assurance of election was integral to faith itself, and consequently the believer was freed "to give all his attention to the effort to mould the world and society according to the Will of God."[77] In later Calvinism and Puritanism assurance was seen as conditional on one's obedience to the claims of the Gospel. This vision of a holy community is not to be confused with the eternal kingdom of God; it is best understood as a secular sign of this kingdom. Coercion plays a significant role in such a community because its citizens are still sinners, and their sinfulness must be restrained, if necessary by the sword.

The privatization of religion was singularly absent in both Pietism and Puritanism. More than the Pietists, the Puritans sought to influence the political order directly because of their vision of a holy commonwealth. They rightly perceived that God's Word calls not only for the conversion and nurture of people's souls in the fellowship of the church but also for the creation of a new social order where righteousness reigns.[78]

The vision of a holy commonwealth is in our estimation still viable, though it must be considerably qualified in the light of the pluralistic religious basis of modern industrial nations. The disturbing thing about Watergate was not just the private immorality, which was rightly denounced by the general populace, but the lack of any comparable outcry against the immorality in the wider public realm as practiced in the higher quarters of the government of that time. We are thinking here of the bombing of open villages in Viet Nam, the terminating of welfare aid, and the growing disparity between rich and poor. Yet against the New Left we maintain that only one who holds to absolute standards in private life can also consistently hold to absolute or transcendent norms in public life.

Liberation and political theology today generally stands within the Augustinian and Calvinistic "Christ transforming culture" tradition, though it very easily slides into a "Christ of culture" position, especially where Christianity is virtually equated with democratic socialism. Jürgen Moltmann, who draws upon Pietism as well as the Reformation, is adamant that the Christian faith teaches the need for personal, inward change as well as a change in circumstances and structures. The decision of faith entails a breakthrough into meaning as well as a commitment to social justice. Yet in Moltmann salvation is emptied of its supernatural content and too easily becomes identified with liberation for human dignity and responsibility. In his view the purpose of the incarnation is to enable man to learn to accept and bear his humanity.[79]

Hans Küng in his social-critical theology is more concerned than Moltmann to differentiate the Christian meaning of salvation from political and economic liberation, though he sees the one leading into the other.[80] Redemption, which is liberation by God, sets man free to enter the struggle for emancipation, which is man's self-liberation. At the same time, Küng also conceives salvation primarily as the realization of man's humanity rather than deliverance from the condemnation of hell or transformation into the image of God's glory.

THE LIFE OF PRAYER

While evangelical piety focuses attention on the agonizing needs of the world, it does not lose sight of the truth that all social service must be grounded in a life of prayer. Prayer is the very "soul of faith" (Calvin), and its neglect means the demise of true religion. Joseph Sittler has rightly observed: "Love is the function of faith horizontally just as prayer is the function of faith vertically."[81] Prayer is both a gift and a command: it is a command made possible by an outpouring of divine grace. For John Preston prayer is the "banquet of grace," so it can be said that "a man of much prayer is a man of much grace."[82]

The founders and luminaries of the Reformation as well as of later Evangelicalism were all people of prayer. Luther spent several hours in prayer daily. Philip Spener rose every morning while it was still dark for private prayer and afterward assembled his entire household for morning prayers. John Wesley rose at 4:00 A.M. for several hours of prayer and meditation. The great missionary outreach of evangelical Protestantism in the eighteenth and nineteenth centuries was grounded in the intercessory prayer of very dedicated yet humble people.

Biblical or evangelical prayer, it should be noted, differs from the prayer of primitive religion and even from the prayer of mysticism. Friedrich Heiler, in his monumental work *Prayer: History and Psychology*, compares five different types of prayer in the phenomenology of religion.[83] Primitive prayer is motivated by fear and need and seeks to persuade and even control the divine power or powers for its own purposes. Its goal is the attainment of earthly aims and escape from misfortune. Ritual prayer formalizes the spontaneous petitions in primitive religion, but the magical intent is even more obvious. Vain repetitions and incantations are performed by a priestly caste. Philosophical prayer reduces prayer to resignation or thanksgiving. In mysticism prayer becomes contemplative adoration of the infinite, and petition, if it is allowed at all, is seen as a lower or carnal form of prayer. Prophetic prayer, which Heiler associates with the biblical religions, consists of spontaneous petitions made out of love as well as need and for the purpose of fulfilling God's will in the world. It is the pouring out of the heart before God more than the elevating of the mind to God (as in mysticism).[84] It is based on the presupposition that God is supremely personal and hears and answers petitions made with sincerity of heart, though in his own way and time. Heiler's depiction of prophetic prayer is amazingly close to our own understanding of evangelical prayer.

True prayer is not only resignation and submission but striving with God, pleading with God, seeking to change the ways of God with his people so that his ultimate will might be more surely or fully accomplished. God's ultimate purposes are unchangeable, but his immediate will is flexible and open to change through the prayers of his children. Prayer is "filial reciprocity" (Forsyth), for it entails a dialogic encounter whereby man proposes and God disposes (Prov. 16:1, 33). Such prayer often takes the form of complaint and question (Exod. 5:22, 23; Pss. 44:23, 24; 55:17; Jer. 12:1), since God wants us to understand his decisions, and only by searching and questioning do we understand.

Evangelical prayer is based on the view that a sovereign God can and does make himself dependent on the requests of his children. He chooses to realize his purposes in the world in collaboration with his people. To be sure, God knows our needs before we ask, but he desires that we discuss them with him so that he might work with us as his covenant partners toward their solution. There is, of course, a time to submit as well as a time to strive and wrestle with God in prayer, but this should come always at the end of prayer and never at the beginning. Moreover, our submission is not a passive resignation to fate but a relinquishing of our desires and requests into the hands of a living God to answer as he wills.

While petition is dominant in evangelical prayer and is indeed present to some degree in all prayer which takes its inspiration from the Bible, it must not be regarded as the only mode of prayer. True prayer also takes the form of thanksgiving, confession, and adoration. Forsyth maintained that adoration should be present at both the beginning and culmination of our prayers since, if they remain exclusively petitionary, they become incurably anthropocentric and bereft of reverence to God. On the other hand, the complementary modes of prayer presuppose petition, since we must ask God to accept and crown our sacrifices of praise and thanksgiving and also to hear our confessions. We could not approach the throne of grace apart from faith in the Mediator Jesus Christ who prays for us and in us, and who presents our sacrifices and intercessions to the Father. This is why all Christian prayer should be offered in the name of Jesus.

With the shift in theology to a panentheistic or pantheistic stance, prayer has come to be reinterpreted as soliloquy, reflection on life or meditation on the ground of being. Moltmann contends that one can no longer pray *to* God but only *in* God, that is, in the spirit of God.[85] Schleiermacher, who denied the efficacy of petitionary prayer, believed that prayer should take the form only of gratitude, resignation, or meditation. Tillich sees prayer as an openness to the ground or depth of being rather than a petition to alter the ways of God. In some circles prayer is understood as a consciousness raising experience which brings us into tune with the infinite. In others prayer is reduced to a technique whereby we come to know ourselves in a new way. Or it is a method by which one arrives at inner serenity.

True prayer is neither a magic formula nor a therapeutic technique. Rather it is a dialogic encounter with the living God whose Spirit enables us to pray and who prays for us in groans too deep for words when we cannot adequately verbalize our needs (Rom. 8:23, 26). In prayer we do not so much ascend to God as he descends to us and meets us on our level (cf. Isa. 64:1, 5). In the outpouring of his Spirit we are enabled to give voice to our complaints and trials and seek for his aid and mercy. We do not tap into spiritual power (as today's pop mysticism would have it), but receive power from on high and are therefore enabled to pray from the innermost depths of our being.

Prayer is not so much an address directed to God as a spontaneous outburst of praise and supplication in response to God's gracious outreach to man. Prayer will invariably take the form of structured address and of ritualized formula because man, in his weakness, desires a crutch in his relationship with the divine. But in those moments when he is impelled by the interior movement of the Spirit to cry out to God as a child to his loving father, he transcends the prayer of rote and enters into biblical or prophetic prayer, the conversation of the heart with God.

We do not deny the rightful and necessary place for a structured order of worship when God's people come together to praise God and to hear his Word. Christian prayer is not only private but also corporate, and the latter especially lends itself to set or prescribed forms. Nor do we rule out the possibility that read prayer in a liturgical service, either on the part of the pastor alone or by the congregation, can be genuine prayer if it proceeds from the heart. Yet more often than not in a church where liturgy is emphasized over free prayer the liberating movement of the Spirit is impeded. James Denney, who here reflects the Protestant bias against high churchism, nonetheless gives a timely word of warning: "A liturgy, however beautiful, is a melancholy witness to the quenching of the Spirit: it may be better or worse than the prayers of one man, but it could never compare for fervour with the spontaneous prayers of a living church."[86]

WORLDLY CHRISTIANITY

Our concern in this section is not with holiness in the world but with worldliness in the church. When the church becomes acculturized and secularized, it can no longer penetrate the world as a leaven; instead, it contributes to the vacuity and dissolution of the surrounding culture.

Syncretistic mysticism is one manifestation of a worldly or cultural Christianity. The Gnostics in the early church sought to come to terms with the Hellenistic mythos by reinterpreting Christianity as one of the ways to salvation from the prison of materiality. They held up *gnosis* (knowledge), which enabled the soul to escape from the flux and change of life and to find assurance of immortality. The dualism of spirit and matter, which was endemic to Platonism, persisted in Gnosticism. Manichaeism, another form of syncretism, sought to absorb elements from Zoroastrianism, Judaism, and Christianity. The body was depicted as a material prison in which the soul was confined. Salvation was based on right knowledge of man's true nature and a desire to return to the realm of light. In the neo-Platonic mysticism which infiltrated Christianity, it was taught that the world of sense is entirely opposed to the Idea of the Good. Against these various heresies Augustine saw in the life of this world the radiance of the heavenly world.

Biblical Christianity teaches not escape from the world into a heavenly realm but the renewal of both heaven and earth by the transforming grace of Christ. H. Richard Niebuhr rightly maintains that Christ "does not direct attention away from this world to another; but from all worlds, present and future, material and spiritual, to the One who creates all worlds, who is the Other of all worlds."[87]

Legalism is another form of worldly Christianity. In this heresy one's salvation is held to be conditional upon one's moral rectitude. Holiness is viewed as a human achievement rather than as a gift of God. One of Paul's primary tasks in his Epistle to the Galatians was to combat the legalism of the Judaizers, who made circumcision a prerequisite to entry into the family of God.

Perhaps the most subtle form of works-righteousness is faith-moralism, in which lip service is paid to the doctrine of justification by faith, but faith is seen as a human work or virtue. We must remember that faith is not a virtuous quality within man but the new creation of grace that enables man to believe, to hope, and to obey. Arminius opened the door to faith moralism by regarding faith as the first cause of justification, not the instrument by which man accepts justification. In his opinion the faith which resides in man as a potential quality is the basis for the imputation of righteousness. This stands in contrast to the Reformation principle that "justification is the utterly paradoxical imputation of righteousness to the sinner, in contrast to his moral condition, and without regard to the moral alteration in him."[88]

It was against the legalism of the Jews that Paul reminded his hearers that we do not have a righteousness of our own based on law (Phil. 3:9). Instead our righteousness is based on faith in the atoning sacrifice of Christ, which alone entitles us to heaven. "Our purest works," declared J. C. Ryle, "are no better than filthy rags, when tried by the light of God's law."[89] It is not the quantity of our moral exercise but the quality of our faith that makes us effective ambassadors of Christ (Forsyth).

Antinomianism is the opposite peril of legalism. Here it is maintained that because salvation is assured through the grace of Christ, the Christian is thereby freed from the obligations of the law. Free grace becomes cheap grace, since it saves but does not rule the lives of its subjects. Luther opened the door to this pitfall by conceiving of holiness as God's productivity and activity, not man's. Insofar as man can do nothing apart from God's grace, this is a viable position, but it overlooks the fact that man is called to a holy life on the basis of grace. The early Barth also reflected antinomian tendencies in his devastating critique of the pietism and moralism that characterized culture-Protestantism. "Depth of feeling, strength of conviction, advance in perception and in moral behaviour," he averred, "are no more than things which accompany the birth of faith. Being of this world, they are in themselves no more than unimportant signs of the occurrence of faith."[90] Yet our Lord tells us that if we do not bear fruit in works of piety and love, we will lose the grace that is given to us (Matt. 25:14–30).

Modern evangelicalism frequently depicts sanctification as simply yielding oneself to God. Its motto is: "Let go, and let God." This ignores the truth that Scriptural holiness entails warfare and struggle in carrying forward the banner of Christ. In the words of Bishop Ryle: "A holy violence, a conflict, a warfare, a fight, a soldier's life, a wrestling, are . . . characteristic of the true Christian."[91]

The law of sowing and reaping is not annulled by the Gospel of grace but altered and redirected. In Christ we reap what he sows, that is, peace, righteousness, hope, and love. Outside of Christ we reap what we ourselves sow, that is, enmity, discord, terror, and death. Yet the believer is only in Christ when he abides in Christ and walks in his light. We turn away from Christ when we take his law for granted, when we acknowledge him as Savior without following him as Lord, when we do what we please and not what pleases Christ. We also find ourselves outside of Christ when we trust in our own efforts and goodness as the ground of our security.

Eudaemonism is another temptation that beguiles many people to embark on a spurious road to holiness. This is the ethical stance of Aristotle, which sees the goal in life as man's own well-being or happiness. In medieval Catholicism holiness was viewed as a higher happiness, but the Aristotelian motif was still very pervasive.[92] The equation of holiness and happiness was also extremely prevalent in Protestant Pietism. This is a subtle error, since Christians may very well be happy as the world understands it. But when happiness is made a Christian goal, the values of this world have usurped the cross of Christ. Then egocentric religion has supplanted theocentric religion. It is important to bear in mind that being happy *(eudaemonon)* is qualitatively different from the state of being blessed *(makarios)*, which Christ extols in the beatitudes. Luther pointed to this difference when he described the hallmark of the Christian life as a "comforted despair." Calvin agreed that "this life, taken by itself, is full of unrest, trouble and misery, and not really happy from any point of view."[93] What the Christian can be assured of is not the absence of conflict but the gladness of knowing that his sins are forgiven. The Christian is summoned to bear the cross sometimes even at the expense of his own physical and emotional well-being (cf. Ps. 44:22). He will nevertheless have in the midst of his suffering an inner joy, and in the midst of his anguish a peace that passes all understanding.

Worldliness also infiltrates the church whenever a sacramentalist mentality becomes dominant. Here forgiveness is assured through the sacraments without any clear call to repentance or summons to obedience. In this kind of objectivism salvation is something conferred on us through the ministrations of the church rather than something that one must appropriate through a lifelong struggle.

Other forms of objectivism are predestinarianism, which locates salvation completely outside us in the eternal decrees of God, and Christomonism, where sanctification is said to take place in Christ and not in the sinner. "Christ in you," then becomes a status objectively realized in Christ for all people, not a promise subjectively attained in faith and obedience.[94]

Worldliness even asserts itself in perfectionism, particularly when those who aspire to Christian perfection fall into the delusion that they have arrived. We need to take seriously Paul's confession: "Not that I have already obtained this or am already perfect; but I press on to make it my own, because Christ Jesus has made me his own" (Phil. 3:12). Paul reminds us that perfect holiness will not be attained until the end of our journey: "He who began a good work in you will bring it to completion at the day of Jesus Christ" (Phil. 1:6).

James Dunn, a trenchant critic of current revivalism, gives these words of wisdom:

The antithesis between the inward man and the flesh is not overcome and left behind, it continues through and beyond the shout of thanksgiving—as a continuing antithesis between mind and flesh. . . . *The religious experience of the believer is characterized by paradox and conflict—the paradox of life and death, the conflict of Spirit and flesh.* It is a religion of *Anfechtung*—of faith always assailed by question and doubt, of life always assailed by death, of Spirit always assailed by flesh.[95]

Religious enthusiasm is still another perversion of Scriptural holiness. Here the attention is focused not on ethical fruits or the cross of suffering but on extraordinary experiences which function as outward signs of sanctity. Among the signs prized by enthusiasts through the ages have been the stigmata, dreams, miracles, visions, speaking in tongues, and dancing in the Spirit. The Puritans encouraged people to look for such signs or evidences as zeal, love, and faith, but they distrusted any claim to extraordinary gifts or experiences. There is nonetheless a danger when religion becomes conscious of itself as a religion. True sanctity is oblivious to its own merits. Our Lord warns that the left hand should not know what the right hand does (Matt. 6:3). Loud boasts of folly should not be mistaken for religious certainty (cf. 2 Pet. 2:18). While grace will have visible effects in our lives that can be discerned by others, grace itself is hidden and imperceptible to the senses. In this light we can appreciate Barth's remark: "Grace is and remains always in this world negative, invisible, and hidden; the mark of its operation is the declaration of the passing of this world and of the end of all things."[96]

The call to holiness is also distorted by a certain kind of social activism that confuses kingdom righteousness with social justice and Christian charity with humanitarianism. Ritschl laid the ground work for an unbiblical Social Gospel by asserting that the purpose of justification is to serve the ethical striving for the attainment of the perfect society of persons. Forgiveness was seen as the divine companionship that enables the sinner after every defeat to arise and resume his ethical task. Only by engaging in civic work for the common good, by being faithful to one's social calling, is it possible to be true to the example of Christ. The later Ritschlians substituted the phrase "the brotherhood of man" for the "kingdom of God." The current theologies of revolution and liberation which see the kingdom of promise ushered in by revolutionary struggle and warfare reflect a secularizing of the Gospel call to holiness.[97]

Finally, we must warn against the technological morality which is manifest in the human potential and pastoral psychology movements. When the religious or moral life is based on the techniques of psychology and related social sciences rather than the authority of Scripture and the spiritual wisdom of the church tradition, group dynamics becomes a surrogate for the *koinonia,* and counseling takes the place of confession. The goal in life is now self-fulfillment and personal integration rather than the great commission. The seeds of this current focus on the quest of the self for wholeness and health are to be found in Pietism and Puritanism, where the keeping of spiritual diaries was encouraged to lay bare the soul's struggle for holiness. It is ultimately rooted in the Eros piety of Hellenistic philosophy and religion.

The values of the technological society have even penetrated the bastions of conservative evangelicalism, where some of its spokesmen are now advocating a technology of the spirit to inculcate Christian virtues in man by human conditioning.[98] In some Lay Witness missions people use spiritual growth charts to gauge their spiritual progress empirically. Fasting and tithing are sometimes portrayed as tried and true methods for insuring physical and spiritual well-being. The clinical psychologist Millard Sall, who identifies himself as evangelical, argues that the reward of faith is "maturity and enrichment," that the right use of the Bible and psychotherapy can bring people "the highest satisfaction and enjoyment possible."[99]

This technological morality is also glaringly apparent in the school of Positive Thinking and the neo-transcendentalist movement (Christian Science, Unity, New Thought), which depict health and prosperity as the inevitable concomitants of right thought and action. In this orientation prayer is reduced to a method of attaining personal satisfaction and social success.

One danger in this new form of culture-religion is that holiness becomes a result of technique and therefore something within man's power. Another peril is that sanctity is confused with sanity, holiness with healthfulness. Emotional stability is valued more highly than the zeal and madness of faith. The aim is to be absolved from bad feelings, not to repent of sins. Philip Rieff scores the ethical stance of modern psychotherapy, including that which has a Christian guise: "A man can be made healthier without being made better—rather, morally worse. Not the good life but better living is the therapeutic standard."[100]

Evangelical Christianity stands in diametrical opposition to the technological morality by its insistence that holiness is a product of God's supernatural grace and not of human technique. It is election by grace, not the rational discovery and application of spiritual laws, that places one in the kingdom of the redeemed. Biblical faith does not deny the place for spiritual disciplines but stresses that these have no value apart from the secret inward work of the Holy Spirit, and they are designed to bring our actions into conformity not with the canons of scientific rationality but with the will of God, which is perceptible only to the eyes of faith. Moreover, the goal of the Christian life is seen not as personal integration or wholeness nor as the realization of human potential but rather as the sacrifice of the self to the cause of the kingdom and the glory of God. Jesus Christ, the pattern for Christian living, had neither a long life nor a tranquil one. He was accused of insanity because of his fervency and boldness in faith (Jn. 10:20). Yet in emptying himself and giving himself for the welfare of his fellow human beings, he exemplified that perfect wholeness which is at the same time perfect holiness, for he was integrated not with the standards of the world but with the will of the living God, the ground and goal of all human existence.

NOTES

1. I agree with J. Sidlow Baxter in his criticism of the Victorious Life and Higher Life movements in which sanctification is generally depicted as wholly the work of Jesus Christ within and not also the work of the believer empowered by Christ. It seems that in those movements we do not ourselves battle against temptation but let Christ dispose of it while we stand by as onlookers. See J. Sidlow Baxter, *A New Call to Holiness* (Grand Rapids: Zondervan, 1975).

2. Adolf Harnack, *History of Dogma,* vol. 2, trans. Neil Buchanan (New York: Russell & Russell, 1958), p. 228.

3. Martin Luther, *Luther's Works,* vol. 14, ed. Jaroslav Pelikan (St. Louis: Concordia, 1958), p. 93.

4. Luther, *Luther: Lectures on Romans* Ed. & Trans. Wm. Pauck, p. 127.

5. *Ibid.,* p. 189.

6. Martin Luther, W.A. 37, 357.

7. *Luther's Works,* vol. 27, p. 87.

8. Luther generally saw justification and regeneration as correlative, whereas Melanchthon was inclined to regard regeneration as following upon justification. The latter view renders faith purely cognitive rather than regenerative and creative as well.

9. John Calvin, *Institutes of the Christian Religion,* III, 16, 2 ed. John T. McNeill, trans. Ford Lewis Battles (Philadelphia: Westminster Press, 1960), p. 800.

10. *Institutes* I, 2, 1 ed. McNeill., p. 41.

11. Cf. Calvin: "Christ, through whom we have returned to favor with God, is set before us as a model, the image which we should express in our own lives." *Corpus Reformatorum, Calvini Opera* 1, 1125.

12. *Corpus Reformatorum, Calvini Opera* 45, 481.

13. Calvin, *Institutes* II, 16, 7, ed. McNeill, p. 512.

14. Calvin, *Institutes* III, 3, 9, ed. McNeill, p. 601.

15. See Kenneth Ronald Davis, *Anabaptists and Asceticism* (Scottdale, Pa.: Herald Press, 1974).

16. Jonathan Edwards, *Treatise Concerning Religious Affections.* In *Works of Jonathan Edwards,* ed. John E. Smith, Vol. 2 (New Haven: Yale University Press, 1959), p. 387.

17. See Norman Pettit, *The Heart Prepared: Grace and Conversion in Puritan Spiritual Life* (New Haven: Yale University Press, 1966).

18. Philip Jacob Spener, *Pia Desideria,* ed. and trans. Theodore G. Tappert. (Philadelphia: Fortress Press, 1964), p. 95.

19. Walter Marshall, *The Gospel-Mystery of Sanctification* (London: Oliphants Ltd., 1954), p. 99.

20. In Marie E. Richard, *Philip Jacob Spener and His Work* (Philadelphia: Lutheran Publication Society, 1897), p. 46.

21. Charles Spurgeon, a nineteenth-century heir of Pietism and Puritanism, declared: "If you cannot keep good company and avoid the circle of dissipation, do not profess to be followers of Christ, for He bids you come out from among them and be separate." *The Treasury of Charles H. Spurgeon* (Westwood, N.J.: Fleming H. Revell Co., 1955), pp. 78, 79.

22. John Preston, *The Saints Qualification* (1637). Cited in Irvonwy Morgan, *Puritan Spirituality* (London: Epworth Press, 1973), p. 118.

23. Albert Outler, ed., *John Wesley* (New York: Oxford University Press, 1964), p. 378.

24. Karl Barth, *Church Dogmatics* II, 2, ed. G.W. Bromiley and T. F. Torrance (Edinburgh: T & T Clark, 1969), p. 576.

25. Dietrich Bonhoeffer, *The Cost of Discipleship,* trans. R. H. Fuller (London: SCM Press, 1959), p. 79.

26. *Ibid.,* p. 105.

27. *Ibid.,* p. 267.

28. Dietrich Bonhoeffer, *Letters and Papers from Prison,* ed. Eberhard Bethge (New York: Macmillan, 1972).

29. Paul Tillich, *Systematic Theology,* vol. 2 (Chicago: University of Chicago Press, 1957), pp. 176 ff.

30. Hans Küng, *Justification,* trans. Thomas Collins, Edmund E. Tolk, and David Granskou (New York: Thomas Nelson, 1964).

31. Edwards, *Treatise Concerning Religious Affections,* pp. 387–388.

32. For Calvin both justification and sanctification exist in their own right, and neither is to be subordinated to the other. Both are necessary for the Christian life. See François Wendel, *Calvin,* trans. Philip Mairet (London: Collins, 1963), pp. 255– 257. To be sure, in his *Institutes* Calvin deals with regeneration before justification, though it could be argued that his purpose in doing so was to highlight justification. See the editorial comment in *Institutes,* III, 3, 1, ed. McNeill, p. 593.

33. Some Reformed theologians, such as Kohlbrügge and the early Barth, erred on the other side and emphasized justification to the detriment of sanctification.

34. Heinrich Heppe, *Reformed Dogmatics,* ed. and rev. Ernst Bizer, p. 566.

35. Morgan, *Puritan Spirituality,* p. 75.

36. Martin Luther, W.A. 57, 102, 15. Cited in Gordon Rupp, *The Righteousness of God* (London: Hodder & Stoughton, 1963), p. 200.

37. Bonhoeffer, *The Cost of Discipleship,* p. 152.

38. Calvin, *Institutes,* III, 2, 21, ed. McNeill, p. 567.

39. *John Wesley's Forty-Four Sermons,* 12th ed. (London: Epworth Press, 1975), p. 475.

40. In the Swedish Pietist Paul Peter Waldenström the Lutheran doctrine of forensic justification is called into question, and salvation is said to consist in imparted rather than imputed righteousness. Waldenström's teachings were influential in the formation of the Mission Covenant Church in 1878, though the precise relationship between justification and sanctification has been left open in that communion. See Julius Bodensieck, ed., *The Encyclopaedia of the Lutheran Church,* vol. 3 (Minneapolis: Augsburg, 1965), pp. 2450–2451.

41. Abraham Kuyper, *The Work of the Holy Spirit,* trans. Henry de Vries (Grand Rapids: Eerdmans, 1966), p. 270.

42. Thomas Torrance, *Kingdom and Church* (Fair Lawn, N.J.: Essential Books, 1956), p. 101. "Sanctification is not a response of man that must be added to justification, but the continual renewing and re-enacting in the believer of a justification that is made once and for all."

43. See Regin Prenter, *Spiritus Creator,* trans. John M. Jensen (Philadelphia: Muhlenberg Press, 1953), pp. 87, 245.

44. Richard Jensen, *Touched by the Spirit* (Minneapolis: Augsburg, 1975), p. 118.

45. J. Sidlow Baxter rightly reflects that "although human effort is . . . powerless in itself to *maintain* inwrought holiness after the Holy Spirit has wrought the . . . miracle within us, yet human cooperation is all the while necessary in resisting encroachments of evil upon the sanctified territory, in cultivating prayerful responsiveness to the Holy Spirit, and in carefully culturing those *conditions* which are required for a continuing experience of holiness." *A New Call to Holiness,* p. 142.

46. Jensen would possibly not disagree here, since he appears to mean that sanctification is alien to the being of the natural man. But can we even say this if we affirm that man in his created being is good and not evil? Regeneration does not negate but transforms the being of man.

47. Karl Barth, *A Shorter Commentary on Romans,* trans. D. H. van Daalen (London: SCM Press, 1959), p. 65.

48. *Present Truth,* vol. 4, no. 1 (February 1975), p. 48. If pressed, Robert Brinsmead will recognize that the Holy Spirit, as well as the Father and Son, plays a role in our justification, and that we are not effectively justified until the Spirit produces faith within us. I agree with Brinsmead that we are justified by the righteousness of Christ, which is outside ourselves. But we must make contact with this righteousness by faith, which is a subjective work of the Holy Spirit (and which has an experiential side). My position is close to Brinsmead and to *Present Truth* (now known as *Verdict* magazine), but my emphasis is not the very same in this area.

49. Our Reformed fathers made a helpful distinction between "active justifi-

cation," which takes place in the tribunal of God (Rom. 3:20; Gal. 3:11) and "passive justification," which takes place in the heart or conscience of the believer. See Louis Berkhof, *Manual of Reformed Doctrine* (Grand Rapids: Eerdmans, 1933), p. 259.

50. *The Works of Bonaventure,* IV, trans. José de Vinck (Paterson, N.J.: St. Anthony Guild Press, 1966), p. 37.

51. *Luther's Works,* vol. 29, p. 139.

52. *Corpus Reformatorum* Vol. 79, *Calv. Op.* 51, 186.

53. John Calvin, *Golden Booklet of the True Christian Life,* trans. Henry J. Van Andel (Grand Rapids: Baker Book House, 1975), p. 18.

54. Philip Spener, *Pia Desideria,* p. 80.

55. For a perceptive discussion of regeneration and Christian perfection in Spener and Francke see Dale Brown, *Understanding Pietism* (Grand Rapids: Eerdmans, 1978), pp. 95 ff.

56. John Bunyan, *Justification by an Imputed Righteousness* (Swengel, Pa.: Reiner Publications, 1970), p. 67.

57. J. C. Ryle, *Holiness,* reprint ed. (London: James Clarke, 1956), p. 39.

58. Quoted in J. Mcleod Campbell, *The Nature of the Atonement* (New York: Macmillan, 1895), p. 124.

59. This reflects Luther's view that, apart from God's merciful judgment, the good works of the Christian can only be counted as "mortal sin."

60. The Westminster Shorter Catechism, Q. 37. In Philip Schaff, *The Creeds of Christendom,* vol. 3 (New York: Harper & Bros., 1919), p. 684.

61. Robert Monk argues that regarding the doctrine of Christian perfection Wesley is remarkably similar to the Puritan John Preston, who envisioned a perfection of intention or dedication that nevertheless does not exclude the continuation of human infirmities, which he recognized as sins. This perfection of the "sound heart" is an imperfect perfection, which presses on toward the ultimate perfection obtained when the taint of sin is taken from man at death. Both Preston and Wesley conceived a perfection that demanded continual increase in love. Monk does not suggest that Wesley derived his ideas from Preston but rather that this doctrine was present in the Puritan tradition and that Wesley was familiar with its formulation. See Robert C. Monk, *John Wesley: His Puritan Heritage* (Nashville: Abingdon Press, 1966), pp. 113–118.

62. Wesley himself sometimes employed this term, but he regarded it as unwise and finally decided to refrain from using it, since it conflicted with his view that even a person encompassed by the love of God still commits involuntary transgressions.

Those in the Holiness movement who have held to the eradication theory, namely, that sin is extirpated in the second blessing, are more likely to speak of sinless perfection. That branch of the Holiness movement that stresses the counteraction of sin in the second blessing emphasizes victory over sin rather than sinless perfection (e.g., the Keswick Convention).

63. J. Sidlow Baxter, *A New Call to Holiness,* p. 171.

64. *The Journals of Søren Kierkegaard,* ed. and trans. Alexander Dru (London: Oxford University Press, 1951), p. 413.

65. *Ibid.,* p. 174.

66. Barth, *Church Dogmatics,* II, 2, p. 770.

67. P. T. Forsyth, *God the Holy Father,* reprint ed. (London: Independent Press Ltd., 1957), p. 124.

68. John Calvin, *Commentary on the Book of Psalms,* vol. 1, trans. James Anderson (Edinburgh: Calvin Translation Society, 1845), p. 526.

69. Martin Luther, *A Commentary on St. Paul's Epistle to the Galatians,* ed. Philip Watson, p. 505.

70. Bonhoeffer, *The Cost of Discipleship,* p. 257.

71. *Luther's Works,* vol. 27, p. 332.

72. That the Christian will sense that he is being used by God as a witness and sign of God's power and holiness is made clear by Paul in II Cor. 1:12. At the same time, the genuine Christian will forever be aware of his unworthiness before God and will forever marvel that God's power is made perfect through weakness (II Cor. 12:9).

73. Bonhoeffer, *The Cost of Discipleship,* p. 239.

74. Calvin, *Golden Booklet of the True Christian Life,* p. 36.

75. Friedrich Schleiermacher, *The Christian Faith,* vol. 2, ed. H. R. Mackintosh and J. S. Stewart. (New York: Harper Torchbooks, 1963), p. 517.

76. John Preston, *The Doctrine of Self Denial* in his *Four Godly and Learned Treatises,* 3, 3rd ed., (London: T. Cotes, F. M. Sparke, 1633) p. 227. Cf. Richard Sibbes: "It is a dastardly thing for a Christian to be cowardly, because he hath death and hell conquered, and everything is made serviceable to help him to heaven." In *The Complete Works of Richard Sibbes* Ed. Alexander Balloch Grosart. Vol.III (Edinburgh: James Nichol, 1862), p. 441.

77. Ernst Troeltsch, *The Social Teaching of the Christian Churches,* vol. 2, trans. Olive Wyon (London: Allen & Unwin, 1950), p. 589.

78. The Calvinist vision of a new social order is admirably stated in Abraham Kuyper, *Christianity and the Class Struggle,* trans. Dirk Jellema (Grand Rapids: Piet Hein, 1950).

79. Jürgen Moltmann, *The Crucified God,* trans. R. A. Wilson and John Bowden, 2nd ed. (New York: Harper & Row, 1973), p. 231. Moltmann claims to be expressing Luther's position on this matter, but, as Bengt Hoffman documents in his *Luther and the Mystics* (Minneapolis: Augsburg, 1976), Luther, in line with the mystical tradition, saw the goal of the incarnation as man's elevation into glory.

80. Hans Küng, *On Being a Christian,* trans. Edward Quinn (Garden City, N.Y.: Doubleday, 1976), p. 571.

81. Joseph Sittler, *The Structure of Christian Ethics* (Baton Rouge: Louisiana State University Press, 1958), p. 64.

82. John Preston, *The Fullness of Christ for Us* (London: J. Oakes, John Stafford, 1640) p. 22.

83. Friedrich Heiler, *Prayer: History and Psychology,* ed. and trans. Samuel McComb (New York: Oxford University Press, 1958).

84. The metaphor of the pouring out of the heart to God is clearly set forth in Isa. 26:16; Lam. 2:19; Pss. 119:145–147; 142:2; and Heb. 5:7.

85. Moltmann sees God not as a "heavenly person" but as a dynamic "eschatological process." He breaks with monotheism and embraces a Hegelian form of panentheism. See *The Crucified God,* pp. 247–249.

86. Cited in J. Oswald Sanders, *The Holy Spirit and His Gifts* (Grand Rapids: Zondervan, 1970), p. 99.

87. H. Richard Niebuhr, *Christ and Culture* (New York: Harper & Bros., 1951), p. 28.

88. Otto Heick, *A History of Christian Thought,* vol. 2 (Philadelphia: Fortress Press, 1966), p. 232.

89. Cited in *Present Truth,* vol. 4, no. 1 (February 1975), p. 61.

90. Karl Barth, *The Epistle to the Romans,* trans. from 6th ed. Edwyn C. Hoskyns (London: Oxford University Press, 1975), p. 39.

91. Ryle, *Holiness,* p. xvi.

92. In the theology of Thomas Aquinas we see Christian ethics combined with the ancient ethics of self-fulfillment, with its natural virtues. For Tillich's discussion of eudaemonism in Thomas see Tillich, *A History of Christian Thought* (New York: Harper & Row, 1968), pp. 196–198.

93. Calvin, *Golden Booklet of the True Christian Life,* p. 69.

94. This orientation can be discerned in the early Barth, but in his maturity he definitely made a place for sanctification as a regenerative process within the believer which reflects and attests his perfect sanctification accomplished in Christ.

95. James D. G. Dunn, *Jesus and the Spirit* (Philadelphia: Westminster Press, 1975), pp. 315, 338.

96. Barth, *Epistle to the Romans* Ed. Hoskyns, p. 103.

97. We see this secularizing process especially in Gutierrez and Colin Morris. Though Moltmann and Küng seek to maintain a Christian identity in social involvement, it seems that the Christian message is also compromised in their theologies.

98. Dr. Paul W. Clement of the Fuller Graduate School of Psychology advocated such a technology of the spirit at the International Conference on Human Engineering and the Future of Man, at Wheaton College, Wheaton, Ill. (July 21–23, 1975).

99. Millard Sall, *Faith, Psychology, and Christian Maturity* (Grand Rapids: Zondervan, 1975), p. 126.

100. Philip Rieff, *The Triumph of the Therapeutic* (New York: Harper & Row, 1966), p. 58.

IV.
THE CRUCIALITY
OF PREACHING

So faith comes from what is heard, and what is heard comes by the preaching of Christ.

Romans 10:17

I am certain that when I enter the pulpit to preach or stand at the lectern to read, it is not my word, but my tongue is the pen of a ready writer.

Martin Luther

God . . . deigns to consecrate to himself the mouths and tongues of men in order that his voice may resound in them.

John Calvin

With preaching Christianity stands or falls because it is the declaration of a Gospel. Nay, more—far more—it is the Gospel prolonging and declaring itself.

P. T. Forsyth

Preaching is "God's own Word." That is to say, through the activity of preaching, God himself speaks.[1]

Karl Barth

He has put His Word in our mouth. He wants it to be spoken through us. If we hinder His Word, the blood of the sinning brother will be upon us. If we carry out His Word, God will save our brother through us.

Dietrich Bonhoeffer

PREACHING AS A MEANS OF GRACE

The cruciality of preaching in the plan of salvation is already very much in evidence in the Old Testament. We read that Moses was appointed by the Lord to confront Pharaoh with the divine summons to release the people of Israel from their slavery: "Now therefore go, and I will be with your mouth and teach you what you shall speak" (Exod. 4:12). When Moses hesitated, God chose Aaron as a partner for His unwilling servant with the promise that He would also be with

71

Aaron's mouth and teach them both what to say and do (Exod. 4:15).

The prophets of Israel definitely saw themselves as the mouthpieces and instruments of the Word of God. They were appointed to proclaim both the grace and the judgment of God. They were messengers of doom but also heralds of glad tidings (Isa. 40:9; 61:1). They were servants of the Word, not its creator or originator (Jer. 25:4, 8). They were sent forth not only with the Word but also with the Spirit, since it is the Spirit who fills their words with meaning and makes their hearers receptive to the divine message (see Isa. 48:16; 61:1).

Like the prophet Isaiah Jesus perceived his role as a preacher of good news to the poor (Luke 4:18, 43). It was not simply his person but his Word that was the means of salvation to lost sinners: "Truly, truly, I say to you, he who hears my word and believes him who sent me, has eternal life" (John. 5:24; cf. 6:63). Moreover, he commissioned his disciples to be heralds of the Word (cf. Matt. 28:19, 20; Mark. 16:15; Luke 10:1, 2). That the words of his disciples in the event of preaching are indeed the very Word of God is evident in this remark of our Lord: "He who hears you hears me, and he who rejects you rejects me. . . ." (Luke 10:16; cf. Mark 13:11).

The sacramental nature of preaching is further attested in the writings of the apostle Paul. It was Paul's deep-felt conviction that the preaching of the Gospel is the divinely-appointed means by which people come to salvation: "Faith comes from what is heard, and what is heard comes by the preaching of Christ" (Rom. 10:17). And again: "Since, in the wisdom of God, the world did not know God through wisdom, it pleased God through the folly of what we preach to save those who believe" (1 Cor. 1:21; cf. 15:1, 2; 2 Cor. 5:20). Paul believed that the words of the apostles were so united with the Word of God that this Word was truly conveyed through their words. He thanked God constantly, he told the Thessalonians, "that when you received the word of God which you heard from us, you accepted it not as the word of men but as what it really is, the word of God, which is at work in you believers" (1 Thess. 2:13). He saw himself as under a divine mandate to preach, and he knew that he would fall under divine judgment if he spurned this injunction: "Woe to me if I do not preach the gospel!" (1 Cor. 9:16).

A similar emphasis is reflected in other epistles of the New Testament. In Titus we read that "at his appointed season he brought his word to light through the preaching entrusted to me by the command of God our Savior" (1:3 NIV). Peter declared: "You have been born anew, not of perishable seed but of imperishable, through the living and abiding word of God. . . . That word is the good news which was preached to you" (1 Pet. 1:23, 25). The Book of Revelation attributes the triumph over the devil not only to the atoning sacrifice of Christ but also to the preaching of the Gospel: "They overcame him by the blood of the Lamb and by the word of their testimony" (Rev. 12:11 NIV).

Despite the early synthesis of Christian and Hellenistic values and beliefs, the fourth century witnessed a partial renewal of biblical preaching. John Chrysostom in the East and Augustine in the West were both characterized by a thorough knowledge of the Bible as well as of human nature. Through their oratorical skills and biblical expositions they won many souls to Jesus Christ and his kingdom. Chrysostom, unfortunately, did not always rise above the doctrinal errors of his day in his praise of alms, celibacy, and monasticism as meritorious works. His view of sin and its remedy also tended to be more moral than evangelical. Augustine often lapsed into allegorical interpretation in his treatment of Scripture, but the truth of the Gospel nonetheless shone through his expository lectures.

In the medieval period the preaching of the Gospel was more and more subordinated to the sacrifice of the Mass, and the visual came to be stressed over the aural in the service of worship. Preaching itself was reduced to homilies or exhortations on moral themes; this was especially apparent in Gabriel Biel and other nominalists.

The rise of mysticism further eroded the cruciality of the preaching of Christ in man's salvation. The mystics maintained that God acts without instrumentality and without ideas (Eckhart). Their aim was to ascend beyond the rational to an intuitive apprehension of God in himself. Preaching was simply an external aid by which one was drawn to focus attention on the suprarational and suprahistorical. In the New Testament church the content of preaching was Christ crucified, risen, and coming again. In the preaching of Meister Eckhart there was little about the events of salvation-history but much about the birth of Christ in the soul.

At the same time, the evangelical strand asserted itself ever again in Roman Catholic spirituality. Augustine (as we have seen) and Bernard of Clairvaux were noted for their expository preaching. Thomas Aquinas gave evangelism priority even over contemplation. In his judgment "the highest place in religious orders is held by those which are directed to teaching and preaching. . . . For even as it is better to enlighten than merely to shine, so it is better to give to others the fruits of one's contemplation than merely to contemplate."[2] The early Dominicans preached from Holy Scripture. Avoiding the homiletic form as too dull, they sought by their preaching to win souls for Christ. Perhaps the most renowned was Savonarola, in whose piety an evangelical strand can be detected.[3] Another eminent Dominican preacher, Vincent Ferrer, who was instrumental in winning many Jews and Moslems to Christ, had a profound awareness of the sacramental character of Gospel preaching: "When a preacher preaches the Word of God and is not concerned with poets . . . or how to flatter the listeners with sonorous phrases . . . but preaches only the Word revealed by God, it is not he who preaches, but the Holy Spirit in him, or Christ Himself."[4]

Edwin Charles Dargan offers this somewhat critical appraisal of preaching in the later middle ages:

> Though there was much and very effective preaching . . . and though it attracted great multitudes of hearers, yet in quality and character it did not escape the faults inherited from the long ages of departure from a true Biblical standard. . . . The use of Scripture was often only sad misuse—it was either neglected wholly or served merely as a pretext for wholly unscriptural or even antiscriptural teachings. . . . The merit of works, the saving value of ordinances, penances, and the like, were presented, to the detriment of gospel truth and sound Christian morals. The glory of the Virgin, the legends of saints and martyrs crowded, and sometimes crowded out, the history and doctrine of Scripture. . . . Yet amid all this failure and perversion the main distinctive truths of Christianity were ably and sincerely presented, and by many earnest voices the saving power of Christ was told, and thousands were brought to his cross. Sin was searchingly analyzed and boldly denounced, and to the ever-present springs of human action appeal was constantly made.[5]

Contemporary Catholicism is seeking to recover the crucial significance of preaching in the life of the church. The Second Vatican Council affirmed that the sermon should draw its content primarily from Scripture and "its character should be that of a proclamation of God's wonderful works in the history of salvation."[6] Pope Paul VI declared that "preaching is the primary apostolate," and this "is above all the ministry of the Word." "No other form of communication can take its place," he asserted, "not even the enormously powerful technical means of press, radio and television."[7]

With the rediscovery of the full meaning of the Gospel, including the themes of substitutionary atonement, salvation by grace, and justification by faith, the Reformation ushered in a new age of biblical preaching. It can be said that Gospel preaching became a third sacrament in the Reformation, replacing the sacrament of confession and absolution.

Martin Luther, in particular, was noted for his elevation of preaching as the primary means of grace—even above Scripture:

The Gospel is really not a document, but wishes to be a spoken word, which recites the content of the scripture, just as Christ did not write but only spoke. He did not call his teaching scripture but Gospel, that is, good news or proclamation. That is why it must not be described with the pen but with the mouth.[8]

According to Luther the Holy Spirit has bound himself to the preaching of the Word as the channel by which he convinces sinners of the truth of the Gospel. Indeed, "there is no other means of attaining faith than by hearing, learning, and pondering the Gospel."[9] The preacher is only a mouthpiece of the living Christ himself: "Those who are now proclaiming the gospel are not those who really do it; they are only a mask and a masquerade through which God carries out his work and will. You are not the ones who are catching the fish, God says, I am drawing the net myself."[10]

Luther maintained that the gospel preacher should convict people of their sins and then comfort them with the promise of redemption through the atoning sacrifice of Jesus Christ. He should generally include in his message a call to repentance or conversion. The sermon itself should consist of an exposition of a biblical passage and usually should not exceed twenty minutes in length. As he declared, "I would not have preachers torment their hearers, and detain them with long and tedious preaching, for the delight of hearing vanishes therewith, and the preachers hurt themselves."[11]

John Calvin, too, was convinced of the indispensability of Gospel preaching for realizing the promise of redemption: "It is true, that the sinner receives remission by the ministry of the Church; but not without the preaching of the gospel. Now, what is the nature of that preaching? That we are cleansed from our sins by the blood of Christ."[12] For Calvin, as for Luther, there is generally no direct bestowal of grace apart from human instrumentality: "The word goes out of the mouth of God in such a manner that it likewise goes out of the mouth of men; but God does not speak openly from heaven; but employs men as his instruments."[13] In his view preaching is a mighty instrument in the hands of the Lord "for both the awakening of faith, and for the building up of the people of God in faith."[14]

Calvin stressed the decisive role of the Holy Spirit in making the word effectual in the lives of people. In his understanding the Spirit must work not only within the preacher but also within the hearer. There is no benefit from the word of preaching "except when God shines in us by the light of his Spirit; and thus the inward calling, which alone is efficacious and peculiar to the elect, is distinguished from the outward voice of men."[15] Calvin was emphatic that there is no necessary accompaniment of the word of the sermon by the Spirit: the Spirit acts and speaks as he wills. God is sovereign even in the preaching of his Word, and preaching becomes effectual "where it pleases God by the secret power of his Spirit to work in this manner."[16] For Calvin the Spirit can work even apart from the preaching of the church, though preaching is the ordinary or usual means of his working.[17]

In the developing Protestant orthodoxy an emphasis was placed on the objective reality and efficacy of the Word of God in preaching, though this efficacy was generally tied to the illuminating work of the Holy Spirit. It was asserted by the Second Helvetic Confession that "the preaching of the Word of God is the Word of God."[18] The preaching of the Gospel has validity despite the moral failings of the preacher: "The Word itself which is preached is to be regarded, not the minister that preaches; for even if he be evil and a sinner, nevertheless the Word of God remains still true and good."[19]

The preaching in Protestant orthodoxy frequently took the form of polemics in which the Calvinistic or Lutheran doctrinal position was defended against opposing views. Learned discourses on abstract doctrinal themes where the intellectual acumen of the preacher was displayed were not infrequent. Doctrinal rectitude came to supplant gospel simplicity in many pulpits. This was more true in full-blown scholastic orthodoxy than in early Protestant orthodoxy.

Puritanism and Pietism signaled a reaction against the stultifying worship of orthodox services and the recovery of evangelical gospel preaching. The Puritan preachers were called "spiritual preachers" in contrast to the "witty preachers" of the ecclesiastical establishment.[20] They thought of preaching not as reflection upon moral or theological themes but as the confrontation of sinful man with a righteous God. Their emphasis was on simplicity, directness, and sincerity. For John Preston "the Word must be presented in a spiritual manner, plain and unadorned."[21] The preacher should not make a pretense of superior virtue or wisdom but instead identify himself with his hearers as only a sinner saved by grace. He should preach "as a dying man to dying men" (Richard Baxter). The dynamic of the preacher's appeal was grounded in his own experience, though the actual experience was rarely mentioned. At the same time, it was vitally important that there be a certain congruence between the preacher's life and message, since only a person united with Christ in faith and love could preach in the power of the Spirit.

In Puritan preaching there was an urge to evangelism: every sermon should be geared to bringing people to a personal decision of faith. Moreover, the Puritans sought to reach the common man for the Gospel and not just an intellectual or cultural aristocracy. William Perkins, Lecturer at Great St. Andrews Church, Cambridge, used an open-air pulpit to win the ear of the masses. George Whitefield preached on street corners, in church yards, and in open fields.

John Bunyan (d. 1688) saw the preaching of the Gospel as such a momentous event that he approached it with great trepidation. "Though trembling," he wrote, "I used my gift to preach the blessed gospel, in proportion to my faith, as God had showed me in the holy Word of truth."[22] The goal of preaching is not to share information about God or the Christian religion but to bring sinners to a saving knowledge of the Lord Jesus Christ: "In all my preaching . . . my heart has earnestly cried out to God to make the Word effectual to the salvation of souls."[23] Bunyan acknowledged that sometimes he was actually "in real pain, travailing to bring forth children to God."[24] He was never satisfied "unless there has been some fruit." Like many other Puritan preachers he recognized that it is not human effort or preparation but the work of the Holy Spirit that makes a sermon effectual for salvation:

Sometimes I have noticed that a word cast in, by the way, has done more than all the rest of the sermon. Sometimes when I thought I had done the least, then it developed that the most has been accomplished; and at other times when I thought I had really gotten hold of them, I found I had fished for nothing.[25]

Philip Spener, who spent most of his working years in the pastorate and whose sermons sparked a revival in his parish in Frankfurt, exemplifies the stance of German Pietism on worship and preaching. In his view preaching should be directed toward the heart and not merely toward the mind of man. He criticized the continual preaching of the law in Lutheran pulpits and called every preacher above all to announce the good news of salvation. He also condemned the prevailing custom of exhibiting learning in the pulpit as this was reflected, for example, in quotations from foreign languages and concentration on obscure doctrinal points. Nor should the preacher go out of his way to introduce controversy in the pulpit. The hallmark of an evangelical sermon is apostolic simplicity. Spener wanted the Bible to be allowed to speak to the church and thereby be instrumental in the reformation of its life and worship. For this reason he warned against dependence on the predetermined texts (pericopes) while the rest of the Scriptures remained largely untouched.

Spener urged those who preach the Gospel to bear in mind that they speak not the words of men but the power of God. They should take care not to mingle with the preaching of the Word of God any thoughts of their own. At the same time they must give diligent and reverent preparation to their sermons, for to preach simply and profoundly requires much study. Only in this way can they make sure that what they preach is the Word of God and not the word of man.

If the Gospel is the Gospel of Christ, we are thereby admonished, that as the preacher should desire to preach nothing else so the hearers should desire to hear nothing else; not human trifling and merry tales to produce laughter in the church; not deep speculation which none of the hearers can understand . . . not the histories or empty services of the saints . . . nor yet mere morality; for although it is proper that morality should be impressed upon the Church, it is not its first and immediate aim, but is to be awaited as a result, not looked to as a means.[26]

In the modern period Friedrich Schleiermacher is of special interest, since he illustrates the profound change that preaching underwent in neo-Protestantism. For him proclaiming God meant testifying to the reality of one's own experience of God. The tenets of the Christian faith are only derivatives of the inner state of man. The Word is of secondary importance, for the divine is ineffable. What is of primary importance is not doctrinal fidelity but the cultivation of piety or religiousness. In his sermons Schleiermacher did appeal to the Bible, but his aim was not to confront his hearers with the judgment and grace of a holy God but to awaken the God-consciousness within all people and to encourage moral effort. What happens in the service of worship is not the proclamation of the mighty acts of God but the communication of one's awareness of the divine Spirit in human life.[27] He never preached from the Old Testament, since he regarded its portrayal of God as pre-Christian. Schleiermacher reflects the subjectivistic slant in Christian mysticism and Pietism. The dialectic that was maintained in early Pietism between the Word of God in Scripture and the human response in faith and obedience was sundered in his emphasis on religious experience.

P. T. Forsyth, on the contrary, remained true to the dominant evangelical strand in the tradition of Pietism. In his view preaching should be centered on the power of the cross of Christ to redeem fallen mankind. Jesus should be presented as the Savior and Lord of the world and not as elder brother or exemplar of a higher religious consciousness. Forsyth lamented the fact that modern preaching lacks the note and energy "of spiritual profundity and poignancy as distinct from spiritual sympathy, and of moral majesty as distinct from ethical interest."[28] Such is "ultimately due to the loss of conviction as to a real, objective, and finished redemption, and to the disappearance from current faith of a real relation to the holiness and the wrath of God."[29] He regarded with special disfavor "subjective, psychological preaching," which is "weak," "exhausting," and "dangerous."[30] "Analyse the Gospel in reference to the soul," he recommended. "You are a minister of the Word, not of the soul."[31] Forsyth called for a return to biblical, evangelical preaching in which the content of the sermon would be derived from the Scriptural witness, not from one's own religious experience. Too often, he observed, the preacher reads his own message into the Bible instead of reading God's message out of the Bible.

In more recent years Karl Barth has sought to lay the foundation for a recovery of biblical, evangelical preaching, though he diverges at certain points quite markedly from the tradition of the evangelical revival. Barth speaks of both the impossibility and the necessity of preaching God's Word.[32] The task is impossible because the finite cannot bear or carry the infinite (finitum non capax infiniti), but it is necessary because the very existence of the church depends upon the preaching and hearing of the Word. Barth contends that through our feeble and broken witness God acts and speaks. He does not speak so much in our words as with our words so that in the event of preaching people hear the veritable Word of God. Preaching, like the sacraments, is more properly a sign or testimony of grace than a means of grace, for it witnesses to the grace poured out for all people in Jesus Christ. At the same time it can certainly be regarded as a means to the knowledge of grace and thus, in this secondary sense, a means of grace, since through preaching the Spirit of God grants us knowledge of what God has done for us in Christ. And this knowledge is not simply cognitive but also regenerative in that it affects the being as well as the intellect of man.

The content of our preaching, says Barth, should be the announcement of God's grace and judgment which has taken place on behalf of all humankind in Jesus Christ—in his incarnation, crucifixion, and resurrection. "God was in Christ reconciling the world to himself" (2 Cor. 5:19) is the pivotal text in Barth's theology. According to him this means that the world is already reconciled to God in that Jesus Christ, Representative Man and Revealing God, by virtue of his sacrifice of

obedience dispels the enmity between God and man. His confession of
sin on behalf of man signifies and ratifies man's acknowledgement of
and gratefulness for God's forgiveness. Yet though the world is reconciled to God, it is not yet redeemed because mankind has not yet been
awakened to the truth and significance of God's reconciling work in
Christ.

In our preaching, Barth contends, we do not offer people salvation
but proclaim a finished work of salvation. Through the word that is
proclaimed the congregation receives a practical awareness of a salvation that is already theirs. We do not call our hearers to decision but
remind them of God's decision on their behalf actualized in Jesus
Christ. This is not to deny that the Spirit of God may reach out through
our preaching and effectuate a conversion of life in our hearers, but we
ourselves cannot do this or even hope to do this by preaching. Our
responsibility is to make known the conversion of all humankind to
God that has already taken place in Jesus Christ. The Spirit of God will
in his own way and time enable people to enjoy the benefits of this
conversion, but it is not the task of the church. This means that we
approach unbelievers not as sinners but as virtual brothers, since they,
too, stand within the sphere of grace and redemption, though as yet
they do not know it. The preacher is therefore a herald of good news
but not a winner of souls, an ambassador of Christ but not an agent of
his ongoing work of salvation. Christ alone is the Savior of souls, and
his work of salvation has already been effected and completed in his
sacrificial life and death. Nor should the preacher warn of the terrors
of God's judgment because these terrors have already been borne by
Jesus Christ on behalf of all humanity. It is "necessary to speak of
human sin and error, but only in order to show that sin is annihilated
and error destroyed."[33]

Our difficulty with Barth at this point is that he tends to see preaching not as an instrument or agency of salvation but only as a testimony
to a salvation already completed. Salvation was realized in the faith of
Jesus Christ, he says, and our own faith is simply an acknowledgement
of this great salvation. Perhaps our difference with Barth lies in emphasis rather than substance, since he, too, insists that what has already been accomplished must be apprehended and appropriated by
sinful man in the here and now. Yet in his depiction of the cross of
Christ as the reconciliation of all mankind to God, he diverges from the
biblical and Reformation witness that this reconciliation has validity
and reality only for faith and that the world of unbelief continues to
stand under the wrath and judgment of God. Preaching, therefore, is

not only a witness to reconciliation but a means of reconciliation. Barth can be appreciated for his reminder that God's reconciling grace and love extend to all, that the atoning work of Christ is done on behalf of all, that justification and sanctification are intended for all. But what has been accomplished on behalf of all mankind de jure does not become a concrete reality for us until we receive and surrender to the risen living Christ who confronts us in the word of the sermon. And this surrender is not only an acknowledgement of a salvation accomplished for us but also a decision for a salvation that is applied to us and enacted in us.[34]

Although noticeably influenced by Barth, Dietrich Bonhoeffer retained the Lutheran doctrine that the finite can bear the infinite *(finitum capax infiniti)* and therefore saw the preacher not simply as a witness to Christ but as a Christ to his neighbor through the word that he speaks. As Bonhoeffer's biographer put it: "The word of the sermon has, and is, the presence of Christ."[35] The sermon has not an accidental but an organic and integral relationship to the Word of the living Christ. "Nothing", Bonhoeffer insisted, "is more concrete than the real voice of Christ speaking in the sermon."[36] He did, of course, also acknowledge the concrete presence of the Word in Scripture and the sacraments, but thought it essentially and primarily noticeable in the preached Word. His position is made unmistakably clear: "He has put His Word in our mouth. He wants it to be be spoken through us. If we hinder His Word, the blood of the sinning brother will be upon us. If we carry out His Word, God will save our brother through us."[37] Bonhoeffer rightly perceived the urgency in the preaching of the Gospel. People are dying in their sins and need to be told the good news that a Savior has come to them and is ready to receive them. "Time is precious, and multitudes are still waiting for the message of the gospel. . . . To tell men that the cause is urgent, and that the kingdom of God is at hand is the most charitable and merciful act we can perform, the most joyous news we can bring."[38]

This does not mean that the Word of salvation should be proclaimed indiscriminately. In his *Letters and Papers from Prison* Bonhoeffer maintained that there is a time to speak but also a time to remain silent.[39] The church should remain silent when it has so falsified its message that it is compromised before the world. It should also be silent when its message becomes a facilitator of sociological conformity or when its message is a plea for its own existence. He believed that the secularization of the faith made it supremely difficult to proclaim the Word of faith in its purity and power and that therefore the church

should seek to witness simply by Christian presence, vicarious identification with the poor and despised of the world. He envisioned a period
of silence and struggle, but in the end it would once again be the
proclaimed Word that would renew the church. When the Word is
proclaimed again in power, however, it will be a dereligionized Word,
a Word liberated from its captivity to a religio-cultural tradition of the
past. It will be a Word expressed not in the archaic language of Zion,
an unnecessary stumbling block to the man come of age, but in a new
language capable of being understood and assimilated by secularized
man.

While appreciating many of Bonhoeffer's insightful observations
and recommendations, we nonetheless have certain reservations. His
view that there are periods when the church should refrain from direct proclamation of the Gospel message has some merit, particularly
when this message is compromised in the inner circles of faith itself.
At the same time it could be argued that this is precisely the time
when the message needs to be uttered by those who have been
granted spiritual and theological discernment. In those situations
where people refuse to hear or where the hearers of the message are
already acquainted with it but have spurned it, there is no merit in
direct proclamation, and the ambassador of Christ should then either
remain in an underground role or go on to other fields where people
may be more receptive (Luke 9:5; Matt. 7:6; Acts 16:6). We can think
of some theological seminaries and church colleges that have lost
their first love and where the message in its authentic purity and
power would be resisted or even ridiculed. Here it is better to remain
silent as far as public proclamation is concerned, though one must
never give up personal witnessing among his fellow human beings,
and this would certainly include the classroom. The point is that even
in the most hopeless situations we should look for some opportunity
to speak about Christ, and while one must keep silent on occasion,
one should never remain silent on principle. Bonhoeffer seems to
imply that in this present postwar period we must not go beyond the
Word (as in mysticism) but prepare ourselves to hear the Word when
God speaks it again in all its truth and power. We believe that God is
speaking now, though only those with the eyes and ears of faith can
hear and understand. But it is incumbent on those who hear to declare it to others.

We also have questions about Bonhoeffer's insistence on speaking
the Word in a new language of a nonconfessional and nonreligious
character. We agree with Barth that there can be no substitute for the

language of Zion or Canaan, the language of the Bible. To be sure, we must utilize new imagery in clarifying and illuminating biblical concepts, but we can never abandon the uniquely inspired language of Canaan. Nor can we ever lightly forego the confessional language of the church tradition. Paul Tillich, who has tried to translate the biblical concepts into modern parlance, has acknowledged that none of the new expressions can ever contain the richness and depth of meaning that are included in such original words of the religious tradition as "grace" and "sin."[40] Bonhoeffer's plea for a new language is not made in the interest of apologetics (as is the case with Bultmann and Tillich) but rather with the intention of clarifying the meaning of the kerygma, which will forever be a stumbling block and folly to the cultured despisers of religion. Like Barth, Bonhoeffer accepts the Anselmian methodology of faith seeking understanding as opposed to the understanding preparing the way for faith (as in Thomas Aquinas). He rightly sees that faith is free to employ new thought-forms and imagery to illumine its object, the Word of God, but he goes too far when he suggests that the religious language of the Bible and the church tradition is thereby superseded.

PREACHING THE WHOLE COUNSEL OF GOD

It is imperative that in our preaching we proclaim the whole counsel of God (Acts 20:27), and this includes the Law of God as well as the Gospel, sin as well as salvation, hell as well as heaven. We should go on to add obedience as well as faith, though not as the condition for salvation but as a practical demonstration of our salvation.

The idea is prevalent in neo-Protestantism as well as neo-Catholicism that the purpose of preaching is not to convict people of sin but simply to assure them of divine forgiveness and acceptance. It is said that everyone is accepted irrespective of belief, conduct, or character. Insofar as God's grace comes to us while we are still in our sins, this is a true statement, but it neglects the complementary truth that though God accepts us as we are, he does not continue to accept us if we remain as we are. He pronounces us righteous for the purpose of making us righteous. He transfers us from the dominion of darkness to that of light (Col. 1:13) so that we might walk in the light. And if we do not earnestly pursue his righteousness, he will spew us out of his mouth (Rev. 3:16).

The Gospel is not only an announcement of unfathomable grace but an invitation to surrender in faith and repentance. It also includes a call to ethical obedience. Barth's emphasis has been on the first, while the Pietist concern has been with the second and third. All these facets are evident in Isaiah 44:22: "I have swept away your transgressions like a cloud, and your sins like mist; return to me, for I have redeemed you" (cf. Isa. 45:22).

It is interesting to compare Barth and Edwards in this area. Barth believes that the preaching of the Gospel "does not imply that the hearer is called to make a decision. A decision, if it is made, is a matter between the individual and God alone and is not a necessary element in preaching."[41] We should call upon our hearers to acknowledge the salvation that has already been procured for them by Christ and then to live as liberated people. We do not ask them, however, to accept the offer of salvation so that they might be truly saved. Jonathan Edwards, on the other hand, contends that because of the moral inability of the natural man, he is unable to make a bona fide decision for Christ. We should therefore call upon him to seek for salvation, since he can do this through his own power, though not without the aid of the Holy Spirit.

Our position is that through the preaching of the Gospel a new freedom is given which enables the person in sin to repent and cleave to the grace and mercy of Christ. The hearer can make a decision for Christ, though not on the basis of his own power or wisdom. The Holy Spirit is poured out on all who hear the good news of what God has done for us in Christ, but the Spirit can be quenched and grieved by those who taste of its power and then reject the Gospel (cf. Matt. 13:5–7). Those who hear the Gospel and refuse to heed its call damn themselves, for they had the opportunity but squandered it. If they accept, of course, the credit goes to the grace of God, since it was the Spirit who enabled them to accept. On the other hand, if they refuse, the blame is on them, since their hardness of heart did not allow the Spirit to have full sway in their lives. Therefore, the Gospel is to one a "savour of death unto death" but to another a "savour of life unto life" (2 Cor. 2:16 KJ).

We must preach not only the good news of God's mercy and love but also the bad news of his wrath and judgment on sin. Apart from the preaching of God's holiness and wrath his love is misunderstood as a sentimental love that only soothes instead of the holy love that purifies and redeems. The Gospel apart from the Law becomes a pill that tranquilizes, not a medicine that stings but also heals. The goal of preaching is indeed to make known "the unsearchable riches of Christ" (Eph. 3:8), but this is only possible when our sins have been exposed by the search-light of his law.

Norval Geldenhuys expresses our own attitude on this matter:

> This preaching of repentance must always be an inherent element in the Gospel-preaching of the church. Firstly, the sinfulness of sin should be pointed out, as well as God's wrath against it, followed by the inexorable demand for true repentance, and then there should be a summons to have faith in Jesus, the Savior. Without the preaching of the need for repentance the message of the church would degenerate into sentiment.[42]

To preach Christ's love and to be silent regarding his holiness and wrath is to misconstrue him as a divine Helper rather than a mighty Savior. His cross is wrongly understood as only a symbol of creative love rather than an atonement for sin. We would do well to heed these perceptive remarks of John Wesley: "To preach Christ, is to preach what He hath revealed, either in the Old or New Testament; so that you are then as really preaching Christ, when you are saying, 'The wicked shall be turned into hell, and all the people that forget God,' as when you are saying, 'Behold the Lamb of God, which taketh away the sin of the world!' "[43]

When we urge the preaching of the Law of God as well as the Gospel we mean the Law not only as a mirror of man in his sin (its first use) but also the Law as a guide to the Christian life (its third use). Conse-quently, the preaching of the whole counsel of God entails ethical instruction and admonition as well as the exposure of sin and the offer of salvation. To preach the Law only as a guide for Christian living, however, is to fall into the abyss of moralism, since we then lose sight of the biblical truth that the Law condemns even those who aspire to righteous living and that man's only hope is the free grace of God revealed and enacted in Jesus Christ.

We should also bear in mind that when we warn of God's coming judgment in our preaching of the Law and Gospel, we must never ignore the complementary truth that God is also gracious and that his mercy is everlasting. Nor should the person in sin be depicted as only a despicable worm or spider (as in Edwards' preaching), but he should be told that he is created in the image of God and that he stands under the sign of God's gracious election and infinite compassion. Francis Schaeffer reminds us that man is not nothing but something; indeed, he is a little lower than the angels (Ps. 8:5 KJ), and this is why God's love pursues him. Luther advised: "Sinners should not be upbraided in such a way that they are only wounded and driven to despair; but they should be cherished again, so that they are encouraged to be obedient. But this will happen if they are never reproved without mixing in some praise of them."[44]

When we preach about sin in the light of God's law, we should not remain with sin in the abstract but also include a condemnation of specific sins. We are thinking of social sins as well as individual sins, for only in this way does our preaching become prophetic. We must indeed censure the more obvious sins of adultery, stealing, murder, alcoholism, and drug addiction, but we must go on to bring under the scrutiny of God's judgment the social maladies of air and water pollution, nuclear and germ warfare, indiscriminate abortion, racial and sex discrimination, and the exploitation of the poor by slum landlords and ruthless business concerns. Karl Barth is right that all sermons will have political overtones, though we should not preach politics as such. The bane of so much conservative evangelical preaching today is that sin in its social and political dimensions is scarcely touched upon, while personal transgressions of the moral code of the culture are sometimes given undue attention. This, of course, is simply another kind of capitulation to the culture, since law-abiding and respectable citizens are left secure in their sins, while only the weak are condemned.[45]

Evangelicals profess to accept the whole of Scripture and criticize liberals for accepting only what is congenial in Scripture. John Warwick Montgomery scores evangelicals for their lack of consistency: "But why don't we follow our own advice? The liberals use the visible scissors and paste of destructive biblical criticism while we employ the invisible scissors and paste of selective hermeneutics: we preach only those texts that do not make us socially uncomfortable."[46]

To preach the whole counsel of God means to apply the Gospel and Law to the whole of life. The preaching that concentrates solely on the concern for personal salvation is termed by Berkouwer a "salvation-egotism." It can also be described as a simple Gospel reductionism, which was already attacked by Wesley, since it neglected the call to social as well as personal holiness. To preach only sin and salvation is also to ignore the truth that the Gospel answers not only the problem of sin and guilt but also the problem of meaninglessness, which is particularly acute in our time.

The task of the church is to afflict the comfortable by the preaching of the Law and to comfort the afflicted by the preaching of the Gospel. The comfortable are not really afflicted unless the Law is directed to them personally, not only to their individual transgressions but also to their complicity in social and political sin. Yet the word of condemnation must never be the last word in the sermon. Every sermon that claims to be biblical should contain the message of salvation, the glad tidings that a Mediator has identified himself with us and intercedes for us. Every sermon should be a heralding of the good news of God's grace revealed in Jesus Christ, for otherwise the person in sin is left in disillusionment and despair. Indeed, unless his sins are exposed in the light of God's grace and love as well as God's law, man will never really know himself as a sinner in need of redemption. The Law by itself can provoke feelings of guilt, but only the Law in conjunction with the Gospel can produce conviction of sin as well as the hope of redemption.

In our proclamation of God's law against sin we as preachers must not exempt ourselves from the judgment of this law, as Reinhold Niebuhr reminds us: "A preacher is the mediator of God's judgment and also of his mercy. He may claim to preach with great courage; but he also must recognize how he is himself involved in the sins against which he is preaching. Mercy, humility, and charity must come out of this recognition."[47]

Finally, the afflicted should not only be comforted but they should also be challenged to decision and obedience. They should not only be given the promise of the Gospel but also the imperative of the Gospel (the Law in its third use). We should make clear that salvation is assured not only by the work of Christ but also by the decision of faith made possible by the gift of the Holy Spirit. Salvation turns into damnation if it is spurned and rejected (cf. Heb. 12:25). But it becomes the wellspring of peace and joy, the balm of Gilead, when it is accepted and appropriated in repentance and faith.

REFORMED WORSHIP

Reformed worship is centered about the preaching and hearing of the Word of God. We are here using the word *Reformed* in its widest sense to include the whole of evangelical Protestantism, the hallmark of which is the appeal to the authority of the Bible over the church tradition and mystical experience. This kind of spirituality was most clearly identifiable in the Reformation and in early Calvinism and Puritanism. Reformed motifs were rediscovered in the neo-orthodoxy associated with Barth, Brunner, the Niebuhrs, and Bonhoeffer. One can even speak of a Reformed Catholicism (in the style of Küng and Kilian McDonnell). Reformed theology sees the church under the Word and not as the master of the Word or even its guardian. Bonhoeffer cogently expresses the relationship between Word and church from a biblical perspective:

The Word of God . . . enters the Church by its own self-initiated movement. It is wrong to suppose that there is so to speak a Word on the one hand and a Church on the other, and that it is the task of the preacher to take that Word into his hands and move it so as to bring it into the Church and apply it to the Church's needs. On the contrary, the Word moves of its own accord, and all the preacher has to do is to assist that movement and try to put no obstacles in its path.[48]

It is not the visual but the aural that is given paramount attention in Reformed worship. For Barth, " 'liturgy' means the proclamation of the mighty acts of God by which the congregation is established and in the celebration of which it permits itself to be established anew, again and again."[49] "In the sermon," says Heiko Oberman, "the Word of God meets the faithful with authority. There the apocalyptic event takes place wherein the real dimensions of the created world are revealed."[50] Bultmann here speaks for Calvinists as well as Lutherans: "It is not the consecration of the priest but the proclaimed word which makes holy the house of God."[51] According to Bultmann it is the Greeks and not the Hebrews who stressed sight over hearing. To see God is to make an object of him and so "to be able to stand upright in his presence."[52] On the other hand, "hearing is a sense of being encountered, of the distance being bridged, the acknowledgment of a speaker's claim on us."

At the same time we should bear in mind that preaching is not the whole of worship. Forsyth rightly observes: "Preaching is the Church's supreme appeal to the world, but it has lost power because it has been made the chief or only function of the Church, which is really to worship. Preaching is a form of worship, worship is not a form of preaching."[53] For Calvin the culmination of the worship service is intercessory prayer, not the sermon. Both Luther and Calvin regarded the blessed sacrament of the Eucharist as the high point of a service of worship, though this is always the sacrament in the context of the Word. Moreover, only the Word is necessary for corporate worship.[54] The Pietists saw free prayer, the singing of hymns, and testimonies as also significant and highly beneficial in the service of worship.

In modern evangelicalism preaching has come to preempt worship to such an extent that the personality and gifts of the preacher are deemed more important than the praise and adoration of God. Robert Webber voices this complaint: "Part of the problem is that we have made our churches into centers of evangelism and instruction. The focus of our services is on man and his needs instead of God and His glory."[55]

We need to recall that it is not only the preached Word but also the celebration of the sacraments that creates and sustains the fellowship of Christ. Bonhoeffer remarks: "The word of preaching is insufficient to make us members of Christ's Body; the sacraments also have to be added. Baptism incorporates us into the unity of the Body of Christ, and the Lord's Supper fosters and sustains our fellowship and communion . . . in that Body."[56] Forsyth advises: "Our idolatry of the popular preacher needs to be balanced by more stress on the Sacraments. There the common gift comes out, the administrant fades away."[57] The sacraments were ordained by Jesus Christ as channels and bearers of his Word. They are described by Emil Brunner as "the divinely given flying buttresses which save the Church from collapse."[58]

The sacraments are the visible Word or the visible form of the Word. Yet this very manner of speaking points to the fact that there can be no sacrament apart from the proclaimed and read word of Scripture. The sacrament is a supplement to the Word but not a substitute for it. While the sacraments are supremely helpful in the application of the fruits of our salvation, the Word alone is indispensable for salvation. There is no fullness of the Church without the sacraments, but there can be true fellowships of believers apart from the sacraments.

Catholic theology has traditionally emphasized the Mass over the sermon as the focal point of the service, but evangelical voices in that communion have continued to make themselves heard. Bernardino of Siena (1380–1444) recommended: "If thou canst do only one of these two things, hear the Mass, or hear a sermon, thou shouldst rather leave the Mass than the preaching."[59] Bernard of Clairvaux averred, "It is not the absence but the contempt of the sacrament that damns."[60] Augustine stoutly affirmed that the celebration of the Eucharist should always be accompanied by the preaching of the Word. In our day Kilian McDonnell is one who regards the preaching of the Gospel as primary, though he sees the Eucharistic celebration as part of that proclamation.[61] Hans Küng maintains that in the Lord's Supper Christ becomes present not through the ritual or elements but through the word that is preached. As he puts it, "The word here has not primarily the function of consecrating and transforming, but of proclaiming and testifying."[62]

Both the mainline Reformers had a high view of the sacraments, but they also insisted on the priority of the proclaimed Word. Luther asserted: "For the word can exist without the sacrament, but the sacrament cannot exist without the word. And in case of necessity, a man can be saved without the sacrament, but not without the word; this is true of those who desire baptism but die before they can receive it."[63]

Calvin was adamant that Christ is really present by his Spirit in the sacraments which he ordained. Yet they must never preempt the place of the Gospel: "I do not, indeed, deny that the grace of Christ is applied to us in the sacraments, and that our reconciliation with God is then confirmed in our consciences; but, as the testimony of the Gospel is engraven upon the sacraments, they are not to be judged of separately by themselves, but must be taken in connection with the Gospel, of which they are appendages."[64] For sacraments "to beget faith," they must be united with the preaching of the Gospel.[65]

Despite his sacramental bent Bonhoeffer nevertheless looked with reserve on the liturgical movement which sought to restore litanies, the weekly Eucharist, pericopes, and symbols. "With cultic endeavors," he warned, "we are in danger of wanting to add something to the preached word, of attempting to lend a particular style of expression to it. But it may not be and does not need to be so undergirded."[66]

A similar distrust of the liturgical movement is reflected in Reformed theologian Hans-Joachim Kraus: "Orders of worship are good and necessary, but more and more their liturgical formalism solidifies a ritualistic procedure in which only one person presides—the priest-like pastor. . . . Where the authority of preaching declines, the attempts to make worship liturgical and formal increase."[67] Kraus advocates a rediscovery of charismatic gifts in trying to break through liturgical ossification, but (at least in this particular discussion) he makes no attempt to relate these to the sacraments.

In our reservations concerning formalistic and sacramental worship, we must not deny the sacraments their rightful place. The Word and the sacrament are complementary, even though the second is more or less dependent on the first. The Word needs the sacrament in order to become concrete in the life of the congregation. The sacrament needs the Word in order to give meaning and direction to the congregation. On the road to Emmaus the two men who accompanied Jesus heard his message and also broke bread with him. Their eyes were opened to his identity in the breaking of the bread, but previous to that their hearts burned within them while he talked with them on the road and opened to them the Scriptures (Luke 24:30–32). Their conversion was not fulfilled until the time of their sacramental eating.

In his controversy with his Catholic and sectarian opponents Luther was compelled to place perhaps undue emphasis on the Word. He could even say: "Where God's Word is not preached, it were better if people did not sing, read, or assemble at all."[68] The sacrament should generally not be celebrated apart from the proclaimed word, but certainly people can join together in fellowship singing, Bible study, and prayer apart from any formal preaching. Preaching is indispensable for complete worship, but only prayer (in sung or spoken words) is absolutely essential for worship itself.

A sanctuary in a truly Reformed church will be based on the principle of the congregation gathered to hear and adore the Word of God. A divided chancel is not true to the peculiar emphases of either Luther or Calvin, though its demise was effected only in Reformed Christendom. The early Calvinists and Puritans believed that the preached Word should never be separated from the Word read from Scripture. Instead, the sermon should be an exposition of what has been previously read. In a Reformed church the pulpit will be in a prominent position not remote from the people; ideally it will be in the center and slightly raised. Below the pulpit facing the congregation will be the communion table (or table altar).[69] This arrangement points to the biblical and Reformed truth that the sacrament is dependent on the Word for its reality and efficacy.

The blessed sacrament should be celebrated frequently, but not too frequently, since sacramental participation in the mystery of Christ's passion and death must be preceded by self-examination and confession of sins. There is also the danger of the sacrament becoming too commonplace if it is celebrated too often.[70] The sacrament must not be reduced to a fellowship or agape meal, for it signifies a real participation in the body and blood of Christ (1 Cor. 10:16). Here people are confronted by the living Christ, who makes himself present in a way even more intimate and awe-inspiring than in the hearing or reading of the Word.

Reformed worship should not be overstructured, thus allowing for the freedom of the Spirit to change and redesign worship. It will generally include, in addition to the preaching and hearing of the Word of God, the reading from the Old Testament as well as the New, prayers of praise and thanksgiving, confession of sins and assurance of pardon, intercessory prayer, and the singing of hymns to the glory of God. For the pastor to face the altar in prayer is decidedly un-Reformed, since this betrays a hidden belief in the localized presence of Christ. (Such a practice is also very bad acoustically.) Choirs, testimonials, and invitationals are not integral to Reformed worship, though they may enhance it on occasion. The stress in Reformed Christianity is on the congregation praying and singing in unison as well as hearing the Word of God as a corporate body.

Reformed worship will also be characterized by a sense of the numinous. Worship is not a social get-together but a state of being grasped by the holy God. We worship not for the sake of mutual edification but to give glory and honor to God. Yet in addition to the sense of the awesome presence of God, Reformed worship has a certain joyous spontaneity. Where the Spirit of the Lord is, there is freedom, confidence, and joy. Bonhoeffer declares: "The Word of God demands a great deal of reserve and awe, but it demands an even greater confidence and joyfulness in its power and might."[1] We would add that the Word of God also creates a sense of expectation, since where God's Word is truly preached and heard, there people are converted, reconciled, and renewed in their faith.

BIBLICAL VERSUS CULTURAL PREACHING

There is no doubt that cultural preaching has largely supplanted biblical preaching, at least on the American scene, and this holds true in conservative as well as liberal churches. While studying in New York City, Bonhoeffer was dismayed to find that preaching had been "degraded to marginal ecclesiastical observations about events of the day," with "the quoting of edifying instances . . . willing descriptions of one's own religious experiences, to which of course no binding character is attributed in practice."[2] Daniel Jenkins has labeled American preaching as "anecdotal" and "trivial." At its best such preaching provides an emotional uplift, but very rarely does it result in spiritual rebirth.

There is much preaching, to be sure, that "sticks to the Gospel" outwardly but makes no attempt to relate the Gospel to the concrete situation where people find themselves. Forsyth's advice was to "refuse to bow to the spirit of the age," but "at least to speak the language of that age, and address it from the Cross in the tone of its too familiar sorrow."[3]

Gospel preaching should be biblical as opposed to sectarian. It should concern itself with the whole counsel of God and not with the party line of the denomination. It should be a faithful exposition of the text and not an unconvincing appeal to the text in support of preconceived opinions.[4] It should be both evangelical in content and ecumenical in outreach: it should seek to bring the whole world into submission to Christ. Sectarian preaching is present when an emphasis on predestination makes superfluous a call to conversion or when eternal security is upheld in such a way as to make people secure in their sin. A sectarian gospel is also evident when free grace is preached to the exclusion of the call to holiness. Another kind of imbalance is apparent where sanctification is magnified over justification. It is by no means time-worn formulas that will satisfy the spiritual yearnings of our people but a fresh word from God which judges all human constructs and systems. Our commission is to preach not Calvinism or Lutheranism or Wesleyanism but the biblical Gospel in all its breadth, depth, and power.

At the same time the biblical preacher will not neglect doctrine for religious experience or ethics. He will eschew doctrinal complexities but will try to make clear the doctrinal distinctives of biblical faith. He will not seek to fathom mysteries unknown but declare mysteries revealed. As Luther put it: "Doctrinal truth should be preached always, openly, without compromise, and never dissembled or concealed."[75] Luther was particularly emphatic that preaching should include a defense of salvation by grace and justification by faith alone. "Preaching must faithfully adhere to doctrine," said Barth, "that is, to the Confession of our faith, which is not a summary of the religious ideas drawn from our own inner consciousness but a statement of what we believe and confess because we have received it and have heard the Word of Revelation."[76] James Boice rightly urges that we should "preach the great doctrines of Scripture and not withhold them in the mistaken notion that they are too deep or too 'theological' for our people."[77] Furthermore, we should also expose all subjective, untrue thought systems in the light of the Word (Bonhoeffer).

An anti-intellectualism pervades modern evangelicalism, which gives preaching an experiential rather than a doctrinal or biblical cast. Calvin contended that "none will ever be a good minister of the Word of God, unless he is first of all a scholar."[78] The right preparation for preaching is not only prayer but also study, and study not just of the Bible but of the theology of the Church through the ages. To be sure, we are to preach Christ and not theology, but we are to present the right understanding of Christ, and this entails theology. Our preaching must be grounded in a personal encounter with the living Christ, but it must be informed by biblical and theological study. We must speak in the power of the Spirit, but we must think theologically if we are truly to preach the biblical Christ. Dogma is not the aim of our preaching, but it is a condition for it (Bonhoeffer).

Again, biblical preaching will carry the ring of authority. According to Emil Brunner, "soundness of doctrine is only one point of view from which the preaching of the Church may be judged; the other is that of sincerity, 'power,' and authority."[79] So much preaching today is eclectic rather than exclusivistic; it is characterized by an uncritical openness to the spirit of the age rather than an urgency to bring the good news of redemption to lost sinners. More often than not it takes the form of an edifying discourse on spiritual or moral themes in contrast to a definitive pronouncement concerning God's act of salvation in Jesus Christ. Jesus himself preached with authority (Luke 4:32, 36), and so must his followers through the ages. Kierkegaard's complaint is still valid: "Authority is a specific quality either of an Apostolic calling or of ordination. To preach simply means to use authority; and that is exactly what is completely and utterly forgotten in these times."[80] In a similar vein Karl Barth laments: "Is not the very fact that so wretchedly little binding address is heard in the Church accountable for a goodly share of her misery—is it not perhaps *the* misery?"[81]

It should be borne in mind that the authority in preaching should center not on the personality or talents or wisdom of the minister but on the Word. Bonhoeffer warns against a temptation that seems particularly prevalent in current evangelism: "Every cult of personality that emphasizes the distinguished qualities, virtues, and talents of another person, even though these be of an altogether spiritual nature, is worldly and has no place in the Christian community; indeed, it poisons the Christian community."[82]

Biblical preaching will also be kerygmatic rather than apologetic in nature. It will not seek to defend the validity of the claims of the Christian religion but instead herald the good news of reconciliation and redemption through the death and resurrection of Jesus Christ. Our task is simply to let down the net (the Gospel), and Christ will bring in the fish (Luke 5:1-10). Christ, said Luther, "should and must be preached in such a way that, in both you and me, faith grows out of, and is received from, the preaching. And that faith is received and grows when I am told why Christ came, how men can use and enjoy Him, and what He has brought and given me."[83] We do not need to prove Scripture but to expound Scripture in the light of its goal and content—the cross of Christ. We are not called to discover a point of contact with our hearers, since the Word of God creates its own response. God sends forth his Word, and it does not return to him void (Isa. 55:11). Neither should we seek to correlate the Gospel message with the questions of our hearers (as Tillich and Brunner advise);

rather we should so confront them with the Gospel that they are moved to ask the right questions. We are to begin with the Word of God in Scripture and then relate it to the cultural situation; we do not begin with man's existential predicament and then try to discover whether Scripture throws any light upon it.

Kerygmatic preaching is based not on topics of current interest but on the Scriptural message, which has abiding relevance. Consequently, it takes the form of an elucidation of this message rather than a discourse on character or conduct. Kerygmatic preaching is sacramental rather than ethical because through this preaching sins are forgiven and hearts and minds transformed.

Biblical preaching will likewise be evangelical as opposed to moralistic. It will be based on the principle of the sovereignty and all-sufficiency of grace rather than the possibilities for righteousness inherent within man. This means that fidelity to the Word of God is more important than an appeal to the understanding or emotions of our hearers. If man's conversion has its source in divine grace instead of the freedom of the will, the hope of success lies in the action of the Holy Spirit, not in the persuasive powers of the preacher. Augustine wisely observed: "To will is of ourselves, but to will well, both partly and wholly is of grace."[84]

Regrettably, much current revivalistic preaching is Pelagian or semi-Pelagian rather than Augustinian. The desired audience effect hangs not on the preaching but on the total package, which includes awesome settings, dramatic music, careful psychological timing, and altar calls. The altar call as a revival technique did not become fashionable until the first part of the nineteenth century, when it was adopted by Charles Finney; it was singularly absent from the earlier awakenings associated with Wesley, Whitefield, and Edwards, all of whom stressed the priority and all-sufficiency of grace. This is not to deny any place whatever for an altar call, particularly in evangelistic meetings, but preaching itself should contain the invitation. The invitational after the sermon, if it is to be held at all, should be to profess Christ publicly on the part of those who have received him inwardly.[85] There may be times when a special act of dedication and surrender is called for at the close of the service, but Holy Communion should generally be the occasion for this. The loss of the penitential and decision-character of the blessed sacrament partially accounts for the rise and popularity of the altar call.

As has been implied, evangelical preaching stands in contrast not only to moralistic but to psychological preaching as well. The last is indeed a manifestation of a moralistic mentality. The focus is upon sharing one's own experience of conversion or inducing such an experience in others. Paul indicted this general approach when he declared: "For what we preach is not ourselves, but Jesus Christ as Lord" (2 Cor. 4:5). And, as James Denney has trenchantly observed, "No man can at the same time call attention to himself and to Christ."[86] Bonhoeffer also warns against this pitfall: "I am not expected primarily to testify emphatically to my salvation but to the Savior. I cannot save anybody with my human experience."[87] Forsyth was especially critical of what he termed "impressionistic" preaching, by which the minister tries to make an impression upon his hearers rather than to uphold God's Word, even if this arouses displeasure and opposition.

Again, biblical preaching will be charismatic as opposed to formalistic. The preacher will seek to be led by the Spirit even as he speaks (Rom. 15:18, 19). Watchman Nee declares: "A minister of the word ministers with Spirit-taught words. Not only does the Holy Spirit speak words of wisdom with my lips; He teaches me how to speak."[88] This does not deny the necessity for extensive preparation, but, after having prepared, the preacher should rely not on his notes or manuscript but upon the power of the Spirit. Luther makes this poignant observation: "Preachers often go astray in their notes so that they can't go on with what they have begun. It has often happened to me that my best outline came undone. On the other hand, when I was least prepared my words flowed during the sermon."[89] Luther is not arguing against careful preparation but against dependence on one's own resources and wisdom.

Preaching on pericopes or texts selected by the church to fit in with the church year can be a means of quenching the Spirit. Pericopes can be useful as a general guide, but one should be open to the movement of the Spirit even in the selection of the text. We here agree with Paul Holmer:

Surely the pericopes are old and tried, and they probably do not utterly fail the purpose of our faith. But, they also omit a lot, and they tend to make the Bible fit the church practises and the rather demure way that most worshipers have of being domesticated to churchly life.[90]

Charismatic preaching does not necessarily involve a display of emotion on the part of either the preacher or the congregation. Our appeal is not to the feelings of people but to the power of the Holy Spirit. Bonhoeffer rightly criticized "senseless shouting and emotional excitement in preaching and worship. We are witnesses, not the trumpeters of the Last Judgment. That does not, however, exclude from our witness the utmost zeal but rather includes it."[91]

Finally, biblical preaching will be prophetic as well as evangelical and kerygmatic. This is to say it will include the application of the Law to the sins of society. Evangelical power stems from the preaching of the kerygma, but social relevance comes through the preaching of the Law. Those who are called to the ministry of the Word must not be intimidated in the face of public opinion. They must be bold in declaring God's displeasure with social as well as individual sin. Too often, however, prophetic preaching becomes ideological, and what is proclaimed is no longer the divine Word that stands above the polarities in social conflict but the social philosophies of power groups within society. We see this especially in liberal preaching of the social gospel type which is often allied with left-wing causes, but it is also apparent in much conservative preaching which may be biblical in form but ideological in content. In holding up Christ as the direct answer to social problems, conservative preachers often encourage acquiescence to the political status quo, thereby betraying their alliance with the political and economic establishment from which they derive their financial support.

The recent fascination with dialogue preaching, in which two ministers share opinions on some social or theological issue, signifies an evasion of our prophetic mandate. It also indicates an abdication of evangelical preaching, since the focus is on seeking the truth in openness rather than proclaiming it with conviction and certainty. The real dialogue should be between Jesus Christ and the worshipper—Christ speaking through the preacher and the Scripture, and man responding in prayers and hymns of praise.

True biblical preaching is discernible by its fruits. One sign of its authenticity is the experience of conviction of sin and repentance. Another is the creation of a fellowship of love *(koinonia)* and the willingness to enter into costly discipleship. Yet another is the urgency of mission, the desire to bring others into the fold of the saints.

A less welcome but no less inevitable test of biblical preaching is the opposition that it arouses. Such preaching not only disturbs sinners who prefer to be content in their sin but also antagonizes the spiritual powers of darkness which it exposes and overthrows. It was Luther's experience that, "as soon as the Word is preached and as soon as there are people that accept and confess it, the devil quickly appears with all his angels and arouses the world with all its might against this Word, to stifle it and completely destroy those that have and confess it."[92] One should not confuse the opposition of the powers of evil to the Gospel with the understandable resistance of godfearing people to tactlessness, lovelessness, dictatorial methods, or slothfulness on the part of the pastor, all traits which signify infidelity to the Word of God.

Finally, we should note that an awakened and converted congregation will honor the office of preaching. As Bonhoeffer put it: "The congregation which is being awakened by the proclamation of the Word of God will demonstrate the genuineness of its faith by honouring the office of preaching in its unique glory and by serving it with all its powers; it will not rely on its own faith or on the universal priesthood of all believers in order to depreciate the office of preaching, to place obstacles in its way, or even to try to make it subordinate to itself."[93] For the later Bonhoeffer the office of the pastor derives its legitimation from Jesus Christ himself and not from the will of the congregation. A cultural church will be held together by the impact of the personality of the minister. A biblical church, on the other hand, will be sustained by the power and authority of the Word of God and the respect and honor given to the office of preaching. Whereas the spirit of camaraderie will be promoted in a cultural church, the expectation of hope and outgoing love will characterize a biblical church, one that is nurtured and enlivened by the preaching and hearing of the Word of God.

NOTES

1. These words are from Barth's *The Preaching of the Gospel*, trans. B. E. Hooke (Philadelphia: Westminster Press, 1963), which still reflects a sacramental view of preaching. The later Barth was emphatic that preaching is a human response to the divine event of reconciliation and redemption in Jesus Christ and can only attest but not communicate this event, which is ever continuing and living.

2. Thomas Aquinas, *Summa Theologica* Vol. 14, trans. Fathers of the English Dominican Province (London: Burns, Oates & Washbourne Ltd., 1934) pp. 274–275.

3. In his preaching Savonarola was noted for his condemnation of the luxury of the Roman church of his day and its indifference to the poor. The Gospel emphasis is more clearly discernible in his spiritual writings, though it is certainly obvious in many of his sermons. One biographer remarks: "The most powerful impressions made by his preaching were not through his impassioned denunciations of vice and evil-doing, but in his touching and beautiful descriptions of the mercy of God and his love, and in his tender and earnest pleadings with the people to bring their lives into harmony with the divine life of Jesus Christ." In William H. Crawford, *Girolamo Savonarola* (Cincinnati: Jennings and Graham, 1907), p. 95. Another interpreter comments: "His theology was in accord with the Catholic

orthodoxy of his age, having been chiefly formed by Aquinas. But his knowledge of Scripture and his reforming soul encouraged the entrance of many evangelical opinions into his sermons. . . . Besides the scholastic traces, and in spite of the struggle of his better knowledge of Scripture, the allegorical method of interpretation too much prevails and mars the force of his sermons." Edwin Charles Dargan, *A History of Preaching,* vol. 1, reprint ed. (Grand Rapids: Baker Book House, 1974), p. 358.

4. Quoted in Domenico Grasso, *Proclaiming God's Message* (Notre Dame, Indiana: University of Notre Dame Press, 1965), p. 33.

5. Dargan, *A History of Preaching,* vol. 1, pp. 229, 230.

6. Walter M. Abbott, ed., *The Documents of Vatican II* (New York: America Press, 1966), pp. 149, 150.

7. Cited in *The Reformed Journal,* vol. 25, no. 6 (July–August 1975), p. 31.

8. Luther, W.A. 10 I, 1, 17.

9. Martin Luther, *Luther's Works,* vol. 22 (St. Louis; Concordia, 1956), p. 55.

10. Luther, W.A. 17 II, 262–263.

11. Thomas S. Kepler, ed., *The Table Talk of Martin Luther,* (Cleveland: World, 1952), p. 236.

12. John Calvin, *Institutes of the Christian Religion,* IV, 15, 4, Ed. and trans. John Allen (Philadelphia: Presbyterian Board of Christian Education, 1936), p. 585.

13. John Calvin, *Commentary on Isaiah* 55:11. *Corpus Reformatorum, Calvini Opera* 37:291.

14. cf.:"The Gospel is not preached that it may only be heard by us, but that it may as a seed of immortal life, altogether reform our hearts." *Commentary on 1 Peter* 1:23. *Corpus Reformatorum Calv. Op.,* 55:229.

15. John Calvin, *Commentaries on the Epistle of Paul the Apostle to the Romans,* trans. and ed. John Owen (Edinburgh: Calvin Translation Society, 1849), ch. 10.16, pp. 400, 401.

16. John Calvin, *Commentary on the Book of the Prophet Isaiah,* III, 35, 4, trans. William Pringle (Edinburgh: Calvin Translation Society, 1852), p. 65.

17. "He also convinced them without the word, for we know how powerful are the secret instincts of the Spirit." *Commentary on Matthew* 15:23, *Corpus Reformatorum, Calvini Opera,* 45:457. For Calvin, however, this is the exception and not the rule.

18. Arthur C. Cochrane, ed., *Reformed Confessions of the 16th Century* (Philadelphia: Westminster Press, 1966), p. 225.

19. *Ibid.*

20. George Whitefield: "It is not the business of the ministers of the gospel . . . to entertain people with harangues of dry morality, and leave out Jesus Christ." D. Macfarlane, *Revivals of the Eighteenth Century* (Edinburgh, n.d.), p. 32.

21. Irvonwy Morgan, *Puritan Spirituality,* p. 14.

22. John Bunyan, *Grace Abounding to the Chief of Sinners* (Chicago: Moody Press, 1959), p. 94.

23. *Ibid.,* p. 97.

24. *Ibid.,* p. 100.

25. *Ibid.*

26. Cited in Marie E. Richard, *Philip Jacob Spener and His Work* (Philadelphia: Lutheran Publication Society, 1897), p. 20.

27. He declares: "Whether edification takes place in Christian worship largely depends upon the process by which religious self-consciousness comes to be thought and then communicated." Friedrich Schleiermacher, *Brief Outline on the Study of Theology*, trans. Terrence N. Tice (Richmond: John Knox Press, 1966), p. 98.

28. P. T. Forsyth, *Positive Preaching and the Modern Mind* (London: Independent Press, 1953), p. 254.

29. *Ibid.*

30. Harry Escott, ed., *The Cure of Souls: An Anthology of P. T. Forsyth's Practical Writings* (Grand Rapids: Eerdmans, 1971), p. 133.

31. *Ibid.*

32. Karl Barth, *The Word of God and the Word of Man*, trans. Douglas Horton (New York: Harper & Row, 1957), pp. 183–217.

33. Barth, *The Preaching of the Gospel*, p. 17.

34. In his earlier phase Barth was not averse to speaking of reconciliation as being effected through preaching, though he meant the fruits of reconciliation. See *The Preaching of the Gospel*, p. 22. As he matured in his thought, he ever more distinguished the reconciling work of Christ and the revealing work of the Spirit. The Spirit discloses in preaching what has already been enacted and effected for all mankind in the cross and resurrection of Christ.

35. Dietrich Bonhoeffer, *Letters and Papers from Prison*, rev. ed. Eberhard Bethge (New York: Macmillan, 1967), p. xiii.

36. Eberhard Bethge, *Dietrich Bonhoeffer*, trans. Eric Mosbacher et al. (London: Collins, 1970), p. 361.

37. Dietrich Bonhoeffer, *Life Together*, trans. John W. Doberstein (New York: Harper & Row, 1954), p. 108.

38. Dietrich Bonhoeffer, *The Cost of Discipleship*, p. 188.

39. Bonhoeffer, *Letters and Papers from Prison*, ed. Eberhard Bethge (New York: Macmillan, 1972), pp. 280–282, 299–300, 327. Also see his *Ethics*, ed. Eberhard Bethge, trans. Neville Horton Smith (New York: Macmillan, 1962), pp. 84 ff.

40. See Paul Tillich, *The Interpretation of History*, trans. N. A. Rasetzki and Elsa L. Talmey (New York: Charles Scribner's Sons, 1936), pp. 46, 47; and his *The Shaking of the Foundations* (New York: Charles Scribner's Sons, 1952), pp. 153 ff.

41. Barth, *The Preaching of the Gospel*, p. 10.

42. Norval Geldenhuys, *Commentary on the Gospel of Luke*, reprint ed. (Grand Rapids: Eerdmans, 1966), pp. 141, 142.

43. *John Wesley's Forty-Four Sermons*, 12th ed. (London: Epworth Press, 1975), p. 400.

44. *Luther's Works*, vol. 29, p. 184.

45. Evangelicals would do well to remember that Jonathan Edwards spoke out against unethical business practices, rebuking parishioners for denying grazing rights to the poor and for raising the price of their grain in times of poor harvest (*A.D.* magazine, vol. 5, no. 9 [September 1976], p. 28). He also

defended Indian land rights against members of his own congregation and his own relatives (while serving at the frontier Indian mission at Stockbridge after his dismissal from his congregation at Northampton in 1750). We should also bear in mind the politically incendiary preaching of the Scottish Reformer John Knox. Though his sermons were theological in substance, they had far-reaching political and social consequences.

46. Gary R. Collins, ed., *Our Society in Turmoil* (Carol Stream, Ill.: Creation House, 1970), p. 22.

47. Reinhold Niebuhr, *Justice and Mercy* (New York: Harper & Row, 1974), p. 134.

48. Bonhoeffer, *The Cost of Discipleship*, p. 225.

49. Karl Barth, *God Here and Now,* trans. Paul M. Van Buren (London: Routledge and Kegan Paul, 1964), p. 78.

50. Daniel Callahan, Heiko Oberman, and Daniel J. O'Hanlon, eds., *Christianity Divided* (New York: Sheed & Ward, 1961), p. 235.

51. Rudolf Bultmann, *Jesus Christ and Mythology* (New York: Charles Scribner's Sons, 1958), pp. 84, 85.

52. Rudolf Bultmann, *Primitve Christianity in Its Contemporary Setting,* trans. R.H. Fuller (London: Thames & Hudson, 1956), p. 23.

53. P. T. Forsyth, *Congregationalism and Reunion.* (London: Independent Press, 1952), p. 78.

54. Zwingli, unlike Luther and Calvin, restricted the Eucharist to four times a year and saw the worship service oriented about the sermon. He set the pace for the rationalizing of Protestant worship whereby the mystical and sacramental aspects of worship faded into the background.

55. Robert Webber, "Agenda for the Church 1976–2000," *Eternity,* vol. 27, no. 1 (January 1976), pp. 15 ff.

56. Bonhoeffer, *The Cost of Discipleship,* p. 215.

57. P. T. Forsyth, *The Church and the Sacraments,* 2nd ed. (London: Independent Press, 1947), p. 232.

58. Emil Brunner, *Our Faith,* trans. John W. Rilling (New York: Charles Scribner's Sons, 1954), pp. 127, 128.

59. Quoted in Samuel M. Shoemaker, *By the Power of God* (New York: Harper & Row, 1954), p. 128.

60. Cited in Paul Althaus, *The Theology of Martin Luther,* trans. Robert C. Schultz (Philadelphia: Fortress Press, 1970), p. 350.

61. In a personal letter dated February 25, 1976. For McDonnell worship should be seen as the context for the Word.

62. Hans Küng, *The Church,* trans. Ray Ockenden and Rosaleen Ockenden (New York: Sheed & Ward, 1967), p. 219.

63. Luther, W.A. 38, 231.

64. John Calvin, *Commentary on the Epistles of Paul the Apostle to the Corinthians,* II, 5, 19, trans. John Pringle (Edinburgh: Calvin Translation Society, 1849), p. 239.

65. John Calvin, *Institutes of the Christian Religion,* IV, 14, 4, ed. John T. McNeill, p. 1279.

66. Clyde E. Fant, *Bonhoeffer: Worldly Preaching* (Nashville: Thomas Nelson, 1975), pp. 129, 130.

67. Hans-Joachim Kraus, *The Threat and the Power,* trans. Keith Crim (Richmond, Va: John Knox Press, 1971), p. 73.

68. Martin Luther, *Von Ordnung Gottesdiensts,* W.A. 12, 35.

69. We affirm that both symbols—*table* and *altar*—have a place in Reformed Christianity, since the Eucharist is both a fellowship meal and a representation and proclamation of the sacrifice of Christ on Calvary. The Mercersburg movement in the German Reformed church in nineteenth-century America recovered the sacrificial dimension of Eucharistic worship.

70. See Frederick W. Schroeder, *Worship in the Reformed Tradition* (Philadelphia: United Church Press, 1966), pp. 139–147. Our own recommendation is for a monthly observance of the sacrament.

71. Fant, *Bonhoeffer: Worldly Preaching,* p. 173.

72. Bethge, *Dietrich Bonhoeffer,* p. 175.

73. P. T. Forsyth, *God the Holy Father* (London: Independent Press Ltd., 1957), p. 61.

74. Cf. Donald G. Miller: "Unless our message is an unfolding of the meaning of the Scriptures, we are orators and not preachers. And the world will never be saved by oratory—only by God!" In his *Fire in Thy Mouth* (Nashville: Abingdon Press, 1954), p. 109.

75. Martin Luther, *The Bondage of the Will,* trans. J. I. Packer and O. R. Johnston (Old Tappan, N.J.: Fleming H. Revell, 1957), p. 95.

76. Barth, *The Preaching of the Gospel,* p. 30.

77. James Montgomery Boice, "The Great Need for Great Preaching," *Christianity Today,* vol. 19, no. 6 (December 20, 1974), p. 9.

78. Sermon on Deuteronomy 5:23–27. *Corpus Reformatorum, Calvini Opera,* 26:406.

79. Emil Brunner, *Revelation and Reason,* trans. Olive Wyon (Philadelphia: Westminster Press, 1946), p. 157.

80. Søren Kierkegaard, *The ˋresent Age,* trans. Alexander Dru (New York: Harper & Row, 1962), p. 97 n.

81. Karl Barth, *The Church and the Political Problem of Our Day* (New York: Charles Scribner's Sons, 1939), p. 83.

82. Bonhoeffer, *Life Together,* p. 108.

83. Bertram Lee Woolf, ed., *Reformation Writings of Martin Luther,* vol. 1 (London: Lutterworth Press, 1952), p. 368.

84. Quoted in Morgan, *Puritan Spirituality,* p. 33.

85. The invitational, to be sure, can be the occasion for the decision of faith itself, and therefore our recommendation should be taken only as a general principle. We urge, however, that people be encouraged to surrender to Christ and forsake their sins in the situation of the preaching and hearing of the Word, for otherwise preaching is simply a preparation for an extrabiblical devotional practice viewed as the climax of the service.

86. Cited in James McGraw, *Great Evangelical Preachers of Yesterday* (Nashville: Abingdon Press, 1961), p. 8.

87. Fant, *Bonhoeffer; Worldly Preaching,* p. 167.

88. Watchman Nee, *The Ministry of God's Word* (New York: Christian Fellowship Publishers, 1971), p. 187.

89. *Luther's Works,* vol. 54, p. 213.

90. Paul Holmer, "Contemporary Evangelical Faith: An Assessment and Critique." In *The Evangelicals*, eds. David F. Wells and John D. Woodbridge (Nashville: Abingdon Press, 1975) [pp. 68–95], pp. 73, 74.

91. Fant, *Bonhoeffer, Worldly Preaching*, pp. 172, 173.

92. *Luther's Works*, vol. 12, p. 167.

93. Bonhoeffer, *Ethics*, p. 260.

V.

THE PRIESTHOOD OF ALL BELIEVERS

As you come to him, the living Stone . . . you also, like living stones, are being built into a spiritual house to be a holy priesthood, offering spiritual sacrifices acceptable to God through Jesus Christ.

I Peter 2:4, 5 (NIV)

And you have gathered them into a kingdom and made them priests of our God; they shall reign upon the earth.

Revelation 5:10 (LB)

Since he is a priest and we are his brethren, all Christians have the power and must fulfill the commandments to preach and to come before God with our intercessions for one another and to sacrifice ourselves to God.

Martin Luther

Not only ministers but all Christians are made priests by their Savior, are anointed by the Holy Spirit, and are dedicated to perform spiritual-priestly acts.

Philip Spener

The abolition of a special priestly caste and its replacement by the priesthood of the *one* new and eternal high priest has as its strange and yet logical consequence the fact that *all* believers share in a universal priesthood.

Hans Küng

PRIESTHOOD IN THE BIBLE

It is commonly believed that the doctrine of the priesthood of all believers has its basis in the New Testament rather than the Old and that the Old Testament conception of priesthood is superseded and annulled. Yet a careful examination of the Old Testament discloses that the New Testament doctrine is indeed anticipated in the Old. Under the Mosaic covenant the whole nation is to be a "kingdom of priests" and hence a holy people (Exod. 19:6; Lev. 11:44 ff.; Num. 15:40).

104

The sanctity required of the whole people is, however, symbolized in a special priesthood drawn from the tribe of Levi which functioned as a mediator of the covenant. This Levitical priesthood had a representative character. Its members discharged their duties on behalf of the community as a whole. Through their ministrations the true requirements for serving God were continually kept before the eyes of the covenant people. The covenant relationship with God was vicariously maintained by this priesthood in the name of the whole nation. In this way a purified and sanctified Israel was able to serve God and receive his blessing (Zech. 3:1-5).

In the earliest known social pattern of Israel, however, priests as a class did not exist. Any Israelite man could present offerings to God: this was usually the tribal leader or eldest son, for instance, Abraham, Isaac, Jacob, Manoah, and Gideon. Samuel, generally thought of as a prophet, nevertheless fulfilled all the functions of a priest (1 Sam. 2:18; 3:1; 9:13-25). During the early monarchy kings sometimes exercised priestly prerogatives, for example, David (2 Sam. 6:12-19; 24:25) and Solomon (1 Kings 3:15). In Israelite tradition the special priesthood originated at Sinai, with the consecration of Aaron and his sons. At the same time, as we have seen, prophets, judges, and kings also assumed priestly roles on various occasions.

As Israelite religion developed the priestly role was ever more restricted to a special caste. When the temple became a national institution under the kings, the priesthood was given additional prestige. After the return from the exile it assumed an even more important role, since it was religion that now gave Israel its governors, its institutions and meaning, the reason for its being. As the priesthood was increasingly elevated in Hebrew society, the tensions between prophet and priest became steadily more pronounced. The ritual sacrifices of the priests were regarded by prophetic figures as of considerably less value than acts of justice and mercy (Mic. 6:6-8; Amos 5:21-24). It was the sacrifice of a broken heart that was deemed most acceptable before God (Ps. 51:17). The priesthood of the whole people of God was reaffirmed in the messianic prediction of Isaiah: "You shall be called the priests of the Lord, men shall speak of you as the ministers of our God" (Isa. 61:6; cf. Joel 2:28, 29).

By the time of Jesus the authority of the priestly caste had become intolerably oppressive.[1] Beginning in 400 B.C., when the Jews accepted the Torah as their canonical guidebook, the high priest at Jerusalem not only received tithes as an offering but demanded them as a legal requirement. The aristocratic priestly party, the Sadducees, saw in

Jesus a special threat, since he assumed the role of the perfect and great high priest. Jesus did not repudiate the Jewish priesthood nor the sacrificial system of the Temple, but he made clear that the kingdom of God transcends the restrictions of cultus and sacrifice and that the spirit of worship, not the place of worship, is of utmost significance (John 4:23). He also pointed to himself as the true temple of God and thereby incurred the wrath of the high priest Caiaphas (Matt. 26:61; cf. John 2:19–21).

The New Testament is unequivocal that the sacrifices and burnt offerings of the Old Testament priesthood are both superseded and fulfilled in the once for all sacrifice of Jesus Christ on the cross. Whereas the sacrifices of the priesthood under the old covenant were offered repeatedly and could never take away sin, Christ offered for all time a single sacrifice for sin that effects salvation (Rom. 3:25; 8:3; Heb. 10:11, 12). The believer can now enter the sanctuary of God's presence through the blood of Christ and no longer needs the special mediation of a priestly caste. All that is necessary is that we come to God with the full assurance of faith and hope in the promises of Christ (Heb. 10:22, 23).

The priesthood of Jesus finds its type and pattern in the legendary figure of Melchizedek (Gen. 14:18; Ps. 110:4), who "is without father or mother or genealogy, and has neither beginning of days nor end of life" (Heb. 7:3). Christ's priesthood is eternal, for he continues to intercede for us at the right hand of God (Heb. 7:24, 25). Human mediators are no longer necessary, since his Spirit dwells within those who believe. We now have direct access to God through him who died for us and rose again and lives within us by his Spirit.

In Judaism priesthood was hereditary in the tribe of Levi. The priest was a mediator between the divine and human by virtue of his superior knowledge of the supernatural. He was the director and performer of sacrifices offered to the deity.

In the New Testament church, on the other hand, one becomes a priest by being united through faith in the one Mediator, Jesus Christ. Because we are his brethren, we share in his priestly role by offering spiritual sacrifices to God (1 Pet. 2:5). By his Spirit we are enabled to intercede, sacrifice, and counsel on behalf of others. Christ brings our sacrifices and intercessions before the Father and thus renders them acceptable and effectual (1 Pet. 2:5; Heb. 7:25). Christians share in the kingly rule of Christ as well as in his priestly intercession (Rev. 1:6) and therefore fulfill the Old Testament prophecies of the New Israel as a holy nation and royal priesthood (Exod. 19:6; Isa. 42:6; 61:6). The church is indeed established as a "kingdom of priests" (Rev. 1:6, TEV; 5:10; 20:6), who are empowered to preach, sacrifice, and intercede for the world. All its members have been anointed by the Spirit to be witnesses and ambassadors of Christ (cf. Acts 2:17, 18).

THE GIFTS OF THE HOLY SPIRIT

The priesthood of believers, as the New Testament understands this, cannot be adequately understood apart from the gifts of the Holy Spirit. All Christians are called to exercise their priesthood but in different ways, depending on the gifts that have been allotted to them. Calling, indeed, is correlative with charism. The way we serve in the body of Christ is conditional on how we use the charisms that are bestowed on us in faith and baptism (cf. 1 Cor. 7:17 NEB).

Paul was conscious that his own ministry was grounded in the outpouring of the Holy Spirit: "I will not venture to speak of anything except what Christ has wrought through me to win obedience from the Gentiles, by word and deed, by the power of signs and wonders, by the power of the Holy Spirit" (Rom. 15:18, 19). His preaching is here depicted as a manifestation of the Holy Spirit in and through him. In the Epistle to the Hebrews it is declared that the message was spoken first by the Lord and then attested by the apostles "while God also bore witness by signs and wonders and various miracles and by gifts of the Holy Spirit distributed according to his own will" (Heb. 2:3, 4).

The charisms of the Spirit do not refer to innate talents or powers but to potentialities that are created, aroused, and appealed to by the Holy Spirit (Küng). They are wholly dependent on the empowering and renewing activity of the Holy Spirit in the lives of the members of the church. This is why they can be spoken of as manifestations of the Holy Spirit, though they are exercised and applied by the individual Christian.

Charisms are given to all Christians for the purpose of the upbuilding and extension of the body of Christ. Even the gift of tongues, which is for personal edification, nonetheless contributes to the well-being and upbuilding of the church indirectly. When it is united with the gift of interpretation, it serves to edify and instruct others. The charisms are "not special marks of distinction belonging to the few" but "a distinguishing mark of the whole church" (Küng).

However significant the charisms may be in the fulfilling of the mission of the church, they are not the hallmark of being a Christian.

Extraordinary gifts appear among unbelievers as well, and this is why Paul declared that the evidence of true faith is the confession of Jesus as Lord (1 Cor. 12:2, 3). Miracles of healing were evident among the Pharisees as well as among the disciples of Jesus (Matt. 12:27). Caiaphas, the high priest of the Jews, who was not himself a follower of Christ, nonetheless prophesized that Jesus would die not only for the nation but for the whole people of God (John 11:49–52). Jesus cautioned his disciples that they should rejoice not in their ability to do great things for God, in their powers of exorcism and healing, but in their election by God for salvation (Luke 10:17–20).

The gifts of the Spirit are distributed to the whole community of believers, but not everyone receives the very same gift. The Spirit chooses to work through some members of the body of Christ in a different way than through others. The charisms are not uniform but multiform, and therefore there is a diversity in ministry even though there is a oneness in mission. In order to combat anarchic and illuministic tendencies Paul reminds the Corinthians that God has instituted a variety of ministries and orders (1 Cor. 12:28–30). Some persons are called to exercise the public ministries of teaching, preaching, and evangelization. Other charisms, such as admonishing, consoling, wisdom, knowledge, and the discerning of spirits are private endowments given by God for the service of others to be used as the occasion demands. It is incumbent upon all Christians to witness to the faith, but not all are called to witness publicly in the role of apostles, pastors, and evangelists. Jesus appointed the seventy to preach and heal, but when one who was healed asked to serve him as a disciple, he replied that he should instead return to his home community and share the good news with his family and friends (Mark 5:18, 19). In Acts 6:1–4 we read that deacons were appointed to help in the distribution of food to the needy so that the apostles could devote themselves to the ministry of the word. Peter declares that we should use whatever gift is given to us to "serve others, faithfully administering God's grace in its various forms" (1 Pet. 4:10 NIV).

All members of the church have their special call and their personal ministry, even though all do not share in the pastoral ministry. A charism for the exercise of a special ministry can be prayed for (1 Tim. 4:14; 2 Tim. 1:6), but one must be willing to make the sacrifice that the gift requires. Paul urged his hearers to earnestly desire the higher gifts (1 Cor. 12:31), such as prophecy, teaching, and preaching, though he did not denigrate the gift of tongues and regarded it as a salutary aid in prayer and personal communion with God. It is highly probable that

Paul himself spoke in tongues (cf. 1 Cor. 14:18; 2 Cor. 5:13), though he resisted the notion that this is the evidence or sign of having the Holy Spirit (cf. 1 Cor. 12:2, 3).

It is not our intention here to give an in-depth examination of the various charisms of the Holy Spirit, but at least twenty are mentioned in the New Testament. What is important to recognize is that all believers share in the ministry and mission of our Lord Jesus Christ through the charisms that they have received. All ministries, including those exercised by a special commission (e.g., pastor, teacher) are charismatic. Gifts that are not used will atrophy, and this is what happened when sacerdotalism replaced the priesthood of all believers, and formalism usurped the charismatic fellowship of love *(koinonia)* that characterized New Testament Christianity at its best. This, of course, accounts for the Montanist reaction in the second and third centuries, when an attempt was made to regain the free exercise of the gifts of the Spirit.

We need to be reminded that every Christian as a priest and king is directed to some special calling and ministry within the one ministry of Christ. Some are called to be evangelists, pastors, and teachers. Others are appointed to be healers and workers of miracles. Others are given the charisms of knowledge, wisdom, wonder-working faith, exorcism, tongues, and interpretation of tongues. Still others are equipped by the Spirit to serve in an extraordinary way, to admonish and to administer. Some people may be endowed with many of these charisms and others with only a few. All may appear in the lives of a few Christians, since the Spirit acts and moves as he wills, but it seems that every Christian is directed to a particular form of service within the one body, and this means that he will be endowed with particular gifts that will enable him to fulfill this calling. A church where the charismatic gifts in all their variety and wonder are not in evidence is something less than the church founded at Pentecost. A church where the priestly role is restricted to the office of the pastor or bishop is a church where the Spirit has been quenched and grieved. All believers are called to be priests and kings with Christ, and this means all are given the privilege of interceding and sacrificing for their brethren; yet the way in which we exercise this ministry will vary depending on how the Spirit chooses to manifest himself in and through us.

HISTORICAL DEVELOPMENT

For the purposes of order and propriety the early church was compelled to structure itself, and special offices of pastors and deacons were created. Küng maintains that there is no evidence of a monarchial episcopate in the Pauline communities, though bishops were soon designated to oversee various churches. The earliest bishops, however, were equivalent to pastors or presbyters, and their function was basically administrative and pastoral. The bishops and deacons at Philippi (Phil. 1:1) seem to be comparable to the teachers at Corinth and the "presbyter-bishops" of Ephesus. In 1 Peter (2:25) the chief Shepherd alone is given the title of *episkopos* (bishop), but in Titus the idea of presbyter is replaced by that of *episkopos* (1:7).

By the beginning of the third century the role of bishop became more liturgical in character. The titles "priest" and "high priest" were now applied to the ministry of the bishop, a practice which had earlier been strictly avoided. The first Christian writers to use the words *priest* and *high priest* of the church's ministers were Tertullian and Hippolytus. Küng makes this astute observation: "A genuine sacralizing and ritualizing took effect, especially from the fifth and sixth centuries on: fading of the ministry of the word into the background, the cultic-ritual activity of the minister as the real priestly work, reification of liturgical authority, a special holiness and dignity proper to the office holder."[2] The recognition of the universal priesthood of believers was not wholly lost sight of, however, even though it was not effectively put into practice. Ambrose, who emphasized the sacramental character of the church, could nevertheless affirm: "Everyone is anointed into the priesthood, is anointed into the kingdom, but the spiritual kingdom is also the spiritual priesthood."[3]

In the high middle ages the juridical model of the church reigned supreme, and, except for the protests of charismatic and mystical movements like the Spiritual Franciscans and the Friends of God, it was not adequately challenged. Avery Dulles describes the role of the clergy in this model:

All the functions of the bishop or priest are juridicized. When he teaches, people are obliged to accept his doctrine not because of his knowledge or personal gifts but because of the office he holds. When he celebrates the sacraments, the priest exercises sacred powers that others do not have. According to some theories the priest's "power of the keys" enables him at his discretion to supply or withhold the means of grace, and thus to confer or deny what is needed for salvation—a truly terrifying power over the faithful.[4]

According to Bonaventure the priestly office has a sevenfold function: to instruct in matters of faith, develop virtues, give an example of holiness, intercede through prayers, heal injuries inflicted by enemies, warn against imminent dangers, and repel demonic assaults.[5] He likened the priest to a trustee of the treasures of the faith, a leader and shepherd of the faithful, and a watchman who guards the souls of his people.

The Council of Trent decided that sermons in the strict sense should be reserved for bishops and their assistants. A general ban on lay preaching was officially incorporated in the *Codex Iuris Canonici* (1918), though a layman (Ladovico Nogorola) preached at the Council of Trent itself. Hans Küng argues that, with the change of theological climate in the Catholic Church inaugurated by the Second Vatican Council, the time might be propitious for a restoration of lay preaching.[6]

In its "Decree on the Apostolate of the Laity" the Second Vatican Council sought to make a place for the New Testament doctrine of the priesthood of believers by maintaining that all Christians are sharers in the priestly, kingly, and prophetic role of Christ (Chapter III). It asserted that the laity "should above all make missionary activity their own by giving material or even personal assistance, for it is a duty and honor for Christians to return to God a part of the good things they receive from Him."[7]

At the same time, the idea of the special hierarchical priesthood was stoutly reaffirmed in the Council. It was claimed that our Lord appointed certain individuals who "would be able by the sacred power of their order to offer sacrifice and to remit sins."[8] Such persons "shoulder the sacred task of the gospel, so that the offering of the people can be made acceptable through the sanctifying power of the Holy Spirit."[9] Because of the sacrament of orders, "priests of the New Testament exercise the most excellent and necessary office of father and teacher among the People of God and for them."[10]

More recently Hans Küng has valiantly labored to recover the biblical doctrine of the priesthood of all believers and has definitely gone beyond the Council at various points. Küng vigorously opposes the sacralization of the Church's ministry which sets its holder as a sacred person apart from others and raises him above ordinary Christians to be a mediator with God. "From the dissolution of the special priesthood by the priesthood of the one, new and eternal high priest," he explains, "there follows . . . the universal priesthood of all believers, which has as its concrete content the immediate access of everyone to God, spiritual sacrifices, the proclamation of the word, the carrying out of baptism, the Eucharist, and the forgiveness of sins, and mutual intercession for one another."[11] According to Küng every faithful believer may preach, intercede in prayer, baptize, and administer the elements at the Lord's Supper. He even claims that, because the whole Church has the power to forgive sins, "*every* Christian is fundamentally empowered to take an active part in the forgiving of sins."[12] The power of the keys to bind and loose (John 20:23) is, therefore, not the exclusive prerogative of the clergy. Yet he recognizes that for purposes of church order some of these rights can be limited by the community. He is unwilling to disavow the special role of the pastor in the governance of the church and the special gifts that this role entails. At the same time he allows that, in extraordinary circumstances where no duly ordained pastor is available, a layman may then preside at the Eucharist and even be ordained by fellow laymen for the purpose of baptizing and presiding at the Eucharist. Not surprisingly, Küng's radical departure from the Roman Catholic tradition in this area has elicited some negative reaction in conservative Catholic circles.

The universal priesthood of believers was given special prominence in the Protestant Reformation, particularly by Martin Luther. For Luther, "all Christians are priests, and all priests are Christians. Worthy of anathema is any assertion that a priest is anything else than a Christian."[13] Since Christ is the one high priest, and we are his brethren, "all Christians have the power and must fulfill the commandment to preach and to come before God with our intercessions for one another and to sacrifice ourselves to God."[14] Luther went so far as to avow that any Christian may, in principle, bestow baptism and preside at Communion. He also maintained that "there is no other kind of sin than that which any Christian can bind or loose. There is no other sacrifice than of the body of every Christian."[15] At the same time, he just as vigorously insisted that the public preaching of the Word and the administration of the sacraments be properly done by ministers, who become such by a special calling. In his battle with the enthusiasts he was compelled to reassert the special office of the clergy for the purpose of maintaining church order and discipline. Yet he steadfastly contended for the priesthood of believers not as a substitute for the ministry of the word but as its supplement. In Luther's perspective all Christians are priests by virtue of their baptism, but only a few are ministers through public ordination. The holy priesthood of believers does not exclude the ministry of the word but constitutes its basis and goal. It is the priesthood that designates who are to be ministers and not vice versa.[16] He could even say that priests are "thus greater than mere kings, the reason being that priesthood makes us worthy to stand before God, and to pray for others. For to stand and pray before God's face is the prerogative of none except priests."[17]

For Luther the pastoral ministry is subordinated to the priesthood even in the practice of the private confession of sins. He rejected the ecclesiastical rule that required confession, but yet he saw confession as an indispensable form of the Gospel. When we go to the pastor to confess sins, we should see him first of all as a brother and a Christian and then as a clergyman.[18] Indeed, hearing confession is a priestly service which one may receive from any brother.

The doctrine of the priesthood of all believers is not nearly so pronounced in the theologies of Calvin and Zwingli. For Calvin Christ's priestly work is finished and can in no way be supplemented or repeated by priests of the church. He maintained that Christ never entrusted the function of sacrificing to the apostles nor wished it to be undertaken by any of their successors. Yet he recognized that all Christians must offer spiritual sacrifices to God: first they offer themselves and then they intercede for their brethren.[19] Calvin acknowledged four ministries in the church: pastors, doctors, elders, and deacons. Outside of these official functions, he did not see any special ministries available for believers in fulfilling the great commission. Charismatic ministries such as healing and prophecy were relegated to the apostolic age.

Zwingli explained that the "royal priesthood" of 1 Peter 2 meant that "the Lord Jesus Christ has called all Christians to kingly honour and to the priesthood, so that they do not need a sacrificing priest to offer on their behalf, for they are all priests, offering spiritual gifts, that is, dedicating themselves wholly to God."[20] In Zwingli's discussion of the holy priesthood the Christian as priest offers himself to God, but nothing is said of the ministry of intercession and service to one's neighbor.[21]

The Belgic Confession is typical of the Reformation confessions in elevating the ministry of the Word while slighting or ignoring the priesthood of all believers. Article XXX declares:

We believe that this true Church must be governed by the spiritual policy which our Lord has taught us in his Word—namely, that there must be Ministers or Pastors to preach the Word of God, and to administer the Sacraments: also elders and deacons, who, together with the pastors, form the council of the Church; that by these means the true religion may be preserved.[22]

Surprisingly, the priesthood of believers is also absent from the Augsburg Confession as well as other Lutheran creeds.[23]

It remained for Evangelical Pietism to give the biblical doctrine of the holy priesthood of believers the attention it deserves. Whereas this doctrine received theoretical recognition from Luther and his colleagues, the Pietists gave it tangible expression. Indeed, one of their salient emphases was the priesthood of all believers over the exclusive priesthood of the clergy. Since they attached more importance to spiritual illumination than to education and even ordination, impetus was thereby given to the ministry of the laity.

Philip Spener's contribution to the development of this doctrine is especially significant:

Everybody imagines that just as he was himself called to his office, business, or trade and the minister was neither called to such an occupation nor works in it, so the minister alone is called to perform spiritual acts, occupy himself with the Word of God, pray, study, teach, admonish, comfort, chastise, etc., while others should not trouble themselves with such things and, in fact, would be meddling in the minister's business if they had anything to do with them.[24]

On the contrary, said Spener, "not only ministers but all Christians are made priests by their Savior, are anointed by the Holy Spirit, and are dedicated to perform spiritual-priestly acts."[25] He was convinced that the spiritual priesthood consists in the threefold office of sacrifice, prayer, and the use of God's Word. Any Christian, therefore, may celebrate the sacraments in cases of necessity, especially baptism. In the absence of an ordained preacher the Lord's Supper may also be celebrated, though care should be taken that the one who presides is solid in the faith. Like Luther Spener attacked the idea that without private confession to a priest there is no forgiveness of sins. He criticized the confessional as it was then practiced in some Lutheran circles as a requirement for Holy Communion. Any Christian may confess to a fellow believer and in this way receive absolution.

As a complement to the traditional service of worship, Spener advocated the formation of special assemblies where laypeople could come together for the purpose of mutual consolation and edification. In such an assembly, "one person would not rise to preach . . . but others who have been blessed with gifts and knowledge would also speak and present their pious opinions on the proposed subject to the judgment of the rest, doing all this in such a way as to avoid disorder and strife."[26] Women, too, were permitted to give testimonies and prayers at such meetings, and this particularly disturbed those who were rigidly traditionalist or orthodox. In Spener's view every Christian is given the privilege of teaching others, of chastising, exhorting, and converting. Every believer should be concerned about the personal salvation of his fellow human beings and should devote himself to prayer on their behalf.

Yet Spener, like Luther before him, recognized that, though all Christians are called to exercise spiritual functions, not all are called to the public exercise of them. All Christians by virtue of being anointed by the Holy Ghost stand in the spiritual office and in case of need may administer its duties. Yet every Christian will respect and honor those who have been publicly commissioned to the task of shepherding and preaching. The spiritual priesthood does not encroach on the office of the pastor but is its necessary supplement.

The priesthood of all believers was given additional impetus in the Wesleyan movement. Wesley was unwilling to discard the notion of a separated ministry, but he was adamant that the laity too must participate in the evangelistic mandate of the church through personal witnessing, intercession, Bible study, and deeds of mercy. In his perspective it seems that we are all priests by regeneration, not by baptism. The vision of the holy priesthood is epitomized in Annie Matheson's missionary hymn:

> Tell every man on earth,
>   The greatest and the least,
> Love called him from his birth,
>   To be a king and priest.[27]

The charismatic gifts, especially the so-called extraordinary gifts, were more in evidence among the Anabaptists and radical Pietists than in the mainstream evangelical movement. Prophecy, healing, discerning of spirits, miracles, and glossolalia were present in some Anabaptist circles, though the emphasis was always upon a life of contrition and penitential suffering. The baptism of martyrdom and blood was regarded more highly than an ecstatic baptism of the Spirit.

Johann Christoph Blumhardt, nineteenth-century German revival preacher, became noted for his ministry of deliverance, which entailed the exorcism of demons. His motto "Jesus is Victor" was later adopted by Karl Barth as the salient theme of his theology.[28] Through his Christ-centered emphasis Blumhardt succeeded in overcoming the subjectivism that marred much latter-day Pietism.[29]

Radical Pietism, which gave birth to religious communities and new sects, stressed the need for a continual openness to the movement of the Spirit. The Community of True Inspiration (Amana Society) accorded special recognition to divinely attuned individuals *(Werkzeuge)* who fell into trance-like states and uttered prophecies with authority. New revelations and spiritual healings have figured prominently in the Catholic Apostolic church (Irvingites), the Christian Catholic church (Doweyites), and the New Apostolic church. Among the Plymouth Brethren the idea of a separated clergy is wholly rejected, and any layman illumined by the Spirit can give a special address at meetings or officiate at the Lord's Supper. While speaking much of the gifts of the Spirit, the Brethren have emphasized preaching, evangelism, and prayer and not the more spectacular gifts.

In original Quakerism, too, there was no ordained clergy, and every follower of Christ was believed free "to speak or prophesy by the Spirit" (Robert Barclay). George Fox averred that Christians receive a part of the ministry through "the exercise of their spiritual gifts in the church."[30] The sacraments were regarded as being mainly relics of primitive magic. Prophecy, healings, and new revelations were not uncommon in the early history of Quakerism.

The gifts of the Spirit have been especially pronounced in the Pentecostal and neo-Pentecostal movements, with particular emphasis on glossolalia and spiritual healing. Glossolalia is generally considered the evidence of the baptism or infilling of the Holy Spirit, an experience thought to be subsequent to conversion. Yet other gifts are also given prominent attention, gifts which have been minimized or ignored in mainline Protestantism: the working of miracles, discerning of spirits, prophecy, and the word of knowledge. Regrettably, not as much importance is attached to the less spectacular gifts of teaching, administration, and lowly service, though these gifts are not neglected. While preaching is still highly regarded in the mainstream of Pentecostalism, in some sects preaching is seen as less significant than personal testimonies and healing ceremonies. David du Plessis, an ecumenical Pentecostal, voices this complaint: "I have seen too many shouting Christians go to sleep when the Word is preached. They live on 'milk' and choke on the 'meat' of the Word."[31] In the Catholic Apostolic church, which combines charisma and liturgy, preaching has generally been restricted to ten minutes, and ritual is given precedence. The openness of many Pentecostals to new revelations reflects a spiritualistic orientation in which God's direct guidance to an individual takes precedence over the Bible.

Nonetheless, those of us in the Reformed tradition should recognize that Pentecostalism at its best has recovered the charismatic dimension of New Testament Christianity. The spirit of prophecy is still alive in the charismatic churches, though admittedly it has led to certain excesses. Moreover, the priesthood of all believers is a vibrant reality in these churches. Because of the recognition of the gifts of the Spirit many doors have been opened to spiritually sensitive laymen to engage in a priestly and evangelical ministry. Women too have found a ministry even in the pulpits of Pentecostal churches, and this has been generally denied to them in historical Protestantism.

In Protestant liberal theology the priesthood of believers has been affirmed in such a way as to undercut the idea of a special ministry of the word and sacraments. Theologians who were markedly influenced by the Enlightenment sought to overcome the distinctions between clergy and laity. The pastor was no longer a father figure who speaks God's authoritative word but a fellow-traveler on life's journey who shares the insights and wisdom that he has accumulated on the way. In Schleiermacher's words: "Let there be an assembly before him and not a congregation. Let him be a speaker for all who will hear, but not a shepherd of a definite flock."[32] In the view of this theologian, "every man is a priest, in so far as he draws others to himself in the field he has made his own and can show himself master in; every man is a layman, in so far as he follows the skill and direction of another in the religious matters with which he is less familiar."[33] For Schleiermacher the priestly capacity is something to be gained through the cultivation of religious feeling. Because he recognized a diversity of gifts, he came to accept the place for an ordered ministry but not as a special class removed from the laity. The task of those who develop their religious sensibilities is not to absolve from sin or intercede in prayer but to share religious insights and experiences and guide their fellow human beings in the quest for meaning and reality.

Despite the attack of liberals upon a special ministry under the Word, they developed their own sacerdotalism, but it was based on cultural rather than religious considerations. The Puritans in England and America complained that the liberal clergy sought preeminence over their brethren by virtue of education and worldly honors.[34] It was the Puritans who criticized the preoccupation of the liberal clergy with a guaranteed annual income and job security. In Puritan religion the pastors should be essentially concerned with upholding the faith and shepherding and nurturing the flock that is their charge.

The biblical doctrine of the priesthood of believers is conspicuously apparent in Dietrich Bonhoeffer, who maintained that all Christians must intercede, witness, exhort and reprove, and give counsel. In order

to unburden oneself of guilt one need not go to an ecclesiastical superior or trained counselor but should feel free to approach a Christian
brother or sister, since it is this person who now stands in Christ's
stead. For Bonhoeffer, "the most experienced psychologist or observer
of human nature knows infinitely less of the human heart than the
simplest Christian who lives beneath the Cross of Jesus. . . . In the
presence of a psychiatrist I can only be a sick man; in the presence of
a Christian brother I can dare to be a sinner."[35] Bonhoeffer did not deny
the need for an overseer or pastor so long as the pastoral ministry was
one of service rather than of domination: "Pastoral authority can be
attained only by the servant of Jesus who seeks no power of his own,
who himself is a brother among brothers submitted to the authority of
the Word."[36] Whereas in his early theology Bonhoeffer saw the authority of the pastor derived from the congregation, he later regarded it as
originating from Christ himself.[37]

THE MINISTRY OF THE WORD AND SACRAMENTS

In the light of this brief historical survey it is now appropriate to
examine the precise relation between the priesthood of believers, in
which all Christians share, and the special ministry of the Word and
sacraments. This special ministry is not separate from the priesthood
of believers but the pivotal ministry within it. In the Old Testament we
read that the people of Israel were called to the service of the glory of
God (Isa. 42:6), but also special persons, prophets, were directed to
particular tasks (Isa. 6:8, 9; 50:2). Every believer was commissioned to
a holy vocation, but some were appointed shepherds and guardians of
the faith (Jer. 23:1–4; Isa. 63:11; Ezek. 3:17 ff.; 33:7). The priesthood as
a special caste was abolished by Jesus Christ, but the concept of a
special pastoral ministry remained. This special ministry was anticipated by the prophet Malachi when he declared: "The lips of a priest
should guard knowledge, and men should seek instruction from his
mouth, for he is the messenger of the Lord of hosts" (Mal. 2:5–7). Here
the priest is seen not as one who offers sacrifices but as one who gives
guidance and direction in the faith.

The ministry of the Word has its basis not only in the priesthood of
believers but also in the messianic commissioning of the apostles by
Christ. Only some were commissioned by our Lord to preach the Word
to the nations. This is to say that the ministry of the Word, like some
of the other special ministries of the church (evangelist, deacon, elder),

is a divine office. It is at the same time a charismatic ministry, since it is made possible by spiritual gifts which accompany the divine calling. Paul makes clear that this office is of divine institution: "I became a minister according to the divine office which was given to me for you, to make the word of God fully known" (Col. 1:25; cf. Rom. 15:15, 16). In his address to the elders of Ephesus he points out that this office is one of shepherding and preaching: "Take heed to yourselves and to all the flock, in which the Holy Spirit has made you guardians, to feed the church of the Lord which he obtained with his own blood" (Acts 20:28; cf. 2 Tim. 4:1–4; Titus 1:7–9). He also affirms that this ministry is based on a special charismatic endowment: "Of this gospel I was made a minister according to the gift of God's grace which was given me by the working of his power" (Eph. 3:7).

The rite of ordination was already present in the New Testament church, though the idea was probably taken from Judaism. We read that Moses laid his hands on Joshua, imparting to him the spirit of wisdom needed for his work (Deut. 34:9). In the New Testament the ritual probably took the form of the laying on of hands with intercessory prayers, as described in the commissioning of the seven (Acts 6:3–6; cf. 1 Tim. 4:14; 2 Tim. 1:6). We concur with Küng that ordination is not a sacrament in the New Testament sense of being instituted by Christ. Nonetheless, it is a spiritual event where the Spirit is active through the laying on of hands. Ordination is a sign of the special apostolate of the ministries of leadership. It is a ratification of charism but not its precondition. It signifies "the public calling of a believer to the ministry of leadership, in which the Church recognizes and confirms God's calling."[38]

Hans Küng's efforts to recover the priesthood of all believers for the church have not prevented him from acknowledging the special ministry of the Word and sacraments. "All Christians," he says, "have authority to preach the word, to witness to their faith in the Church and in the world, to 'missionize.' But only pastors with a special calling, or those commissioned by them, have the particular authority to preach in the meetings of the community."[39] In Küng's view the pastor is "a special person in the community, since he is authorized as one with special powers to exercise a special ministry in the public life of the community."[40] He has the authority to found and govern communities, to unite and build up communities, to preach the word in the public assembly, to baptize and celebrate the Lord's Supper, and to bind and to loose from the bondage of sin. "His authority is guaranteed by the gift of the Spirit, which was called down on him by his vocation and through the laying-on of hands and the praying over him; and this vocation must constantly be renewed, the gift of the Spirit must constantly be revived."[41] For Küng the fundamental apostolic succession is that of the Church itself and of every Christian and consists of an objective keeping of the faith of the apostles, which must be concretely realized ever again. At the same time he affirms a special apostolic succession of the ministries of leadership. Reformed Christianity would heartily concur in his view that those preachers who remain faithful to the apostolic message stand in the apostolic succession.[42]

In some respects Küng's position is closer to Luther's than to traditional Roman Catholicism. Luther affirmed the priesthood of all believers, but he also contended for the special ministry of the Word and sacraments. "For although we are all equally priests," he declared, "still not all of us can serve and minister and preach."[43] This ministry, in his judgment, is divinely instituted by Christ but is also certified and authorized by the congregation of believers. Luther saw no contradiction between these two derivations of the ministry—one from above and the other from below, that is, from the priesthood of believers. In both cases the office is willed by God, though it is willed indirectly through the universal priesthood.

Luther was adamant that there must be a divine or inward call as well as the outward call from the congregation before one could become a minister of the Word. Because this ministry is ultimately based on the divine calling, it carries a heavy responsibility but also the assurance that the minister of the Word can prevail against the forces of sin and darkness through the power of the Spirit: "We who are in the ministry of the Word have this comfort, that we have a heavenly and holy office; being legitimately called to this, we prevail over all the gates of hell."[44]

What Luther did not sufficiently recognize is that there are other special ministries that might also require special rites of commissioning, for instance, evangelists, healers, deacons and deaconesses, sisters and brothers of mercy, and so on. At the same time, these should be regarded as auxiliary ministries to the ministry of the Word, since the latter is a ministry of apostolic leadership.

One danger in holding to a special ministry of the Word is sacerdotalism. This means that the minister comes to be viewed as a mediator between man and God. His office is seen as necessary for people to make contact with God. He is also regarded as more holy than other Christians by virtue of being nearer to God. Sometimes in the circles of sacerdotalism the priest or pastor is likened to the neck and Christ to the head. The laypeople represent the lower parts of the body and cannot reach the head apart from the mediation of the priest. Sacerdotalism is present not only in Roman Catholic and Orthodox Christianity but also in the New Apostolic church, the Catholic Apostolic church, and the Church of the Latter Day Saints, all of which maintain a special apostolic or priestly order. Admittedly, such tendencies can also be detected in the churches of the Reformation.

Luther sought to guard against sacerdotalism by maintaining that the pastor is not elevated above the congregation but is responsible to the congregation as its shepherd and overseer. His primacy is one of service, not moral superiority. His representative activity does not exclude but instead includes the cooperation of the community. Paul Althaus gives this interpretation of Luther's position:

The call to an office in the church does not convey a special Christian status but only the special ministry of word and sacrament to the community. There is no indelible character. There is a distinction between the called clergyman and the layman only because of the office: not because of what they are but because of what they do.[45]

A quite different peril that can subvert the ministry of the Word is secularism. Here the minister is no longer shepherd and herald but facilitator and counselor. His role is to build up the autonomous powers of the people who come to him for help, not to speak to them an authoritative Word from God. Langdon Gilkey, in advocating a new role for the pastor-priest, sees him as a peer rather than an authority figure. He is at best "an advisor and counselor in man's personal quest for fulfillment."[46] The counselee himself replaces the priest "as the final judge with regard to his own spiritual health, i.e., as to what law applies and as to whether the law and its rule really help in this case."[47] In this new concept of priesthood there is "little authority and practically no moral objectivity but possibly new and greater opportunities for real ministry."[48]

In some circles today, both Catholic and Protestant, the gifts that are most prized in a minister are personnel managment and skills in human relations.[49] Under the pervasive influence of the business mentality, efficiency in administrative and financial matters is given more weight than biblical fidelity. The rules of the ministerial game are being proficient and being friendly but avoiding any show of religious particularity or dogmatism. Ivan Illich makes this caustic comment: "Clerical technocracy is even further from the gospel than priestly aristocracy. And we may come to recognize that efficiency corrupts Christian testimony more subtly than power."[50]

Thomas Torrance sees a new Protestant sacerdotalism emerging that replaces the humanity of Christ by the humanity of the minister and obscures the Person of Christ by the personality of the minister.[51] It is the dynamism of the minister that mediates the Word of God to man and mediates the worship of man to God. The sermon is no longer an exposition of the Word of God but a presentation of the opinions of the minister. What we find, Torrance observes, are psychological priests. The therapeutic counseling of the minister has displaced the pastoral ministry of Christ.

Our position is that the pastor is an authority figure and a servant figure at the same time. He has been placed in his role by Christ himself through the inward calling of the Holy Spirit, though the congregation must recognize and ratify what Christ has done. The pastor must not lord it over the congregation but be an example of patience and humility. He must give guidance and direction when necessary. He is a resource person to be sure, but even more he is a spiritual director and confessor. He must not be detached from his people but must identify himself with their trials and sufferings. He must intercede for them daily in prayer. He must preach the word in season and out of season (2 Tim. 4:2), and this entails exposing false teaching as well as expounding the truth (Titus 1:10–14). He must be a model of holiness in keeping with his greater responsibility (Titus 2:7). He must "exhort and reprove with all authority" (Titus 2:15), though he must speak the truth always in the spirit of love (1 Cor. 16:14;1 John 3:18). He must seek to please God above all and not his congregation, but he must place no unnecessary stumbling blocks before his people that might prevent them from accepting and following the Gospel. He will be willing to share authority with gifted laypersons of the congregation, who are also priests, but he will not abdicate authority by simply parroting the prejudices of his people. His aim is not to help people adjust to their social and cultural environment but to direct them to God so that they will then be inspired to change their environment. He will see his role as a shepherd rather than a fellow seeker, since he has been entrusted with a commission to make known the Gospel (1 Cor. 9:17, 18). At the same time he will also see himself as a servant who will subordinate himself to his people in their requests and desires, who will make himself continually available to his people as an ambassador of Christ and an agent of reconciliation.

Such a pastor will inspire those in his care also to be priests, to be intercessors and witnesses to the truth at home and at work. He will welcome reproof from his fellow Christians so long as it is done in charity and is based on Scripture. A church directed by such a pastor will indeed be a holy priesthood where all share in some way in the priestly and kingly and prophetic ministry of Christ. The gifts of the Holy Spirit will be in evidence not only in the pulpit but in Sunday school classes, youth groups, and prayer and Bible study groups. The laity will be the missionary arm of the church, for it is through their outreach in the community that the spiritually lost will hear the good news and will be brought into the worship and life of the church.

TOWARD A CATHOLIC BALANCE

In offering a constructive statement of the doctrine of the church and its ministry we must do justice to both cultic and charismatic dimensions if we are to remain true to our biblical and catholic heritage. In Protestantism there has been a noticeable tendency to downplay the institutional side of the church in favor of charisma and koinonia.

The Lutheran church historian Rudolf Sohm propounded a typology of religious association which graphically depicts how the original religious enthusiasm of the church was eroded by a creeping ritualism and formalism. While New Testament Christianity was characterized by a dominance of spirit (charisma), in early Catholicism charisma was transferred to the office of the hierarchy. Then later we see the extension and transfer of charisma from office to thing (sacrament). Whereas in the New Testament church the Spirit was a moving reality in the life and experience of believers, it finally became objectified in the sacraments.

Contrasting the church as an institution with the ecclesia, a communion of persons, Emil Brunner declares that the ecclesia alone is the body of Christ and that it alone was given "the promise of invincibility and eternal durability."[52] The church ideally should be the vessel of the ecclesia, but too often it presents an obstacle to the growth of the ecclesia through sacramentalism and sacerdotalism.

James Dunn too emphasizes the charismatic over the cultic and institutional aspects of the church: "Christian community is not primarily sacramental in character; baptism and the Lord's Supper express community and thereby consolidate community, but they neither create it nor do they form its basis; as all Christians as members of a Christian assembly are charismatics, so *all have immediate access to grace, all may be the channel and instrument of grace to others.*"[53] He maintains that Paul conceives of authority in dynamic terms, not in terms of office or fixed form.

While there is much truth in the traditional Protestant criticism of ecclesiasticism, we must nevertheless recognize that the church is an institution as well as a communion of persons, that it entails structure and cultus as well as charisma. It is not historically accurate to portray the New Testament church as simply a spontaneous fellowship of love directed by charismatic leaders. Jesus himself instituted an apostolic office through his commissioning of the twelve, and Paul upheld permanent ministries of apostles, pastors, evangelists, and teachers, though he also saw these ministries as gifts or charisms and not simply as offices (Eph. 4:11). In the pastoral epistles it is quite evident that the ministry is regarded as a special office in the church, though again the charismatic dimension is not denied. We cannot go along with Ernst Käsemann's contention that Paul's theory of order does not rest on "offices, institutions, ranks and dignities." Käsemann maintains that, in the Pauline view, "authority resides only within the concrete act of ministry as it occurs."[54] But this overlooks the fact that Paul considered his own ministry a divine office (Rom. 1:1–5; Col. 1:25; 2 Tim. 1:11) and that his polemic against the Corinthian church was intended to bring religious enthusiasm under the direction of apostolic and ecclesiastical authority.

Hans Küng in his book *Why Priests?* is more Protestant than Catholic in his critique of ecclesiasticism. He maintains that "there can be no office among the followers of Jesus that is constituted simply through law and power corresponding to the office of state potentates; nor can there be an office that is constituted simply through knowledge and dignity corresponding to the office of the scribes."[55] Yet Jesus himself likened his ministers to scribes who have trained for the kingdom of heaven (Matt. 13:52). He also declared: "I send you prophets and wise men and scribes, some of whom you will kill and crucify. . . ." (Matt. 23:34).

Thomas Torrance presents a quite different view. Far from thinking that the priesthood of the church is dissolved in the general body of believers, he holds with Calvin that the priesthood of the church is "imaged in the midst of the community of believers in the form of a divinely instituted ministry, an episcopate held in a united capacity by those called and ordained to the ministry of Word and Sacraments."[56] This episcopal order is "placed within the Body and partakes of its inner cohesion in mutual service and love, but at the same time it involves diversities of function and distinctions in order, through which Christ exhibits Himself as actually present in the Church as its only Bishop and Master."[57]

Von Allmen insists that there is only one authentic ministry, namely, that of the Word and sacraments, and this has its basis not in the priesthood of believers but in the Messianic commissioning of the apostles.[58] The ministry, he contends, is based on a special grace or calling and is not merely a matter of how the church organizes itself. This contrasts with the view of many Catholic scholars today who are thinking of the pastoral office no longer in terms of its sacral-consecratory function but of its socio-ecclesial function. The role of the priest is to coordinate and integrate the various charisms in such a way as to build up the community of faith.

Avery Dulles is critical of this tendency to see the special priesthood as simply a mode of service in the church rather than a sacramental or ecclesiastical office.[59] Yet he is also cognizant of the dangers in the sacral concept of the priesthood which "can lead to a superstitious exaltation of the priest as a person possessed of divine or magical powers." Such a person, he recognizes, can "become removed from the rest of the community and surrounded with an aura of cultic holiness more redolent of paganism than of Christianity."[60]

We believe that Luther has preserved the right catholic balance in seeing the pastoral office as derived both from its divine institution by Christ and from the priesthood of believers. We cannot go along with Von Allmen and Torrance in regarding ministerial representation as issuing only from above downward and not also from below upward. In our view the ministry is a mode of service within the priesthood of believers, but it is at the same time a service that entails authority and responsibility over the whole community of faith. It derives its authority from God himself and yet through the priesthood of believers. The ministry of the Word and sacraments must not be downgraded (as in a spiritualistic egalitarianism), but it must also not be unduly elevated (as in sacerdotalism).

We see the church as a sacramental and ecclesiastical institution as well as a charismatic fellowship of love. Charisma must be directed and channeled by the pastoral or ecclesiastical office, though we recognize that too often the clerics extinguish rather than fan the flame of the Holy Spirit.

An authentically catholic church is a church under the Word, and this means that the clerical office is also under the Word. Every Christian layman as a fellow priest has the right and obligation to challenge his ecclesiastical superiors if they stray from the clear teaching of the Word. The Spirit does not work independently of the Word but, on the contrary, seeks to bring the Word to bear on the life of the church. The gifts of the Spirit are bestowed in order to draw us closer to the Word and not to go our independent ways.

Too often the priesthood of all believers has been geared to the interest of religious individualism rather than to the service of the corporate missionary witness of the church. We need to recover the biblical and catholic doctrine of the royal priesthood of the church, and Luther can here be a sure and safe guide. Paul Althaus contrasts Luther's position with that of later individualistic Protestantism:

Luther never understands the priesthood of all believers merely in the "Protestant" sense of the Christian's freedom to stand in a direct relationship to God without a human mediator. Rather he constantly emphasizes the Christian's evangelical authority to come before God on behalf of the brethren and also of the world. The universal priesthood expresses not religious individualism but its exact opposite, the reality of the congregation as a community.[61]

The priesthood of all believers is based on the sovereign authority of Jesus Christ as the sole head and ruler of the church, not on the consensus of the people. Mark Noll rightly points out that Luther "replaced the role of the oligarchical few, not, as we in America are inclined to believe, with the rule of the democratic many, but with the rule of the eternal Son of God who was active in all true members."[62] The current practice in Protestant denominations of running the church through committees generally leaves out the one thing needful, the subjection of group consensus to the authority of the Word of God as revealed in Holy Scripture. One consecrated believer who truly wrestles with the Scripture in order to discover God's will may indeed be closer to the truth than his peers who are more concerned with the survival and advancement of the church as an institution. The priesthood of all believers does not necessarily mean majority rule but obedience to the sovereign rule of the one high priest, Jesus Christ. Democratic methods may indeed be preferable to oligarchical dictation in determining the will of God, but these methods themselves must be subjected to the judgment of a still higher criterion, the voice of the living Christ speaking in Scripture.

The keys of binding and loosing (Matt. 16:19) have been given to the whole church to be exercised first of all and especially by those in the office of pastoral leadership. Yet every Christian as a priest has access to these keys. Every Christian can hear confession of sin and grant absolution on the basis of the indwelling of the Spirit of Christ in all the members of his body.

While the priesthood "is common to all Christians, not so is the ministry," declares the Second Helvetic Confession, rightly reminding us that the priesthood and the ministry of the Word are not the same.[63] And yet it goes too far when it affirms that the two are "*very different from one another*" (italics added).[64] All Christians are called to the apostolate and not just those who are commissioned to oversee congregations and preach the Word publicly. All Christians are summoned to sacrifice themselves for the salvation of the world and the advancement of the kingdom of God in the world. Every Christian should be an evangelist, in the sense that he is placed under the divine obligation to give testimony to his faith before the world.

The creeds of the Reformation were accustomed to say that the two hallmarks of the church are the preaching of the Word and the right administration of the sacraments. But even more fundamental is the urgency of mission, and this should entail not simply correct preaching but preaching with a zeal for souls. In this perspective baptism is conceived not simply as entrance into the body of the church but as dedication to the conversion of the world. Confirmation then becomes not merely a renewal of baptismal vows but the ordination of the laity to the apostolate. The Lord's Supper is not just a memorial of Christ's past sacrifice but a participation in his present intercession for the sins of the world. Charismatic gifts are to be accepted not only because of their aid in personal and mutual edification but also, and above all, because of their indispensability in fulfilling the great commission.[65] By these gifts the Holy Spirit empowers us for mission, and this indeed is the vocation of the holy priesthood of believers. The priesthood of believers cannot make reparation for sin, for this has been taken care of by Christ, but it can and must bear witness to the once for all atonement for sin. And it does this through intercessory prayer, sacrificial deeds of kindness and mercy, bringing assurance of pardon for sin, and missionary preaching. Through the charismatic gifts available to us may we rededicate ourselves to this high and holy calling.

NOTES

1. In the words of Henri Daniel-Rops: "The priesthood had thus come to form an exclusive caste, very conscious of itself and full of contempt for others, a caste to which one had to belong . . . before one could pride oneself . . . on one's noble lineage—a caste, furthermore, that was often hated by the common people and the lower clergy." In *Daily Life in the Time of Jesus,* trans. Patrick O'Brian (New York: Hawthorn Books, 1962), p. 422.

2. Hans Küng, *Why Priests?* trans. Robert C. Collins (Garden City, N.Y.: Doubleday, 1972), p. 54.

3. Roy J. Deferrari, trans. *Saint Ambrose: Theological and Dogmatic Works* (Washington, D.C.: Catholic University of America Press, 1963), p. 298.

4. Avery Dulles, *Models of the Church* (Garden City, N.Y.: Doubleday, 1974), p. 153.

5. *Works of Bonaventure,* IV, trans. José de Vinck, (Paterson, N.J.: St. Anthony Guild Press, 1966), p. 256.

6. Hans Küng, *The Church,* p. 378.

7. Walter M. Abbott, ed., *The Documents of Vatican II* (New York: America Press, 1966), p. 502.

8. *Ibid.* ("Decree on the Ministry and Life of Priests" Ch. I, Art. 2), p. 534.

9. *Ibid.,* p. 535.

10. "Decree on the Ministry," ch. II, art. 9, p. 552.

11. Küng, *Why Priests?* pp. 41, 42.

12. Küng, *The Church,* p. 380.

13. *Luther's Works,* vol. 40, (St. Louis: Concordia, 1958), p. 19.

14. Martin Luther, W.A. 12, 308.

15. *Luther's Works,* vol. 40, pp. 34, 35.

16. Cyril Eastwood states Luther's view in this way: "The Christian is a member of the universal priesthood by baptism, but he is given a special task within that priesthood by the call of God which is confirmed by the congregation." Note that the call to the ministry comes directly from God, but it takes effect only in the priesthood. It is authorized first by God but then also by the priesthood in that the latter must ratify and confirm the divine call. Cyril Eastwood, *The Priesthood of All Believers* (Minneapolis: Augsburg, 1960), p. 44.

17. Bertram Lee Woolf, *Reformation Writings of Martin Luther,* Vol. I, p. 366.

18. See Paul Althaus, *The Theology of Martin Luther,* trans. Robert C. Schultz (Philadelphia: Fortress Press, 1970), pp. 316–318.

19. "We can offer nothing, until we offer to him ourselves as a sacrifice; which is done by denying ourselves. Then, afterwards follow prayers, thanksgiving, almsdeeds, and all the duties of religion." Calvin, *Commentaries on the Catholic Epistles,* trans. and ed. John Owen (Edinburgh: Calvin Translation Society, 1855), p. 65.

20. Ulrich Zwingli, *Clarity and Certainty of the Word of God,* trans. G. W. Bromiley. In *Library of Christian Classics,* vol. 24 (Philadelphia: Westminster Press, 1953), p. 88.

21. See T. W. Manson, *Ministry and Priesthood: Christ's and Ours* (Richmond, Va.: John Knox Press, 1958), p. 37.

22. Philip Schaff, ed., *The Creeds of Christendom,* vol. 3 (New York: Harper, 1919), p. 421.

23. There is only a scant reference to "the mutual conversation and consolation of brethren" in the Smalcald Articles (1537), and this hardly does justice to the biblical concept of the priesthood of all believers. See Theodore G. Tappert, trans. & ed. *The Book of Concord* (Philadelphia: Fortress Press, 1959), p. 310.

24. Philip Spener, *Pia Desideria,* p. 94.

25. *Ibid.,* p. 92.

26. *Ibid.,* p. 89.

27. Cited in Eastwood, *The Priesthood of All Believers,* p. 214.

28. See Karl Barth, *Church Dogmatics,* IV, 3, a, pp. 165–274.

29. Karl Barth, *Protestant Theology in the Nineteenth Century* (Valley Forge, Pa.: Judson Press, 1973), pp. 643 ff.

30. In D. Elton Trueblood, *The People Called Quakers* (New York: Harper & Row, 1966), p. 110.

31. David du Plessis, *The Spirit Bade Me Go* (Plainfield, N.J.: Logos, 1970), p. 106.

32. Friedrich Schleiermacher, *On Religion: Speeches to Its Cultured Despisers,* trans. John Oman (New York: Harper & Row, 1965), p. 175.

33. *Ibid.,* p. 153.

34. In Alan Heimert, *Religion and the American Mind* (Cambridge, Mass.: Harvard University Press, 1968), pp. 159 ff.

35. Dietrich Bonhoeffer, *Life Together,* pp. 118, 119.

36. *Ibid.,* p. 109.

37. He declares that the preaching office "is established *in* the congregation and not *by* the congregation, and at the same time it is *with* the congregation." Bonhoeffer, *Ethics,* ed. Eberhard Bethge, trans. Neville Horton Smith (New York: Macmillan, 1963) p. 294.

38. Küng, *Why Priests?,* p. 90.

39. Küng, *The Church,* p. 439.

40. *Ibid.,* p. 440.

41. *Ibid.*

42. "The apostolic succession of pastors is not something that occurs automatically or mechanically through the laying-on of hands. Faith is a prerequisite and a condition; it must be active in the spirit of the apostles. This succession does not exclude the possibility of error or failure, and so must be tested by the faithful as a whole." Küng, *The Church,* p. 442.

43. Bertram Lee Woolf, ed. *Reformation Writings of Martin Luther,* Vol. 1, p. 367. Cf.: "Certainly all Christians are priests. But not all are pastors, for beyond the fact that a man is a Christian and a priest, he must also have an office and a parish that he has been commanded to serve." Luther, W.A. 31 I, 211.

44. *Luther's Works,* vol. 26, p. 20.

45. Althaus, *The Theology of Martin Luther,* p. 328.

46. Langdon Gilkey, *Catholicism Confronts Modernity* (New York: Seabury Press, 1975), p. 76.

47. *Ibid.*

48. *Ibid.,* p. 78.

49. One observer comments: "Priestly emphasis on mediating the Holy is giving way to models taken from education ('resource person'), science ('catalyst'), medicine ('enabler') and sports ('team builder')." John Conrad Wilkey, *The Meaning of Ordination in the United Methodist Church as It Relates to the Ministry of the Laity,* unpublished Doctor of Ministry thesis, University of Dubuque Theological Seminary, 1977, p. 80.

50. Ivan Illich, *Celebration of Awareness* (New York: Doubleday & Co., 1970), p. 75.

51. Thomas Torrance, "Justification." In *Christianity Divided,* ed. Daniel J. Callahan et al. [pp. 283–305], p. 302.

52. Emil Brunner, *The Misunderstanding of the Church,* trans. Harold Knight (Philadelphia: Westminster Press, 1953), p. 117.

53. James Dunn, *Jesus and the Spirit* (Philadelphia: Westminster Press, 1975), p. 298.

54. Ernst Käsemann, *Essays on New Testament Themes,* trans. W. J. Montague (London: SCM Press, 1964), p. 83.

55. Küng, *Why Priests?,* p. 39.

56. Thomas Torrance, *Royal Priesthood* (Edinburgh: Oliver & Boyd, 1955), p. 92.

57. *Ibid.*

58. From a lecture in Dubuque Theological Seminary Chapel, February 27, 1969. Cf. Jean-Jacques Von Allmen, *Le Saint Ministère* (Neuchâtel: Editions Delachaux et Niestlé, 1968), esp. pp. 55 ff.

59. Dulles, *Models of the Church,* p. 156.

60. *Ibid.,* p. 158.

61. Althaus, *The Theology of Martin Luther,* p. 314.

62. Mark A. Noll, "Believer-Priests in the Church: Luther's View," *Christianity Today,* vol. 18, no. 2 (October 26, 1973), [pp. 4–8], p. 7.

63. Arthur C. Cochrane, ed., *Reformed Confessions of the 16th Century* Second Helvetic Confession, ch. 18, p. 271.

64. *Ibid.*

65. While Paul, in his treatment of the charismatic gifts, emphasizes their value in building up the body of Christ, Luke is concerned with how they aid in the mission of the church to the world. The gift of tongues, for example, is associated by Luke with inner release and endowment for missionary service, whereas in Paul its purpose is said to be personal edification and thereby only indirectly building up the church. It should be noted, however, that Paul also shows how the gifts relate to mission and evangelism (cf. 1 Cor. 14:24, 25; Rom. 15:18, 19; 2 Cor. 12:12; Heb. 2:4; 2 Tim. 1:6–8). In the fuller perspective of Paul's teaching it is necessary to build up the church so that the church can then give a united and effectual witness before the world.

VI.
TWO KINGDOMS

He has rescued us out of the darkness and gloom of Satan's kingdom
and brought us into the kingdom of his dear Son.

Colossians 1:13 LB

And if thou be not in the kingdom of Christ, it is certain that thou
belongest to the kingdom of Satan, which is this evil world.

Martin Luther

Goodness is a realm; and there is a realm of evil. Each is spiritually
against the other. If the other world has a king, there is also a prince of
this world; and there can be no peace except in a complete victory, so
that such a war shall never be again.

P. T. Forsyth

The fundamental biblical opposition is not between flesh and Spirit,
creature and Creator, but between the Creator of the flesh and its
destroyer, between God and the devil, Christ and Satan, the Holy Spirit
and the Unholy.

Philip S. Watson

THE BIBLICAL TESTIMONY

Biblical religion speaks of two kingdoms in irrevocable conflict with
one another—the kingdom of God and the kingdom of the world, also
known as the kingdom of Satan. This dualistic vision runs throughout
the Scriptures, though the two kingdoms go under many different
names. This is not a metaphysical dualism, as in Zoroastrianism, since
the devil is seen as a fallen angel, superior to man but greatly inferior
to God. Yet it signifies a moral dualism which recognizes that evil is the
antithesis to good and that there can be no compromise between these
two forces.[1]

In the Old Testament the two kingdoms antithesis is already evident in Genesis 1, where light is separated from darkness. Some medieval theologians see this as implying the separation of good and bad
angels. In the Garden of Eden the serpent typifies the antigod force
which is already active in the good creation and which provides man

with the occasion for sin. It is prophesied that the Messiah will crush the head of the serpent; that is, he will overthrow its dominion, though not without being wounded in the struggle (Gen. 3:15; Isa. 27:1; cf. Rom. 16:20).

In ancient Hebraic tradition the source of evil was both the watery chaos and the personification of this chaos in the dragon called Leviathan. We read that the chaos appeared at the beginning of the creation (Gen. 1:1, 2) and was prior to the formation of the earth and life on the earth; yet this chaos or darkness was definitely not co-eternal with God and, indeed, did not exist apart from the will of God (cf. Isa. 45:7). In the Genesis account the *têhom* (the deep) is the philological equivalent of Tiamat, the personified chaos monster in the Babylonian myth. Leviathan, derived from the Canaanite Lotan, was related to both the Babylonian Tiamat and the Greek Hydra. It was also associated with Behemoth, a spirit of the desert, and even more closely with the sea monster Rahab as well as with that primal symbol of evil, the serpent (cf. Isa. 27:1; Amos 9:3; Job 26:13). In Hebraic thought the darkness and its personification in Leviathan signified not just recalcitrance and deficiency but destructive creativity (cf. Job 3:5, 6; Dan. 7:7). In Job 41:33, 34 Leviathan is pictured as the king of all the sons of pride.

It is difficult to pinpoint the precise time in Israel's theological history when Leviathan became identified with Satan, the angelic messenger of death who became God's adversary, but this identification is significant in the concept of the two kingdoms, since it indicates a rupture within the order of God's creation itself. It means that the powers of darkness contain within themselves the light of God's good creation, that they have a heavenly origin.[2] In the Apocalypse of John the dragon, the serpent, the devil, and Satan are all equated (Rev. 12:9; 20:2; cf. 11:7; 13:1 ff.).

Israel was originally depicted in the Old Testament as the elect people of God called to be a kingdom of priests and a holy nation (Exod. 19:6). The adversary was portrayed as the kingdoms of this world, the "kingdoms of the idols" (Isa. 10:10). Slowly but surely it dawned upon the prophets of Israel that God's kingdom is a spiritual one and that Israel, like every other nation, stands under the judgment of this kingdom. It was recognized that the kingdom of God is an "everlasting kingdom" (Dan. 4:3) and that it "rules over all" (Ps. 103:19). That Israel would indeed be taken up into this spiritual kingdom came to be an eschatological hope and promise. God will realize his purposes through the people of Israel, and when his work is fulfilled they shall be called "the city of righteousness, the faithful city" (Isa. 1:26; cf. 9:7). This city will be one without walls: the Lord will be a wall of fire around her and the glory in her midst (Zech. 2:5).[3]

In Daniel's vision of the four beasts (Dan. 7), we witness the rise and fall of four empires and then the coming of a fifth kingdom typified by a human figure, the Son of Man. The beasts emerge out of the sea, the evil domain of chaos (Dan. 7:2, 3). The fifth kingdom is the kingdom of God incorporated in the people of Israel. At the end time God will set up a kingdom that shall never be destroyed and that will break in pieces the kingdoms of this world, and it shall stand forever (Dan. 2:44).

In the developing theology of the Old Testament, it was recognized that behind the kingdoms of men is a strategy of evil, a dominion of darkness that directs the destiny of nations. Exodus 12:23 refers to an angelic destroyer who is nonetheless under God, the supreme power, and is used by God.[4] Job speaks of a "king of terrors" who drives man from light into darkness (Job 18:14–18; 41:33, 34).[5] Isaiah contrasts the "city of righteousness" (1:26) with a "city of chaos" (24:10)[6] governed by the hosts of heaven (Isa. 24:21). Daniel envisages angelic princes behind the kingdoms of this world: the good prince Michael is the protector of the Jews, whereas an evil angel is the defender of Persia (Dan. 10:13). While the immediate reference in Isaiah 14:12–14 is to the downfall of an earthly tyrant, we have an unmistakable allusion to Day Star or Lucifer, the fallen angel of Ugaritic mythology; though he aspires to be God, he shall finally be thrust down into the pit, and his power shall be taken from him (cf. Ezek. 28).[7] The pseudepigraphal book of Enoch also speaks of the rebellion and overthrow of disobedient angels (10:4–6, 11–12; 54:3–5; cf. Gen. 6:1–4; Jude 6; Rev. 9:1).

The idea of a kingdom of darkness led by an angelic adversary of God and man is very pronounced in the intertestamental and New Testament periods.[8] God has set up his kingdom in the midst of a fallen world, but antigod powers, angels of violence, have tried to overthrow it by force (Matt. 11:12).[9] In attacking the kingdom of Christ the demonic powers sealed their ultimate destruction. Yet where Christ is not acknowledged as King and Lord, these powers continue to hold sway over the world (1 John 5:19). Satan, indeed, is called the "god" and "prince" of this world (2 Cor. 4:4; John 12:31). Through his cross and resurrection victory Jesus Christ "disarmed the principalities and powers" (Col. 2:15; cf. 1:13), but they still wield a modicum of power (through man's continuing sin), though now as usurpers. All their rights and privileges have been taken from them, but they continue to wage war, even though they have been defeated and dethroned. Paul confesses that our battle is not with flesh and blood but with "the world rulers of this present darkness . . . the spiritual hosts of wickedness in the heavenly places" (Eph. 6:12). Jesus Christ, through his resurrection, has bound the prince of darkness so that he cannot prevent the missionary expansion of Christ's church (cf. Luke 11:21; Matt. 12:29), though he still possesses destructive power within his own domain, the sphere of unbelief. St. Augustine likened the devil to a mad dog which is chained: it can instill fear through its barking, but it cannot harm those who are united with Jesus Christ and are thereby out of its reach (cf. Col. 2:20).

We are told that at the end of the age Satan will again be loosed to persecute the saints and deceive the nations (Rev. 20:7–8; Ezek. 38–39), but his final attack will be to no avail, for his doom has already been assured. The "great city" of the world (Rev. 17:18; 18:18) will ultimately be overthrown, and the "beloved city," the city of God (Rev. 20:9), will reign triumphant. In the last days the city of God will be surrounded by the forces of wickedness (Rev. 20:9), but because God has made the cause of the saints his own, they shall persevere and gain the victory. The beast, the false prophet, and the devil will all finally be thrown into the lake of fire (Rev. 19, 20), and the kingdom of this world will become "the kingdom of our Lord and of his Christ" (Rev. 11:15). The holy city, the new Jerusalem, will come down from heaven; night will be no more, for the Lord God will be the light for all his people (Rev. 21, 22).

It is important to recognize that Satan's rule in this world does not indicate a kind of ownership of creation. This indeed was a gnostic doctrine—that the world legally belongs to Satan, and therefore it is bad and everything in it is evil. The Evil One's proper abode is not the earth but the deep, the abyss of darkness (cf. Job 41:31, 32; Rev. 9:1; Jude 6), though originally he dwelt in the heavens close to God. This world is neither the realm of light nor the realm of darkness but the battleground between light and darkness. The church is an island of light in a sea of darkness, but its light is spreading. The holy catholic church is not on the defensive but on the offensive. Through the word that it proclaims it evicts the demons from their strongholds (cf. Luke 11:20). Having overthrown the devil, Christ and his angelic armies pursue their severely wounded adversary (Rev. 19:11–16). The gates of hell[10] will not be able to prevail against the advancing forces of the kingdom of heaven (Matt. 16:18), and the legions of darkness will finally be compelled to capitulate. While admittedly much of this is figurative language, it nonetheless points to realities that form an integral part of the biblical vision. The Bible vividly, but also accurately, describes events in both superhistorical and historical time which have happened, are happening now, and will happen in the future.

The whole world already belongs to Jesus Christ, but large parts of it still remain mesmerized by the spell that the devil casts upon it. This world is both enemy-occupied territory and the theater of God's glory. It is in this light that we can understand these words of our Lord: "I do not pray that thou shouldst take them out of the world, but that thou shouldst keep them from the evil one" (John 17:15). The call of the New Testament is not flight from the world but the conquest of the world by means of the Gospel.

DEVELOPMENT IN CATHOLIC THOUGHT

The biblical dualistic perspective was quite pronounced among the patristic fathers, both Greek and Latin. Indeed, they generally interpreted the atonement as the victory of Christ over the demonic powers of darkness. They understood the Christian life as a daily battle against these same powers.

It was Augustine who articulated the two kingdom theory in systematic fashion. In his well-known work *The City of God* he depicted world history in terms of an ongoing conflict between the city of God *(civitas dei)*, which is composed of the regenerate, faithful remnant and is reflected in but not identical with the church, and the city of the world *(civitas terrena)*, which is under the dominion of the powers of darkness. He traced the origins of the city of the world to the fall of the angels. The devil was sinful from his creation, since he did not abide in the truth from the beginning, though his nature was created good. The devils hold in bondage the worshippers of a plurality of gods, but they can never seduce the church. While Augustine did not identify the city of God with the church nor the city of the world with the state, the former was increasingly associated in his thinking with the church and the latter with the secular kingdom.

Augustine saw the state as a consequence of and remedy for sin. Here he broke with the classical understanding in which the state was said to be rooted in a "compact of justice" (Cicero). Though the state is very much penetrated by the city of the world, he nevertheless envisioned the possibility of a Christian state which would oppose the city of the world. Only Christian states have justice.

In Augustine's view the cleavage between the two cities continues into eternity: "After the resurrection, when the general judgment has been held and concluded, there will remain two cities, each with its own boundaries—the one Christ's, the other the devil's; the one embracing the good, the other, the bad, with both consisting of angels and men."[11] The community of faith has been predestined to eternal life, whereas the members of the earthly city have been predestined to eternal damnation.

For the most part, Augustine understood the church as the form or first fruits of the kingdom of God, though he sometimes practically equated them.[12] Reinhold Niebuhr rightly criticizes him for assuming that the church as an historical institution can never become a vehicle of evil and never really stands under the judgment of God.[13]

The dualistic perspective continued in the thought of Thomas Aquinas, but the polarity that commanded his attention was that between nature and grace. These are not opposed to one another but complementary. Thomas sees the kingdom of nature as the portal to the kingdom of grace. Just as reason is fulfilled by revelation, so nature is completed in supernature. Just as natural law is complemented by revealed law, so natural virtues are fulfilled by theological virtues.

Thomas did not develop a theology of the kingdom of God, but he sometimes virtually identifies this kingdom with the church. At other times the kingdom is viewed eschatologically as the court of heaven. The church as the community of the redeemed exists in tension with the secular order, which reflects both the goodness of creation and the ravages of sin.

On the whole, Thomas envisages the state in a positive light, just as he regards nature positively rather than negatively. Following Aristotle, he derives the idea of the state from the very nature of man. For Thomas even a non-Christian state is endowed with some positive value, whereas for Augustine the pagan state virtually embodies the *civitas terrena.* Just as spiritual power is ordained to the supernatural end of man, so temporal power is ordained to the natural good of society. While the norm for the state is natural law, the norm for the church is revealed law. Thomas holds that evil rulers must be resisted because the natural law is higher than the will of the state; politics is subordinate to ethics.

In Thomistic thought the church is both a mystical community and a structure of power. As the custodian of the divine law it assists in the ordering of the temporal life. The temporal power, moreover, is subject to the spiritual just as the body is subject to the soul. Because the divine law goes beyond the natural law, the state can and should receive guidance from the church.

Thomas, more than Augustine, was willing to recognize the live possibility of a Christian state. In this case state and church must work in partnership. The difference is mainly in function, since both are under the kingship of Christ. Yet he always stressed the subordination of the temporal to the spiritual.

Did Thomas admit the reality of a kingdom of darkness arrayed against both church and state? This idea is certainly present in his writings, but it is not systematically developed. The devil and his hosts, he says, "are powerful and great, possessing an immense army against which we must fight."[14] For Thomas the demons belong to the order of nature, not the order of grace. Though they were created in grace, they have fallen from their supernatural position. They are now deprived of grace, but they have not lost their natural gifts. They abuse their nature for evil, but they still have a nature that includes some aspects of the good.[15] According to Thomas, while nature is perfected by grace, sin is annulled by grace.

Despite the occasional surge of biblical realism, the dichotomy between the city of God and the city of the world was, for the most part, downplayed in the mainstream of medieval thinking after Augustine. This is partly because of the pervading influence of neo-Platonism, which was present to a degree also in Augustine. In Anselm's *Fall of the Devil* Satan is no longer the furious mutineer who seeks to overthrow God's authority and replace it with his own but instead a misguided angelic figure who tries to increase his happiness in a disorderly way.[16] In Thomas' theology Satan has a necessary place in the graded hierarchy of being. Sin is understood as privation and deficiency of knowledge, for evil cannot have a formal cause.[17] According to Hall, Thomas "wishes to say that there is a sense in which the desire to be like God is good, and also that it was impossible for Satan to do what he *knows* is wrong (since to *know* the good is to do it)."[18] In both Anselm and Thomas we see "the intellectual form of the unified medieval culture which suppresses chaos within its powerful will to order."[19]

The neo-Platonic subversion of the biblical concept of the demonic is strikingly illustrated by a magnificent miniature in a ninth-century manuscript copy of a work by Gregory of Nazianzus.[20] Satan is pictured as a nobly dressed, graceful youth whose angelic appearance is qualified only by a mauve coloration which contrasts with the pink glow of his fellow angels. Good and evil are no longer seen in terms of an antithesis between being and anti-being but as a difference in the degree of being. In this kind of thinking evil is not an invading force that seeks to overturn the good but, instead, the omission of good.

In Meister Eckhart, whose mysticism also bears the incontestable stamp of neo-Platonism, the principal polarity is between nature and spirit rather than between God and an anti-god power. The primal sin is individuation, separation from the source or ground of being, and man's greatest need is reunion with this ground. Because "evil . . . is nothing but a defect or shortcoming,"[21] the answer to evil is to realize the presence of God within the soul. The way to become a Son of God is to "live according to reason, according to the spirit and not according to the flesh."[22] For Eckhart membership in the kingdom of God lies not in outward ordinances of the church but in mystical union with the God within.[23] In the thought of this theologian, it seems, the two kingdoms are the unity of the Godhead and the world of multiplicity.

Not that the reality of the devil was denied in the mystical tradition of the church; indeed, many of the great saints and mystics had graphic encounters with the devil. Yet those who tended toward pure mysticism viewed evil as only a fleeting shadow that does not really disturb reality in itself. The absolute opposition between a good and an evil power is overcome, since all distinctions are lost in God, all opposites are transcended.

REFORMATION AND POST-REFORMATION PERSPECTIVES

The reality of two kingdoms in dire conflict was nowhere given more cogent expression than in the theology of Martin Luther. Luther perceived the demonic not merely as the absence of light but as an assault upon it. In this view the devil is a creative, dynamic power superior to man though inferior to God. His chief sin was to try to be like God, and this is why he was cast out of the heavens. His strategy is to bring humankind in subjection to his will, and if it were not for the cross of Christ he would indubitably have succeeded.

Luther sees a qualitative distinction between the two kingdoms. God's kingdom is one of grace and mercy, whereas the kingdom of the world is one of wrath and severity. Christ's kingdom is invisible and spiritual, and its weapons are spiritual: the preaching of the Gospel, prayer, and works of love. The devil's kingdom, on the other hand, is temporal and is ruled by strict laws enforced by the sword. Those who believe in Jesus Christ and are reborn by his Spirit belong to the kingdom of God. Those who still dwell in unbelief belong to the devil's kingdom, which is "a disordered chaos of darkness."[24]

Luther recognizes that these kingdoms are not equal. God exercises his sovereign power through the kingdom of darkness as well as through the kingdom of his Son, but in different ways. Through the devil God rules by his left hand, by his wrath. Through Christ God rules by his right hand, by his love and mercy. God uses the devil to accomplish his hidden purposes, to bring judgment upon the world. Luther could even speak of the great conquerors in history as the "demonic masks'" of God. Occasionally he described the Turk as both "God's rod" and "the devil's servant."

In addition to the two kingdoms *(Reichen)*, Luther also acknowledged two governments *(Regimenten)*, church and state. Sometimes he referred to these as two kingdoms, but the context usually indicates that the state is then seen as being under the sway of the kingdom of the world.[25] In his view Satan roams about in both governments. It is a great mistake to identify the state with the kingdom of the devil. He could even say that God has specifically instituted the secular government against the kingdom of the world, understood as the kingdom of Satan. It was Luther's belief that the secular government contributes to the preservation of earthly life. Blessings as well as judgment come through this government, though these are physical not spiritual blessings.

While in Luther's perspective the state is characterized by law and power, the church is distinguished by mercy and love. God rules over the state through the Lordship of Christ and the partial domination of the devil. Yet the devil can also penetrate into the visible church, and this accounts for the appearance of false prophets and antichrists. The invisible church, the kingdom of God, on the other hand, is impervious to the demonic assaults.

The connection between the two governments can be seen in the individual Christian as he lives out his vocation. He is a citizen of two realms, the temporal (state) and the spiritual (kingdom of God), and, therefore, he has different responsibilities and tasks. Yet the two realms are not separated but are held together in paradoxical tension. The secular tasks of the Christian must always be informed by a spiritual goal. The Christian is summoned to carry the Gospel into the structures of life.

In Luther's understanding Christ is Lord of both state and church. Jesus Christ rules over all peoples and nations as God or as a member of the Godhead, but in his humanity he reigns only in the Church, in the community of faith. He is ruler of all but Savior only of those who believe.

Calvin, too, perceived that against the kingdom of righteousness is arrayed "the empire of wickedness," the kingdom of the devil. He, too, affirmed two kingdoms engaged in irrevocable warfare. Following Augustine, he believed that the object of the devil's attack was both to injure God and to destroy man. Satan is not an independent and self-sustained lord of this world, as in Manichaeism, but he is called the prince of this world because "by God's permission, he exercises his tyranny over the world."[26] Just as "the church and fellowship of the saints has Christ as Head, so the faction of the impious and impiety itself" have "their prince who holds supreme sway over them."[27]

Whereas Luther understood the kingdom of God as the hidden realm of faith, Calvin regarded it as the area in which God establishes his reign in Christ. Like Augustine he practically identified the kingdom of Christ with the church. He believed that this kingdom could be advanced by the exercise of power, both civil and spiritual. Luther, on the other hand, considered the renunciation of power as a hallmark of being in the kingdom. For Calvin the kingdom of God will be fulfilled in the renovation of the earth, not in its dissolution (as in Luther).

Calvin also spoke of two governments, church and state, but he did not see an antithesis between them, as did the early Luther. Instead, they complement one another, and this is why he could speak of a "twofold government." The difference between them is in function. Both serve the Word of God, and both employ coercion.[28] The state protects public morality and promotes civil justice, whereas the church preaches the righteousness of the kingdom, which is the transcendent norm for civil law. For Calvin, social welfare is properly the concern of the church as well as of the state. The church should give moral support to the state, and the state should give temporal support to the church.

While Luther emphasized the state as a dike against sin, Calvin saw the state as a means by which people show their calling to lives of servanthood. Calvin envisioned a positive role for the temporal government, just as he perceived the law of God in mainly positive terms. The law was understood not only as a restraint and as a taskmaster that drives people to the Gospel (as in Luther), but also and primarily as a guide for them in their Christian life as they seek to realize their vocation in secular society.

Unlike Luther, Calvin entertained the idea of a holy community in which both church and state are under the revealed law of God. This holy community was not the kingdom of God but a "corporate community that was neither purely religious nor purely secular, but a compound of both."[29] The lines between church and state are still maintained, but because they cooperate in maintaining the social order, it is better to speak of a duality rather than a dualism in Calvin's thinking in this area.

Yet Calvin is as dualistic as Luther in his perception of the antithesis between the two kingdoms of Christ and the devil. In contrast to the milder scholastic view, Calvin believed that Satan's goal is to rob God of the government of the world and claim it for himself.[30] Yet though his power over the reprobate is very real, his influence over the elect is limited and temporary. At the same time, Calvin assigned Satan a very exalted position among the enemies that enslave man. In his doctrine of the atonement Calvin brought together the patristic *Christus victor* motif, in which Christ redeems man from bondage to the devil, and the satisfaction theory of the Latin fathers.[31]

The moral dualism present in Luther and Calvin was even more pronounced in the left-wing Reformation among the Anabaptists. In the Anabaptist view the two kingdoms, that of Christ and that of Satan, are distinct from each other in every essential detail. In the words of one interpreter: "The kingdom of God is eternal and heavenly oriented, dominated by the spiritual, and submissive to the rule of God; but the kingdom of Satan is temporal, this-worldly oriented, dominated by the fallen flesh, proud, and disobedient to the rule of God."[32] Such an understanding could indeed facilitate political quietism, but it also resulted among some of the radical Anabaptists in revolutionary activity designed to overthrow the kingdom of the devil and bring in the kingdom of God.

In the evangelical revivalism of the Pietists and Puritans the two kingdom idea figured very prominently, and as a consequence foreign missions were instituted to expel the devil from his controlling position in the pagan nations. In the Pietist vision the world was under the power of the Evil One, but through the preaching of the Gospel his power could be overthrown. Many of the Pietists and Puritans looked forward to a latter-day glory for the church in which there would be a worldwide harvest of souls. This would be a time when the demonic powers would be routed and the kingdom of God would everywhere be advancing. The Puritans envisaged holy commonwealths, religio-political communities governed by the revealed law of God, which would function as outposts of righteousness in a still unredeemed world. From these outposts the warfare against the powers of darkness could be carried forward to completion.

Unlike many of the Pietists, who were influenced by Lutheranism, the Puritans generally affirmed the Calvinist doctrines of eternal security and predestination and therefore believed the cause of righteousness to be invincible and the doom of the adversary already sealed. Once one belongs to the "Kingdom of Grace," John Preston maintained, he can never be robbed of it. If one is not in this kingdom, then he is in the "Kingdom of Destruction" and predestined to hell for eternity.[33]

In the nineteenth century, with the rise of premillennialism and dispensationalism, evangelicals came to take a much more pessimistic view of human history. It was held that the church is now entering its twilight period, and Christ's kingdom, which signifies a restoration of the historic Davidic kingdom, will be inaugurated at his second coming. The kingdom of the world, which is under the domain of Satan, was believed to be present, while the kingdom of Christ, the millennial age, was depicted as future. The church, comprised of the remnant of true believers called out of the world, will be taken up by Christ into heaven before the great tribulation preceding the second coming. Yet the dispensationalists also contend that Christians will share in the rule of the kingdom.

MODERN DISCUSSION

With the rise of the Enlightenment in the late seventeenth and eighteenth centuries a monistic orientation supplanted that of biblical dualism, and the whole world was viewed as the family of God. The devil was demythologized to become the adverse consciousness rooted in ignorance and disregard of the divine law. For William Blake the good and evil angels are complementary rather than opposing forces. Love joined to Energy is the "marriage of Heaven and Hell." As Schleiermacher saw it, belief in a continuing kingdom of Satan would weaken joyful courage and be destructive of Christian love.

In the modern view the fundamental cleavage is not between God and the devil, heaven and hell, holiness and sin, but between nature and freedom or flesh and spirit. Kant envisioned an ethical commonwealth in which all people would come to live according to an enlightened conscience. Marx and Engels heralded a "kingdom of freedom," which they identified with the classless society. Troeltsch referred to a kingdom of freedom that was opposed to the determinism of nature.

Albrecht Ritschl was convinced that the whole world was progressing toward the kingdom of God, which he defined as "the organization of humanity inspired by love." Like Kant he conceived of this kingdom as an ethical ideal which can be partially attained through benevolent action. Both church and state should serve the kingdom of God by promoting and nurturing moral perfection. The principal dualism in Ritschl is between nature and spirit, the world and the kingdom. While he referred to a "realm of sin" opposed to the kingdom of God, he meant by sin a social contagion, bad influences emanating from our collective life. Sin is a failure to realize ethical values and gain mastery over instinctual drives. The vocation to which we are called is to establish moral dominion over nature and thereby prepare the way for the union of mankind in the kingdom of God.

The note of biblical dualism is more evident in Walter Rauschenbusch, though, like Ritschl, he rejected belief in demons and Satan. While Ritschl tended to see the kingdom of God as supramundane impinging on history, for Rauschenbusch it was a historical force now at work in humanity. In his understanding sin is selfishness, especially corporate selfishness. The church, which is a fellowship of worship, exists for the purpose of the kingdom, which is a fellowship of righteousness. Any advance in social righteousness is an advance of the kingdom of God and a part of redemption. The kingdom of God is "the Christian transfiguration of the social order."[34] While Ritschl conceived of the kingdom as a transcendent ethical ideal, Rauschenbusch envisioned a kingdom of God on earth, a universal brotherhood of man under the fatherhood of God. Nonetheless, it was his conviction that the kingdom of God would come not by peaceful development alone but through conflict with the kingdom of evil. "If we consent to the working principles of the Kingdom of Evil," he warned, "and do not counteract it with all our strength, but perhaps even fail to see its ruinous evil, then we are part of it and the salvation of Christ has not yet set us free."[35] Rauschenbusch believed that in the battle for social justice the forces of evil would be uprooted, and the millennial hope would then be realized.

Unlike Ritschl and Rauschenbusch, Paul Tillich sees the demonic in cosmic and not merely sociological terms, though he, too, refuses to accept the idea of a supernatural demonic adversary to God and man. For Tillich the demonic has reference to a power of evil that precedes human sin and that perverts the good "into a mixture of form-creating and form-destroying energy in history."[36] Against the Enlightenment view Tillich understands the demonic not as deficiency in goodness but as "perverse and powerful affirmation." It signifies the distortion of the sacred rather than its denial. In line with his Lutheran background Tillich perceives a continuous battle "going on between divine and demonic structures" in history.[37] He speaks of a demonic kingdom opposed to the kingdom of God, but he understands this mainly in terms of an underground conspiracy against the will and purpose of God rather than a kingdom equal or analogous to that of God.

In addition to this Lutheran dualism, however, Tillich also shares the Enlightenment concern for unity and universality. He contends that the kingdom of God embraces all peoples and all movements, though in its transhistorical dimension it signifies the eschatological consummation and fulfillment of history. The kingdom of God is reflected in the Spiritual Community, which includes the church as well as secular and non-Christian religious movements outside the church. All of these are vulnerable to penetration by the demonic, though the church is less open to such incursion than secular movements because it has the principle of resistance in itself. The manifest church is the visible body of believers, while the latent church, or the Spiritual Community in its latency, signifies the world that has not yet come to the realization of the victory of the kingdom of God. Tillich maintains that one cannot reach the transcendent kingdom of God without participating in the struggle of the inner-historical kingdom of God.

This same uneven mixture of Reformation and Enlightenment motifs can be discerned in Reinhold Niebuhr. For Niebuhr the kingdom of God is beyond history, not as a supernatural realm but as a transcendent ideal. The kingdom of God is the ideal world, one that cannot be perfectly attained within history. Its perfect realization means the end of the world as we see it in the crucifixion of Jesus Christ who embodied this ideal. The two kingdoms are the heavenly and the earthly, the ideal and the actual, this world and the coming kingdom of God. "The kingdom of truth," Niebuhr says, is "not the kingdom of some other world. It is the picture of what this world ought to be."[38] The real world moves toward the ideal world, but there is no automatic progress. As civilization advances, so the possibilities of retrogression and evil also increase. The kingdom always impinges on man's every decision and is involved in his every action. It is always coming, but it is never here. Its principal hallmark is suffering love, which is realized only at the edge of history. The attainable goal within history is mutual love or justice. The church is the community that heralds the coming of the kingdom, but this coming is always conceived eschatologically.

Niebuhr allows for the reality of the demonic, but in his thought the demonic is simply a symbol for the possession of the self by something less than the Spirit of God. It represents a force of evil that precedes human sin. But Niebuhr does not accept the idea of a personal angelic power who presides over a kingdom that seeks the overthrow of the kingdom of God.

In Karl Barth, too, we witness a partial convergence of Enlightenment monism and Reformation dualism.[39] Barth understands evil as the Nothingness, a negative reality that is given a provisional existence by God in order to set it off from his good creation. It exists by God's not-willing rather than by his willing. It is the antithesis that is set apart from the thesis, but it is not included in any new synthesis, as in Hegel. The Nothingness was already marked for dissolution and destruction at the creation, and its capability for injury was completely removed at the crucifixion and resurrection of Jesus Christ. At the same time, it continues to have a semblance of power because of its capability for deception. In itself it is powerless and nonexistent, but in the spell that it casts upon the creature it gains a pseudo-power, one that is given to it by man the sinner. Even though objectively it has been done away with, it continues to mesmerize and beguile those who do not know or trust in Jesus Christ.

Although Barth occasionally speaks of a kingdom of Satan, he means by this not a kingdom arrayed against the kingdom of God but a kingdom that is already behind us and all people, a pseudo-kingdom that has been disarmed and defeated. While the Nothingness "still is in the world," he says, "it is in virtue of the blindness of our eyes and the cover which is still over us, obscuring the prospect of the kingdom of God already established as the *only* kingdom undisputed by evil."[40] The kingdom of Christ signifies not just the community of faith, as in Augustine and Calvin, but the world of humanity in its totality. It is "greater than the sphere of Israel and the Church. But it is in this sphere, and in it alone, that it is believed and known that the kingdom of the world is His, and not the devil's."[41] The world is no longer bewitched, but exorcised, for Christ's victory is complete and final. The church constitutes the "inner circle" of the kingdom of Christ, and the world or state the "wider circle." The world is, in effect, the invisible church or, as Tillich would say, the church in its latency. With the coming of the kingdom of God the principalities and powers of the world crumble away and, moreover, are now forced into the service of this superior kingdom, even against their will.[42] Those who in themselves are disobedient "are claimed and absorbed by the act of His obedience."[43] The kingdom cannot remain a merely external fact hanging over them: "They themselves have to be within it."[44] For Barth the "righteousness of the kingdom" means "a real, the most real determination of human life; to which every man willingly and wittingly or not, is subject."[45] Yet only those can actively participate in it who take up their cross and follow Christ.

Barth also distinguishes between the kingdom of grace, which now includes the whole world, and the kingdom of glory, which refers to the future of the world as redeemed. Glory signifies the fulfillment and revelation of grace, just as grace represents the restoration and renewal of nature. God's work of creation, reconciliation, and redemption comprises a unified unfolding of his redemptive purposes from all eternity. But this work excludes and negates the kingdom of the Nothingness, which has been shorn of any real, ontological power.

Bonhoeffer also mirrors this concern for the unity of creation and redemption, which implies the ultimate harmony and reconciliation of the church and secular state. He attacks thinking in terms of two spheres—the natural and supernatural, the temporal and the spiritual. He affirms two realms, church and state, but only one kingdom, the reign of Christ which includes all of existence. "The kingdom of God," he says, "exists in our world exclusively in the duality of church and state."[46]

Yet at the same time, Bonhoeffer acknowledges the existence of a demonic power that penetrates into God's good creation as an alien force but that is dispelled by the preaching of the Gospel. His vision of the immediate future is not optimistic: "The older the world grows, the more heated becomes the conflict between Christ and antichrist, and the more thorough the efforts of the world to get rid of the Christians."[47] At the same time, he is insistent that the world is not divided between Christ and the devil, since it completely belongs to the former: "Any static delimitation of a region which belongs to the devil and a region which belongs to Christ is a denial of the reality of God's having reconciled the whole world with Himself in Christ."[48] The devil must serve Christ even against his will: "He desires evil, but over and over again he is compelled to do good."[49] The "realm or space of the devil is always only beneath the feet of Jesus Christ."[50] Bonhoeffer, therefore, will not speak of a world that is spiritually lost, separated from the redemption of Christ.

In modern neo-Catholicism the kingdom of God is depicted as all-pervasive and all-inclusive, though it is said that man can resist and deny the work of grace around and within him. For Karl Rahner it is possible to conceive of the " 'evolution' of the world *towards Christ,* and to show how there is a gradual ascent which reaches a peak in him."[51] In his thought we live in a redeemed world and not merely a redeemable world. Thomas O'Meara sees the kingdom of God as "the deeper kingdom of history," which, in a sense, already includes all people, at least in intention, since all are "surrounded by presence."[52] This new optimism is also mirrored in Tad Guzie:

The world is God's family, before and apart from baptism. . . . It is not baptism that brings us into the world of grace. The grace and love of God is already here, it is freely given, it surrounds our existence, and we are in contact with it from the first moment of our life.[53]

Not surprisingly, the apostolic and patristic vision of two kingdoms of light and darkness has been kept very much alive within the fold of Eastern Orthodoxy. Evgeny Barabanov, a Russian Orthodox layman, perceives "not only an opposition between the Church . . . and a totalitarian system, but also a more fundamental opposition, that between the Church and the world."[54] He calls for active participation in the political and economic life of the world, but accompanied by a vigorous renunciation of its temptations and vanity. According to Thomas Hopko, American Orthodox theologian, "There is a cosmic battle going on between the children of light and the children of darkness—and we must be bold enough to say that there are children of light who are not formal members of the Church, and children of darkness who are."[55]

Within contemporary Protestantism Jacques Ellul gives a strong reaffirmation of the idea of two diametrically opposed kingdoms. Contrary to the prevailing view, "Satan is still as such the prince of this world. It belongs to him. . . . Its power, riches, progress, and history are under his control. It is he who institutes capitalisms and imperialisms. It is he who establishes states and triggers revolutions."[56]

Though Ellul follows Barth in contending that the powers of darkness have been decisively defeated by Christ, he nonetheless acknowledges the reality of their continuing threat:

We must accept the fact that the powers defeated by Christ are still at work, that they refuse to admit their defeat and are struggling more violently than ever. They do gain local victories, and their violence forces us to believe in their power (still real over us), whereas in truth they are subject to Christ.[57]

A THEOLOGICAL REAPPRAISAL

As we see it, the fundamental dichotomy is not between nature and grace, time and eternity, spirit and matter, but between sin and holiness, light and darkness, God and the devil. The devil's kingdom, the kingdom of darkness, is not equal with God's kingdom, but its goal is to injure God as well as to subjugate man. Nor is this kingdom a complement to the kingdom of light (as in William Blake) but instead its antithesis. The kingdom of the world is not simply one mode of the universal rule of God (as in much neo-Lutheranism and Barthianism) but an adversary to the kingdom of God. Both kingdoms are spiritual, and their warfare is essentially invisible, though it inevitably assumes visible expression.

The devil represents not the satanic principle of negation but perverse and powerful affirmation (Tillich), the assault upon goodness and not simply the absence of goodness. Evil is what builds, creates, animates, inspires—as well as what destroys (Martin Buber). We accept the traditional or orthodox view of the devil and his hosts as fallen angels superior to man but inferior to God. The devil is not simply the chaos in its dynamic manifestation (as in Barth) but a superhuman intelligence with a strategy and purpose of his own; this is why man is unable to repel or escape from the power of evil by means of education or knowledge.

In addition to the two kingdoms there are two spheres or dimensions, the spiritual and the temporal, which are correlated with church and state. Much of the current criticism of Luther's two kingdom theory is directed to his idea of two governments which are distinct and yet integrally related to one another. The revolutionary implications in Luther's theology cannot be fully appreciated until we see behind the two governments of church and state the two kingdoms of light and darkness. It was Luther's conviction that the kingdom of the devil must be vigorously resisted wherever it intrudes, in the church as well as in the state. In modern thought Luther's doctrine of the devil is deemed mythological and, therefore, does not receive the attention it deserves.

This is not to deny that Luther's doctrine, which saw the purpose of the state as a dike against sin, played into the hands of those who were concerned primarily with upholding rather than changing the secular order. Yet when this doctrine is viewed in the wider perspective of the cosmic conflict between light and darkness, it can be a powerful impetus to cultural transformation, as is evidenced in Augustine and Calvin.

We see the two governments of church and state as two modes of the divine rule. While the state is instituted for the purpose of preservation, the church is established by Christ for the purpose of redemption. Material blessings derive from the state, spiritual blessings come through the church. Through common grace, which is everywhere at work, the state can arrive at civil righteousness, but the church is preeminently concerned with spiritual righteousness, which is given by the Holy Spirit in the new birth. The state is not a separate or autonomous kingdom in competition with the church, but a government community that strives for law, order, and justice. It is designed to serve man in the temporal and material side of his existence. It must never claim absolute homage and obedience, and when it does so, it becomes demonic and must consequently be resisted by God-fearing people. Because the temptation to arrogate unconditional power to itself is almost irresistible, particularly where there is no Christian contingent within its domain, the state often falls under the sway of the powers of darkness. We read in Revelation 17:18 that the woman of sin, the mother of harlots, gains dominion over the kings of the earth.

The kingdom of God is both a future reality beyond history and present now in the community of faith. It exists now in the midst of the faithful, though it is not to be equated with any visible institution. The church is the vessel or the instrument of the kingdom rather than the kingdom itself. The kingdom is basically future, but it is present now in the hearts of those who believe. It is mirrored and anticipated in the company of believers, but it will not be fulfilled until the end of the world.

Having been cast out of the heavenly realm, the devil and his legions have invaded the earthly realm, and he has thereby become the "prince of this world." Though he was mortally wounded by the cross and resurrection victory of Christ, he continues to fight on. Indeed, the demonic powers become more destructive and virulent as the kingdom of God advances.

Jesus Christ is Lord of both the church and the world, even that side of the world that has fallen under the sway of the powers of darkness. Yet he is Lord in a direct and saving way only of the church. Luther declared that while "God is the Lord of all nations," he is not "the God of all nations. For he's not the God of those who don't have his Word."[58] Christ exercises his saving work only in the community of faith, but he exercises his preserving and judging work everywhere.

We reject the Barthian idea of a Christocracy where Christ is portrayed as being in direct control of the structures and institutions of the secular order. Nor can we subscribe to Barth's view that the Gospel is the criterion for the political order. We here agree with Brunner: "The State will never, never be governed by the Word—in the sense of the Gospel—but exclusively by the word of the Law, quite simply by the Decalogue, which is not the actual 'Word' of Christ."[59] Christ exercises his Lordship indirectly through rebellious principalities and powers, but in the role of Judge, not Savior. He rules over the powers of darkness while at the same time negating and restraining them. The works of darkness are made to serve God's will, even though outwardly they are against his will.

When John refers to the kingdom of the world becoming the kingdom of our Lord and of his Christ (Rev. 11:15), he has in mind the possessions and subjects of the devil, not the devil's government, which will be destroyed. G. B. Caird gives a proper translation: "The sovereignty of the world has passed to our Lord and to his Christ."[60] The Living Bible version is: "The kingdom of this world now belongs to our Lord, and to his Christ."

As has already been indicated, the deepest meaning of the kingdom of the world is that it is a "dominion of darkness" (Col. 1:13) that has deceived the nations and even, at times, confused the church. It refers not simply to the temporal government or civil jurisdiction but to this government as it is presently under the sway of the powers of darkness. The shadow that the anti-god power casts over the nations accounts for the tensions and discord between church and state.

Ideally, both church and state should be allied in the struggle against evil, and this ideal can be approximated where the state is infused with Christian values. While the sword of the state is physical force, the sword of the church is the Word of God. The state should seek not simply to preserve law and order (as in Luther), but also to serve the cause of justice. Its goal should be not so much a holy community as a just society. The rational ideal of justice must be united with the suprarational ideal of perfect love if creative justice is to become a reality. A holy community, in the older Calvinist sense, presupposes faith in Jesus Christ by the overwhelming majority of the constituency. It is questionable whether this particular vision can ever be realized in our modern pluralistic world, though it can be attained to a degree in smaller towns and villages.

The Christian should not be mesmerized or paralyzed by the evils in the world, since he has the certain knowledge that the principalities and powers have already been disarmed by Jesus Christ (Col. 2:15). One interpreter astutely comments: "It is with bare fists or broken swords that they thus rush around, while we are given the armour of God, and (so long as we put it on . . .) we shall stand our ground."[61] The demonic powers were irrevocably defeated by Jesus Christ on his cross, but they still exert power and influence where Christ is not acknowledged as Lord and Savior. Their weapons are rendered ineffectual against the power of faith, though even with their broken weapons they can still win minor victories against those who persist in unbelief. Despite the fact that nations rage against her, the city of God will remain secure, since the Lord dwells in her midst (Ps. 46:4, 5).

Until Christ comes again in glory, the church is engaged in an unceasing struggle with the dislodged powers of darkness. These powers can be vanquished only by the Word of God, not by the sword, though the chaos that they engender in society can be held in check by the sword. In the words of Torrance: "Until Christ comes the Church is engaged in warfare and her weapon is the Word of God, for it is through the majesty of the Word that disorder is subdued to order, and the deformed state of the Church is reformed to conformity with Christ."[62] Though the devil vents his fury against the people of God because he knows his time is short, they will be able to withstand and emerge victorious by the power of the blood of the Lamb and the word of the Gospel (Rev. 12:11, 12).

We, as the ambassadors of Christ, cannot build his kingdom, but we can serve it. We cannot bring in the kingdom, but we can prepare the way for it. The kingdom of Christ is presently hidden in the structures of history, but its revelation and consummation are still ahead of us in the absolute future of God. We can be instruments in its advance within present history, but we cannot determine this advance, since the wind of the Spirit blows where it wills (John 3:8). We cannot force the hand of God, but we can pray that his kingdom will come on earth as well as in heaven (Matt. 6:10). Moreover, our prayers as well as our spoken and lived witness are indeed used by the Spirit in extending and furthering the kingdom in this world.

NOTES

1. Cf. Nathan Söderblom: "All attempts within Christianity to escape from or to overcome dualism have weakened the fearless sense of reality within the gospel or else have led to the incredible result of locating dualism in the very nature of God." Cited by Gustaf Aulén in "Nathan Söderblom as Theologian," *Una Sancta,* vol. 24, no. 1 (1967), [pp. 15–30], p. 18.

2. In the Babylonian creation story Tiamat was not just a personified monster of the deep but a Babylonian goddess, mother of the gods of the pantheon.

3. We see this prediction fulfilled in the church, which is indeed an eschatological community, since it lives between the times of the two advents of Christ. The New Jerusalem from heaven will have walls, as is made clear in Revelation 21.

4. Origen, in his *Contra Celsum* 6. 43, identifies this destroyer with the devil, the agent of God's wrath against the Egyptians.

5. Marvin Pope identifies "the king of terrors" with the middle-eastern god Mot, the god of the netherworld and the chief of demons. See Marvin H. Pope, *Job* (Garden City, N.Y.: Doubleday, Anchor Bible, 1965), p. 126.

6. Edward J. Young makes these apposite comments on the city of chaos: "In this picture the city becomes in actual fact what it already was in nature.

Through their sins its inhabitants had introduced desolation and confusion into the world, and so the place of their dwelling becomes a desolation like the beginning. The nature of the city was desolation; the destiny and final end of the city will also be desolation." In Young, *The Book of Isaiah,* vol. 2 (Grand Rapids: Eerdmans, 1974), p. 164.

7. Jewish apocalyptic writers generally interpreted the "bright morning star" (Lucifer) of Isaiah 14:12–15 as referring to the fall of one of the heavenly host. It was not uncommon in the Old Testament and in Jewish tradition to identify angels with stars. The banished angels in the Book of Enoch are likened to stars falling from heaven. See Jeffrey Burton Russell, *The Devil* (Ithaca, N.Y.: Cornell University Press, 1977), pp. 194–197.

8. This is especially true of the intertestamental apocalyptic literature. *The Assumption of Moses* depicts the eternal kingdom of righteousness as being established by the direct intervention of God without any mediator. In 10:1 we read: "Then his kingdom shall appear throughout all His creation. And then Satan shall be no more, and sorrow shall depart with him."

9. For further elucidation see James Kallas, *The Significance of the Synoptic Miracles* (Greenwich, Conn.: Seabury Press, 1961), p. 73.

10. The "gates of hell" in Matthew 16:18 (KJ) clearly refers to the city of darkness, not the realm of the dead, since the latter could not engage the church in mortal battle. See R. C. H. Lenski, *The Interpretation of St. Matthew's Gospel* (Columbus, Ohio: Wartburg Press, 1943), p. 628. See infra, p.207, note 53.

11. Louis A. Arand, trans., *St. Augustine: Faith, Hope and Charity* 4th ed. (Westminster, Md.: Newman Press, 1963), p. 104.

12. Cf. Augustine: "Therefore the Church even now is the kingdom of Christ, and the kingdom of heaven." *The City of God,* Bk. 20 ch. 9. In *The Basic Writings of Saint Augustine* vol. 2, ed. Whitney J. Oates (New York: Random House, 1948), p. 524.

13. Reinhold Niebuhr, *The Nature and Destiny of Man,* vol. 2 (N.Y.: Charles Scribner's Sons, 1951), p. 139.

14. Thomas Aquinas, *Commentary on Saint Paul's Epistle to the Ephesians,* trans. Matthew L. Lamb (Albany, N.Y.: Magi Books, 1966), p. 238.

15. Thomas Aquinas, *Summa Theologica,* I, Q. CIX. In *Basic Writings of Saint Thomas,* vol. 1 ed. Anton G. Pegis (New York: Random House, 1945), pp. 1012, 1013.

16. One interpreter makes this astute comment: "He is assumed to know that his sin will not overthrow God's order and appears more like a small boy who is about to steal some of his mother's cookies." Charles Hall, *With the Spirit's Sword* (Richmond, Va.: John Knox Press, 1968), p. 57.

17. For Thomas evil has an imperfect form but not a single form that makes it a single unity. The angels sinned through pride, but pride is a defective act. It means falling short of the form that was proper to them.

18. Hall, *With the Spirit's Sword,* p. 58.

19. *Ibid.,* p. 58.

20. *Ibid.,* p. 56.

21. Meister Eckhart, *Selected Treatises and Sermons,* ed. and trans. James M. Clark and John V. Skinner (New York: Harper, 1958), p. 196.

22. Raymond B. Blakney, ed. and trans. *Meister Eckhart* (New York: Harper, 1941), pp. 291–292.

23. Eckhart: "Some good people are hindered by being outwardly too zealous for the blessed sacrament of our Lord's body, so that they never receive it in reality. They expend too much diligence on superfluous things and are never joined to the truth—for truth is to be found within and not in visible phenomena." Blakney, *Meister Eckhart,* p. 198.

24. Martin Luther, *The Bondage of the Will,* trans. J. I. Packer and O. R. Johnston, p. 133.

25. See Paul Althaus, *The Ethics of Martin Luther,* trans. Robert C. Schultz (Philadelphia: Fortress Press, 1972), pp. 51–53.

26. John Calvin, *Commentary on the Gospel According to John,* vol. 2, trans. William Pringle (Edinburgh: Calvin Translation Society, 1847), p. 104.

27. John Calvin, *Institutes of the Christian Religion,* I, xiv, 14, ed. John T. McNeill, p. 174.

28. For Calvin the juridical and moral coercion of the church must be clearly distinguished from the punishing sword of the state. Yet the church wields positive power when it corrects and admonishes its members by imposing discipline upon them. See Sheldon S. Wolin, *Politics and Vision* (Boston: Little, Brown, 1960), pp. 173–175.

29. Wolin, *Politics and Vision,* p. 168.

30. John Calvin, *Commentary on Matthew* 4:8.

31. See Hall, *With the Spirit's Sword,* pp. 100–109.

32. Kenneth Ronald Davis, *Anabaptism and Asceticism,* (Scottdale, Pa: Herald Press, 1974), p. 141.

33. Irvonwy Morgan, *Puritan Spirituality,* pp. 10, 11.

34. Walter Rauschenbusch, *A Theology for the Social Gospel* (New York: Macmillan, 1917), p. 145.

35. *Ibid.,* p. 92.

36. James Luther Adams, in Paul Tillich, *The Protestant Era* (Chicago: University of Chicago Press, 1948), p. 304.

37. Tillich, *The Protestant Era,* p. xxi.

38. Reinhold Niebuhr, *Beyond Tragedy* (New York: Charles Scribner's Sons, 1937), p. 277.

39. There was no conscious attempt on the part of Barth to incorporate Enlightenment ideas into a Reformation perspective, but he was unwittingly influenced by the Enlightenment through his concentrated exposure to Schleiermacher and Kant in the period of his academic theological study. See Donald G. Bloesch, *Jesus Is Victor!: Karl Barth's Doctrine of Salvation* (Nashville: Abingdon Press, 1976), pp. 72–103.

40. Karl Barth, *Church Dogmatics,* III, 3, ed. G. W. Bromiley and T. F. Torrance (Edinburgh: T & T Clark, 1969), p. 367. (Italics added).

41. Karl Barth, *Church Dogmatics,* II, 2, p. 571.

42. "Here on this earth and in time, and therefore in the immediate context of all human kingdoms both small and great, and in the sphere of Satan who rules and torments fallen man, God has irrevocably and indissolubly set up the kingdom of His grace, the throne of His glory, the kingdom which as such is superior to all other powers, to which, in spite of

their resistance, they belong, and which they cannot help but serve."
Barth, *Church Dogmatics,* II, 2, p. 688.

43. *Ibid.,* p. 693.

44. *Ibid.* The immediate context indicates those who are called to be Christians, though the wider context makes clear that this calling goes out to all. Only those who respond and obey actually enjoy the benefits of the kingdom and are members of this kingdom in the true and proper sense. While all are ordained for fellowship with God, only some actually enter into and enjoy this fellowship.

45. Karl Barth, *Church Dogmatics,* II, 2, p. 690.

46. John D. Godsey, *Preface to Bonhoeffer* (Philadelphia: Fortress Press, 1965), p. 40.

47. Dietrich Bonhoeffer, *The Cost of Discipleship,* p. 240.

48. Bonhoeffer, *Ethics,* (New York: Macmillan, 1965), p. 204.

49. *Ibid.*

50. *Ibid.*

51. Karl Rahner, *Theological Investigations, I,* trans. Cornelius Ernst (Baltimore: Helicon Press, *1965), p. 165.*

52. Thomas O'Meara, *Loose in the World* (New York: Paulist Press, 1974), p. 119.

53. Tad Guzie, in *National Catholic Reporter,* vol. 13, no. 12 (January 14, 1977), p. 9.

54. Evgeny Barabanov, "The Schism Between the Church and the World." In *From Under the Rubble,* Alexander Solzhenitsyn et. al., trans. Michael Scammell (Boston: Little, Brown, 1974) [pp. 172–193], p. 181.

55. Thomas Hopko, *The Spirit of God* (Wilton, Conn.: Morehouse-Barlow, 1976), p. 120.

56. Jacques Ellul, *The Ethics of Freedom,* trans. & ed. Geoffrey W. Bromiley (Grand Rapids: Eerdmans, 1976), p. 81.

57. Jacques Ellul, *The Meaning of the City,* trans. Dennis Pardee (Grand Rapids: Eerdmans, 1970), p. 166.

58. *Luther's Works,* vol. 54, p. 57.

59. Emil Brunner, *The Christian Doctrine of Creation and Redemption,* trans. Olive Wyon (Philadelphia: Westminster Press, 1952), p. 318.

60. G. B. Caird, *A Commentary on the Revelation of St. John the Divine* (New York: Harper & Row, 1966), p. 141.

61. John Richards, *But Deliver Us from Evil* (New York: Seabury Press, 1974), p. 90.

62. Thomas Torrance, *Kingdom and Church,* (Fair Lawn, N.J.: Essential Books, 1956), p. 136.

VII.
THE CHURCH'S
SPIRITUAL MISSION

And the twelve summoned the body of the disciples and said, "It is not right that we should give up preaching the word of God to serve tables."

Acts 6:2

We are interested, of course, in the *amelioration* of society; and much is gained for its amelioration that we are so. But what society radically needs is *salvation;* and it is salvation that the Church offers to all.

P. T. Forsyth

It is not the primary . . . task of the Church to create, to change, to improve the social order. The task of the Church lies beyond any social order, because its task is to preach the Gospel of Jesus Christ, the Kingdom of God which transcends all social orders, the good and bad alike.

Emil Brunner

This proclamation [the Gospel] cannot allow itself to be changed or transposed into any . . . plan for saving men by the solution of political, economic or social problems.

Karl Barth

The Church has at times become too much like the secular state to do justice to the spiritual mission of the Church and its connection with the mystery of Christ.

Avery Dulles

The concept of the spiritual mission of the church has lent itself in the past to grave distortions, and this is why it must be carefully defined. Various southern denominations after the Civil War were accustomed to using the term *spiritual mission* because it served to assuage the guilt of the church on the issue of racial segregation and discrimination. Similarly some churches in our day have stressed the spiritual aspect of the church's mission in order to avoid coming to grips with controversial social questions that are at the same time moral questions.

We propose to show that the biblical understanding of the church's spiritual mission entails preaching the Law in its social dimension as well as the Gospel. At the same time, we must avoid the opposite error of politicalizing the Gospel, by which we lose sight of the spiritual mission of the church altogether.

THE NEW TESTAMENT PERSPECTIVE

While the Old Testament tended to conceive of the kingdom of God as a restored earth and the deliverance which God effects as political-social, the New Testament gave a spiritual interpretation of salvation which did not deny its social implications but pointed beyond history to an eternal kingdom. This move away from a purely political conception of salvation is already discernible in the prophetic books of the Old Testament, especially the apocalyptic book of Daniel.

In Luke 4:18, 19 Jesus declares:

The Spirit of the Lord is upon me, because he has anointed me to preach good news to the poor. He has sent me to proclaim release to the captives and recovering of sight to the blind, to set at liberty those who are oppressed, to proclaim the acceptable year of the Lord.

These words are drawn from Isaiah 61:1, 2 and 58:6, where the context clearly indicates a social-political deliverance. But that Jesus is definitely not thinking of political liberation is made clear in Luke 7:22: "Go and tell John what you have seen and heard: the blind receive their sight, the lame walk, lepers are cleansed, and the deaf hear, the dead are raised up, the poor have good news preached to them." Jesus came to offer deliverance from the power of sin and death rather than from political and economic bondage, though when one's heart is changed one will then be enabled to confront the ruling powers of the world with the proper wisdom and motivation. Nonetheless, inward emancipation from sin does not necessarily result in outward liberation from the adverse circumstances of life, though it does give one patience and contentment in the midst of adversity.

That Jesus conceived of salvation primarily in eschatological and spiritual terms accounts for the fact that his message was a stumbling block to the Jews. The Messiah that was expected by Israel was not the Messiah who appeared (Reinhold Niebuhr). The Zealots finally turned against Christ because he refused to accept the role that they assigned him—that of a political Messiah.

Jesus rebuked the multitudes whom he had fed with the loaves and fishes because they did not recognize the sign in the miraculous meal, namely, the inbreaking of the eschatological kingdom of God (John 6:27; cf. 6:40). The work that he required of his hearers was not the building of a new social order but faith in the messenger of God (John 6:29). Jesus called his disciples to the work of mission and evangelism: "The harvest is plentiful, but the laborers are few; pray therefore the Lord of the harvest to send out laborers into his harvest" (Matt. 9:37, 38; cf. John 4:35). The great commission given by the risen Christ to the apostles was the proclamation of the remission of sins through his death and resurrection: "Thus it is written, that the Christ should suffer and on the third day rise from the dead, and that repentance and forgiveness of sins should be preached in his name to all nations, beginning from Jerusalem" (Luke 24:46–47; cf. Matt. 28:18, 19; Mark 16:15). Because the apostles understood their mandate as the ministry of the Word, they appointed deacons to care for the material needs of the congregations so that they could devote all their time to the preaching of the Gospel (Acts 6:1–4).

Paul also understood his commission as the heralding of the Gospel, not as the improvement of human society. He declared that grace was given to him "to preach to the Gentiles the unsearchable riches of Christ, and to make all men see what is the plan of the mystery hidden for ages in God who created all things. . . ." (Eph. 3:8, 9). The preacher of the Gospel is to give single-minded devotion to his Commander in the holy warfare of the saints and should not become "entangled in civilian pursuits" (2 Tim. 2:3, 4). Paul warned that "the kingdom of God does not mean food and drink but righteousness and peace and joy in the Holy Spirit. . . ." (Rom. 14:17). In his view the purpose of the Gospel is not to provide people with happiness and security in this world but instead life with God in eternity.

At the same time, it should be recognized that in the mind of the New Testament this was a spiritual mission to be lived out in the midst of this world and not in some other world (John 17:15). The vision of the New Testament was the spiritual *in* the secular, not divorced from the secular. Moreover, the kingdom of God was viewed not as an individualistic, private affair but as a new society in which the brethren in the faith would share their goods with one another (Acts 4:32–37) and open their homes as hospitality houses (Heb. 13:1, 2). The dichotomy is not between the spiritual and the social but between the spiritual and the profane. Küng astutely remarks: "Jesus had no directly political, but a thoroughgoing 'religious' message and mission, which of course later had incisive 'political' implications and consequences."[1] The spiritual message of our Lord had far-reaching social implications because it brought to people a new set of values that promoted a yearning for a new social order. Though the kingdom of our Lord is not of this world (John 18:36; Heb. 13:14), it must be witnessed to and demonstrated in this world. We are not to remain within the confines of a spiritual ghetto but are summoned to go "outside the camp, bearing abuse" in his name (Heb. 13:13).

WITNESS OF THE CHURCH TRADITION

In the battle with Gnosticism the early church had to emphasize the goodness of creation and the Christian's responsibility in society. It also had to make clear that the spirituality of the kingdom does not entail escape from the body but instead the resurrection of the body. At the same time, the church fathers fully concurred with the author of Hebrews that in this life "we have no lasting city, but we seek the city which is to come" (Heb. 13:14). This world is a vale of tears whose temporary pleasures cannot be compared with the glory that is still to be revealed. Yet this world is also the battleground in which our eternal destiny is decided, and this means that it becomes more, not less, significant when related to the heavenly new Jerusalem.

St. Augustine perceived that the Christian community had an obligation not only to bring people to Christ and build them up in the faith but also to infuse the secular order with Christian values so that the heads of state might give indirect support to the church in its heavenly mission. He concluded that the pagan states had been ruined because of the worship of false gods and that idolatry contains the seeds of social anarchy. The mission of the church is to instill true piety, which is the genuine worship of the true God and which is also the foundation for personal and social righteousness. Without justice, he believed, there can be no society, but without piety there can be no justice.

Churchly involvement in the secular order can, of course, be abused. Luther's protest was directed in part against the medieval church's temptation to clericalism, by which it sought the power and goods of this world. The mission of the church, he insisted, was not to expand either its temporal or spiritual power but to give glory to God by upholding his Word. Luther sought to substitute evangelism for ecclesiastical imperialism and proselytism:

Evangelism means nothing other than preaching, the speaking forth of God's grace and mercy, which the Lord Jesus Christ has earned and acquired through his death. . . . It is a vocal preaching, a living Word, a voice which can be heard throughout the whole world, a message that is publicly proclaimed so that men can hear it everywhere.[2]

The Christian community is also summoned to obedience by demonstrating the love of God before the world. Yet the final goal of our works of love is that the heathen might "hear our doctrine, and then be converted."[3]

Despite Calvin's impassioned concern with building a holy community in this world, he, too, emphasized the spiritual mission of the church. If Christ had permitted himself to be made king, he said, "his *spiritual* kingdom would have been ruined, the Gospel would have been stamped with everlasting infamy, and the hope of salvation would have been utterly destroyed."[4] For Calvin, "Christ's spiritual kingdom and the civil jurisdiction are things completely distinct,"[5] though the latter must always be informed by the values of the former. The pastor must always remember why he has been ordained, that he is the ambassador of God to declare the forgiveness of sins through Jesus Christ, "that he is sent to procure the salvation of souls."[6] This missionary mandate of the church, however, is not just the prerogative of the clerics, but of all members of Christ's body. Torrance puts his finger on the tremendous missionary impetus in Calvin's theology: "Those who do not endeavour to bring their neighbours and unbelievers to the way of salvation plainly show that they make no account of God's honor, and that they try to diminish the mighty power of His empire."[7]

Standing in the Reformed tradition is P. T. Forsyth, who wrote at a time when the social gospel was penetrating English theology and church life. In opposition to a merely social Christianity he argued that the "largest and deepest reference of the Gospel, is not to the world or its social problems, but to Eternity and its social obligations." While acknowledging that the Gospel carries with it the incentive for social reform, he was also keenly aware that a concern for social reform does not necessarily carry with it the Gospel. "The Church has been at its best," he concluded, "when it did not mix with political transactions in the way of ruling prerogative or direct control. Its true influence is that of its apostolic Word and its moral character."[8] He was adamant that the mission of the church not be confused with humanitarianism: "Mere fraternal service to the world does not yet secure Christ's purpose with the world. Christ the Helper is not yet Christ the Saviour. Merely to help and bless the world is not yet to secure it for the

Kingdom of God."[9] He perceived that the "chief danger today is not the ceremonial ritual, but the moral and social ritual,"[10] which stems from the idea that people "are to be saved by welldoing, by integrity, by purity, by generosity, by philanthropy, by doing as Christ did rather than trusting what Christ did, by loving instead of trusting love."[11]

Forsyth made his witness in a period when some theologians were saying that the essence of the Gospel lies in the brotherhood of man under the fatherhood of God. The mission of the church was thereby misconstrued as building the kingdom of God on earth. Forsyth's aim was to recall the church to its apostolic mission—the proclamation of God's grace revealed in Jesus Christ:

The greatest product of the Church is not brotherly love but divine worship. And we shall never worship right nor serve right till we are more engrossed with our God than even with our worship, with His reality than our piety, with His Cross than our service. It is well to dream and to talk much of brotherly love. But the brethren who love best and the love that loves longest are made by the Gospel.[12]

Perhaps no theologian in recent years has wrestled with the meaning of the church's mission more assiduously than Karl Barth. As a pastor in Safenwil, Switzerland, before his teaching career, he came to know and identify with the needs of the working people in his region. Very early in his ministry he gave wholehearted support to the Social Democratic Party, and it has even been suggested that his theology is best understood as a rationale for his commitment to socialism.[13] This is a grave misinterpretation of Barth's position, however, since even at Safenwil he protested against the identification of any social ideology with the kingdom of God. As he put it: "Pacifism and social democracy do not represent the kingdom of God, but the old kingdom of man in new forms."[14] The enlightened Christian will be sensitive to the crying needs in the secular community, and he will work to meet these needs, but this does not mean that the Gospel itself should be understood as a political manifesto. In no uncertain terms he declared: "I regard the 'political pastor' in any form as a mistake, even if he is a socialist. But as a man and a citizen . . . I take the side of the Social Democrats."[15] The Gospel itself transcends "all morality and politics and ethics," which have no saving power in themselves, and this is true "even of so-called Christian morality and so-called socialist politics."[16]

Barth broke with many of his friends in the religious socialist movement in his conviction that humanity cannot build the kingdom of God on earth but can only wait for God to act in his own time and way, though it can set up signs and parables of the coming of the kingdom. He insisted that the Gospel "cannot allow itself to be changed or transposed . . . into any plan for saving men by the solution of political, economic or social problems."[17] This is his subtle rejoinder to those who would confuse the heavenly and earthly kingdoms: "Clever enough is the paradox that the service of God is or must become the service of man; but that is not the same as saying that our precipitate service of man, even when it is undertaken in the name of the purest love, becomes by that happy fact the service of God."[18]

Barth has no intention of excluding the concern for social justice and reform from the Christian mission, but his position is that in our preaching we should endeavor to transcend partisan politics. All social ideologies stand under the judgment of the Word of God, though this does not mean that one is not preferable to another in the concrete situation in which we find ourselves. Barth can even speak of the "political mission" and "political responsibility" of the church,[19] but here he means that the church must be willing, in its proclamation, to speak out against social evils without necessarily aligning itself with any political or social platform.[20] During the church conflict in Germany he himself preached sermons that bordered on the incendiary because of their political overtones, though their basic emphasis was on upholding Jesus Christ as the one and only Lord. While seeking to underline the unity between theology and praxis,[21] Barth stoutly contended that theology must not be politicized nor politics theologized.

The primary content of the church's preaching should be the Gospel of reconciliation and redemption which involves the announcement of judgment as well as grace manifested in Jesus Christ. Barth can perhaps be criticized for his view that the Gospel proclamation is simply an announcement of a redemptive event in the past and that the purpose of our preaching is to give people knowledge of this event by which they are already saved. Yet it must not be forgotten that for Barth the knowledge that is communicated through our preaching is not merely intellectual knowledge but creative power which effects the conversion of those who receive and hear. In this light we can understand these words of his: "There can be no doubt . . . that in the delivering of the Christian message it is also a matter of saving souls, of inviting and helping men to personal being, possession and capacity in the kingdom of grace and salvation, and therefore to participation in the supreme good and all the other goods which it includes."[22]

While he recognizes the political thrust and implications of the preaching of the Gospel, Barth stands with Forsyth in resisting any attempt to equate the Gospel with humanitarianism or politics:

The Church must remain the Church. It must remain the inner circle of the Kingdom of Christ. The Christian community has a task of which the civil community can never relieve it and which it can never pursue in the forms peculiar to the civil community. It would not redound to the welfare of the civil community if the Christian community were to be absorbed by it . . . and were therefore to neglect the special task which it has received a categorical order to undertake. It proclaims the rule of Jesus Christ and the hope of the Kingdom of God.[23]

Emil Brunner also voiced misgivings at the confusion of humanitarianism and social welfare programs with the Gospel. Emphasizing, like Barth, the transcendental and eschatological nature of the Gospel, he agreed that a church which is not, as such, an evangelizing church is either not yet or no longer the church. The primary or essential task of the church is not to change or improve the social order but rather "to preach the Gospel of Jesus Christ, the Kingdom of God which transcends all social orders, the good and bad alike."[24] Brunner recognized that we need to sound the prophetic note of judgment in our proclamation, but it must be aimed finally at the man in sin and not simply at the symptoms of sin. "Religion," he said, "does not merely criticise one form of civilization or another but casts doubt upon civilization itself and upon humanity, because it casts doubt upon man."[25]

For Brunner "Christian action in the world is not one of progressive building up," as in liberal social gospel theology. Instead, "it resembles a sortie from a fortress more than a campaign of conquest, which goes forward from stage to stage." Christian action needs always "to return to the starting-point . . . in order that it may not become something different, or something wrong."[26] The lines between the church and world will remain intact until the end of history.

Dietrich Bonhoeffer brings into the picture something new in that the main thrust of his witness is to deplore the spiritualization of the church's mission by which the Gospel is removed from the cares of the world, and the kingdom becomes other-worldly. Bonhoeffer saw that the Christian community must be concerned with social justice and material need as well as the righteousness of the kingdom. Sometimes the church must address itself to the penultimate—the area of temporal concerns—before it addresses itself to the ultimate—the issues that concern one's eternal destiny. "To give bread to the hungry man," he said, "is not the same as to proclaim the grace of God and justification to him, and to have received bread is not the same as to have faith. Yet for him who does these things for the sake of the ultimate, and in the knowledge of the ultimate, this penultimate does bear a relation to the ultimate."[27] Bonhoeffer found the supernatural only in the natural, the holy only in the profane, the revelational only in the rational. At the same time, "what is Christian is not identical with what is of the world. The natural is not identical with the supernatural or the revelational with the rational."[28]

Bonhoeffer, too, was opposed to the politicalizing or secularizing of the Gospel, despite the fact that some of his interpreters have been led to embrace a secular Christianity. In his view, "the realm of the spiritual office" must never be confused with "the realm of secular government."[29] The mission of the church is to preach the message of redemption but always with the understanding that this redemption has implications in every area of man's existence: "Instead of the solution of problems, Jesus brings the redemption of men, and yet for that very reason He does really bring the solution of all human problems as well . . . but from quite a different plane."[30] The Church must not be confused with a "national community like the old Israel," since Christ's word of nonresistance "removes the Church from the sphere of politics and law." Yet the church, nonetheless, has a "political character" in its doctrine of sanctification. "The world is the world and the Church the Church, and yet the Word of God must go forth from the Church into all the world, proclaiming that the earth is the Lord's and all that therein is."[31]

At the Second Vatican Council the spiritual character of the mission of the church was reaffirmed, as we see in the "Decree on the Apostolate of the Laity": "For this the Church was founded: that by spreading the kingdom of Christ everywhere for the glory of God the Father, she might bring all men to share in Christ's saving redemption."[32] It declares that the "mission of the Church concerns the salvation of men, which is to be achieved by belief in Christ and by His grace. Hence the apostolate of the Church and of all her members is primarily designed to manifest Christ's message by words and deeds and to communicate His grace to the world."[33]

Avery Dulles reflects the apostolic concern of the Council when he laments: "The Church has at times become too much like the secular state to do justice to the spiritual mission of the Church and its connection with the mystery of Christ."[34] He is insistent that the church "must constantly preach that human salvation consists principally in a life beyond our earthly experience."[35] Dulles here opposes the secularizing trends present in the new Catholicism as well as in current Protestantism, where biblical theology has been largely supplanted by political theology.

REINTERPRETING THE CHURCH'S MISSION

In recent years the church's task has been reinterpreted to mean something other than the great commission given by Jesus to his apostles. Some have sought to politicalize the Gospel so that it now is seen as a message of political liberation. The women's liberation movement understands the Gospel as a manifesto for social egalitarianism (Rosemary Ruether, Mary Daly). Then there are those who psychologize the Gospel by reducing its content to an interior state of consciousness. Some have even sexualized the Gospel so that it comes to signify deliverance from sexual frustration and repression (D. H. Lawrence, Wilhelm Reich). We also have those who religionize or spiritualize the Gospel so that it is portrayed as a style of piety or a quest for a higher righteousness. Closely related to this group are those who privatize the Gospel so that it is made to apply only to the religious or personal side of one's life. This is the perennial gnostic temptation which bifurcates life into outer and inner realms, with the latter alone having genuine significance. The battle today is not so much for the Bible as for the Gospel, since the innermost content of the church's proclamation and mission is being altered.

Special attention should be given to the politicalization of the Gospel, which seems to be the principal challenge to the evangelical church in our time. This misunderstanding was already evident in the old social gospel movement (e.g. Walter Rauschenbusch), where the mission of the church was perceived as the creation of a new social order characterized by freedom and justice. In our day Gustavo Gutiérrez contends that to build the human community is also to save. Social revolution, even violent revolution, for the sake of liberation from political and economic oppression "is a salvific event. . . . It is the historical realization of the Kingdom."[36] Similarly, Langdon Gilkey maintains that "the task of the church is that of liberating and humanizing God's world."[37] Rubem Alves champions a political humanism which he understands as "a new type of messianism which believes that man can be free by the powers of man alone."[38] According to Jürgen Moltmann the mission of the church is not to convert people to the Christian religion but to plant the seeds of liberation in the hearts and minds of the oppressed.[39] A World Council of Churches document, *The Church for Others*, advocates not "Christianization, bringing man to God through Christ and his church," but instead "humanization," in which conversion is now thought of on the corporate level, "in the form of social change."[40] André Biéler asserts that the mission of the church is "perpetually to present to the world the goals of peace, non-violence, liberty, solidarity, disarmament, classless society, global society, etc., and to work for their political realization."[41] In this kind of thinking the self-development of the oppressed peoples of the Third World, in effect, supplants the call to evangelize the heathen. Many of the liberation theologians refer to themselves as Christian Marxists because they see Marx as the outstanding social prophet of the modern industrial era.

In the human potential and pastoral psychology movements, the Gospel is reconceived as a call to realize human possibilities and discover one's identity in a chaotic world.[42] The aim is no longer to awaken people to Christ's great work of remitting sin and guilt through his death and resurrection but to relieve people of guilt feelings. O. Hobart Mowrer contends that most pastoral counseling today is patterned after secular psychotherapy, the aim of which is not repentance and restitution but insight into one's self.[43] Philip Rieff points to the secularizing influences in group therapy:

Group psychotherapy follows the form of commitment therapy without its doctrinal content. It is as if Wesley's famous classes continued to meet, for intense supportive discussions, without the basic conceptual scheme expressed in the theology, merely reaching out for temporary relief from the dialectic of despair and hope generated by the traditional culture.[44]

There is no doubt that salvation and mental health are integrally related and that the gift of salvation will bring identity and meaning into a person's life and thereby impart a certain degree of stability. At the same time, the call to obedience which comes from the cross entails the disciplining of one's passions and feelings and a willingness to stand against the predominating values of the surrounding culture. The cross liberates one from the anxiety of meaninglessness, but it does not exempt one from conflict with one's fellow human beings and the threat of persecution by the powers of the world. The believer may well be placed under a more severe emotional stress than the unbeliever, and his only comfort is that he is upheld by one whose peace remains after peace with the world has dissipated and whose joy is not dependent on the changing circumstances of life (as is the case with a purely human happiness).

A syncretistic or universalistic outlook also characterizes avant garde theology. John B. Cobb, Jr., claims that Jesus is important as the historical personification of liberating love but that other Christ-Figures likewise attest the movement of the divine within man.[45] For Robert McAfee Brown the church's mission is no longer to bring Christ to the lost of the world but to find Christ already among them.[46] The reason for mission is that Christianity brings us into contact with love and creativity and offers a sense of joy in a world of fear. Fred Brown argues in his *Secular Evangelism* that the task of evangelism is not to evangelize per se but "to help people to understand their unconscious spirituality; to perceive the nature of God's presence and activity in the world; to find a greater measure of true fulfillment by consciously cooperating with God whom . . . they already know by some other name."[47] John Macquarrie upholds a "global ecumenism," which rules out missionary effort to convert pagans and instead enlists enlightened people of every world religion to minister to the loveless and unloved masses of humanity.[48]

Not surprisingly, voices have been raised in protest against these perversions of the Gospel. Catholic lay theologian Ralph Martin sounds this note of caution: "An apostolate which deals only with the material and psychic needs of man is seriously truncated; only when the spiritual situation is changed through repentance, faith, baptism for the forgiveness of sins and the gift of the Spirit has the specifically Christian mission been fulfilled."[49] Torrance suggests that evangelical convictions are being submerged "by *consciously meritorious involvement* in socio-political issues, which is associated with a serious degeneration of genuine ethical substance and indeed a widespread moral laxity of the individual in our society."[50] Julius Lester, a black theologian associated with *Katallagete* magazine, laments the fact that modern Protestantism has become a "politicized Christianity."[51] "As long as the Church thinks that it should and can change the world, the Church will be a caucus group within the Democratic Party." Despite his genuine concern with the social implications of the Gospel, John R. W. Stott warns:

The kind of ecumenism which concentrates exclusively on questions of social justice . . . on eliminating racial discrimination, hunger, poverty and war, forgets the Christian saying which is "sure and worthy of full acceptance, that Christ Jesus came into the world to save sinners," and forgets also His plain commission to the church to proclaim repentance and forgiveness to all nations.[52]

Probably the foremost critic of the new theology is Jacques Ellul, lay theologian in the Reformed church in France. Though a lawyer by profession and intimately involved in the political process, he makes clear that politics can at most put bandages on the wound; it cannot eradicate the source of man's affliction. Ellul concludes that, for all the current emphasis on social Christianity, "an unbiased and unprejudiced reading of the Bible shows that converting men to their Lord is the work Christians are called to do."[53] The conversion that we should aim for is not to any particular political philosophy but to a whole new orientation toward life, the world, and God. "If this conversion fails to take place," he says, "all the constitutional devices, all studies on economic democracy, and all reassuring sociological inquiries on man and society are vain efforts at justification."[54]

Interestingly enough, Hans Küng, despite his openness to the theology of liberation and his concern for social justice for the oppressed, draws a sharp line of distinction between redemption and emancipation (in the political sense). Redemption "means liberation of man by God, not any self-redemption on man's part."[55] Emancipation, on the other hand, means the "liberation of man by man, it means man's self-liberation." Emancipation should grow out of redemption, but it must never be confused with the latter, for otherwise we are again in the morass of Pelagianism.

EVANGELISM AND SOCIAL CONCERN

The two dangers that confront the church today are divorcing the kingdom of God from politics and economics and maintaining that the kingdom is realized through politics and economics. While a privatistic evangelicalism and an acculturated liberalism (where the Gospel is psychologized) are guilty of the first error, the liberation theologies often fall into the second error. Robert Bellah voices our own sentiments: "Religion and morality and politics are not the same things, and confusing them can lead to terrible distortions. But cutting all links between them can lead to even worse distortions."[56]

The apostolic mandate is to preach the Gospel, not a political program, but this Gospel has tremendous social and political repercussions. Moreover, this mandate includes teaching the new converts to be disciples, and one dimension of discipleship is social service. True evangelism "will show that no single aspect of human life and human suffering lies outside the concern of Christ and his Church."[57] Carl

Henry indicts those who would limit the demands of the Gospel to the decision of faith: "The Gospel of Christ contains more than the assurance of divine forgiveness and new life; it includes also the seed of human dignity and freedom. To obscure this essential fact is no less to imperil the human soul than to neglect personal evangelism."[58] To his discredit Charles Hodge concluded that "both political despotism and domestic slavery, belong in morals to the *adiaphora,* to things indifferent."[59]

Embracing the Gospel means being willing to give a public testimony to the freedom of Christ and the law of grace in the face of the political religions of nations, races, and classes (Moltmann). It entails not only taking up the cross in service to the unfortunate in society but also engaging in political programs for social change. Though morality cannot be legislated, social justice can be, and this is the cultural mandate of the church, which is fulfilled indirectly by its members working as a transforming leaven in the secular stations of life. The injunction in Proverbs 31:8 is: "Speak up for people who cannot speak for themselves. Protect the rights of all who are helpless" (TEV). Martin Luther King acknowledged that the force of civil law could not make whites love blacks as brothers, but it could protect blacks from whites who regard them as less than brothers.

Social service *(diakonia)* sometimes takes chronological priority over the preaching of the Gospel since, if our hearers are in dire physical distress or material need, they will not listen to our message until these immediate concerns are dealt with. Everett Harrison makes this trenchant observation: "Missionaries who would prefer to spend most of their time in spreading the good news are drawn into the task of food distribution because they find that people in a near starving condition are so benumbed by their plight that they cannot concentrate on their spiritual need and are literally unable to take in the message of salvation."[60] Peter Claver, a Catholic missionary to African slaves, remarked: "We must speak to them with our hands, before we try to speak to them with our lips." He understood that concrete service like the distributing of medicine, food, or brandy to black slaves could also prove to be a potent witness to the love of Christ and would probably make his hearers more receptive to the message of salvation. Social service in this sense is pre-evangelism, which is also necessary in fulfilling the great commission. Prayer, of course, is another form of the ministry of pre-evangelism (cf. Col. 4:3).

Social service, which in this context includes social action, should also be regarded as a fruit and evidence of the Gospel. It should follow the Gospel proclamation as a demonstration of our gratefulness for the redemption purchased for us by Christ. When Martin Luther King walked across the forbidden park in Birmingham or up the road from Selma, it was after such holy observances as a black gospel service.[61]

The way to regain social relevance in our preaching is to rediscover the social imperatives of the law of God, which certainly form a part of God's Word. We need to address ourselves to social as well as personal evils in society when we preach against sin. We must not only herald the good news of God's grace but also warn of God's impending judgment on a disobedient people. It is not up to the church to implement the law—this is the task of the state—but the church must preach the law as well as offer guidelines to government officials through its public pronouncements. Political decisions should always be informed or shaped by theology, and this goal can be realized not only by Christian officials in government reflecting on their faith but also by formal counsel given by the church to the government.

However important the cultural mandate of the church, we must continue to maintain the theological priority of evangelism and conversion. Jacques Ellul, in his exposition of the Book of Jonah, avers:

Here we have the entire answer to social sin. Not reforms first. Nineveh will not, for example, acquire new social structures or a new government. Neither is it because men will *individually* repent and begin leading a righteous, pious, holy life. It is rather the event that seems impossible to us: the conversion of an entire population *and* its government.[62]

Moral counsel, Reinhold Niebuhr reminds us, is one of the tests of true prophecy. In addition to pronouncing woe upon injustice wherever it may be found, the truly prophetic church will reveal the way of God more perfectly by suggesting alternatives to specific sinful practices. In this way the prophetic admonition is not exclusively negative but also holds out hope for a better life. Despite his indictment of popular American revivalism, with its concern for individual conversions, Reinhold Niebuhr acknowledges that "social sensitivity can be derived from the conscience of our individual religious life."[63] Alan Heimert has documented the thesis that Calvinist or evangelical religion in the eighteenth century planted the seeds of the American Revolution, with its democratic and egalitarian impulses derived from the Gospel. Liberal or rational religion, on the other hand, sought to maintain the cultural and political status quo.[64]

The Gospel itself is a stick of dynamite in the social structure, and this is why both communist and fascist dictatorships almost invariably place a restriction on its heralds and ambassadors. The Gospel has politically revolutionary implications because it desacralizes the holy places of culture-religion; it demythologizes the myths which society has created for itself and by which it is enabled to survive; and it calls into radical question the current absolutes that enthrall the political and academic establishments and that have their source in man's idolatrous imagination. In short, the Gospel is a direct threat to the pantheon of the gods, whether these go under the names of science, sex, the national heritage, the racial consciousness, the proletarian utopia, or any other. The Gospel poses an unmistakable challenge to every kind of political totalitarianism which demands from its subjects unconditional allegiance, even if it should use the cloak of Christianity to broaden its appeal.

Our chief motivation for spreading the Gospel, however, is not to overturn oppressive social structures or disturb the existing social order but instead to witness to God's incomparable grace in Jesus Christ and thereby save souls from sin, death, and hell. It is a matter of eternal salvation that people be brought into the kingdom of Christ, and this in itself should furnish the incentive to preach and witness to the truth of the Gospel. We wholeheartedly concur with this admonition of Norval Geldenhuys: "In spite of all failures in the past, the church of Christ must again and again renew its energetic attempts under His guidance to gather in souls for His kingdom, and must do this not merely in the 'shallow waters' but in the 'deep water'—not only in the vicinity of settled ecclesiastical life, but also among the great masses of people where the need is so great."[65]

Bonhoeffer, in his *Cost of Discipleship,* where his evangelical stance is most noticeable, warns that

nothing could be more ruthless than to make men think there is still plenty of time to mend their ways. To tell men that the cause is urgent, and that the kingdom of God is at hand is the most charitable and merciful act we can perform, the most joyous news we can bring. The messenger cannot wait and repeat it to every man in his own language. God's language is clear enough. It is not for the messenger to decide who will hear and who will not, for only God knows who is "worthy"; and those who are worthy will hear the Word when the disciple proclaims it.[66]

A recent survey reported in *U.S. Catholic* revealed that in Catholic France only 11 percent of the people regard the preaching of the Gospel as the foremost task of the church, and 75 percent see the continuing existence of the church more as a social institution than as a specifically Christian institution.[67] The statistics from America would be somewhat different, but in the mainline denominations evangelism understood as winning people to Christ and thereby saving them from eternal death would definitely be considered a secondary task of the church, and in many circles it would be dissociated completely from the church's mission. It is indeed imperative that we recover the evangelistic zeal and urgency of the first-century church and carry the flag of the Gospel into the pagan world of our time, seeking to bring all peoples into submission to the one Lord and Savior, Jesus Christ.

NOTES

1. Hans Küng, *On Being a Christian,* trans. Edward Quinn (Garden City, N.Y.: Doubleday, 1976), p. 338.

2. Martin Luther, W.A. 12, 259.

3. *Luther's Works,* vol. 29, p. 57.

4. John Calvin, *Commentary on the Gospel According to John,* I, 6, 15, trans. William Pringle (Edinburgh: Calvin Translation Society, 1847), p. 234. (Italics added).

5. John Calvin, *Institutes of the Christian Religion,* IV, 20, 1, ed. John T. McNeill, p. 1486.

6. John Calvin, *Corpus Reformatorum, Calv. op.* LIII, p. 235.

7. Thomas Torrance, *Kingdom and Church,* p. 162.

8. P. T. Forsyth, *The Church and the Sacraments* (London: Independent Press, 1947), p. 78.

9. *Ibid.,* p. 120.

10. P. T. Forsyth, *God the Holy Father* (London: Independent Press, 1957), p. 128.

11. *Ibid.*

12. Forsyth, *The Church and the Sacraments,* p. 25.

13. See Friedrich-Wilhelm Marquardt, *Theologie und Sozialismus* (München: Chr. Kaiser Verlag, 1972).

14. Eberhard Busch, *Karl Barth,* trans. John Bowden (Philadelphia: Fortress Press, 1975), p. 101.

15. *Ibid.,* p. 88.

16. *Ibid.,* p. 84.

17. John Baillie and Hugh Martin, eds., *Revelation* (London: Faber & Faber, 1937), p. 81.

18. Karl Barth, *The Word of God and the Word of Man,* p. 276.

19. Karl Barth, *Against the Stream,* ed. Ronald Gregor Smith (London: SCM Press, 1954), p. 151.

20. *Ibid.,* pp. 22, 23.

21. Barth criticized the German Confessing Church, which he had helped found, for fighting only for itself, for the freedom and purity of its proclamation

and keeping silent over the persecution of the Jews, the horrendous treatment of political opponents of the Third Reich, and the suppression of the press by the government. Busch, *Karl Barth,* p. 273.

22. Karl Barth, *Church Dogmatics* IV, 3 b. p. 563.

23. Barth, *Against the Stream,* p. 22.

24. Emil Brunner, *The Church in the New Social Order* (London: SCM Press, 1952), p. 7.

25. Cited in *The British Weekly* Vol.XCV, No. 4290 (May 8, 1969), p. 9.

26. Emil Brunner, *The Mediator,* trans. Olive Wyon (Philadelphia: Westminster Press, 1947), p. 616.

27. Dietrich Bonhoeffer, *Ethics* (New York: Macmillan, 1965), p. 137.

28. *Ibid.,* p. 199.

29. *Ibid.,* p. 95.

30. *Ibid.,* p. 355.

31. Dietrich Bonhoeffer, *The Cost of Discipleship,* p. 252.

32. Walter M. Abbott, *The Documents of Vatican II* (New York: America Press, 1966), p. 491.

33. *Ibid.,* p. 496.

34. Avery Dulles, *Models of the Church* (Garden City, N.Y.: Doubleday, 1974) pp. 153, 154.

35. Avery Dulles, *The Resilient Church* (Garden City, N.Y.: Doubleday, 1977), p. 23.

36. Gustavo Gutiérrez, *A Theology of Liberation,* trans. Sister Caridad Inda and John Eagleson (Maryknoll, N.Y.: Orbis Books, 1973), p. 177.

37. Langdon Gilkey, *Catholicism Confronts Modernity* (New York: Seabury Press, 1975), p. 199.

38. Rubem Alves, *A Theology of Human Hope* (Washington: Corpus Books, 1969), p. 17.

39. Jürgen Moltmann, *The Church in the Power of the Spirit,* trans. Margaret Kohl (New York: Harper & Row, 1977), pp. 83ff., 150ff.

40. *The Church for Others* (Geneva: World Council of Churches, 1968), pp. 76ff.

41. André Biéler, *The Politics of Hope,* trans. Dennis Pardee. (Grand Rapids: Eerdmans, 1974), p. 118.

42. For a damning indictment of humanistic psychology in and outside the church today, see Paul C. Vitz, *Psychology as Religion: The Cult of Self-Worship* (Grand Rapids: Eerdmans, 1977). Vitz gives special attention to the deleterious influence of Carl Rogers on the pastoral care movement today.

43. O. Hobart Mowrer, *The Crisis in Psychiatry and Religion* (Princeton, N.J.: Van Nostrand, 1961).

44. Philip Rieff, *The Triumph of the Therapeutic* (New York: Harper & Row, 1966), pp. 77, 78.

45. John B. Cobb, Jr., *Liberal Christianity at the Crossroads* (Philadelphia: Westminster Press, 1973), pp. 108–116.

46. Robert McAfee Brown, *Frontiers For the Church Today* (New York: Oxford University Press, 1973), p. 43.

47. Fred Brown, *Secular Evangelism* (London: SCM Press, 1970), p. 20.

48. John Macquarrie, *Principles of Christian Theology* (New York: Charles Scribner's Sons, 1966), pp. 394, 395.

49. Ralph Martin, *Unless the Lord Build the House* (Notre Dame, Indiana: Ave Maria Press, 1972), p. 40.

50. Thomas Torrance, *Theology in Reconciliation* (Grand Rapids: Eerdmans, 1975), p. 277.

51. Julius Lester, "Come, Come, Ye Saints All Is Well" in *Katallagete,* vol. 5, no. 1 (Spring 1974), pp. 12–13.

52. John R. W. Stott, *Christ the Controversialist* (Downers Grove, Ill.: Inter-Varsity Press, 1972), p. 188.

53. Jacques Ellul, *Violence,* trans. Cecelia Gaul Kings (New York: Seabury Press, 1969), p. 149.

54. Jacques Ellul, *The Political Illusion,* trans. Konrad Kellen (New York: Alfred A. Knopf, 1967), p. 234.

55. Hans Küng, *On Being a Christian,* p. 430.

56. Robert Bellah, "American Civil Religion in the 1970's" in *Anglican Theological Review* (July 1973), (Supplementary Series) [pp.8–20], p. 20.

57. Peter Beyerhaus in *Christianity Today,* vol. 18, no. 13 (March 29, 1974), p. 49.

58. Carl Henry in *Christianity Today,* vol. 19, no. 20 (July 4, 1975), p. 65.

59. Cited in Donald Dayton, *Discovering an Evangelical Heritage* (New York: Harper & Row, 1976), p. 129.

60. Everett F. Harrison, "The One Ministry of Our Lord: Proclaiming the Good News/Healing the Body." In *World Vision,* vol. 19, no. 6, (June, 1975) [pp. 9–11], p. 11.

61. See Henry H. Mitchell, *Black Preaching* (Philadelphia: J. B. Lippincott, 1970), p. 217.

62. Jacques Ellul, *The Meaning of the City,* trans. Geoffrey W. Bromiley (Grand Rapids: Eerdmans, 1970), p. 69.

63. Reinhold Niebuhr, *Justice and Mercy* (New York: Harper & Row, 1974), p. 110.

64. Alan Heimert, *Religion and the American Mind* (Cambridge, Mass.: Harvard University Press, 1966).

65. Norval Geldenhuys, *Commentary on the Gospel of Luke,* 6th ed. (Grand Rapids: Eerdmans, 1966), p. 183.

66. Dietrich Bonhoeffer, *The Cost of Discipleship,* p. 188.

67. *U.S. Catholic,* vol. 40, no. 6 (June 1975), p. 20.

VIII.
THE PERSONAL RETURN
OF CHRIST

Hark, your watchmen lift up their voice, together they sing for joy; for eye to eye they see the return of the Lord to Zion.

Isaiah 52:8

Christ, having been offered once to bear the sins of many, will appear a second time, not to deal with sin but to save those who are eagerly waiting for him.

Hebrews 9:28

From the Scriptures you will learn also of His second manifestation to us, glorious and divine indeed, when He shall come not in lowliness but in His proper glory, no longer in humiliation but in majesty.

Athanasius

To all He will appear in the ineffable glory of His kingdom, in the radiance of eternity, and in the boundless might of divine majesty accompanied by the army of angels.

John Calvin

Redemption does not mean that the world and we ourselves within it evolve in this or that direction. It means that Jesus Christ is coming again.

Karl Barth

CURRENT ISSUES IN ESCHATOLOGY

Perhaps the foremost issue in current eschatology is the nature of the kingdom of God. Did Jesus preach an inbreaking of a supernatural kingdom in the imminent future, or did he see the kingdom realized in his own ministry and teachings? Should the church preach an eschatological kingdom or one that is present now in the fellowship of believers?

According to Albert Schweitzer Jesus definitely thought within the framework of apocalyptic and therefore envisioned the imminent, catastrophic establishment of a new age of righteousness completely different from the present age.[1] Yet Schweitzer maintained that Jesus was mistaken in his expectations and that the kingdom "must be understood as something ethical and spiritual, rather than supernatural, as something realized rather than expected."[2]

C. H. Dodd champions what he calls "realized eschatology," which means that the kingdom came to be known as an experienced reality in the life of Jesus and in his resurrection.[3] Jesus' eschatological imagery only symbolizes the abiding truths of a moral universe. Eternal life is a present reality for the community of faith. The kingdom is not a future time when the world will be recreated but a timeless eternity, a state of inner communion with God.

Rudolf Bultmann propounds what might be termed a realizing eschatology, since the eschaton is said to be realized anew in the decision of faith. Seeking to demythologize the apocalyptic framework of Jesus' thinking, he arrives at the position that the kingdom signifies the power of grace and forgiveness experienced by man in the decision of faith and surrender. In his theology the kingdom is internalized; it is the "presence of eternity" in time. There is no cosmic redemption, but Bultmann does affirm the reality of personal freedom through contact with the preaching of the kerygma. The kingdom of God is never established in history, since people are always sinners. The end of the world means the end to inauthentic existence in the crisis of repentance and faith.

Ernst Käsemann holds that it is not the message of the historical Jesus but the Christian kerygma that has an apocalyptic thrust. While taking for his point of departure the apocalyptic preaching of John the Baptist, Jesus preached the immediacy of a God who is near at hand. Apocalypticism originated not with Jesus but in the post-Easter enthusiasm of the primitive church. Käsemann does not simply wish to discard apocalyptic imagery but rather to reinterpret it in such a way that certain themes that seem integral to it are preserved—for example, the realization of sonship and freedom through the forgiveness of sins.[4] The kingdom of God is "the kingdom of freedom" exemplified and actualized in "the freedom of Jesus."[5]

Reflecting the tradition of Christian mysticism, Paul Tillich spiritualizes the kingdom, seeing it as the manifestation of the presence of God within history, though in its eternal fulfillment it stands above history. The accent in Tillich's thought is on eternal life rather than the second coming of Christ and the end of world history. In his view history will forever remain ambiguous and marked by conflict.

From a quite different perspective T. A. Kantonen seeks to make a prominent place for the realization of the promises of Christ on earth as well as in heaven and thereby upholds a millennial age prior to the second advent.[6] He distinguishes between the kingdom of Christ, the present reign of Christ, and the eternal kingdom of God, which is still to come. The kingdom of Christ includes the church but is not limited to it. The church in the millennium will still be the church militant; the demonic powers will be unleashed for a final stand at the end of the millennial age.

Also representing a futuristic eschatology is George Eldon Ladd, who contends that the kingdom involves two great moments: a fulfillment within history, which has taken place in the coming of Jesus Christ, and a consummation at the end of history. He draws a sharp distinction between the new order inaugurated by Christ and the eschaton, or age to come. The kingdom of the future will be realized in two stages: an interim millennial kingdom subsequent to the second advent and the final consummation, which "will introduce a redeemed order whose actual character transcends both historical experience and realistic imagination."[7]

Seeking to unite futuristic and realized motifs, Karl Barth posits three forms of the return of Jesus Christ.[8] The first is the resurrection, which has already occurred and which is the basis of all other manifestations of Christ. The second is the outpouring of the Holy Spirit at Pentecost, which is a present reality in the church. The third is the parousia, by which Christ reveals and confirms to the whole of creation what has already been accomplished for the salvation of the world through his death and resurrection. For Barth the first coming of Christ is inaugurated eschatology, whereas the second coming is consummated eschatology. The great events of the end of the world have already taken place in the resurrection and ascension of Christ, but they have still to take place in the history of the community of faith.

When we turn to the theologies of hope and liberation we are presented with a decidedly this-worldly rather than other-worldly emphasis. For Pannenberg the coming kingdom is not a supernatural intervention into history but the destiny of present society. In Gilkey's view, "hope is directed at a human well-being in the new historical world of the future."[9] Moltmann speaks of the fulfillment of history rather than a kingdom "beyond history."[10] He is careful not to claim that man creates his own future but that he acts "in the light of the promised future that is to come." Christ's coming is not eternity breaking into history but "the opening up of history." The eschatological hope is seen as "the *humanizing* of man" and "the *socializing* of humanity."[11]

A present-day proponent within Catholicism of what might be termed intrahistorical fulfillment is Johannes Metz. He sees the future that the church hopes for "emerging" and "arising" in the here and now. In place of an otherworldly eschatology he proposes "a creative and militant eschatology" which seeks the overthrow of oppressive power structures in society. The this-worldly character of his theology of hope is apparent in this statement:

Our eschatological expectation does not look for the heavenly-earthly Jerusalem as that ready-made and existing, promised city of God. This heavenly city does not lie ahead of us as a distant and hidden goal, which only needs to be revealed. The eschatological City of God is *now* coming into existence, for our hopeful approach *builds* this city. We are workers building this future, and not just interpreters of this future. The power of God's promises for the future moves us to form this world into the eschatological city of God.[12]

This brings us to the relation between eschatology and futurology in current theological study. Metz argues that the Christian community needs to mobilize the "political" potentiality of its faith and hope by making the future the object of enlightened technological planning.[13] While Moltmann does not wish to equate *futurum*, that which grows out of the present, with *parousia*, that which comes from the other side, the focus of his attention is on liberation from political and economic oppression. The new element that appears in the story of Christ, he says, is not merely the prospect of a once for all end of history or a life after death but the humanizing of this present world.[14] One critic offers these trenchant comments:

Moltmann moves so far away from a one-sided emphasis on the so-called last things to a total eschatological outlook that he almost forgets to mention these last things. When he mentions them, however, they are generally described as earthly, man-endeavored goals, such as peace for all creation and socializing of humanity.[15]

Teilhard de Chardin is an outstanding example of one who synthesizes eschatology and futurology so that the eschaton becomes the climax of an evolving process within the universe in which humanity plays a creative role. Through hominization man emerged from the animal world to the noosphere, and through christification the evolutionary process will come to fulfillment with everything being received into Christ. Teilhard understands evil as the negative aspects of disorder and failure which accompany every breakthrough into the future. The apocalyptic vision of an anti-god power that outwardly challenges God's supreme position and threatens man's well-being is completely absent from his thinking.

From the evangelical side there have been attempts to do justice to the dimensions of the Christian hope that concern man's historical future without confusing this with the eschatological hope. Paul Rees is sure that, "there is a future that is *now* for diseased people who need healing and impoverished people who need bread. No, this is not the millennial future or the eternal future, which is in God's hands. It is the less than perfect but available future that is in man's hands—by God's ordering."[16] What Rees and other progressive evangelicals are saying is that penultimate hopes can at least be partially realized through Christian social involvement, though the ultimate hope, the kingdom of God, is a gift for which we can only wait and pray.

The issue of life after death has been a perennial one in theology and continues to occupy the attention of theologians of all stripes. There are some who deny the reality or even the relevance of this subject in Christian eschatology. For Gordon Kaufman the Christian hope pertains to this world only, to a reign of God under the conditions of historical existence. Schubert Ogden, writing from the perspective of process theology, declares: "What I must refuse to accept, precisely as a Christian theologian, is that belief in our continued subjective existence after death is in some way a necessary article of Christian belief."[17] Bultmann has also expressed complete skepticism concerning a life hereafter.[18]

Oscar Cullmann argues for the resurrection of the body as opposed to the Greek idea of the inherent immortality of the soul.[19] Yet he maintains that those who die in Christ are granted immortality as a gift. They are still in time, but it is an interim state of nakedness that looks forward to fulfillment at the second advent.

For Tillich there is no immortality in the sense of continued self-conscious existence beyond the grave. At the same time, he affirms a return of selfhood to Godhood with the self still maintaining its own identity. The power of love alone is immortal, but we participate in this love. In his view there is no intermediate state but the present reality of eternal life, a reality that is not eradicated at death.

Kantonen, on the other hand, vigorously upholds an intermediate state in which spirits with bodily form wait to be further clothed.[20] There is no natural immortality, but there is the immortality of a personal relationship with Christ. He is clearly committed to the doctrine of the communion of saints understood as spiritual solidarity between the living faithful and the dead who are in Christ.

In the theology of Karl Barth eternal life is not a second life beyond our present life but the reverse side of this life, which is still hidden from us. It should be understood as "this life in relationship to what God has done in Jesus Christ for the whole world and thus also for us."[21] Eternal life means the life of the age to come, which we now have access to in faith. Our resurrection has already taken place in the resurrection of Jesus Christ, in whom we and all humankind are included. Yet there will be various manifestations of this: our life now in Christ is one manifestation of our resurrection, and our future life in the kingdom of God is another.

The principal tension in the history of theology in this area is between the mystical tradition, which has its roots in Platonism and neo-Platonism, and the biblical, personalist tradition. The former stresses the immortality of the soul and redemption from the flesh. The latter emphasizes the resurrection of the body, the transformation of the material. While the mystics look forward to a timeless eternity, the prophets of biblical history speak of a new heaven and a new earth (cf. Isa. 66:22; Rev. 21:1).

Still another issue that preoccupies current theology is the final consummation. Does history have a twofold outcome in which believers will be separated from nonbelievers for eternity, or is all of history directed to God and his kingdom? Here we see the tensions between an eschatological universalism and a moral dualism, both of which have biblical support. The dominant current in modern theology is universalistic, though other views are also evident. The chief problem is the reconciliation of God's justice and his love. Liberal theology (à la Ritschl) subsumes God's justice under his love; the idea of a wrathful God is regarded as primitive and outmoded. Other related issues are whether heaven and hell are states of mind or ontological realities and whether the idea of purgatory has any merit. All these questions will be dealt with at length in the next chapter.

THE SECOND ADVENT

In realized eschatology the second coming of Christ is dissolved to mean simply the return of the Holy Spirit at the day of Pentecost. This event is often interpreted by liberal theologians in a figurative way as referring to the gradual permeation of society by the ethical principles of Christ.

Our position seeks to do justice to the elements of truth in both realized and futuristic eschatology. The fulfillment of time *(kairos)* occurred in the incarnation of Christ (Mark 1:15), but the consummation of history is an event still to take place in the future. This consummation, however, will be ushered in by the personal, visible return of Jesus Christ to our present world. The day of deliverance (D-Day) has already happened in the cross and resurrection of Christ, but the day of total victory (V-Day) is still ahead of us.[22] Both these times can be referred to as the "Day of the Lord" since they both involve the epiphany of the Son of God in human form.[23]

Jesus Christ has come, but he is coming again. Hebrews assures us that "Christ, having been offered once to bear the sins of many, will appear a second time, not to deal with sin but to save those who are eagerly waiting for him" (9:28; cf. 1 John 3:2). "Then he will send you Jesus, your long-heralded Christ," Peter declares, "although for the time he must remain in Heaven until that universal restoration of which God spoke in ancient times through all his holy prophets" (Acts 3:20, 21 Phillips).

While Christ came in his first manifestation as the suffering servant, he shall come again the second time as the conquering king and judge. Mark depicts "the Son of man coming in clouds with great power and glory" (Mark 13:26; Matt. 26:64; Jude 14, 15). The Book of Revelation describes the heavens opening and Christ descending with armies of angels (Rev. 19:11 ff.). He will come as King of kings and Lord of lords, triumphing over the forces of evil (Rev. 19:11–16). He will come not in the body of his humiliation but in glory.

The parousia of Christ is portrayed as unexpected, like the coming of a thief in the night (1 Thess. 5:2; Matt. 24:42–44; Luke 12:39–40). It will take people by surprise, and therefore every believer must maintain constant vigilance (1 Thess. 5:2, 3; Rev. 3:3; 16:15). The parables in Matthew 24 and 25 all deal with a Lord or bridegroom whom we will meet and whose coming we should anticipate with watchfulness. We should make certain that our lamps always contain the oil of faith in Christ, for otherwise we shall be left out in the cold (Matt. 25:1–13).

Moreover, it is made clear that the coming of Christ will be visible. Jesus himself maintained that all the tribes of the earth would *see* the Son of man coming in his glory (Matt. 24:30; 26:64). The two angels on Mount Olivet announced: "This Jesus, who was taken up from you into heaven, will come in the same way as you saw him go into heaven" (Acts 1:11). In the words of St. John: "Every eye will see him, every one who pierced him; and all tribes of the earth will wail on account of him" (Rev. 1:7).

Likewise, the apostolic testimony is that Jesus will appear in bodily form. It will not be simply the spirit of Christ but Jesus Christ in his glorified humanity who will confront humanity in the last days (cf. Acts 1:11; 3:20, 21; Heb. 9:28; Rev. 1:7). This is consonant with the biblical witness that Jesus rose in body and in spirit and will come again to judge the living and the dead.

The purpose of the second coming of Christ is to introduce the future age by inaugurating and completing two mighty events: the resurrection of the dead and the last judgment. Both the righteous and the wicked will be resurrected to appear before the judgment throne of Christ (cf. Matt. 12:36, 37; 25:32; Rom. 14:10; 2 Cor. 5:10). Although the righteous will not be exempt from the judgment (Matt. 13:30; 40–43; 47–50; 25:31–46), they have the certain confidence that the Judge is at the same time the Savior who purchased their redemption by the shedding of his blood. The demonic hosts, too, will be judged in "the great and terrible day of the Lord" (Matt. 8:29; 1 Cor. 6:3; 2 Pet. 2:4). This juridical work of Christ will be shared by the angels (Matt. 13:41, 42; 24:31; 25:31); he will be assisted also by the saints in glory (Ps. 149:5–9; 1 Cor. 6:2, 3; Rev. 20:4). The last judgment will follow immediately after the resurrection of the dead (John. 5:28, 29; Rev. 20:12, 13).

Christ's coming signifies the end of the old aeon, and the beginning of the new heaven and the new earth. The old earth and heavens will pass away with a loud noise, and the elements will be dissolved with fire (2 Pet. 3:10). This event is described as a "regeneration" of the whole of existence (Matt. 19:28 KJ). It will be cataclysmic and irreversible. We affirm not simply the dissolution of the world (as in Luther) nor its renovation (as in Calvin) but its transformation into a new heaven-earth on which all the biblical promises concerning the future glory of Jerusalem will be fulfilled. Yet this Jerusalem is no longer the earthly city but a heavenly city having the glory of God (Rev. 21:2, 10). The glory of the holy city far surpasses that of the lost paradise (Hendrikus Berkhof). It is not so much a restoration as a new creation.

The parousia signifies not merely the unveiling of what has already been accomplished in Christ but a new work of salvation. Yet it will not be entirely new, since it will ratify and crown the one great work accomplished on the cross. It signifies the execution and fulfillment of all preceding judgments. The purpose of reconciliation will be completed on the day of redemption when God will be all in all.

There is nothing that we can do to inaugurate the drama of the last things. But the knowledge of the coming victory of Christ should encourage us in steadfast devotion to the work of the Lord, confident that this work will not be in vain but will receive its reward (1 Cor. 15:58). We cannot build the kingdom of God, but we can herald its coming and call upon people to prepare themselves for it. We can set up parables of the coming kingdom by a concrete demonstration of Christian love and righteousness (K. Barth).

Though the parousia will be sudden and unexpected, the Bible nonetheless speaks of signs for those who have the eyes to see and the ears to hear. They are not empirical evidences or proofs but reminders to the faithful that his coming is on the horizon. Among these signs are the appearance of antichrists (1 John 4:3; 2 John 7; Matt. 24:24); the coming of a world dictator (Rev. 13:7); the revival of the occult (1 John 2:18; 1 Tim. 4:1; Matt. 24); the ingathering and conversion of the Jews (Isa. 11:11; Luke 21:24; Rom. 11); the proclamation of the Gospel to all peoples (Matt. 24:14); the wholesale destruction of peoples and nations by fire (Joel 2:3; Rev. 8:7, 8); great earthquakes and famines (Rev. 6:12; 18:8; Luke 21:10, 11); a falling away from faith accompanied by false prophets with signs and wonders (Matt. 24:10–11, 24; 1 Tim. 4:1; 2 Tim. 4:3, 4; 2 Thess. 2:3, 9); the widespread persecution of believers (Dan. 11:44; Matt. 24:9, 10; Mark 13:9, 12, 13; Luke 21:12–17); an unprecedented increase in lawlessness (Matt. 24:12; Luke 21:9); and remarkable eclipses of the heavenly bodies and their fall to earth (Isa. 13:10; 24:23; Joel 2:30, 31; Matt. 24:29; Rev. 8:12). We concur in the judgment of Anthony Hoekema that many of these signs are present in every age to remind the faithful of the approaching end, but there will be an intensification of these signs before the final day.[24]

A subject much debated in conservative circles is whether we are in the last days now. For both Calvin and Barth the last days refers to all time between the resurrection of Christ and the last judgment; it signifies an interim period before the approaching end. This is the time when Christ destroys every rule and every authority and power before delivering the kingdom to the Father (1 Cor. 15:24). Yet though we are in the last days, we are not yet at the last day, the day of the parousia itself. The New Testament describes this day as near at hand, not that it will happen tomorrow but that it may happen within the lifetime of every believer.

Certainly the crisis of death is also a last day even in the spiritual sense. Christ meets us in the hour of death as well as at the time of the end of all things (cf. 1 Sam. 28:19; Luke 23:43; Acts 7:54–60). Scholars generally agree that the rich man in Luke 12:20, who is called to give an account of his stewardship, refers to a purely personal parousia. Winklhofer observes: "Whenever death occurs, there is a parousia of the Lord, a manifestation of his power and glory."[25]

It can also be argued that whenever the Gospel is preached, the day of judgment is imminent. Because the Gospel is a prolongation of the new age already inaugurated in the life, death, and resurrection of Jesus Christ, this new age confronts people in the here and now, calling them to decision. An eternal Gospel was given to the angel to proclaim to all peoples: "Fear God and give him glory, for the hour of his judgment has come" (Rev. 14:7). Because the new age overlaps the old age, the eschaton can even now be anticipated in faith and repentance. The church is indeed an eschatological community ever waiting and looking forward to the consummation of a reality already experienced in its midst.

In this light we can appreciate Bonhoeffer's admonition to be constantly prepared for our Lord's imminent return:

The Church has never forgotten Christ's promise of his imminent return, and she has always believed that this promise is true. The exact manner of its fulfilment remains obscure, but that is not a problem for us to solve. This much is clear and all-important for us today that the return of Jesus will take place suddenly. That fact is more certain than that we shall be able to finish our work in his service, more certain than our own death.[26]

The eschaton signifies both the *finis* (chronological end) and *telos* (goal) of history. It is not the merely future in the sense of an extension of history but the absolute future. Quenstedt contends: "The resurrection will occur on the last or latest of all days, and will place an end to the vicissitude of worldly things, and therefore to time itself."[27] Yet though time in the sense of *chronos* will then be at an end, time in the sense of *kairos* (fulfillment) will continue. Eternity must not be misunderstood as timelessness but as a new quality of time. Time is not dissolved or overcome (as in the Greek conception) but instead transformed and fulfilled. Likewise, eternity should not be misconstrued as spacelessness but as an intensified life with God in a new time-space dimension.

THE RESURRECTION OF THE DEAD

In the early history of Israel there was only a faint intimation of life after death. Sheol was the realm of the departed, and at first it was believed that there was no conscious existence in this state. Gradually Sheol came to be filled with more content, and a kind of conscious immortality was affirmed, though this was based on an inescapable relationship with God rather than inherent potentialities within the soul. Job rises to the sublime assurance that the living God whom he

trusts will be his Vindicator and that after death, in at least one glorious moment of conscious existence, he will see his Maker face to face
(Job 19:25). A similar sentiment is expressed in Psalm 17:15: "I shall
see thy face, and be blest with a vision of thee when I awake" (NEB).

It was in connection with the messianic hope of the nation that the
idea of the resurrection of the body arose (cf. Isa. 26:14–19; Dan. 12:2;
Ezek. 37). By the intertestamental and New Testament periods the idea
of resurrection was stoutly defended by many of the leaders within the
Jewish community, especially among the Pharisees. Some Palestinian
believers in the resurrection taught the restoration of exactly the same
body that was laid away (cf. 2 Baruch 50:2).

In the New Testament the resurrection of God's people gains its
meaning and purpose from the resurrection of Jesus Christ, our Savior
and Elder Brother. Paul declares: "If Christ has not been raised . . . then
those also who have fallen asleep in Christ have perished" (1 Cor. 15:17,
18). "But in fact," he continues, "Christ has been raised from the dead,
the first fruits of those who have fallen asleep" (verse 20). The resurrection does not involve getting rid of the body but the changing of "our
lowly body to be like his glorious body" (Phil. 3:21). His bodily resurrection is a sign and guarantee of our future resurrection, when we shall
be raised like him in a body incorruptible.

The resurrection connotes not the resuscitation of the flesh but the
renewal of the person. *Soma* can mean body in the earthly, physical
sense (here it is identical with *sarx*), but it can also refer to "the self"
or "breath," and it is in this latter usage that we can speak of the
resurrection of the body. The resurrection entails both soul and body,
but it negates the "flesh," which is the power of death. Soul and body
should be distinguished (cf. Matt. 10:28; 1 Thes. 5:23), but soul always
seeks some kind of bodily form. The body is necessary as a means of
fellowship, communication, and identification. When the Bible affirms
the resurrection of the body, it means the renewal and restoration of
the whole person, soul and body. It means the raising up of man in the
totality of his individual, personal existence.

In the early church there was a considerable difference of opinion
concerning the composition of the resurrected body. Tertullian taught
that the new body will not lack any of the elements of the body placed
in the grave. Origen, on the other hand, spiritualized the resurrection
altogether so that, at the end of man's pilgrimage, there will be a
complete destruction of the body.[28] Paul's view is different from each
of these positions. According to the apostle it is sown a natural body,
but it is raised a spiritual body (1 Cor. 15:44). Just as the seed is buried

in the ground and its material wrapping decomposes, so our fleshly body will die and decay. But just as there is a continuity between the seed and the new plant because the creative power of God gives a new form to the life which sprouts from the seed, so there will likewise be a continuity between our fleshly existence and our spiritual body. Some of the church fathers used the apt illustration of a caterpillar, cocoon, and butterfly to point out the change in the *soma* of the believer from *sarx,* which by its very essence decays, into *doxa,* the body in the state of glory.

This brings us to the question of whether the body of our risen Lord was also different from his earthly, physical body. It is our conviction that Jesus, too, was given a new body, since "he appeared in another form" (Mark 16:12). His appearance was indeed altered after his resurrection. Mary Magdalene, his disciples on the seashore, and the two men on the way to Emmaus did not at first recognize him. Yet there was, at the same time, a perfect continuity between his resurrection body and the old body because he was sinless, and, therefore, his physical body was not subject to corruption. We believe in a substantial identity between the old and new bodies of Jesus, but even here there was no resuscitation (as with Lazarus) but a transformation or transfiguration. This must not be taken to mean that only the spirit of Christ rose from the dead, for as our Lord said, "A spirit has not flesh and bones as you see that I have" (Luke 24:39). Yet his new body was at the same time spiritual, and some would contend that it steadily became more spiritualized or, at least, invisible. His body passed through the grave clothes, leaving them undisturbed except that they no longer contained anything. He ate food on the Emmaus road and also bread and fish with his disciples (John 21:13), but he could, at the same time, pass through closed doors (John 20:19, 26; Luke 24:33–37). He did not want to be touched, for he had not yet ascended to the Father (John 20:17). At the Ascension, when he was elevated into heaven, he was virtually invisible (Acts 1:9). On the Damascus Road, when he spoke to Paul and his companions, he was not visible to the naked eye (Acts 9:7). Yet this may legitimately be viewed as one of the postresurrection appearances of our Lord (cf. 1 Cor. 15:8).

The resurrection in the biblical perspective occurs in a series of stages. The first resurrection of the dead is regeneration, when the dead in sin are raised to new life through faith in Jesus Christ. Our Lord declares: "I am the resurrection and the life; he who believes in me, though he die, yet shall he live, and whoever lives and believes in me shall never die" (John 11:25, 26; cf. 5:24; Rom. 6:11; Eph. 2:4–6; Col.

2:12; 1 John 3:14). Some theologians (e.g., Martensen) have speculated that the new resurrection body might already be in the making within the present mortal body and be ready for occupation at death. Luther intimates that this body itself undergoes an inward change by the work of "the Holy Spirit who sanctifies and awakens even the body to this new life, until it is completed in the life beyond."[29]

It is also possible to speak of the resurrection on the day of death, when the souls of believers are translated into paradise. Advocates of an amillennial position generally view the "first resurrection" referred to in Revelation 20:6 as the elevation into glory of those who have died in Christ.[30] Just as Jesus was put to death in the flesh but made alive in the spirit (1 Pet. 3:18), so all the saints will experience the travail of death, but they will immediately be received into the presence of Christ (cf. Acts 7:54–60).[31] In this light we can understand Paul's words that to live is Christ, but to die is gain (Phil. 1:21). That he has in mind the time of death is made abundantly clear in subsequent verses: "What I should like is to depart and be with Christ; that is better by far; but for your sake there is greater need for me to stay on in the body" (Phil 1:23, 24 NEB). In the parable of the rich man and Lazarus Jesus says: "The poor man died and was carried by the angels to Abraham's bosom" (meaning paradise) (Luke 16:22). And he promised the repentant thief on the cross: "Truly, I say to you, today you will be with me in Paradise" (Luke 23:43). In John Bunyan's *Pilgrim's Progress* the passage through the river of death leads immediately to the heavenly city.

Even unbelievers are carried through death by virtue of their inescapable relationship to the living God (cf. Dan. 12:2; Acts 24:15). Yet this is not a resurrection unto life but a descent into the shadowy existence of hades, the nether world of spirits. This is not yet hell, since hell *(gehenna),* like heaven, is a reality in the ultimate future. Hades, like paradise, refers to the immediate hereafter, but it is the hereafter for the spiritually lost. Here the souls who do not know Christ or who have rejected him exist in a state of inner torment or lostness, waiting for the general resurrection and the last judgment (cf. Luke 16:19 ff.). It should nonetheless be pointed out that God is present in this so-called realm of the dead, and is in absolute control (cf. 1 Sam. 2:6; Job 26:6; Pss. 86:13; 139:8). This realm is not outside the compass of the Gospel, since our Lord preached to the spirits who were in prison (1 Pet. 3:19, 20).

It has been a matter of theological controversy whether the souls of the saints in the intermediate state of paradise are clothed in bodily form. In our judgment Cullmann errs by denying any continuity in bodily existence in the immediate hereafter. Even Samuel, who came back from the other side of the grave, was depicted as being wrapped in a robe and having the appearance of a god (1 Sam. 28:13–14). The saints on the Mount of Transfiguration were definitely in bodily form, for Peter even wished to make booths for them (Matt. 17:1–4; Mark 9:2–5). In the book of Revelation the saints in paradise are described as being "clothed in white robes" (Rev. 7:9; 6:11). The two witnesses in Revelation 11 are raised bodily into heaven. It was a common understanding in biblical times that the dead are clothed in some kind of body (1 Cor. 15:35). The inward man who persists after death includes the somatic as well as the psychic part of man.

Some sects have portrayed the souls after death as in a state of soul-sleep. Even Luther entertained this idea for a time.[32] Yet such a view is a profound misunderstanding. The term *sleep* in the New Testament is a euphemism for death, a euphemism which indicates the manner of dying to some extent and also the meaning of death for the Christian. Those who die in Christ (1 Thess. 4:15–16) have the terror of death behind them; they are now at rest (Rev. 14:13). Because Christ is risen, the dead in Christ do not perish in death (1 Cor. 15:17ff). The term *sleep* is therefore theological and eschatological, not anthropological. What Paul means by falling asleep in Christ corresponds to what Hebrews means by entering God's rest (see Heb. 4). Jeremias contends that the idea of soul-sleeping is foreign to the entire New Testament as well as to late Judaism.

The souls in the state of paradise already experience the glory of God (cf. Col. 1:12). Paradise is not a state of nakedness as is hades;[33] it is not the underworld but the realm of glory. Indeed, we are said to be closer to God in paradise than in our earthly, bodily existence (2 Cor. 5:6–8). Yet because of their identification with the sufferings and tribulation of the church militant on earth, the saints in paradise are keenly aware that the perfection of all things is still in the future.[34] Their state is one not only of *beatitudo* but also of *expectatio,* expectation and waiting (cf. Heb. 11:40; Rev. 6:11). Though they have the vision of God, they await the general resurrection of the dead at the second advent of Christ. Though they have perfect love and perfect holiness, they still do not have perfect peace or perfect joy, since they intercede for their brethren on earth "under the altar" and cry "How long?" (Rev. 6:9 ff.; 8:3, 4). As it is stated in Hebrews 11:40: "Apart from us they should not be made perfect." Pierre-Yves Emery maintains that the departed saints "will wait until the end of the world for us, the believers still on earth, to fulfill their ministry, their works, their crown, their joy."[35] There is progress in their knowledge and in their mode of service, but they do not progress toward salvation, since they already have salvation through Christ's atonement. Christ is both our justification and sanctification (1 Cor. 1:30), and his righteousness becomes our own through faith.

What is important to underscore is that the resurrection body is a new creation. There is no inherent immortality of the soul.[36] The person who dies, even the one who dies in Christ, undergoes the death of both body and soul. Yet, as Thomas Aquinas said, though the soul experiences death as the form of the body, it lives on in a new form. The soul is not disembodied but is further clothed, putting on a heavenly dwelling (2 Cor. 5).[37]

We come now to the question of how the resurrection at death is related to the resurrection on the last day, to the consummation of all things that will be ushered in by Christ's second coming. The resurrection is not only an event but also a process that will be fulfilled only at the parousia (cf. John 5:25 ff.; 6:39; 2 Cor. 3:18; 4:14–18). In John 5 Jesus speaks of two resurrections within one short utterance (24–29). Revelation 20 also refers to two resurrections, though not quite in the same sense. The last day is not to be confused with the moment of death (cf. 2 Tim. 2:18; 4:6–8). Some believe that the parousia will be essentially an apocalypsis, that is, a revelation in bodily or earthly form of what we already are in Christ. We concur that the final resurrection will be a public revelation, yet not only this but also a transfiguration, a putting on of the incorruptible body that shall endure throughout eternity.

Church tradition generally holds that the disembodied spirit will be united with the natural body that died on earth. The truth in this conception is that nothing of significance is really lost. The untruth is that this denies that the final body is a new creation rather than the mere restoration of what has been before. There is a substantial, but not an exact, material identity between the final glorified body and the earthly body.

The general resurrection signifies the transfiguration of matter itself. The books of the prophets speak of a new heaven and a new earth. We shall witness the materialization or making visible of what is now invisible. In the words of Irenaeus: "Not only is matter susceptible of salvation but the salvation of man, the resurrection, implies the salvation of matter."[38] Yet we affirm not the restoration of an earthly material existence but the transformation of matter into spirit. The eternal glory, of which paradise is an anticipation, shall then encompass the whole of the created order, for God will be all in all (1 Cor. 15:28; Eph. 1:10).

THE MILLENNIUM

Apart from biblical inerrancy no doctrine has caused greater division in evangelical Christianity in the present day than the millennium. Though the biblical references to a millennial kingdom are minimal, they have given rise to elaborate theologies based on the reality of such a kingdom. Because the millennial hope has been a source of inspiration to Christians throughout the history of the church, impelling many toward a missionary vocation, it merits serious consideration. The polemical overtones of this doctrine make it especially significant for those who are concerned with the catholicity and unity of the church.

The key passage in the New Testament is Revelation 20:2, 3:

And he seized the dragon, that ancient serpent, who is the Devil and Satan, and bound him for a thousand years, and threw him into the pit, and shut it and sealed it over him, that he should deceive the nations no more, till the thousand years were ended. After that he must be loosed for a little while.

Millenarians or chiliasts (from *chilios,* the 1,000 years) also appeal to 1 Cor. 15:23 ff. where Christ is depicted as delivering the kingdom to God the Father after destroying every rule and authority and power. It is said that he must reign until he has put all his enemies under his feet, and this reign is interpreted in some circles as referring to an interim messianic reign following his second coming but before the end of the world.[39]

There are, of course, many passages in the Old Testament that envision a restoration of the glory of Israel in which Jerusalem will become the pivotal center in a new world era characterized by peace and prosperity. Those who reject the chiliast position see these particular Old Testament prophecies fulfilled in the church, the new Israel. The conception of an intermediate messianic kingdom before the age to come is found in some Jewish apocalypses from the period between Paul and Revelation (2 Baruch 30:1; 2 Esdras 7:26–30). There is no messianic reign in such typical apocalypses as Isaiah 24–27, Daniel, the Assumption of Moses, and the Apocalypse of Abraham.

In the history of the church three general positions have developed concerning the millennium. The first, which is called premillennialism, understands the millennium as a messianic, interim kingdom inaugurated by the second coming of Christ, in which he will reign on earth for 1,000 years (or an indefinite period) before the last judgment and end of the world. This is chiliasm properly so-called. In the dispensational brand of premillennialism Christ is said to have two parousias, one to the saints at the time of the rapture, when they are taken into heaven before the tribulation that will befall the world, and then a second, in which he sets up the millennial kingdom on earth after destroying the beast and false prophet (see Rev. 19). Extreme dispensationalists speak of two gospels, the gospel of grace and the gospel of the kingdom. The first is for the Gentiles and the second for the Jews. The kingdom gospel will be in effect during the time of the millennium. While classical premillennialists see the church enduring the tribulation prior to the millennial age, the dispensationalists see the true church as being exempt from this tribulation, and are therefore termed *pretribulational,* meaning that Christ will appear to his elect before the tribulation.

Premillennialism has a long and varied history. It was adopted by many theologians in the early church period, including Cerinthus, Papias, Justin Martyr, Irenaeus, Methodius, Tertullian, Montanus,[40] Hippolytus, and Lactantius. Cerinthus depicted the future kingdom of Christ as providing sensual pleasures: eating, drinking, and marriage festivities. In the middle ages premillennialism virtually faded into oblivion, but it was revived among some of the Anabaptists in the sixteenth century. In the seventeenth century a view approaching premillennialism was advanced by a German Calvinist, Johann Heinrich Alsted, who was a delegate to the Synod of Dort in 1618. During this century premillennialism gained ground in England, where it was especially evident among the Puritan Fifth Monarchy Men, but then fell out of favor. In the nineteenth century it was revived by Edward Irving, founder of the Catholic Apostolic church, and John Nelson Darby, one of the founding fathers of the Plymouth Brethren.[41] Thereafter premillennialism came to be associated ever more closely with dispensationalism, though dispensational ideas were already developed by the Dutch Pietist theologian Cocceius in the seventeenth century. Dispensational views were entertained by Henry Moorhouse, R. A. Torrey, and Dwight L. Moody (though Moody, in particular, was not dogmatic on this issue) and were given wide circulation in the Scofield Reference Bible, devised by C. I. Scofield.

Among contemporary advocates of premillennialism are George Eldon Ladd, Oscar Cullmann, H. Bietenhard, G. R. Beasley-Murray, and Heinrich Quistorp. Those who defend a dispensational viewpoint include John Walvoord, Charles Ryrie, Hal Lindsey, Dwight Pentecost, Lewis Sperry Chafer, Arno C. Gaebelein, and René Pache. For scholars like Cullmann, Bietenhard, and Quistorp, who reflect the concerns of the salvation-history school, the millennium is an end-historical category signifying the last period of the dominion of Christ over this age in which God closes off the history of the world. It is the "final act" of Christ's kingship, in which the church "will appear as part of the coming age." The millennium is "neither a purely spiritual nor a purely earthly kingdom, but an intermediate one which no longer belongs to this aeon—but neither does it wholly belong to the new world-aeon of God."[42]

Chiliast ideas were opposed by both Origen in the Eastern church, who allegorized the millennium, and Augustine in the Western church, who identified the millennial kingdom with the church. For Augustine the binding of Satan has taken place in the resurrection of Jesus Christ, though this is only a relative binding, since the demonic powers are still active. This amillennial interpretation, already foreshadowed in the early church in Barnabas,[43] Gaius of Rome, and Ticonius (d. 400), became the dominant view in the Roman Catholic church and the churches of the Reformation. In the modern period it has such noted representatives as Louis Berkhof, G. C. Berkouwer, Theodore Graebner, Emil Brunner, George L. Murray, Nelson B. Baker, Anthony Hoekema, Edmund J. Fortman, Hans Schwarz, Leon Morris, Floyd Hamilton, Thomas Torrance,[44] and Michael Wilcock.[45] Helmut Lamparter takes a position that combines elements of amillennialism and premillennialism.[46]

Amillennialists generally hold that the kingdom of God is now present in the world as the victorious Christ rules his people by the Word and Spirit. At the same time, they look forward to a future, glorious, perfect kingdom on the new earth in the life to come. They perceive the forces of evil gaining momentum as world history draws to an end and predict a time of persecution and tribulation for the church prior to the parousia. In his *Church Dogmatics* IV, 3 b Barth maintains that the "growing greatness of the Word of God" in the course of history also means a deepening of darkness and contradiction. Berkouwer echoes the position of many amillennialists in his assertion that the vision in Revelation 20 is "not a narrative account of a future earthly reign of peace at all, but is the apocalyptic unveiling of the reality of salvation in Christ as a backdrop to the reality of the suffering and martyrdom that still continue as long as the dominion of Christ remains hidden."[47] Amillennialists see world history after the resurrection of Christ as both the gospel age and the age of the Spirit.

The third position, postmillennialism, envisions a millennial period within history prior to the parousia but not identical with the whole history of the church. In this conception there will be a golden age for the church in which the Gospel will be preached to all nations, and then the end will come (cf. Matt. 24:14). The harvest of history will also see the conversion of the Jews to Christ or at least the restoration of a significant number of the descendents of Israel (cf. Isa. 11:11ff.; Zech. 12:10; Rom. 11:12). Postmillennialists generally make a place for the appearance of an antichrist toward the end of the millennium, but his time will be short since the parousia is then imminent. While premillennialists and amillennialists are inclined to view this present age with pessimism and to picture the church as a citadel of light in a world that is falling ever more into darkness, postmillennialists are optimists, believing that many of the promises of Christ will be realized within history and not simply in a life hereafter. Postmillennialists have often appealed to Ezekiel 36:27 ff. which proclaims the promise of the transformation of the external order of society through inner spiritual renewal. Psalm 102:16 (KJ) has also figured in postmillennial speculation: "When the Lord shall build up Zion, he shall appear in his glory." Likewise, Malachi 4:3 has been used in support of this credo: "And you shall tread down the wicked, for they will be ashes under the soles of your feet, on the day when I act, says the Lord of hosts" (cf. Dan. 2:44).

Postmillennialism was already anticipated in the church father Eusebius of Caesarea, who interpreted the victory of the church during the reign of Constantine as the beginning of the "millennium." As has been indicated, a postmillennial strand was also evident in Montanism, though it was overshadowed by the premillennial emphasis.[48] Postmillennialism experienced an upsurge in the middle ages, being reflected in utopian spiritualistic movements. Foremost of these was the Joachim movement, which divided history into three stages—those of Father, Son, and Spirit. The first period, resting on the Father, was said to be characterized by law and fear. The second, the time from the coming of Christ up to the thirteenth century, was the period of the Son, earmarked by grace and faith. The third and final period was believed to be inaugurated by St. Benedict and commencing in its fullness in 1260; this is the period of the Spirit, dominated by love and zeal. The age of the Spirit was to be an order of monks, just as the age of the Father was an order of the married and the age of the Son an order of priests. Joachim of Fiore, who devised this scheme, thought of himself as still belonging to the second period, though each of these periods overlaps somewhat. In contrast to Montanism nothing is said of a visible reign of Christ on earth after the dispensation of the Spirit.

Postmillennialism reappeared among some of the Anabaptists who spoke of the dawning of the "age of the Spirit" which would precede the eschaton. Melchior Hoffman saw himself as one of the two witnesses foretold in Revelation who were appointed by God to prepare people for the final judgment. He also referred to the "time of grace," the interval of time between the appearance of the witnesses of the last day and the coming of that day itself in which there would still be the possibility of a choice.

The real heyday of postmillennialism was in the seventeenth and eighteenth centuries, which witnessed the flowering of the evangelical movements of Pietism and Puritanism. In the early Evangelical vision the future of history belongs to Jesus Christ, and his kingdom will be manifested in power and glory before his coming again. The millennial age is a time characterized by the overflowing of the fulness of the Spirit, though Christians will still be in conflict with indwelling sin and will continue to face temptation and death. The church in the millennial age is still the *ecclesia militans,* not the *ecclesia triumphans.* Both Pietists and Puritans saw the millennial hope as the fulfillment of the great commission, and this accounts for their intense preoccupation with world mission and evangelism. Among the guiding lights of postmillennialism in early Evangelicalism were Philip Spener, Daniel Whitby, John Owen, Samuel Rutherford, William à Brakel, John and Charles Wesley, and Jonathan Edwards. The expectation of the worldwide establishment of the kingdom of Christ is reflected in Isaac Watts' great hymn, "Jesus Shall Reign Where 'er the Sun." J. A. Bengel is claimed by both post- and premillennialists, though it seems that chiliasm gained ascendency in his thinking, since he expected the second advent of Christ to come in 1836. Among the later Pietists Johann Christoph Blumhardt (b. 1805) looked forward to a new age of grace prior to the parousia of Christ; this new age would be characterized by an outpouring of the gifts of the Holy Spirit.

In more recent times postmillennialism can count among its adherents Charles Hodge, Benjamin Warfield, A. H. Strong, and James Orr. Even Walter Rauschenbusch can be considered a postmillennialist in a qualified sense because of his expectation of a kingdom of God on earth. In our day classical postmillennialism, which might be called the chiliasm of the church, is defended by T. A. Kantonen, Iain Murray,

Loraine Boettner, and Hendrikus Berkhof. A more secularized form of postmillennialism, which envisions the golden age as one of justice and equality for all people, has been entertained by Johannes Metz, Rubem Alves, Harvey Cox, Jürgen Moltmann, and Martin Luther King. King was a postmillennialist of a sort in so far as he envisioned the "Beloved Community" being actualized within history. Moltmann seeks to establish some continuity with the older postmillennialism when he claims that Israel and the church have different callings and that the state of Israel "is a sign of the end of the dispersion and the beginning of Israel's homecoming."[49]

Among the cults and sectarian movements the Shakers, who took the name "the Millennial Church," affirmed what might be termed a realized millennium, since they saw the second coming occurring in the illumination of their founder, Mother Ann Lee.[50] Seventh-day Adventists, Mormons, Christadelphians, Jehovah's Witnesses, and the Worldwide Church of God are all premillennial in some sense. The Seventh-day Adventists, however, do not envision a reign of Christ on earth but, instead, Christ reigning in heaven with his saints during the millennial period, when the earth will be divested of all human habitation.

Each of these three basic positions on the millennium has certain strengths and certain weaknesses. Premillennialism should be given credit for not spiritualizing away the prophecy in the Book of Revelation and for recognizing that some of God's promises will be realized on earth as well as in heaven. It has the additional merit of taking seriously the biblical promises to the people of Israel that they will at last see a restoration of the glory of Israel, though this glory is understood in nationalistic terms, and this we cannot accept. Premillennialism, and particularly the dispensational strand, has also kept alive the expectancy of the imminent return of Christ.

In delineating the weaknesses of premillennialism we have to confess that, at least in its traditional form, it cannot be regarded as a viable option from our standpoint. First, the premillennialists generally make the kingdom of God into an earthly and national kingdom, whereas the New Testament describes it as spiritual and universal. Again, while the Bible speaks of the resurrection of the just and unjust in a single breath (Dan. 12:2; John 5:28, 29; Acts 24:15) and the resurrection of the righteous as occurring at the end of time (John 6:39, 40, 44, 54; 11:24), premillennialism separates the resurrection of the righteous from that of the wicked by a period of 1,000 years. It also divorces the last judgment from the second coming of Christ, though the inseparability of these events is testified to in Matthew 16:27; 25:31–32; Jude

14, 15; 2 Thessalonians 1:7–10; and Revelation 22:12. The dispensational view of the rapture of the church before the great tribulation and the coming of the Son of Man for the destruction of the antichrist contradicts Matthew 24:29–31, which depicts the Son of Man gathering his elect from the uttermost parts of the earth after the tribulation (cf. Mark 13:27). Dispensational premillennialism is based on the supposition that the Old Testament prophecies concerning the future of Israel must have a literal fulfillment, but this is entirely untenable in the light of the New Testament identification of the church as the true Israel. Since many premillennialists hold that the saints in resurrected bodies will join Christ in his reign on the new earth over persons who are still sinners in the flesh, we have the extraordinary picture of perfect saints in glorified bodies mingling with mortal creatures in a so-called millennial paradise. Does not this smack more of mythology than biblical eschatology? It should be noted that some of these objections do not apply to the premillennialism of Cullmann, Bietenhard, and Quistorp. George Eldon Ladd, too, has kept himself free from some of the extravagant speculation of chiliasm.[51]

Postmillennialism has more Scriptural support than is commonly realized. First, wherever the binding of Satan is referred to in the New Testament, it can be seen to be related to the work of Christian mission, and this is a salient postmillennial emphasis (cf. Luke 10:17, 18; John 12:20–32). Satan's binding means his inability to deceive the nations, to prevent the Gospel from being proclaimed with power and efficacy to the nations (Rev. 20:3). Again, the outpouring of the Holy Spirit in the last days can be regarded as a latter-day glory for the church, even though the first outpouring occurred on Pentecost.[52] Moreover, by upholding the effectual evangelization of the nations, postmillennial theology bids us take seriously the church's mandate to conquer the world for Jesus Christ. Our Lord's promise that the gates of hell will not prevail against his church (Matt. 16:18 KJ)[53] presents a picture of a church that withstands and overcomes the principalities and powers of the old aeon (see Rev. 12:11). In postmillennialism the saved will be not a remnant called out of the church but a great multitude from every tribe, people, and tongue (cf. Rev. 7:9). The chief merit in this position is that it recaptures the note of optimism that characterized at least a large part of the apostolic church in its belief that the whole world belongs to Jesus Christ. Postmillennialists could never speak as dispensationalists do of a twilight of the church.

Nonetheless, there are certain serious objections to a postmillennial view, especially one that ignores or underplays the continuation of demonic power in the world and also in the church on this side of the parousia. First, the contention that the whole world will gradually be won for Christ and that the life of all nations will, in the course of time, be transformed by the Gospel is not in harmony with the New Testament picture of the end of the age. Many postmillennialists appeal to the parable of the leaven, which seems to anticipate a transformation of the whole creation by the Gospel (Matt. 13:33; Luke 13:21), but nowhere is it stated that this transformation will take place wholly within earthly history. Those postmillennialists who see the present age passing almost imperceptibly into the coming age misunderstand the apocalyptic character of the Gospel message of Jesus, which envisions the kingdom coming by supernatural intervention. The modern idea that natural evolution and the efforts of man in the fields of education and social reform will gradually bring in the perfect reign of the Christian spirit conflicts with the New Testament affirmation that the kingdom is wholly a gift of God. This idea, of course, does not characterize classical postmillennialism and signifies a secularization of that vision. Again, the postmillennial tendency to interpret the first resurrection in Revelation 20:4, 5 as the elevation of the martyrs for the purpose of reigning with Christ, as distinct from the general resurrection of the righteous, seems to call into question the fact that all Christians are enjoined to confess their faith under trial and persecution, and all Christians are destined to reign with Christ as priests and kings (1 Cor. 6:2; Rev. 1:6, 9; 5:9, 10).[54] Finally, the expectancy of the imminence of Christ's return is definitely undermined by the postmillennial emphasis on the return of Christ only after a period of unparalleled prosperity for the church and also for the nations.

It might be supposed that we endorse amillennialism because of our difficulties with the other two positions. Yet this is not necessarily so, despite certain obvious strengths in amillennialism. Its chief merit, though it has this in common with many postmillennial views, is that it acknowledges that the New Testament represents the great events of redemption, namely, the second advent, the resurrection, the last judgment, and the end of the world, as occurring in roughly the same span of time.[55] The only indication that any of these events are separated by 1,000 years is given in Revelation 20:4–10 which can lend itself to another interpretation. We are persuaded by such scholars as Hoekema and Wilcock that the events of Revelation 20 should not be conceived as chronologically following Revelation 19, which depicts the parousia. Revelation 20 is a flashback that recapitulates the triumph of Christ over the adversary from a slightly different angle; there are other examples of such flashbacks in the Book of Revelation.[56] Again, amillennialism reminds us that the binding of Satan in Revelation 20 must be related to the binding of Satan in the Gospels, where it is described as taking place already in the ministry, death, and resurrection of our Lord (cf. Mark 3:27; Matt. 12:29; Luke 10:18, 19; John 12:31–32).[57] We also agree with the amillennialists' interpretation of the 1,000 years as symbolic, referring more to the quality than to the quantity of time.[58] 2 Thessalonians 2, which describes the end of the church age, bears a remarkable similarity to Revelation 20, which describes the end of the millennial age. In the former we find the man of lawlessness who is restrained but who will break out of this restraint just before the coming of our Lord in glory. But he will be destroyed when Christ comes again, just as the dragon in Revelation 20 will be destroyed.

Yet, for a number of reasons, we are not happy with amillennialism despite its strong exegetical foundations. First, it too easily falls into a church imperialism, especially where the kingdom of Christ is identified with the visible church (as in Augustine and Calvin).[59] Second, there is a tendency, at least in some circles, to be overpessimistic concerning the course of world history: the church is viewed as a remnant in a world that is still wholly under the spell of the powers of darkness, despite the fact that Revelation 20 depicts Satan as being so bound that he cannot deceive the nations any further. Third, those who embrace an amillennial posture are inclined to spiritualize the kingdom and make it primarily other-worldly (the heavenly side of the church),[60] whereas the kingdom of Christ as portrayed in the New Testament has strong this-worldly dimensions as well. Their focus of attention is usually on the life hereafter rather than the events of the last days, on immortality rather than the harvest of history, on the vision of God rather than the great commission to go into the world with the Gospel.

Finally, amillennialism tends to take away the expectancy of Christ's second coming by seeing this coming realized, at least in part, in the gift of the Holy Spirit to the church. The view advanced by Calvin and Barth that we are already in the last days (since we are living in the period between Christ's resurrection and second advent) is acceptable so long as a role is still given to the last day (as distinct from the last days) and so long as the biblical signs of the imminent appearing of Christ are not disregarded.[61] It should be acknowledged that the churches of the Reformation have never recovered the eschatological consciousness characteristic of the New Testament church, and this accounts for the rise of chiliastic sects that have accentuated the cruciality and imminence of the second coming of Christ.[62]

In seeking to break through the impasse that presently besets the evangelical world on this question, we need to look more closely at Revelation 20, which supposedly describes the millennium. After a careful examination of this text we are persuaded that it is a description of the age of the church from the viewpoint of the millennial triumph experienced by the martyrs and confessors in heaven. The millennium signifies not just the church age but that side or aspect of the church age where the rule of the martyrs and confessors is manifest. Unlike the parallel passage in 2 Thessalonians 2, where the mystery of lawlessness is said to be at work even after the resurrection of Christ, here Satan is described as being in a *shut* or *sealed* pit. Before Christ Satan is completely powerless: this is the meaning of Satan being bound. Yet we also know that outside of Christ Satan can still cause injury and affliction. So long as we remain in Christ, we will participate in his kingly and priestly rule (Rev. 1:6), but once we turn away from Christ, the devil regains some of his power. The beast that was slain is revived (Rev. 13:3; 17:8) and can thereby cause more trouble, even for Christians. The devil has been likened to a mad dog that is chained (Augustine). He is powerless to harm us when we are outside his reach, but once we enter his circle we expose ourselves again to injury and harm.

Toward the end of the church or gospel age, when the church will face severe persecution and defection, Satan will regain some of his power over the nations (Rev. 20:7, 8). The devil will seek to realize his ends through the figure of an antichrist. Evil will be embodied in a person or temporal power that will pose a direct threat to the existence of the church (cf. Dan. 7:25; 2 Thess. 2:4; 1 John 2:18, 22; Rev. 13:7, 8). The antichrist will not be able to overthrow Christ's church, however, and will finally be deposed by Jesus Christ himself at the parousia.

It is possible to speak of a millennial dawn in every era of missionary outburst and expansion, since wherever the Gospel is proclaimed the utter defeat of Satan is further revealed and confirmed. In the light of Scripture one can affirm that a period in the temporal future before the end will be characterized by the messianic glory of Christ's conquering kingdom (cf. Ps. 108:5; Hab. 3:3ff.; Ezek. 37:26–28; Matt. 13:31–32, 47–50; 24:14).[63] We see this glory as a prolepsis of the ultimate, promised future of the kingdom of God. Before the end the Gospel will be carried into every region of the earth, and great remnants of the original Israel will be united with the church (Isa. 11:11–16; Rom. 11:12).

This coming breakthrough in Christian mission is not the 1,000 year reign, since Christ is already enthroned, but a period associated with the end time when history is rapidly approaching its climax, a period that will be followed by the antichrist and great tribulation. It is even likely that the great missionary effort of the church will be accompanied by a rising tide of demonic opposition, though this opposition will not be truly effective until apostasy and defection take root within the church itself.

What is being proposed here is a postmillennialism within the framework of a modified amillennialism. The millennial glory is the glory of the church triumphant, the church in paradise, but this glory has been and will be manifest in the history of the church on earth, in those periods when the banner of the Gospel is carried forward into the centers of worldly power (Hab. 3:12, 13). This does not mean that the church will be exempt from suffering and battle—even in paradise, since the church triumphant identifies itself with the travail of the church militant. This is not a call to romantic optimism but, instead, a summons to confidence and courage in the knowledge that Christ has utterly defeated the powers of evil, and this defeat will become more and more manifest as the church fulfills the great commission.

We take issue with the view prevalent in Barthian circles that the whole world is now the kingdom of Christ. With Paul we affirm that all things are not yet subjected to Christ de facto (1 Cor. 15:24–28). The kingdom of Christ counts in its membership only the community of faith, though it will be manifest throughout the world in this dispensation.[64] Its power and glory will extend throughout history, even though large parts of humanity still remain mesmerized by the spell of the powers of darkness. The reach of its impact is far wider than the immediate boundaries of the church, though only those who steadfastly adhere to Christ effectively participate in its fellowship and mission. The millennium is best understood not as a condition already actualized in all its power and efficacy but as a drama that is being unfolded on the screen of history as the church penetrates the darkness of the world.

Calvin's picture of the kingdom continually advancing in the world does justice to both postmillennial and amillennial motifs. Though the kingdom of God has been inaugurated in Jesus Christ, he says, we should pray "that he assiduously increase and advance it, until it reach the summit of its power; which we hope for only at the last day, when God, having reduced all creatures to order, will alone be exalted and preeminent, and thus be all in all."[65] A postmillennial note can also be detected in these words of Calvin's: "The light of the gospel must shine over the whole earth before God gives Satan a free hand. . . . I think I hear Paul speaking of the calling of all peoples and declaring that the grace of God must be offered to the whole earth so that the impiety of men should stand out clearly.[66]" That the parousia is to be connected with the triumph of the church rather than its demise is made evident in Psalm 102:15, 16 (NEB): "Then shall the nations revere thy name, O Lord, and all the kings of the earth thy glory, when the Lord builds up Zion again and shows himself in his glory" (cf. Mal. 4:3).

Just as the church as a whole will experience the glory of the millennium, so every Christian may experience this glory if he will only seek and pray for it. This is the truth in the Holiness doctrine of the second blessing, which refers to personal renewal of faith and victory over temptation not in some other world but in this life. Paul asserted that "we are more than conquerors through him who loved us" and that nothing "will be able to separate us from the love of God in Christ Jesus our Lord" (Rom. 8:37, 39). The eschaton can be anticipated and partially realized now through the outpouring of the Holy Spirit, but it will not be revealed in its full splendor and power until the parousia of Christ. The future world is already breaking into the present world, but this present world has still to be taken up into the future world. We thus seek to hold together the truths in both realized and futuristic eschatology.

We do not anticipate within history a pure church which is required to separate from the institutional church (as in dispensationalism). The church will remain a mixture of wheat and tares until the final judgment (Matt. 13:24–30, 36–43). Yet there will be a defection from the church and, therefore, a likely division within the church before the coming of Christ. But even the faithful remnant cannot claim purity in the sight of God, since it, too, will be, at the most, a church of sinners that lives solely by the grace of God.

The truth in chiliasm is that the kingdom of Christ has this-worldly as well as other-worldly dimensions, that the consummation will include a new earth as well as a new heaven. Chiliasm arose as a valid protest against spiritualizing and Platonizing tendencies in the early church. Yet chiliasm errs by seeking a heaven on earth in the here and now. It is not content to wait for the revelation of the glory of Christ at the end of time.

Yet we must avoid at all costs the opposite error of looking only to the eschatological or ultimate hope and not seeking to realize penultimate hopes for justice, peace, and brotherhood within human history.

If we abandon the world to the devil, the devil who has been dethroned will seize the opportunity to regain his power, and this has happened ever again when Christians have been lulled to sleep by a false pietism, which is, in effect, quietism. We need to recover the robust and expectant faith of the original evangelicals, whose missionary enthusiasm was accompanied by an outpouring of humanitarian concern and social reform.[67] We need to recover the postmillennial vision of a church on the march, without succumbing to any kind of utopianism or false romanticism. Charles Wesley displayed this kind of faith when he wrote in 1749 in celebration of the revival:

> Now it wins its widening way:
> More and more it spreads and grows,
>   Ever mighty to prevail;
> Sin's strongholds it now o'erthrows,
>   Shakes the trembling gates of hell.[68]

There is reason to look forward not only to persecution and tribulation for the church (as do the premillennialists and many amillennialists) but also to greater advances and triumphs of the church over the world. Yet the millennial hope, which is preeminently realized in the paradise of the blessed, is still a penultimate, not the ultimate, hope. The final hope of humanity rests in Jesus Christ himself—not simply in what he is doing through his church in the here and now but in what he will do at the end of the age when he acts to bring in the eternal kingdom of God in his glorious second coming. This alone is the "blessed hope" (Tit. 2:13), which does not, however, cancel out legitimate this-worldly hopes but places them in the proper perspective. On the basis of this ultimate hope we can step into the future with courage, avoiding both a superficial optimism and a crippling pessimism. We can then sincerely pray that God's will might be done on earth as well as in heaven (Matt. 6:10), knowing that we ourselves can fully expect to see "the goodness of the Lord in the land of the living" (Ps. 27:13) and not only in the life to come.

In seeking to reinterpret the doctrine of the millennium, we have taken into account the valid insights of postmillennialism, though within the framework of a definitely modified amillennialism. Can premillennial motifs similarly be incorporated into this schema? We believe that there is an abiding truth in premillennialism that must not be lightly set aside if we are to do justice to the total biblical witness on this subject. With the premillennialists we affirm that the millennium is an eschatological category, though the glory of the eschaton has already appeared in history in the resurrection of Jesus Christ and the great outpouring of his Spirit at Pentecost. Moreover, there is a sense in which the millennium, understood as the dispensation of the Holy Spirit, is fulfilled in that stretch of time immediately following the second advent of Christ and leading to the new heaven-earth.

At his second coming Christ not only brings an end to the dark and tragic history of a sinful world but also consummates and perfects the millennial glory of an advancing church.[69] The second advent of our Lord predates the millennium as fulfilled in the eschatological triumph over the powers and principalities of this world and the inauguration of the new world aeon of God.[70] Christ, at his coming again, not only subdues the rebellious rulers of this world but also institutes the final judgment prior to the creation of the new heaven and new earth. We read that at the time of this judgment the old earth, the old heavens, and the sea still exist, though they are ebbing away (Rev. 20:11–13). The last great outburst of messianic glory will take place when Christ brings down the curtain on world history, for the durability and triumph of the church will then be made visible to all creation (Isa. 66:18, 19; Ps. 102:15, 16). Christ's millennial reign will come to an end when he delivers the kingdom to the Father (1 Cor. 15:24), who will then bestow upon it the crowning splendor of his eternity. The realization of the universal and all-embracing lordship of Christ will be followed by the final consummation of the universe when God will be all in all (1 Cor. 15:28).

These events at the time of the eschaton will take place in rapid succession, but there is, nonetheless, a sequence of happenings that precede the new heaven and new earth (cf. Isa. 66:18–24; Matt. 13:-40–43; 1 Cor. 15:20–28; Rev. 19:11 ff.; 20:7–15).[71] The old earth does not in and of itself prepare the way for the new earth, but it does experience the glory of the triumphant Christ subsequent to his second coming (Mark 13:26; Luke 21:27).

The millennium can therefore be seen to have four sides: the outpouring of the Spirit upon the church at Pentecost and continuing in all periods of missionary expansion; the paradise of the blessed, where the church triumphant intercedes for the church militant; the great harvest of souls as history moves toward a grand climax; and the final triumph over the adversaries of God and man on the great day of the Lord, inaugurated by his second coming.[72] We have tried to understand the millennium in terms of the church's advancement already evident at Pentecost and culminating in the supernatural intervention of the reigning Christ into history. This advancement is discernible now in various places, but it will be manifest on a worldwide scale toward the end of the age. Even though the church will have to undergo unprecedented tribulation and persecution (Matt. 24:21), through the power of the Holy Spirit it will prove to be invincible and unshakable (cf. Dan. 2:44; Mal. 4:3; Rom. 8:37–39; Rev. 12:11; 17:14; 20:9, 10).

We as Christians can face the future with confidence and hope because we have the certain knowledge that Christ has already won the decisive victory over the powers of darkness and that the future belongs wholly to him and not to the devil, who is now dethroned and in virtual collapse. We can press forward under the banner of the Gospel, upheld by the promise that the meek shall indeed inherit the earth (Matt. 5:5). There is the additional consolation that we are surrounded by a great cloud of witnesses (Heb. 12:1), the saints in paradise, who powerfully aid us by their supplications and intercessions.

While spurning the excesses of both chiliasm and postmillennialism, we have not discarded these options altogether. Our contention is that mainstream Protestantism has too cavalierly dismissed these positions, and the millennium has been spiritualized in the process. We do not wish to promote an artificial synthesis; instead, we have tried to incorporate the abiding insights of these positions in a vision that stands in continuity with the Reformed tradition. The universal realization of the messianic reign of Christ over the earth is still ahead of us in the future, inaugurated by his second advent; here we empathize with premillennialism. Yet parables and signs of this reign are manifest in the history leading to the end-time, the most potent being the conversion of great multitudes of the lost to Jesus Christ through the outpouring of the Spirit and the proclamation of the Word. Such signs are not simply a foretaste but a partial realization of the coming universal lordship of Christ. This is the abiding truth in postmillennialism.

Our intention has been to construct a doctrine of the millennium that includes the note of victory not only over the world powers at the end-time but also over the world powers within our present age. At the same time, we have tried to stay clear of a false church triumphalism that exempts the church from the judgment of God and from the cross of persecution. We have sought to avoid both a crippling pessimism that sees the church as only a tiny remnant besieged by the hordes of darkness and a too facile optimism that underestimates the continuing power of sin and death in the world. The messianic kingdom of Christ is already realized in the birth and life of the church, but it has yet to be consummated when the church is taken up into the eternal kingdom of God. The new age is present now, though hidden in the community of faith, but it will be manifest throughout all the earth when our Lord comes again in glory.

NOTES

1. Apocalyptic is characterized by the belief in two totally distinct and different ages, one under the control of the prince of darkness, the other eternal and perfectly righteous. While prophecy "shows future things as coming forth from what already exists on earth," apocalyptic "shows these future things as coming down out of heaven without involving itself in the connection that these future things bear to the present." (Kuyper). In G. C. Berkouwer, *The Return of Christ,* trans. James Van Oosterom (Grand Rapids: Eerdmans, 1972), p. 308.

2. E. N. Mozley, *The Theology of Albert Schweitzer* (London: Black, 1950), p. 110.

3. C. H. Dodd, *The Parables of the Kingdom,* reprinted. (New York: Charles Scribner's Sons, 1958).

4. See Ernst Käsemann, *New Testament Questions of Today,* trans. W. J. Montague (London: SCM Press, 1969), pp. 101–106.

5. *Ibid.,* p. 124.

6. T. A. Kantonen, *The Christian Hope* (Philadelphia: Muhlenberg Press, 1954).

7. George Eldon Ladd, *Jesus and the Kingdom* (New York: Harper & Row, 1964), p. 333.

8. Karl Barth, *Church Dogmatics* IV, 3 a, pp. 293 ff.

9. Langdon Gilkey, *Catholicism Confronts Modernity,* p. 68.

10. Jürgen Moltmann, *Theology of Hope,* trans. James W. Leitch (New York: Harper & Row, 1965), pp. 222, 223.

11. *Ibid.,* p. 329.

12. Johannes Metz, *Theology of the World,* trans. William Glen-Doepel (New York: Herder & Herder, 1969), pp. 94, 95.

13. *Ibid.,* pp. 154, 155.

14. Jürgen Moltmann, *Hope and Planning* (New York: Harper & Row, 1971), p. 195.

15. Hans Schwarz, *On the Way to the Future* (Minneapolis: Augsburg, 1972), p. 101. In his *The Church in the Power of the Spirit* (New York: Harper & Row, 1977) it is clear that Moltmann acknowledges the eschaton as an event that will bring an end to earthly history as we know it, but his attention is still focused more on the progressive realization of the kingdom of God within history.

16. Paul Rees in *World Vision,* vol. 19, no. 6 (June 1975), p. 23.

17. Schubert Ogden, *The Reality of God and Other Essays* (New York: Harper & Row, 1966), pp. 229–230.

18. Cf. Bultmann: "I don't know anything about immortality. The only

thing we can know is that our earthly life ends with death. Whether there is another life after this one, we don't know." Cited by Kenneth L. Woodward in *U.S. Catholic and Jubilee,* vol. 36, no. 1 (January 1971), p. 13.

19. Oscar Cullmann, *Immortality of the Soul or Resurrection of the Dead?* (New York: Macmillan, 1958).

20. Kantonen, *The Christian Hope,* pp. 39 ff.

21. Eberhard Busch, *Karl Barth,* p. 488.

22. The analogy of D-Day and V-Day is taken from the Second World War: the former signifies the landing of allied troops at Normandy, which was decisive for the future victory, and the latter, the day of the German surrender. This analogy is not the best, since the victory of Christ at Calvary resulted in the complete overthrow of the devil. And yet he continues to fight on even as a defeated foe. Calvary signifies that the warfare is virtually, but not actually, over.

23. For both Barth and Berkouwer the resurrection of Christ connotes V-Day and not simply D-Day. This means that the redemption in the future can only be an unveiling of what has already taken place. See Berkouwer, *The Return of Christ,* p. 75.

With Moltmann we hold that the concept of "unveiling" is inadequate for a full understanding of eschatology and that redemption must be reconceived as an event that takes place in promise and fulfillment. See Moltmann, *Theology of Hope,* p. 228.

24. In Robert G. Clouse, ed., *The Meaning of the Millennium* (Downers Grove, Ill.: InterVarsity Press, 1977), pp. 181, 182.

25. Alois Winklhofer, *The Coming of His Kingdom,* trans. A. V. Littledale (New York: Herder & Herder, 1963), p. 45.

26. Dietrich Bonhoeffer, *The Cost of Discipleship,* p. 192.

27. Heinrich Schmid, *The Doctrinal Theology of the Evangelical Lutheran Church,* trans. Charles A. Hay and Henry E. Jacobs, 3rd ed. (Minneapolis: Augsburg, 1961), p. 644.

28. Origen maintained that "wherever bodies are, corruption follows immediately," so the end of all things will be incorporeal. Origen, *On First Principles,* trans. G. W. Butterworth (New York: Harper Torchbook, 1966), p. 247.

29. Martin Luther, *On the Councils and the Church* W.A. 50, p. 627.

30. In support of this position it should be recognized that Revelation 20 does not teach that the first resurrection occurs just at the beginning of the 1,000 year reign of Christ.

31. The theory that the saints receive their new body immediately upon death has been ably defended by W. D. Davies in his *Paul and Rabbinic Judaism* (London: SPCK, 1962).

32. In his *Commentary on Genesis* Luther later categorically stated: "In the interim, the soul does *not* sleep but is awake and enjoys the vision of angels and of God, and has converse with them." W.A. 43, p. 360.

33. We affirm that even in hades the souls exist in some bodily form, but they exist in a state of deficiency and poverty (cf. Lk. 16:19 ff.). Their bodies lack the durability and glory of the resurrection body of the saints. According to Romano Guardini in his *The Last Things* (Notre Dame, Ind.: University of Notre Dame Press, 1965), only Christ has the perfectly developed spiritual

body. After death the soul is not in nakedness, but there is a lack of complete-ness and wholeness in the spiritual body.

34. Cf. Wesley: "For paradise is only the porch of heaven. . . . It is in heaven only that there is the fulness of joy; the pleasures that are at God's right hand for evermore." Cited in Harald Lindström, *Wesley and Sanctification* (London: Epworth, n.d.), p. 121.

35. Pierre-Yves Emery, *The Communion of Saints,* trans D. J. Watson and M. Watson (London: Faith Press, 1966), p. 126.

36. We have difficulties with Fortman's idea of the natural immortality of the soul. See Edmund J. Fortman, *Everlasting Life After Death* (New York: Alba House, 1976), pp. 41 ff.

37. This passage can also refer to the final resurrection on the last day, and many scholars hold that this is its primary sense.

38. Cited in Robert Gleason, *The World to Come* (New York: Sheed & Ward, 1958), p. 162. See Irenaeus, *Against Heresies* Bk. V, Ch. 3, 5, 6, 7, 12.

39. Berkouwer maintains that I Corinthians 15:23 ff. cannot be used to support chiliasm: "Those who appeal to Paul for a defense of chiliasm must admit that the real motive of chiliasm certainly does not come to the fore in his epistles. The train of thought in I Corinthians 15:23 ff. is not the series: Christ's resurrection, followed by the resurrection of *believers,* and finally by the general resurrection. The emphasis is on being in Christ and the power of His resurrection." (Berkouwer, *The Return of Christ,* p. 302). In our estima-tion Berkouwer's analysis does not do justice to the full intention of this pas-sage, since Paul is certainly pointing to the distinction between the present kingdom of Christ, which will be fulfilled in the eschaton, and the future kingdom of God.

40. Kromminga ably shows that Montanism signified a combination of pre-millennial and postmillennial motifs in that Montanus affirmed a special pe-riod of the Holy Spirit initiated by the new prophecy prior to the second advent of Christ, which inaugurates the millennium. See D. H. Kromminga, *The Mil-lennium in the Church* (Grand Rapids: Eerdmans, 1945), pp. 77 ff.

Tertullian further developed the postmillennial strand in Montanist es-chatology in a dispensational direction: he distinguished between the period of the natural state of righteousness, the period of the law and the prophets, the period of the gospel, and the period of the Paraclete. This last age would be followed by yet another historical period, Christ's visible reign on earth during the millennium (in Kromminga, pp. 78–88). Tertullian might well be consid-ered the spiritual father of modern dispensationalism, though dispensational ideas are also present among a few of the other church fathers.

41. In America a kind of premillennialism was advocated by William Miller, the father of Adventism, though he saw the millennium as part of Eternity. It is interesting to note that the Plymouth Brethren view rather than the Miller-ite gained ascendancy in American evangelicalism.

42. Heinrich Quistorp, *Calvin's Doctrine of the Last Things,* trans. Harold Knight. (Richmond, Va.: John Knox Press, 1955), p. 161.

43. Barnabas has also been claimed by premillennialists, but D. H. Krom-minga presents a convincing case for numbering him among the amillennial-ists. See Kromminga, *The Millennium in the Church,* pp. 29–40.

44. Torrance interprets the millennium as "the sabbatical time of the new humanity which in Christ is wedded to the perfection of eternity. It is in this time, millennium time, that the Church participates as throughout history it lives in union with the risen Christ." It is *"the other side* of the time of this world," which is the time of dark and tragic history. Torrance sees the second coming of Christ as the unveiling and completion of the millennium. Thomas F. Torrance, *Space, Time and Resurrection* (Grand Rapids: Eerdmans, 1976), pp. 101–103.

45. Michael Wilcock presents a convincing case for amillennialism in his commentary on Revelation, *I Saw Heaven Opened* (Downers Grove, Ill.: Inter-Varsity Press, 1975).

46. Lamparter diverges from classical amillennialism by viewing the millennium as the day of the parousia, the harvest of history, and appeals to II Peter 3:8 in support of his position. See his *Die Hoffnung der Christen* (Wuppertal: Aussaat Verlag, 1977), pp. 166–174. Lamparter can also be classified as a premillennialist of a type in that he sees Christ's second coming ushering in the millennial time in which all the final events will occur.

47. Berkouwer, *The Return of Christ,* p. 307.

48. See note 40.

49. Moltmann, *The Church in the Power of the Spirit,* p. 149. Moltmann sees the coming of the universal lordship of Christ partly realized within the structures of history, though the final consummation will not occur until the parousia. In our estimation Moltmann incorporates elements from secular liberation theology while still maintaining continuity with the principal themes of New Testament eschatology.

50. Similarly the Swedenborgians contend that Christ's second coming was fulfilled in the revelations given to Emanuel Swedenborg. Kromminga classifies both Swedenborgianism and Shakerism as theosophical chiliasm, since the millennium is spiritualized to denote an inner order of life.

51. We would have no objection to a premillennial view that sees the second coming of Christ ushering in a new earth on which the millennial promises will be fulfilled, though this new earth is the earth as taken up into eternity. We are also quite willing to entertain the possibility that Christ's victory will take place in a series of stages in which the earth is transfigured in millennial glory prior to its total transformation into an eternal heaven-earth. Yet we see this happening not over a period of a literal 1,000 years but in a very short time span as indicated in Revelation 19:11–21; 20:7–15; and 21:1–4.

52. It is not uncommon for biblical prophecies to have an immediate reference as well as one that relates to the far distant future. Some of the prophecies of Joel were fulfilled at Pentecost (see Ac. 2:17—21) but not those in which the sun is turned to darkness and the moon to blood. It is not unreasonable to expect a deeper and more literal fulfillment of this particular prophecy. Note also that Joel speaks of the latter rain as well as of the early rain (Joel 2:23).

53. The picture in this verse is of a battle between the forces of light and darkness, with the former triumphant. Jeremias sees the powers of hell on the attack against the church. In *Theological Dictionary of the New Testament,* vol. 6, ed. Gerhard Friedrich (Grand Rapids: Eerdmans, 1968), pp. 924–928. The Anchor Bible sees the church as being on the offensive: "The sense here is that

the powers of evil cannot contain or hold in check the new community." In W. F. Albright and C. S. Mann, *Matthew* (Garden City, N.Y.: Doubleday, 1971), p. 196. In Calvin's view the two sides are engaged in mortal conflict, but Christ triumphs over the powers of evil. "The new Church," he says, will "stand triumphant against all the designs of hell." In his *A Harmony of the Gospels Matthew, Mark and Luke,* vol. 2 ed. David Torrance and Thomas Torrance, trans. T. H. L. Parker (Grand Rapids: Eerdmans, 1972), p. 186. Calvin appropriately quotes from I John 5:4 that the faith of the church shall overcome the powers of the world. William Barclay, too, sees Matthew 16:18 as expressing the triumph of Christ over the powers of darkness: "However we take it, this phrase triumphantly expresses the indestructibility of Christ and His Church." In Barclay, *The Gospel of Matthew,* vol. 2, 2nd ed. (Philadelphia: Westminster Press, 1958), p. 159. In this view the gates of hell have no power against the Son of the living God, who has burst the bonds of death (p. 158). For a similar interpretation see Oscar Cullmann, *Peter,* trans. Floyd V. Filson (Philadelphia: Westminster Press, 1953), pp. 201–203.

54. We concur with Reformed theologian Johannes Wollebius that "the apostles (Mt. 19:28), the martyrs (Rev. 20:4), and indeed all believers (I Cor. 6:2) shall judge both the world and the devils; not that Christ will share the glory of judgment with the saints, but that they will approve the sentence and praise the justice and wisdom of the heavenly judge." In John W. Beardslee, ed., *Reformed Dogmatics* (New York: Oxford University Press, 1965), p. 185.

55. Cf. Quenstedt: "Since the second advent of Christ, the general resurrection, the final judgment, and the end of the world are immediately united, and one follows the other without an interval of time, it is manifest that, before the completion of the judgment, no earthly kingdom and life abounding in all spiritual and bodily pleasure, as the Chiliasts or Millenarians dream, is to be expected." In Schmid, *Doctrinal Theology of the Evangelical Lutheran Church,* p. 650. Quenstedt fails to recognize that there must be at least a very brief interval of time between the great events of the last days if Revelation 19 and 20 are to be included in our criterion.

56. See Wilcock, *I Saw Heaven Opened,* p. 193. Revelation 20 could also be an example of synthetic parallelism (prevalent in Hebrew poetic literature) in which the same events are described but carried further.

57. George Eldon Ladd, writing from a premillennial stance, interprets the binding of Satan in Matthew 12:29 as different from his binding in Revelation 20: "The former meant the breaking of the power of Satan that individual men and women might be delivered from his control. The latter binding meant that he should deceive the nations no more." In Clouse, *The Meaning of the Millennium,* p. 189. It should be observed, however, that the same word is used in both cases. Moreover the driving out *(ekballō)* of Satan in John 12:31–32 is derived from the same root as the word used in Revelation 20:3 NEB. "He [the angel] threw [ballō] him [Satan] into the abyss."

58. See Floyd E. Hamilton, *The Basis of Millennial Faith* (Grand Rapids: Eerdmans, 1955): "A thousand, the number of perfection or completion, is held to be the symbolic reference to the perfect period, or the complete period between the two comings of Christ" (p. 35). Cf. Herbert H. Wernecke, *The Book of Revelation Speaks to Us* (Philadelphia: Westminster Press, 1954), p. 149; also

Jacques Ellul, *Apocalypse; The Book of Revelation,* trans. George W. Schreiner (New York: Seabury Press, 1977), p. 208.

59. An imperialism or false triumphalism of the church is also apparent in classical premillennialism, which depicts the church in the millennial age as the *ecclesia triumphans* and no longer as the *ecclesia pressa* (persecuted church). Some forms of postmillennialism succumb to the same danger.

We, too, speak of the triumph of the church, even envisioning the millennium as the triumph of the church over the powers of darkness before the end of the world and the creation of the new heaven-earth. Yet this is not an unqualified triumph, since persecution and oppression still exist, and even intensify, as history draws toward a close.

60. Emil Brunner has asserted that the kingdom of God cannot really enter into this historical world. In his *Eternal Hope,* trans. Harold Knight (Philadelphia: Westminster Press, 1954), p. 76. Similarly, Hans Schwarz maintains that Jesus stood for a kingdom that is "neither of *nor in* this world" (Italics added). In *On the Way to the Future,* p. 155.

61. Calvin gave special recognition to the sign of the persecution and defection of the church before the end, though he generally shied away from a preoccupation with signs, since he believed that the coming of Christ could not be calculated in advance. See Quistorp, *Calvin's Doctrine of the Last Things,* pp. 113, 124. Both the Lutheran Hollazius and the Reformed theologian Hoekema attach special importance to these signs of the end.

62. It can be shown that, though Luther and Calvin rediscovered the forensic meaning of justification, they did not sufficiently recover its eschatological meaning.

63. Ezekiel is germane to this discussion, since Revelation 20 refers to the defeat of Gog and Magog, which is described in Ezekiel 38–39. Moreover, the last chapters of Ezekiel closely parallel the Book of Revelation: the defeat of Edom and the resurrection of Israel to a period of peace and revival (Ezek. 35–37), then the rebellion and defeat of Gog, (38, 39), followed by the vision of the new Jerusalem (40–48). The deepest meaning of the prophecies of Ezekiel concerning the restoration of the nation and the rebuilding of the temple is that they find their fulfillment in the new Israel and the kingdom of Christ. Floyd Hamilton suggests that the "last chapters of Ezekiel must be intended to teach *spiritual truths under the symbolism of the temple and the restored nation!*" In Hamilton, *The Basis of Millennial Faith,* p. 44.

64. Christ in his divine nature already reigns over the whole world, but in his role as Savior he reigns only over the church. The messianic kingdom refers to his reign as the Messiah of the new Israel.

65. J. K. S. Reid, ed. and trans., *Calvin: Theological Treatises.* In *The Library of Christian Classics,* vol. 22 (Philadelphia: Westminster Press, 1954), p. 125.

66. Cited in Quistorp, *Calvin's Doctrine of the Last Things,* p. 120.

67. See Iain Murray, *The Puritan Hope* (London: Banner of Truth, 1971).

68. Cited in *Ibid.,* p. 128.

69. The last outburst of millennial glory at the second coming of Christ is still a proximate, not an ultimate, fulfillment, since the millennial promises are not finally fulfilled until the creation of the new heaven and the new earth.

The church, which participates in Christ's final victory, becomes at the time of the second advent the church triumphant, without ceasing to be the church militant, for it is still engaged in battle.

70. It is not until after the second coming that we can speak of the millennial kingdom including the whole world. The millennial kingdom is being realized throughout history in the missionary advance of the church, but this kingdom will be fulfilled when Christ overthrows the last bastions of worldly resistance on the last day.

71. We see the events of the end of the age taking place in super-history *(Ubergeschichte)*, rather than in history as such, since historical time is being taken up into eternal time.

72. In light of what has been said, the millennial kingdom can be regarded as a twofold kingdom, having an earthly and a heavenly phase, the latter being the paradise of the saints. In its eschatological fulfillment these two phases are merged together, since the earthly is then taken up into the heavenly. The heavenly here connotes not the visible heavens, which will pass away, but the spiritual heaven, which is God's eternity breaking into time. One might say that the glory of paradise is extended to the earth at the time of Christ's second coming.

IX.
HEAVEN AND HELL

And many of those who sleep in the dust of the earth shall awake, some to everlasting life, and some to shame and everlasting contempt.

Daniel 12:2

He who believes in him is not condemned; he who does not believe is condemned already, because he has not believed in the name of the only Son of God.

John 3:18

It is salvation or perdition. Salvation lies ahead; perdition behind—for everyone who turns back, whatever it is he sees.

Søren Kierkegaard

Thou grantest grace even to those who will forever experience the rigour of thy justice.

François Fénelon

The vague and tenuous hope that God is too kind to punish the ungodly has become a deadly opiate for the consciences of millions.

A. W. Tozer

PROMISE AND WARNING

If anything has disappeared from modern thought, it is the belief in a supernatural heaven and hell. Even those who retain some vague idea of heavenly bliss beyond the pale of death are extremely reluctant to give serious credence to the threat of a final judgment and eternal condemnation. On the other hand eternal life understood as the depth dimension of present existence is readily accepted. An advertisement for the movie *The Reincarnate* typifies the modern life and world view: "No Heaven . . . No Hell . . . No Guilt! Eternal life is the only reality!"

While modern thought and theology are ambivalent, if not skeptical, on the question of heaven and hell, the Scriptures are very clear that history will have a twofold outcome. Though the children of Israel, in their early history, were agnostic concerning a transhistorical heaven and hell, they became much more open to this vision in the period of the prophets, particularly during and after the exile. The dualistic motif is especially evident in Daniel: "Many of those who sleep in the dust of the earth shall awake, some to everlasting life, and some to shame and everlasting contempt" (12:2). The expectation of a final, universal judgment is found in several of the major and minor prophets (Isa. 66:15, 16; Ezek. 39:21; Joel 3:1, 2; Zeph. 3:8; Zech. 14). Not all are saved; indeed, those who persist in stubborn rebellion against the living God are spiritually doomed. "They who are far from thee are lost," the Psalmist declares, "thou dost destroy all who wantonly forsake thee" (Ps. 73:27 NEB).

In addition to hades or the realm of the dead the New Testament stoutly affirms the supernatural realities of heaven and hell. These realities are not merely states of mind but time-space dimensions beyond our space and time (cf. John 14:2, 3; Rev. 20–22). Eternity is not simply to be equated with futurity; it signifies the absolute future beyond the merely temporal or historical future.

The twofold destiny of mankind is a constantly recurring theme throughout the New Testament. "Go in through the narrow gate," Jesus urges, "because the gate to hell is wide and the road that leads to it is easy, and there are many who travel it. But the gate to life is narrow and the way that leads to it is hard, and there are few people who find it" (Matt. 7:13, 14 TEV). This passage is not intended to furnish data on the population of heaven and hell but instead to underline the infinite gulf between two ways of life. Our Lord finishes his parable of the last judgment with these words: "And they will go away into eternal punishment, but the righteous into eternal life" (Matt. 25:46). Those who die without faith in Christ as the promised Messiah die in a state of condemnation (John 3:18; 8:24). The author of Hebrews warns of impending doom to those who persist in unbelief and error: "How shall we escape if we neglect such a great salvation?" (Heb. 2:3). Paul also draws a sharp distinction between the two species of humanity, the elect and the reprobate: "To those who by patience in well-doing seek for glory and honor and immortality, he will give eternal life; but for those who are factious and do not obey the truth, but obey wickedness, there will be wrath and fury" (Rom. 2:7, 8). Those whose hopes and goals lie only in this world have become enslaved to the god of this world and are thereby prevented from perceiving the truth (2 Cor. 4:3, 4). Only the righteous will be elevated into glory, while the unrighteous will be thrown into the lake of fire (Rev. 20:14, 15).

At the same time in addition to the moral dualism that runs through the Bible, there is also a universalism that envisions God's grace as everywhere triumphant. "All the ends of the earth," says Isaiah, "shall see the salvation of our God" (Isa. 52:10). The whole world is destined to come to Mount Zion (Pss. 47, 48). Peter declares: "It is not his will for any to be lost, but for all to come to repentance" (2 Pet. 3:9 NEB; cf. Ezek. 18:23). When Paul attributes the evil of unbelief to God's action in hardening hearts (Rom. 9:18), he ends by making this evil provisional and directed to God's ultimate purpose that all should receive mercy (Rom. 11:30–32). Cullmann interprets Matthew 16:18 as giving the promise that the gates of hades (hell or death) shall not be able to "hold out" against the church.[1] The power of the keys therefore implies the possibility of invading "hell," or the realm of death itself. And in the words of James: "Judgment is without mercy to one who has shown no mercy; yet mercy triumphs over judgment" (James 2:13).

Nevertheless, despite the promise of God's mercy to all, the warning is still present that some will be passed over, that some will reject this mercy and thereby doom themselves. The parables of the talents, the faithful and wicked servants, and the wise and foolish maidens show the utter seriousness with which the call to faith and repentance must be taken (Matt. 24:45–51; 25:1–30). The New Testament also gives the additional warning that the wrath and condemnation of God will fall not only upon the outside world but even more upon the sons of the kingdom, those to whom the message of salvation is first delivered. Jesus says that it is the sons of the kingdom who will be cast into the outer darkness (Matt. 8:12; 13:41, 42; 24:45–51). Even the servants who have been set over the household of the Lord will suffer condemnation (Matt. 24:45–51). We can fall from grace through our negligence and stubbornness (2 Pet. 1:9–11). It was the scribes and Pharisees, those who were especially meticulous about keeping the law, whom our Lord excoriated: "You serpents, you brood of vipers, how are you to escape being sentenced to hell?" (Matt. 23:33).

The Scriptures are adamant that God is not mocked and that whatever a man sows, he will also reap (Gal. 6:7). Even in the nether world there is no escape from the wrath of God (Deut. 32:22; Amos 9:2). Yet a way out of our predicament has been provided by the sacrifice of God's own Son. The coming of Christ opens the door not only to heaven but also to hell, since those who reject this offer of salvation are then confirmed in their sins. Those who believe and are baptized will be saved, but those who spurn Christ's salvation will be condemned (Mark 16:16). It is the refusal to believe that prevents people from entering the eternal rest (Heb. 3:18, 19).

The good news has two sides to it: warning and promise. The warning is addressed particularly to the "good" people, to the "religious" people, since these are the ones who claim access to the treasure of the Law and Gospel and who claim to keep the Law. They think that they see, and this is why they shall be made blind (John 9:40, 41). The promise is addressed to sinners (Mark 2:17), that is, those who know and confess their sin and who therefore seek a Savior. They acknowledge that now they do not see as they ought, and this is why they will see in the end (John 9:39).

Shirley Guthrie makes this astute comment:

To whom did Jesus address his gracious words of invitation and promise? To people who were obviously guilty—dishonest tax collectors, prostitutes, political and social outcasts rejected by respectable people. And to whom did he address his sternest warning of hell-fire and eternal misery? He almost never mentioned hell except when he spoke to the scribes and Pharisees—the very moral, very religious, complacent, church-going people of his day.[2]

Our Lord himself declared that the servant who knows his master's will and does not act according to it shall receive a severe beating, but he who does not know and acts wrongly shall receive a light beating. For "every one to whom much is given, of him will much be required; and of him to whom men commit much they will demand the more" (Luke 12:48). Judgment begins indeed with the household of God (1 Pet. 4:17).

The universal atonement of Christ cannot validly be used to argue for a universal final salvation. Rejection must be taken seriously, since one can choose to live in the darkness even while the light shines in the darkness. Some will forfeit eternal salvation, and these of all people are the most to be pitied. The vision of heaven and hell is not only a call to decision but a call to perseverance, for only those who persevere to the end will finally be saved (Heb. 3:6, 14; 6:11, 12).

THE HISTORICAL CONTROVERSY

From the first century onward a conflict has raged between those who defend a universal restoration of all people to the favor of God and those who affirm the harsh reality of divine judgment and hell. Among the church fathers Origen, Clement of Alexandria, and Gregory of Nyssa upheld universalism, whereas Tertullian, John Chrysostom, and Augustine believed in unending torment for those who reject Christ and his Gospel. Origen, as well as some of the other fathers, contended that the salvation of Christ reaches beyond death into hades, where those who still dwell in darkness may be brought to the light.[3] In Origen's view even the devils will finally be led to repentance and restored to God's good graces. The urgency to be baptized and to believe *now* was underlined by John Chrysostom: "If a man cannot enter into the kingdom of heaven unless he be born again of water and the Spirit . . . how without them will it be possible for a man either to escape hell-fire or to reach the crowns which are laid up for us?"[4]

Augustine perceived the world as a schoolhouse or testing ground where one is confronted with decisions that determine one's destiny throughout eternity. According to him, "the prize of victory is eternal life, the penalty for failure is death."[5] Behind man's rejection of the Gospel lies the mystery of predestination. "There are so-called 'sons of hell'," Augustine maintained, "not because they have been born of hell, but because they have been prepared for it, as 'the sons of the kingdom,' are prepared for the kingdom."[6] Not only faith but baptism itself is necessary for gaining salvation. Augustine taught that unbaptized infants are lost or damned, but their punishment is not as severe as for those who commit actual sins.

Following in the tradition of Augustine, Thomas Aquinas contended that a supernatural, eternal hell is as real as its heavenly counterpart. By sinning, one offends the infinite God, and "since punishment cannot be infinite in intensity, because the creature is incapable of an infinite quality, it must needs be infinite at least in duration."[7] He described the horror of being spiritually lost and condemned:

The eternity of damnation is part of the punishment of the damned, and it would not have the true nature of punishment unless it were repugnant to their will. Now the eternity of damnation would not be repugnant to their will unless the damned were aware that their punishment was everlasting. It is therefore a condition of their misery that they know that they can in no wise escape damnation and reach blessedness.[8]

While he saw hell as a necessary concomitant of the justice of God, Thomas did not divorce God's justice from his love. The divine love is related to hell for the purpose of mitigating the sufferings of the damned. In his view the purpose of hell is not exclusively retributive. Moreover, it serves as a deterrent to evil and as a basis for moral order in the universe.

Like Augustine Luther sometimes perceived heaven and hell as the outcome of divine foreordination. He readily acknowledged, with Ezekiel, that God, according to his revealed will, does not will the death of the sinner (Ezek. 18:23, 32; 33:11). According to his "inscrutable will," however, he does will the death of the sinner, and those who are set on the way to perdition are helpless to escape the doom that awaits them.[9]

At the same time, there is another side to Luther's theology, in which he recognized the universal outreach of Christ's love and grace. He could even envisage the possibility of salvation for people who have never actually heard of Christ, and he ventured to hope that Cicero "and men like him" would be saved. Yet he could not conceive of any saving knowledge of God, one representing a right relationship with God, except that which explicitly or implicitly contains Christ.[10]

Calvin, too, affirmed the double predestination to both heaven and hell, but this doctrine was not a predominant motif in his thinking (as in later orthodox Calvinism). In his view Christ's atoning death is offered on behalf of all, though it is efficacious only for those who believe. Calvin did not speak so much of God's love as of his mercy and goodness. Mercy is given to the helpless and undeserving but not necessarily to all. Mercy is not blind (as love is) but discriminating.

Though Calvin tied the rejection of the Gospel on the part of unregenerate man to the secret will of God, he nonetheless traced the immediate cause to man's own sin. Sin does not happen apart from God's will, but man is to blame, since it is man who commits the sin: "Whenever we are deprived of the sense of God's favour, the way has been closed up through our fault; for God would ever be disposed willingly to show kindness, except our contumacy and hardness stood in the way."[11]

In Pietism the idea of universal atonement became more prominent. According to Zinzendorf, "All human souls . . . are designed for salvation."[12] The whole world has been set free by the atoning sacrifice and resurrection of Christ, and it is up to us to acknowledge this and live accordingly. He maintained that many more persons are saved than lost, the latter being the exceptions.

Although rejecting the idea of an eternal hell as the rational consequence of predestination, Kierkegaard saw hell as an overhanging threat and warned against the delusion that all will finally be saved. "Nowadays," he observed, "all of us expect to be saved—and Christ, who certainly is best informed, says: Only few will be saved."[13] If we do away with either the terrors or promises of eternity, "the idea of an imitation of Christ is fantastic. Only the seriousness of eternity can compel and move a man to take such a daring decision and answer for his so doing."[14] In Kierkegaard's eyes there is no neutral ground, it is either salvation or perdition. "Salvation lies ahead; perdition behind—

for everyone who turns back, whatever it is he sees."[15] He was especially irritated with those orthodox churchmen who gave lip service to the doctrine of hell but who were intent only on obtaining a more lucrative position. "Everyone," he said, "who believes that there is a hell and that others go to hell is *eo ipso* a missionary, that is the least he can do."[16]

In Reformed orthodoxy Charles Hodge affirmed the realities of heaven and hell, but he was surprisingly optimistic concerning the triumph of grace in this present world. There was reason to believe, he thought, "that the number of the finally lost in comparison with the whole number of the saved will be very inconsiderable."[17] It was his conviction that all who die in infancy will be saved.

Loraine Boettner also sees a widespread triumph of the grace of God within human history, and this indubitably plays a role in his postmillennialism. He regards the condemnation of the nonelect as "designed primarily to furnish an eternal exhibition, before men and angels, of God's hatred for sin, or, in other words, it is to be an eternal manifestation of the justice of God."[18] He allows for the possibility that strict Calvinism could be consistent with universal salvation: this would occur not where salvation is universally offered to all those who accept but where all are elect despite their demerits. As he sees it, the bridge to heaven is as wide or as narrow, as particular or as universal, as God decides.

In the new Catholicism a monism of grace overshadows the remnants of a moral dualism inherited from Paul and Augustine. For Karl Rahner man, even antecedent to his reception of grace, "is already subject to the universal salvific will of God, he *is* already redeemed and absolutely obliged to tend to his supernatural end."[19] It is not simply a question of whether the world can be saved if it wills: "It *is* in fact saved, as a whole, because God brings it about in Christ that the world does will to be saved."[20] Therefore, we can regard it as the redeemed, not just the redeemable, world. In our preaching, according to Rahner, we should proclaim as a *fact* already realized in Jesus and the saints that salvation history ends victoriously in the triumph of God's grace. At the same time, we should proclaim "as a serious *possibility* that the freedom of each individual may operate to his eternal ruin."[21] Our statements about hell should always be kept open in character, "since they are statements about our possibilities as they are now, and which cannot at present be superseded."[22]

In his noted work *The Divine Milieu* Teilhard de Chardin maintains that, though Christ is destined to be all in all, there are still some souls who seek to spoil the perfection of the final and general union. Yet their miscalculations will be "offset . . . by one of those recastings which restore the universe at every moment to a new freshness and a new purity. The damned are not excluded from the Pleroma, but only from its luminous aspect and from its beatification. They lose it, but they are not lost to it."[23] The existence of hell "adds an accent, a gravity, a contrast, a depth which would not exist without it. The peak can only be measured from the abyss which it crowns."[24] Later, in *The Future of Man,* Teilhard affirms a collective evolutionary development toward an ultrahuman perfection which coincides with the final perfection awaited by all Christians.[25] According to one critic, Teilhard cannot escape from a final universalism.[26]

In neo-Protestantism universalism almost completely dominates the religious scene. Schleiermacher, F. D. Maurice, Tillich, Nels Ferré —all of these scholars and many others uphold the universal restoration of all to God. According to Gilkey "the relevant evils to be overcome are those issues around us here and now, of social injustice and justice, of war and peace, and not a hell threatening hereafter."[27] The Lundensian and Barthian theologies speak of a *Weltrechtfertigung* (world justification), which seems to imply the inevitable salvation of all. Moltmann, who also speaks in this way, argues that "hell does not lie before men. It has been conquered in the cross."[28] In his view, "All are sinners without distinction, and *all* will be made righteous without any merit on their part by his grace which has come to pass in Christ Jesus."[29]

Remarkably absent from current neo-Protestant and liberal theology are the ideas of the righteous wrath of God and the finality of his judgment.[30] At the World Council of Churches Fourth Assembly in Uppsala, Sweden (1968), it was stated in an official document: "Man is lost because he does not know who he is." Nothing was said about standing under the wrath and judgment of God. This brings to mind H. Richard Niebuhr's caustic indictment of nineteenth-century American liberalism: "A God without wrath brought men without sin into a kingdom without judgment through the ministrations of a Christ without a cross."[31]

Even conservative theologians like Walter Künneth and Paul Althaus hold out hope for a universal homecoming. Künneth says that the idea of *apokatastasis* (universal restoration) "represents an ultimate consequence of the doctrine of the aeons, and as such a theological necessity."[32] According to Althaus faith is always on the way from the fear of a possible twofold outcome to a prayerful expectation of a universal homecoming.

C. S. Lewis is one modern who remains steadfast in his defense of a supernatural heaven and hell, though even here one can note certain reinterpretations. If he does not doubt that the lost soul "is eternally fixed in its diabolical attitude," he contends that we cannot be certain "whether this eternal fixity implies endless duration—or duration at all."[33] Hell should be reconceived as the last refuge for the sinner, since this is where the sinner will feel most at home—in the isolation of his self-love.[34]

According to Eastern Orthodoxy people experience a provisional judgment after death on the basis of their faith and works. The souls then enter either heaven or limbo (hades). There they see their future reward or punishment and thus, in anticipation, enjoy blessedness or suffer anguish. While the faithful still on earth may ask God to pardon the tormented souls in hades, their destiny can be changed only by God's mercy.

Among the cults and sects the idea of an eternal hell understood as endless torment has, for the most part, been completely discarded. Sectarian movements that teach conditional immortality, that is, immortality dependent on faith in Christ, are the Jehovah's Witnesses, Seventh-day Adventists, and Christadelphians. In this position those who reject Christ will be resurrected on the last day, and then they will experience anguish terminating in the second death (annihilation). The Mormons teach purification and growth in worlds beyond this world.

Cults that tend toward syncretistic mysticism see both growth and retrogression in this life and beyond. In Spiritualism "the doorway to Reformation is never closed against any soul here or hereafter."[35] Some cults, such as Unity and Theosophy, accept reincarnation whereby the guilty soul works out its karma in successive existences in human history. This idea seems to be contradicted by the author of Hebrews: "And as it is appointed unto men once to die, but after this the judgment: so Christ was once offered to bear the sins of many; and unto them that look for him shall he appear the second time without sin unto salvation" (9:27, 28 KJ).

The idea of purification after death has a long history in the tradition of the Western church. The doctrine of purgatory arose in connection with the ideas of satisfaction and merit; it was said that the reward of heaven cannot be attained until one has paid his debts in full.[36] Purgatory, like many other traditional doctrines, is now being rethought by sensitive Catholic theologians. Ladislaus Boros reinterprets purgatory to mean the point of intersection between life and death. The encounter with Christ at death is our purgatory when we are received into the divine presence through the purifying power of divine love. This converges with the traditional Reformed view that the souls of believers are purified of sin at the moment of death or immediately after death (cf. Rom. 8:18, 23, 30; Heb. 12:23; Rev. 14:5).

Against the modern view of an evolution of grace, which we see in Teilhard and process theology as well as in many of the cults, we affirm a history of salvation and perdition. The forces of good are arrayed against the forces of evil, and our eternal future depends on which army we join. In the knowledge that good will most certainly triumph over evil, we can engage in battle confident of victory. Yet even in this knowledge we cannot close our eyes to the complementary biblical truth that the triumph of good means the destruction and overthrow of evil and those who are allied with evil.

UNIVERSALISM AND PARTICULARISM IN KARL BARTH

Of all theologians in our time none has wrestled with the problem of man's ultimate destiny in the light of Jesus Christ more indefatigably than Karl Barth. He once remarked that theology in its essence is eschatology, and his own monumental work seems to indicate this, though he sees the eschaton not only at the end but also at the center of history, where God became man in Jesus Christ.

In Barth's thought Christ's atonement signifies the objective deliverance and redemption of all humanity. Jesus Christ was both the elected and the reprobate in that he suffered the consequences and penalty of sin on behalf of all. In him all people are elected, and reprobation has become an impossibility for all, since the judgment and hell that deserve to fall upon us instead fell upon him. As Barth perceives it, "God has set up the kingdom of His covenant of grace with man in such a way that He has now finally and efficaciously translated man into this kingdom in the person of His only Son."[37]

The first stage of redemption has been completed in the incarnation and atonement of Jesus Christ, and Barth calls this "reconciliation" (Versöhnung). Yet there is a second stage, whereby people appropriate their redemption in faith. This is the subjective dimension in which the Holy Spirit enables us to recognize and live according to what God has accomplished for us in Jesus Christ. In the third or final stage man's redemption will be revealed for all to see. This is the eschatological unveiling of what has already taken place in Jesus Christ. These last two stages are included and anticipated in the first. Indeed, even before the incarnation the plan of redemption was already set in motion at the creation, since, in Barth's theology, creation serves redemption just as redemption signifies a renewal of creation. The fulfillment or consummation *(Vollendung)* is still in the future, when Christ will come again to set up the eternal kingdom of God. This is why Barth can say that the whole world is now reconciled but not yet redeemed because the fruits of reconciliation are still to be realized for all.

In contrast to much traditional theology Barth maintains that all people are ontologically included in Christ by virtue of his incarnation and atonement. All humanity is united with Christ in a realistic and not just symbolic sense. The world is reconciled as an empirical fact and not just as a legal transaction. This explains Barth's contention that the conversion *(Umkehr)* of man to God has already been effected and that our responsibility is to become aware of who we really are—sons and daughters of God destined for salvation. Faith is primarily a cognitive act by which we are granted illumination concerning the significance of the salvation which Christ accomplished.

It thus seems logical to conclude that Barth is a universalist standing in the tradition of Origen and Gregory of Nyssa. Yet he explicitly disassociates himself from the doctrine of the *apokatastasis,* maintaining that such a doctrine ties God to a metaphysical principle. God's grace is free, and this means that we cannot count on it, especially if we transgress his laws, though we can hope for it because his promise of salvation includes the whole world. We can look forward to it expectantly because we and all humankind have been elected to salvation, though it is only when we believe and obey that we become the elect de facto as well as de jure.

While the universalist motif is very pronounced in Barth, we must not overlook the motif of particularism as well, however subdued. According to Barth despite the fact that all people are children of God in the light of Christ, not all realize their destiny as children of God, at least in human history.[38] If all are called to the vocation of being a Christian, not all are actually set in a Christian fellowship. Yet even those who are still blinded to their true being and destiny in the sight of God are the objects of God's loving care. They are made subjects of the kingdom of Christ even against their will and apart from their knowledge,[39] though they do not actively participate in the fellowship of the kingdom until they are awakened to their true status by the Holy Spirit. Barth makes clear that even in his sinful state man is already released from the prison of the kingdom of Satan and is now placed in the dominion of the kingdom of light: "As the man of sin, and therefore as the liar he is, man stands willy-nilly in this light, being set in it and surrounded by it as it shines in his sphere."[40]

Though the grace of God is for all and surrounds all, Barth recognizes the "impossible possibility" of man's irrational opposition to this grace. If man in his folly persists in his refusal to recognize the light that already shines on him, he lays himself open to God's wrath and judgment. Barth can even say that the man in revolt "stands under the threat and danger of being damned. His condemnation hangs over him like a sword."[41] God's grace is not assured to those who persistently thwart and resist his plan of redemption. Even those whose eyes were once opened to the grace revealed and fulfilled in Jesus Christ cannot take for granted God's continuing favor if they become disobedient and thereby fall back into unbelief. Barth recognizes the grim possibility that one can "imperil one's own life in the Spirit," that one can "surrender again to a different order of life—to the order, or disorder, which stands outside the sphere of grace, which is far from the kingdom of God, and under the wheels of which man can only perish."[42] Barth speaks of the "fatal danger" of unbelief, since for unbelievers it seems that God's sacrifice in Christ has been in vain.[43]

Yet while God's wrath is real, it is not permanent. It is penultimate, whereas his love is ultimate. God's wrath and judgment serve his love and mercy. Those who stand under his wrath at the same time remain under his love and grace, and through the experience of wrath they can again come to know and experience his love. Heaven and hell are not equals in Barth's system. Hell is real because it means the rejection of divine love, and love that is rejected becomes destructive. But heaven is more real, since heaven is eternal, and heaven is the proper destiny not only of the church but of the world. Barth allows for the possibility of hell as an interior reality, as something provisional, a shadow on the world's bright horizon, a painful transition from the state of unbelief to the inevitability of faith. The terrible hell which the Scriptures warn against, hell as an ontological reality, is behind us and all people.[44] It has been done away with by Jesus Christ on the cross, for there he suffered the torments that all deserve to suffer because of sin.[45] "Those who in themselves are disobedient," he says, "are claimed and absorbed by the act of His obedience."[46]

Barth's singular contribution to the theology of hell is twofold.[47] First, the man of unfaith cannot suffer the damnation that Christ suffered for him, though he can still suffer the agonizing experience of God's wrath in his opposition to Christ's love.[48] Second, there is an eschatological limit to the damnation of the creature in his obduracy, since he is marked and predestined for salvation. "If there is also light for them, and hope," Barth declares, "it can only be because and if there is an *eschaton,* a limit, by which even their inescapable bondage is hemmed in from outside."[49] Because God's grace is ultimately invincible and irresistible, the resistance to this grace can only be temporary, and this means that hell has no permanent ontological status.

To Barth's credit he has recovered the integral relation between hell and the love of God and has thereby made both hell and predestination preachable once again. He is correct, in our estimation, that the hell which Christ suffered in our stead is now behind us and all humankind, though an interior hell remains as a sign of both God's judgment and grace. He also reminds us that, in the light of the universal atonement of Jesus Christ, we have grounds for viewing even the non-Christian with hope and optimism, since we know that he, too, is claimed by the love of God. Whereas in much traditional theology the elect are called to hope for the demise of the wicked, in Barth's theology we who have been given the privilege of faith are compelled to hope for the ultimate good even of those who renounce and blaspheme God. We need to pay heed to these words of Shirley Guthrie, Jr., who here speaks out of a Barthian orientation: "If we know that the only hope any of us has is that all of us will one day stand before the Judge who is the 'friend of sinners' (Lk. 7:34), must we not hope *for* rather than *against* the wicked who are his and our enemies?"[50]

Our criticism of Barth is that he breaks the biblical correlation between salvation and faith, so that it is possible to be justified and sanctified without personal faith in Jesus Christ. The sheep-goats dichotomy, which the whole tradition of faith has seen in Matthew 25, is overcome in this theology, since all people are sheep, though they invariably behave like goats. Barth holds out the impossible possibility of damnation, but this is a self-damnation, one that has its basis in man's folly and not in God's decree. Yet this damnation is only temporary because man cannot forever swim against the stream of God's invincible grace. Hell for Barth is not so much an ontological reality in the life to come as a divine judgment in this world. He sometimes leaves open the possibility of a division between people at Christ's second coming,[51] and there seems then to be a place for heaven and hell as eschatological realities. But even in the beyond hell has an eschatological limit, since those who are condemned remain the objects of God's favor. For Barth no limitation can be placed on God's illimitable grace, and this means that even the rejected are only provisionally rejected, since reprobation serves election. In view of the fact that Barth did not complete the fifth volume of his *Church Dogmatics,* which was to deal with the doctrine of redemption or consummation, we shall never know exactly where his thoughts would have finally taken him. He seeks to affirm both the universality of love and grace and the self-destructive character of love to those who reject it. He has helped theology to break through an impasse on this important theme, but in so doing he has not been able to uphold the eternity of hell. The logic of his theology drives him toward an ultimate universalism, though his intention is to transcend the polarity between universalism and particularism.

In Barth's theology the "already" is sometimes emphasized at the expense of the "not yet," and the final redemption therefore becomes only the unveiling of what has happened previously. From this perspective God's saving grace already encompasses the world, so that there is only the one order—redemption.[52] In our view there are still the two orders—preservation and redemption, but we believe that God's saving grace ultimately *will* encompass the whole of creation, though this does not imply the actual salvation of every individual, as we shall point out in the following section.

THE TWOFOLD OUTCOME

In constructing a viable doctrine of heaven and hell for our day, we must try to hold together several complementary truths of revelation: the universal salvific will of God; the sovereignty of grace; and the reality of condemnation, being banished from the kingdom of God. While we must distinguish between God's justice and love, we should not separate them, as was the tendency in the older theology, since this creates a bifurcation within the very heart of God. Hell thereby becomes a coeternal evil and can no longer be reconciled with God's love. We must affirm that God's love goes out to all, that his atonement is intended for all, but at the same time we must recognize that not all accept the atonement. God's grace and love are sovereign, however, and this means that rejection takes place not just in spite of his love but at the hands of his love. We must not make the mistake of saying that God is sovereign *over* his love (as in some kinds of latter-day Calvinism), but we must affirm that God is sovereign *in* his love. But his love is inexorable toward man's sins, for love cannot tolerate sin though it embraces the sinner. It is not because God's love is limited but because it is unlimited that hell as well as heaven is made necessary. God's wrath, indeed, is not only a reaction of God's holiness to sin but also a demonstration of his love, which punishes for the sake of the sinner.

We affirm not an ultimate moral dualism but a duality within an ultimate unity. God will be all in all, and therefore his grace and love will finally encompass all. But this does not mean that his grace and love will be manifest in the same way for every person. For those who reject and deny their Lord and Savior, his love will be destructive and chastening. For those who accept and rejoice in their Savior his love will be restorative and liberating.

The two heresies to be avoided are universalism and double predestination. We must not say that God loves the elect only, since this separates his love from his justice. The other danger is to contend that God must love in the same way. We should remember that God's love is a holy love. Love is not acquiescence in the face of sin but a searing judgment upon sin.

We affirm that both heaven and hell are products of God's love as well as of his holiness. No one can escape from the love of God, even in the nether darkness (Ps. 139:8; Nah. 1:8). Tillich has rightly observed: "Love must destroy what is against love, but not him who is the bearer of that which is against love."[53] God's love destroys the false self-esteem of the sinner, but it upholds the sinner even in his misery. Man is in hell not because God is absent but because he is present, and therefore man is constantly reminded of his guilt and infamy. Hell is exclusion from communion with God, but not exclusion from the presence of God.[54] Even redemptive love is present in hell, but not in the sense that the rejected are brought to redemption; nonetheless, they are ineluctably exposed to redemption.[55]

The metaphor that most nearly describes hell is not a concentration camp presided over by the devil, but a sanitorium for sick souls who are ministered to by Jesus Christ. It is he who has the keys to both heaven and hell (cf. Rev. 1:18; 3:7; 20:1). This view of hell is not based on a higher gnosis arrived at outside the Gospel proclamation, but it is an inescapable inference from various supposedly conflicting affirmations of faith. Hell, too, is within the sphere of the kingdom of God, though it signifies not membership or active participation in this kingdom but alienation from it. Paul says that every knee shall bow and every tongue shall confess Jesus as Lord (Phil. 2:9–11; cf. Rom. 14:11; Isa. 45:23; 66:23, 24), but not every voice will rejoice in the Lordship of Christ. Some will come before the throne of God as sons and daughters, but others as servants, even unwilling servants. God is still glorified even in man's condemnation. His light still shines even in the darkness of man's hell.[56]

We affirm a final harmony of opposites.[57] The eschaton might be likened to a great orchestral composition which contains chords that are dissonant when taken only by themselves but which, nevertheless, contribute to an overall harmony. Hell, like heaven, points beyond tragedy (cf. Dante's *The Divine Comedy*). It is created for those who have deserved it, and therefore it reminds us that we are living in a moral universe. God's will triumphs in hell as well as in heaven. God's glory is exalted even in those who persist in unbelief and error. As Paul expresses it, man's "falsehood enhances God's truthfulness and so increases his glory" (Rom. 3:7) (NIV).

There is no equality between hell and heaven, since hell is included in the dominion of heaven. God's light encompasses all, though not all acknowledge this as the light of salvation. Jacob Boehme aptly declares: "Hell . . . will be hidden in the heavenly kingdom as the night in the day."[58]

Because grace is still grace, we can assume with Thomas Aquinas that the sufferings in hell are mitigated because Christ is present. There is a balm of Gilead even in hell, though there is at the same time real torment and anguish. Fénelon has aptly remarked: "Thou grantest grace even to those who will forever experience the rigour of thy justice."[59]

G. Campbell Morgan has made the ingenious supposition that the fires of heaven and of hell might very well be the same, for the love of God is a consuming fire. The saint would be energized and blessed and fulfilled, while the sinner would be frustrated and tormented. Fire in the Scriptures is indeed a metaphor for both God's love and his wrath.[60]

Many universalists reject the idea that God's justice is retributive, and this is why the doctrine of hell makes no sense to them. They speak of God's justice only in terms of his love. But what does this do to the concept of justice and to meaningful obedience? Love then becomes sentimentality. We affirm that the punishment in hell is both punitive and remedial, though the latter must be understood in terms of preservation rather than purification (as in Nels Ferré).

We do not wish to build fences around God's grace, however, and we do not preclude the possibility that some in hell might finally be translated into heaven. The gates of the holy city are depicted as being open day and night (Isa. 60:11; Rev. 21:25), and this means that access to the throne of grace is possible continuously. The gates of hell are locked, but they are locked only from within. C. S. Lewis has suggested in *The Great Divorce* that where there is a supposed transition from hell to heaven the person was never really in hell but only in purgatory. This, of course, is interesting speculation, and may be close to the truth. Yet we must maintain a reverent agnosticism concerning the workings of God's grace which are not revealed in Holy Scripture. We can affirm salvation on the other side of the grave, since this has Scriptural warrant (cf. Isa. 26:19; John 5:25–29; Eph. 4:8, 9; 1 Pet. 3:19, 20; 4:6); yet we cannot preach that any of those who are banished to hell will finally be saved. Quite the opposite seems to be the case if we take Scripture seriously. We can rest assured that those in hell are in the hands of a God who is both righteous and merciful, and we can trust that his mercy as well as his justice will be manifest among them, though this does not mean final universal salvation.

We must pay heed to the Scriptural warning that where faith is not present, it is impossible to enjoy the bliss and rapture of the kingdom. As Kantonen has wisely observed: "No amount of pity will equip a sea animal lacking lungs to live on dry land. Just so, when faith—the organ by which man lives in God—has atrophied, and the basic life-orientation has become estrangement from God and opposition to him, eternal life in God is unthinkable."[61]

Paul Althaus has aptly defined eternal death as inescapable godlessness in an inescapable God-relationship. Whether God will ever solve this paradox and, as loving Father, transform into his likeness even the most rebellious of his enemies or, as omnipotent Creator, destroy those forms of life that are out of harmony with his new creation, we cannot know on the basis of what is revealed in Scripture. Again we agree with Kantonen: "Hell belongs with Satan and sin and death to that numinous aspect of the divine activity which is not for us to rationalize or moralize."[62]

Hell as well as heaven is the outcome of the atonement. All our sins send us to hell, but only rejection of the grace of God keeps us in hell. We are all predestined to be witnesses and signs of the grace of God, but some will bear witness to this grace in their destruction and thereby be signs of contradiction. Hell is wrongly understood if it is seen primarily as man's self-creation: it is essentially the creation of a loving God for those who refuse the help offered to them in Christ. Hell is not outside the compass of God's mercy nor the sphere of his kingdom, and in this sense we call it the last refuge for the sinner. Edward Pusey voices our own sentiments: "We know absolutely nothing of the proportion of the saved to the lost or who will be lost; but this we *do* know, that none will be lost, who do not obstinately to the end and in the end refuse God."[63]

Charles Spurgeon declared with keen perception: "As sure as God ever puts his children in the furnace, he will be in the furnace with them."[64] He was here thinking of believers who go through the furnace of affliction, but since God calls all into his kingdom, and seeks all for his family, we can assume that God will be present even in the depths of hell. Even the despised and reprobate are claimed for Jesus Christ in some way or other. "Through the Son," says the author of Hebrews, "God made the whole universe, and to the Son he has ordained that all creation shall ultimately belong" (Heb. 1:2 Phillips). Even those who dwell in unbelief are elected by God in Jesus Christ, though not to salvation as such but to the exposure to salvation. As the Representative of the New Humanity Jesus Christ includes in his body only believers. But as the Representative of a fallen race, he encompasses all humanity, both saved and lost.

Whereas hell means a state of continual estrangement from God after the last judgment, heaven signifies a state of intensified fellowship with Father, Son, and Holy Spirit and with the whole company of the saints. "Believers are not only to be with Christ and to behold His glory," says Charles Spurgeon, "but they are to be like Christ and to be glorified with Him."[65] We shall not only reign with Christ, but we shall continue to serve him though as glorified sons and daughters. When the mandate of world evangelization is now completed, we shall be called to higher tasks of service and mission.[66] In the parable of the pounds the faithful servants receive new tasks for the glory of God (Luke 19:11–27). Heaven entails not only the vision of God (1 Cor. 13:12) but loving obedience to God.

Just as hell is created by both the love and justice of God, so the same can be said for heaven. We are assured of heaven not only because of the mercy of God revealed in Christ but also because of the satisfaction of Christ paid to God. Heaven is a free gift, but it is also a prize procured by the merits of Christ, who perfectly fulfilled the law of God in our stead. We are given a title to heaven (by justification) as well as fitness for heaven (by sanctification). Heaven is the outcome of a legal verdict as well as a testimony to the infinite grace of God that goes beyond the law.

Like hell heaven is both a state and a place, though beyond the time and space of human history (cf. John 14:2, 3). It will have no temple, for God himself will be its temple (Rev. 21:22). There will also be no marriage in heaven (Matt. 22:30; Luke 20:35, 36), since the man-wife relationship is now transformed into a brother-sister relationship in Christ. We must not suppose that particular affections will no longer exist, but they must now be seen as having a new basis. Heaven will include a multitude that no one can number (Rev. 7:9). It will have no day or night, since God will be its light (Rev. 22:5). There will also be no suffering in heaven (Rev. 21:4), even though hell will exist outside the gates of the holy city (Rev. 21:27). Hell will not be seen as an evil, but as the place where those who reject Christ are still cared for by Christ—and not simply as Lord and Judge but as Savior and Healer. Heaven includes both a restored earth and a renewed heaven and is therefore better spoken of as a new heaven-earth. It entails not simply spiritual existence but bodily existence as well. Those in heaven shall feast on spiritual food, and drink the water of eternal life (Luke 14:14; Matt. 26:29; Rev. 21:6; 22:1, 2). We should note that the purpose of food and drink is not merely for sustenance but for fellowship as well.

Moreover, there will be real treasures and rewards in heaven (Matt. 6:6, 18, 19, 20; Luke 6:35; 1 Cor. 3:8). We are accepted into heaven on the basis of faith alone, but we are adorned in heaven on the basis of the fruits of our faith. I do not perceive levels in heaven (as I do in the case of hell), but I contend, nevertheless, that there will be distinctions in heaven, though no unlawful discriminations.

Heaven, like hell, is eternal, and yet we should remember that the Greek words *aidios* and *aionios* do not mean "endless" so much as "agelong" or "belonging to the ages." They refer to the quality more than to the length of life, though certainly in the case of those who are in heaven we can affirm their continuance in fellowship with God throughout all ages, since nothing will ever again be able to separate them from his unquenchable and indomitable love (Rom. 8:38, 39).

Peace and joy will reign in heaven, but in hell people will gnash their teeth in the outer darkness (Matt. 8:12; 24:51; 25:30; Luke 13:28). And yet he who is the embodiment of peace and joy will be near to those who remain imprisoned in self. His peace is still present to them, even though this is the cause of their greater anguish.

Just as Abel is the type of the resident in heaven, so Cain is the type of the denizen of hell. Yet we should not forget that God placed upon Cain a sign for his protection, even though he was condemned to wander in a far country. This can legitimately be viewed as the pledge of God's mercy, which was fully revealed in the cross of Jesus Christ. Even Cain is under the sign of the cross, even he is included in predestination to life with God.[67] God will punish our transgressions, but he will not remove from us his steadfast love or be false to his faithfulness (Ps. 89:

31–34), and this applies to both the Cains and the Abels of our world.

May we then hope for the curing of the incurable, for the deliverance of the wretched of the earth? The only sin that is unforgivable is the sin against the Holy Spirit, rejecting and refusing the offer of divine grace (cf. Matt. 12: 31, 32; Mark 3: 28, 29; Heb. 12: 25). The only cure is the cross of Christ appropriated in faith. We should not seek to know more than is revealed, but we do know this: that outside of Christ and faith in his atonement there is no salvation either in this life or in the life to come. We do not need a special message from the dead to prepare now for the judgment that awaits us; we have Moses and the prophets as well as the Gospel of the New Testament, and that is deemed sufficient in the eyes of God (cf. Luke 16: 29–31). Paul proclaimed: "Now is the acceptable time; behold, now is the day of salvation" (2 Cor. 6: 2). Let us make ready to meet our Lord and Savior as he confronts us here and now, for tomorrow may be too late!

NOTES

1. Oscar Cullmann, *Peter,* trans. Floyd V. Filson (Philadelphia: Westminster Press, 1953), pp. 201 ff.

2. Shirley C. Guthrie, Jr., *Christian Doctrine* (Richmond, Va: Covenant Life Curriculum Press, 1968), pp. 398–399.

3. Cf. Origen: "We of the Church assert that the soul of our Lord, stript of its body, held converse with other souls that He might convert those capable of instruction." Cited in J. Paterson-Smyth, *The Gospel of the Hereafter* (New York: Fleming H. Revell Co., 1910), p. 60.

4. John Chrysostom, *Homily on the Priesthood* 3.4. In Francis W. Johnston, *Heart of the Saints* (London: Shand Publications, 1975), p. 69.

5. Cited in Charles N. Cochrane, *Christianity and Classical Culture* (New York: Oxford University Press, 1957), p. 514.

6. *St. Augustine: Faith Hope and Charity,* Trans. Louis A. Arand (Westminster, Md: Newman Press, 1963), p. 48.

7. Thomas Aquinas, *Summa Theologica,* Part III. Q. 99, Art. 1. (English Dominican Trans., London: Burns, Oates and Washbourne Ltd., 1922) Vol. 21, p. 203.

8. Thomas Aquinas, *Summa Theologica,* 22 ae. Q. 18, Art. 3. In *Nature and Grace,* A. M. Fairweather, ed. and trans., *The Library of Christian Classics,* vol. XI (Philadelphia: Westminster Press, 1954), p. 308.

9. Martin Luther, *The Bondage of the Will,* trans. J. I. Packer and O. R. Johnston (Old Tappan, N.J.: Fleming H. Revell, 1957), pp. 166 ff.

10. Philip Watson, *Let God be God!* (London: Epworth Press, 1948), p. 93.

11. *Commentary on Hosea* 2:14. *Corpus Reformatorum, Calvini Opera* 42. 243. Cf. "God would always be ready to relieve us by his goodness, or rather

. . . it would flow down upon us as from a never-failing fountain, if our own ingratitude did not prevent or cut off its course." *Commentary on Psalms* 40:12. *Corpus Reformatorum* 31. 414.

12. Nicholaus Ludwig Count von Zinzendorf, *Nine Public Lectures on Important Subjects in Religion,* ed. and trans. George W. Forell (Iowa City: University of Iowa Press, 1973), p. 62.

13. *Søren Kierkegaard's Journals and Papers,* Vol. I, ed. and trans. Howard V. Hong and Edna H. Hong (Bloomington, Ind.: Indiana University Press, 1967), p. 221.

14. *The Journals of Søren Kierkegaard,* ed. and trans. Alexander Dru (London: Oxford University Press, 1951), p. 313.

15. Søren Kierkegaard, *Concluding Unscientific Postscript,* trans. David F. Swenson (Princeton, N.J.: Princeton University Press, 1944), p. 533.

16. Søren Kierkegaard, *The Last Years,* ed. and trans. Ronald Gregor Smith (New York: Harper & Row, 1965), p. 329.

17. Charles Hodge, *Systematic Theology,* vol. 3 (New York: Scribner, Armstrong, 1874), pp. 879, 880.

18. Loraine Boettner, *The Reformed Doctrine of Predestination* (Philadelphia: Presbyterian & Reformed Publishing Co., 1932), p. 121.

19. Karl Rahner and Herbert Vorgrimler, *Theological Dictionary,* ed. Cornelius Ernst, trans. Richard Strachan (New York: Herder & Herder, 1968), p. 452.

20. Karl Rahner, *Theological Investigations* Vol. 4, trans. Kevin Smyth (London: Darton, Longman & Todd, 1966), p. 273.

21. Karl Rahner, ed., *Encyclopaedia of Theology* (New York: Seabury Press, 1975), p. 437.

22. *Ibid.* Cf. Karl Rahner, *Foundations of Christian Faith,* trans. William V. Dych (New York: Seabury Press, 1978), pp. 443, 444.

23. Pierre Teilhard de Chardin, *The Divine Milieu,* trans. Bernard Wall (New York: Harper & Row, 1960), p. 130.

24. *Ibid.*

25. Pierre Teilhard de Chardin, *The Future of Man,* trans. N. Denny (New York: Harper & Row, 1964), pp. 267 ff.

26. Hans Schwarz, *On the Way to the Future,* p. 131.

27. Langdon Gilkey, *Catholicism Confronts Modernity,* p. 64.

28. Jürgen Moltmann, *The Crucified God,* p. 335.

29. *Ibid.,* pp. 194, 195. (Italics added).

30. Though Sibley Towner seeks to make a place for divine retribution, it is wholly subordinated to the theme of universal redemption. This imbalance becomes glaringly apparent when he declares: "The world was created good and the people in it are already redeemed and are now awaiting the glad word of their redemption." W. Sibley Towner, *How God Deals with Evil* (Philadelphia: Westminster Press, 1976), p. 152.

31. H. Richard Niebuhr, *The Kingdom of God in America* (Hamden, Conn.: Shoe String Press, 1956), p. 193.

32. In Schwarz, *On the Way to the Future,* pp. 148, 149.

33. C. S. Lewis, *The Problem of Pain* (New York: Macmillan, 1962), p. 127.

34. See C. S. Lewis, *The Great Divorce,* reprinted. (London: Geoffrey Bles,

1952), pp. 64 ff. Lewis also opens new ground by including hell in the providential plan of God: "God in His mercy made the fixed pains of Hell." Clyde S. Kilby, *A Mind Awake: An Anthology of C. S. Lewis* (New York: Harcourt, Brace & World, 1969),p. 169.

35. *Spiritualist Manual* (Milwaukee: National Spiritualist Association of Churches, 1955), pp. 194, 195.

36. The only basis for purgatory in the Judaic tradition is 2 Maccabees 12:44, 45, where it is stated that atonement for sin is still necessary after death. This palpably conflicts with the New Testament teaching that Christ made the atoning sacrifice for sin once for all (Rom. 6: 10; Col. 1:22) and that there is no need for further sacrifices (Heb. 1:3; 7:23 ff.).

37. Karl Barth, *Church Dogmatics* II, 2, p. 697.

38. "On the basis of the eternal will of God we have to think of *every human being,* even the oddest, most villainous or miserable, as one to whom Jesus Christ is Brother and God is Father; and we have to deal with him on this assumption. . . . In God's free deed, in Jesus Christ, man *is* God's child. But as long as man lives he remains a pilgrim and a witness. He can only call on God from afar and out of the depth. . . . He does not yet understand himself as the child who enjoys the glorious assurance of belonging to the Father." Karl Barth, *The Humanity of God,* trans. Thomas Wieser and John Newton Thomas (Richmond, Va.: John Knox Press, 1964), pp. 53, 82, 83. Cf. also: "Calling by Him is the future of every man irrespective of the result, and as his future, even if it takes place in his own life only in the most obscure and broken way or not at all, it belongs to the historical existence and situation of every man." Karl Barth, *Church Dogmatics* IV, 3, b, p. 487.

39. Barth writes that in the midst of all human kingdoms, "God has irrevocably and indissolubly set up the kingdom of His grace, the throne of His glory, the kingdom which as such is superior to all other powers, to which, in spite of their resistance, they belong, and which they cannot help but serve." *Church Dogmatics* II, 2, p. 688.

40. Karl Barth, *Church Dogmatics* IV 3, b, p. 482.

41. Karl Barth, *Church Dogmatics* IV 3, a, p. 465.

42. Barth, *Church Dogmatics* II, 2, p. 695.

43. Barth can speak of the work of Christ having "taken place in vain" for those who do not respond in faith. *Church Dogmatics* IV, 3, b, p. 561. Yet this only appears to be the case, since even those who do not respond have been chosen for the family of God and therefore are numbered among the elect.

44. One interpreter comments: "There is a definite distinction between the meaning of hell, damnation and rejection for man and its meaning for Jesus Christ in Barth's doctrine of Election." William John Hausmann, *Karl Barth's Doctrine of Election* (New York: Philosophical Library, 1969), p. 60.

45. "For his sake we have our just damnation, condemnation and rejection behind us and no longer before us." Karl Barth, *A Shorter Commentary on Romans,* trans. D. H. van Daalen (London: SCM Press, 1963), p. 107.

46. Barth, *Church Dogmatics* II, 2, p. 693. Though the immediate reference is to believers, in this very same section Barth maintains that the kingdom of Christ embraces all, that all people, in spite of their resistance, belong to this kingdom "which they cannot help but serve." See pp. 688, 689.

47. This does not imply that we are accepting his contribution uncritically, and our reservations will be candidly expressed. Yet we acknowledge that it bears the stamp of creativity and originality as well as a great measure of biblical fidelity.

48. For Barth, though the one who rejects grace cannot suffer the damnation which Christ has suffered for him and in his place, he can still suffer as a sign of this damnation. But his suffering will, at the same time, be a sign of the grace by which he is saved from this damnation.

49. Barth, *Church Dogmatics* II, 2, p. 496.

50. Guthrie, *Christian Doctrine,* p. 391.

51. "There is a decision and a division, but by Him who has interceded for us." Karl Barth, *Dogmatics in Outline,* trans. G. T. Thomson. (New York: Philosophical Library, n.d.), p. 136.

52. For Barth it seems that salvation history becomes virtually indistinguishable from universal history. In our view salvation history is present only when the Christian mission is carried forward in the conversion and nurturing of souls. This does not mean that God's grace is absent from general history, but this is the grace of preservation, not redemption.

53. Paul Tillich, *Love, Power and Justice* (New York: Oxford University Press, 1954), p. 114.

54. We interpret II Thessalonians 1:9 as referring to an exclusion from man's side but not from God's side. Man shuts himself off from the salvation of the Lord and from the glory of his might, but he cannot escape from this glory (Phil. 2:9–11). Cf. Revelation 14:10, which speaks of sinners in hell being tormented "in the presence of the Lamb."

55. Cf. Karl Barth: "Even in the midst of hell grace would still be grace, and even in the midst of hell, it would have to be honored and praised and therefore announced to the . . . inhabitants of hell." In his *God Here and Now,* trans. Paul M. van Buren (New York: Harper & Row, 1964), p. 35.

56. Cf. Psalm 139:12: "Even the darkness is not dark to thee, the night is bright as the day; for darkness is as light with thee."

57. Paul says that the whole universe, "all in heaven and on earth" will "be brought into a unity in Christ." (Eph. 1:10 NEB). This unity is not a fusion and absorption, however, but a mixture of disparate elements that coexist in an ultimate harmony.

58. Jacob Boehme, *The Way to Christ,* trans. Peter Erb (New York: Paulist Press, 1978), pp. 188–189.

59. François Fénelon, *Christian Perfection,* trans. Mildred Whitney Stillman (New York: Harper & Row, 1947), p. 128.

60. See Isaiah 33:14, 15, where God is depicted as a consuming fire that devours the wicked but does not harm the righteous.

61. Kantonen, *The Christian Hope,* p. 107.

62. *Ibid.,* p. 108.

63. Edward B. Pusey, *What is of Faith as to Everlasting Punishment?* (Oxford: James Parker & Co., 1880), p. 23.

64. Charles H. Spurgeon, *Privileges of Trial.* Cited in Geddes MacGregor, *He Who Lets Us Be* (New York: Seabury Press, 1975), p. 129.

65. *The Treasury of Charles H. Spurgeon* (Old Tappan, N.J.: Fleming H. Revell, 1955), p. 49.

66. It should be noted that the gold and jasper in Revelation 21:18 represent both work and worship. Gold is what one works for, and jasper is conducive to worshiping God in the beauty of holiness.

67. Though all are predestined to life with Christ, we cannot say unequivocally that all are predestined to salvation. God's predestination is realized in two ways: salvation and preservation in the midst of self-damnation.

X.
HOW DISTINCTIVE IS EVANGELICALISM?

For what I received I passed on to you as of first importance: that Christ died for our sins according to the Scriptures.

1 Corinthians 15:3 (NIV)

Whosoever, feeling compunction for his sins, hungers and thirsts after righteousness, let him believe in Thee, who "justifiest the ungodly"; and thus, being justified by faith alone, he shall have peace with God.

Bernard of Clairvaux

Christianity is not the religion of love, but of holy and therefore atoning love, which makes it all the more divine as it makes it less promptly popular.

P. T. Forsyth

The Reformed Confession lays emphasis not so much upon the idea that man is justified by *faith* and not by *works,* as upon the consideration that it is *God* and not *man* who brings about this justification.

Karl Barth

CONFUSION IN TERMINOLOGY

In assessing what is distinctive in evangelical Christianity, we shall recapitulate some themes already discussed but in such a way as to highlight the differences between evangelical and nonevangelical religion. Our intention has been to build bridges between the various strands within the evangelical spectrum, but as evangelicalism looks outward to secularism and the non-Christian religions, it can only remain within its definite boundaries fixed by an authoritative divine revelation in history.

One danger today is that the word *evangelical* is given too broad a connotation, with the result that the distinctive tenets that it has defended in the past are obscured or compromised. Though evangelicalism crosses all denominational lines, it definitely excludes all religion based on law and not on Gospel. The conflict that is presently raging

235

in Seventh-day Adventism on whether salvation is conditional on the keeping of the Sabbath or on the righteousness of Christ alone is a reminder that the sword of faith cuts two ways, creating division as well as unity.[1]

The "new Pietism" reflected in the Faith at Work and higher life movements falls short of genuine evangelicalism because of its focus on regeneration and sanctification to the virtual exclusion of justification. We need to remember that the essence of the Gospel is not Christ coming into our hearts but Christ coming into the world to save sinners. Inner renewal by the Spirit is part of the Gospel when it is related to and grounded in the obedience and death of Jesus Christ, but when presented as the Gospel itself, it can only lead to heresy and confusion.

It is commonly thought that the charismatic renewal signifies a flowering of evangelical religion, but here too we must be cautious. While there is admittedly a fresh zeal for Bible study and a rediscovery of the sanctifying work of the Holy Spirit in neo-Pentecostalism, there is at the same time the legalistic temptation to base justification on a particular kind of religious experience rather than on the perfect sacrifice of Christ on Calvary. One can also detect a synergistic tendency in which salvation is attributed partly to the volitional act of the sinner in addition to the grace of God revealed in Jesus Christ. Many Pentecostals speak of steps that one must go through in order to receive the gift of the Spirit: obedience, repentance, prayer, surrender, and so forth. But is not this a return to the works-righteousness from which the Reformation freed us?

Dispensationalism generally regards itself as evangelical, indeed as the only true evangelicalism, but here again the door is opened to a return to legalism. It is said that in the Old Testament people were saved by "legal obedience," but since the coming of Christ we are saved by grace through faith; yet in the millennial or kingdom age in the future there will be a reversion to a system of meritorious obligation. The theme of salvation by grace is no longer an eternal theme, but limited to a particular dispensation in history.

Some sect groups, such as the Churches of Christ and the Christadelphians, are often treated as branches of evangelicalism, and admittedly in their biblical emphasis they reflect one thrust of authentic evangelicalism. Yet when they make salvation contingent not only on faith but also on baptism and walking the Christian life, they again lose sight of the essence of evangelicalism and indeed of authentic Christianity, namely, the doctrine of *sola gratia* (salvation by grace alone).

While the term *evangelicalism* is often employed to include too much, it is also used to include too little. In conservative Protestant circles it is widely believed that Evangelicalism and Catholicism are contradictory terms, but such is not the case. Admittedly, there is much in Roman Catholicism as well as in Eastern Orthodoxy that contradicts an evangelical stance, but we must not close our ears to authentic evangelical voices in these communions. Karl Barth even acknowledges that Thomas Aquinas was closer, at least in some respects, to the biblical understanding of predestination than Calvin and Luther, since Thomas regarded reprobation as a separate genus, quite apart from predestination, and saw predestination as fundamentally an election to life and to grace.[2] At the same time Barth perceives that in many other respects Calvin and Luther were more true to the Bible than Aquinas, as can be seen, for example, in their attempt to treat the doctrine of election in relation to Jesus Christ.[3]

Where Barth rightly takes issue with Roman Catholicism is not only in its synergistic view of salvation that supposedly is found in Trent, but also and even more in its tendency to accommodate to modern thought through a rationalistic apologetics that undercuts the uniqueness of the biblical revelation. Roman Catholic thought results in a compromised version of the faith, Barth says, "because it is an establishment and justification of the Christian position before the forum of general human thought, and accomplishes the fatal assimilation of the Christian to the human."[4] One modern interpreter of Thomistic theology tends to confirm Barth's critique, since it appears that for Thomas "the house of faith had its foundations firmly set in the soil of common reason and experience."[5] Similarly Rudolf Sohm, the distinguished Lutheran church historian, understands Roman Catholicism as "the religion of the natural man" because it appeals to man's natural religious sense.

At the same time we cannot gainsay that today, as in the past, there are proponents of biblical Christianity in the Roman Catholic communion who vigorously affirm many, if not all, of the salient truths of evangelicalism as delineated in these two volumes. Among these evangelically oriented Catholic scholars are Stanislas Lyonnet, an authority on Paul; Hans Urs von Balthasar, a critic of the current idea of the "anonymous Christian"; Louis Bouyer; Joseph Ratzinger; Lucien Joseph Richard, who holds Calvin in high esteem; Simon Tugwell; Harry McSorley; Stephen Pfürtner; Kilian McDonnell; and W. H. van de Pol.

When we turn to Eastern Orthodoxy, it is admittedly more difficult on first inspection to find points of contact with the evangelical heritage. In Eastern Orthodoxy the salvation model is deification or transfiguration, not penal redemption. At the same time in addition to the mystical theory of the atonement, there is the classic theory of conquest over the powers of darkness, and among many of the early as well as later Orthodox church fathers the idea of expiatory sacrifice was also present. Both the Russian and Greek Orthodox churches have a history of strenuous missionary effort which was sharply curtailed only because of severe persecution first by Moslems and then by Marxists. It must be acknowledged that the patristic fathers are sometimes almost as important as Scripture in Orthodox piety, but the evangelical note has not been completely submerged.[6]

It goes without saying that evangelicalism is diametrically opposed to liberal-modernist Protestantism, which substitutes the authority of religious experience for that of a divine revelation given in sacred Scripture. Harnack, though seeing himself as a defender of Evangelical Christianity, did not begin to fathom the real meaning of the Gospel. For him, as for Ritschl, the essence of the Gospel lay in Jesus' proclamation of the kingdom of God, which is understood in ethical terms. In *What Is Christianity?* he contended that the Gospel concerns the Father, not the Son, and the infinite value of the human soul, not the redemption of the sinner.[7] In Schleiermacher, despite his Christocentric emphasis, the Christian message was transposed into the creative spirituality of man.

It is appropriate at this point to consider what is the hallmark of evangelical faith. We affirm that the watershed of evangelicalism is not the inerrancy of Scripture, not even its divine authority, nor is it the person of Christ or the Trinity. Instead it is the cross of Christ, the doctrine of salvation through the righteousness of Christ procured for us by his sacrificial life, death, and resurrection. It is the cross that gives authority to Scripture, and it is the cross that reveals and confirms the Messianic identity of Jesus as the Son of God. We cannot know the meaning of the cross apart from the Bible or the preaching of the church, but these are only instruments of the Spirit, who alone gives us the proper interpretation as we hear the Word from the mouth of its ministers.

James Orr put his finger on the essence of evangelical faith when he declared: "Christianity is . . . distinctively a religion of Redemption —a great Divine economy for the recovery of men from the guilt and power of sin—from a state of estrangement and hostility to God—to a state of holiness and blessedness in the favour of God."[8] It is the cross that enables us to believe in the miracles of the Bible as well as to discern the real presence of Christ in his church and in the sacraments. But by the cross we mean not only the atoning work of Christ but also the electing and justifying work of the Father and the sanctifying and revealing work of the Spirit. Our salvation has been planned and decreed by the Father, executed by the Son, and applied and unveiled by the Holy Spirit. Evangelical Christianity will forever be solidly trinitarian[9] as well as fundamentally Christocentric.

Evangelical religion places the accent not on a universal God-consciousness, which needs only to be cultivated (as in Schleiermacher), but on the "God-created vacuum in the soul," which can be filled only by Jesus Christ (as with Pascal). It sees the hope of man not in techniques of self-sanctification or in universal education but in the glory of the cross, for it was there that divine grace invaded human history and gave birth to a new humanity.

SUPREME AUTHORITY OF THE WORD OF GOD

Certainly in the area of theological authority evangelical Christianity differs markedly from other philosophies and religions. Its supreme authority is the Word of God revealed and embodied in Jesus Christ and attested and recorded in sacred Scripture. This Word is not simply a past event but a living reality that meets us as we encounter Scripture and the kerygmatic proclamation of the church. It cannot be reduced to words, but it is communicated primarily through words. The Word of God is the Gospel of God, not as a historic testimony buried in the past but as a creative living word, an eternal word that speaks to us in the here and now.

The Word of God takes various forms as it enters human history: the incarnation of Jesus Christ, the prophetic and apostolic witness to Jesus Christ, and the church's proclamation of Jesus Christ. In view of the fact that Christ is the determinative content of the Scriptural witness, this witness is also the Word of God, and since it is an eye- and ear-witness account of the events of redemption, it is the criterion for measuring revelation in the history of the church.

Evangelicalism must not be confused with scribalism, which sees Scripture as a collection of revealed axioms directly available to human reason. Nor is it to be associated with spiritualism, which places the authority of religious experience over that of the written Word. Evangelicalism appeals to the Bible above all other norms, but it is always the Bible as a witness to the self-revelation of Jesus Christ. "The purpose of the God-breathed Scripture," says Berkouwer, "is not at all to provide a scientific *gnosis* in order to convey and increase human knowledge and wisdom, but to witness of the salvation of God unto faith."[10] Similarly Karl Barth declares: "The revelation which has taken place in Christ is not the communication of a formula about the world, the possession of which enables one to be at rest, but the power of God which sets us in motion, the creation of a new cosmos."[11]

Currently the prevailing method in theology is to begin with empirical experience and then seek to validate the Bible wherever this is possible. The modern view stresses subjective certainty over objective infallibility. This anthropocentric orientation is strikingly apparent in Carl Rogers, who long ago discarded objectively given biblical norms: "Experience is, for me, the highest authority. The touchstone of validity is my own experience. No other person's ideas . . . are as authoritative as my experience."[12] Langdon Gilkey, who stands somewhat closer to the center of Christian faith, also reflects this experientialist orientation: "Our theological analysis must begin with man. If we felt sure that the divine word in Scripture was the truth, then the Bible might be our starting point."[13]

Revelation must not be reduced to religious experience, even though it includes within itself the experience of faith that indeed transcends all natural religious experience. Religious experience is the medium but not the source of revelation: the source is the transcendent and living Word of God who meets us in our experience but at the same time challenges it and revamps it. Revelation is always more than religious experience: it is the divine criticism and transformation of religious experience (John Whale).

Nor must revelation be confused with a higher kind of rational knowledge which links up with and builds upon natural knowledge. Revelation overthrows and disrupts human reason, while at the same time placing it on a new foundation. Human reason can serve and explicate revelation, but it cannot of itself lay hold of or make sense of revelation. Both Augustine and Anselm rightly came to the conclusion that we must first believe before we can understand. Calvin, who with Luther, reaffirmed the Augustinian heritage, aptly declared: "Pagan philosophers set up reason as the sole guide of life, of wisdom and conduct; but Christian philosophy demands of us that we surrender our reason to the Holy Spirit; and this means that we no longer live for ourselves, but that Christ lives and reigns within us."[14]

Despite the attempts in modern evangelical circles to resurrect natural theology, it is our conviction that only in Christ are the will and purpose of God fully and truly revealed. We do not dispute the fact that all peoples have a general awareness of God's power and presence, but because of sin this general awareness leads only to a distorted and erroneous knowledge of God and of his moral law. Natural theology can only result in the manufacture of idols, since the true God cannot be identified with the constructs of man's vain imagination. The point of departure in an authentic evangelical theology is not reason, conscience, or intuition but instead the divine revelation given in Jesus Christ and attested and mediated in Holy Scripture.

Some see a basis for natural theology in Romans 2:13–15, where Paul speaks of Gentiles who do by nature what the law requires and thereby show that the divine imperative is written on their hearts. We agree with Augustine and Karl Barth that these are manifestly Gentile Christians, since it is they who have experienced the inward circumcision (Rom. 2:28–29) and have so become partakers of the law of Christ (1 Cor. 9:21). The heart on which is written the work of the law is no longer the natural heart, for it has been turned from a heart of stone into a living heart (Jer. 31:33; Ezek. 11:19). Since all people, Jews and Gentiles, are under the power of sin (Rom. 3:9), it is faith alone that justifies (Rom. 3:30), although those who have faith will invariably be doers of the law because of the love of Christ shed abroad in their hearts (Rom. 5:5). This doing of the law, moreover, is the cardinal evidence of their justification (Rom. 2:13). The conscience that bears witness (Rom. 2:15) is the conscience illumined by the light of faith (cf. 1 Tim. 1:19; 3:9), for a conscience severed from faith in the Christ of the Scriptures cannot lead to the truth (Titus 1:15).

Evangelical theology places the Word of God above church tradition as well as all continuing or supposedly additional revelation. Here it finds itself in conflict not only with the cults (such as Mormonism, Swedenborgianism, and the World Unification Church of Sun Myung Moon, which appeal to new revelations) but also with the Catholic branches of the church that are inclined to elevate tradition to the same level as Scripture. Dyobouniotes, a Greek Orthodox theologian, contends that "apostolic tradition is not just an interpretation of the divine revelation contained in the New Testament, but is also an addition."[15] He therefore holds that there are "two equally valuable sources of doctrine." Carl Feckes declared in 1950, in connection with the then expected dogmatic definition of the Bodily Assumption of Mary: "The primary norm of my Catholic faith is by no means Holy Scripture but the living consciousness of the present-day Church of Christ. If the Church of Christ is indeed . . . the *alter Christus,* the other, the ever living Christ, then she has within herself the clear consciousness of her faith."[16] As we have seen, there is now a growing body of opinion in the Catholic church that affirms Scripture as the only normative source of revelation.[17]

In its emphasis on the historicity and particularity of divine revelation, evangelical Christianity contravenes every form of syncretistic mysticism whose appeal is to the universal awareness of God found in all religions. Radhakrishnan voices a mood that is irreconcilable with the claims of biblical faith: "Religion is not so much a revelation to be attained by us in faith as an effort to unveil the deepest layers of man's being and get into enduring contact with them."[18] The criterion of the biblical Christian is not the deepest within but the Word from without that stands in judgment over all of human existence.

THE TRANSCENDENT GOD

Biblical religion is distinguished from all forms of culture-religion in its affirmation of the utter transcendence of God. God is not "the spirit of the whole" (as in Schleiermacher) but "the Wholly Other" (as in Barth). Culture-religion, Niebuhr observes, seeks "to achieve the eternal and divine by some discipline of the mind or heart, whether mystical or rational," while biblical religion "believes that a gulf remains fixed between the Creator and the creature which even revelation does not completely bridge."[19]

In the history of the church the biblical position was constantly challenged by the Hellenistic view, which conceived the world as in continuity with the being of God. It is crisis, not continuity, that is the hallmark of the biblical understanding of God. The world is not simply an emanation from God, but a creation of God and therefore distinct from its Maker. Eastern Orthodox theologian John Meyendorff rightly maintains that Platonism is "fundamentally irreconcilable with the Biblical concept of creation *ex nihilo*" and has been "the greatest temptation for Eastern Christian thought from the time of Origen."[20]

The whole mystical tradition of the church has a neo-Platonic tinge which stresses the immanence of God over his transcendence and thereby frequently ends up in a type of pantheism or panentheism. This is not true of those mystics who sought to preserve the personalistic element in religion, such as Bernard of Clairvaux and Augustine, though it is true of the more radical mystics, such as Angelus Silesius, who envisioned God as the sum total of existence. In this perspective one cannot see God and all things in God until one has himself "become the All."

The Catholic branches of the church have been especially vulnerable to the infiltration of neo-Platonic mysticism, but many prominent theologians in this tradition have staunchly reaffirmed biblical theism. For Thomas Aquinas God is not a static perfection but the absolutely unlimited Act and Energy. He is not simply the supreme being *(ens)* but the act of being *(esse),* "the very act of being which is prior to all beings."[21] The mystic John of the Cross, while conceiving of a "divine inflowing" in relation to contemplation, nonetheless acknowledged an "infinite distance between God and man."

Certainly the evangelical doctrine of God stands in contradistinction to all forms of Eastern mysticism. In Hinduism the Absolute transcends all opposites and must therefore transcend good and evil. The "Tao" of Lao-Tzu's philosophy is beyond all moral distinctions; it has been aptly described as an all-pervading nonbeing which prefers no one, never taking sides.[22] For Alan Watts God is "the total energy-field of the universe, including both its positive and negative aspects, and in which every discernible part or process is a sort of microcosm or hologram."[23] For the Buddhist scholar Buddhadasa Bhikkhu God includes everything: good and evil, temporality and timelessness, being and nothing.[24] He is the all-embracing impersonal law of nature. In the biblical view, on the other hand, God is the supreme embodiment of the good and excludes and opposes all evil. Evil is willed only in the sense that it is willed to be overcome.

God is utterly transcendent because he is the creator of the world and man. But he also transcends man morally because man is a sinner, whereas God is absolute holiness. God is indeed "wholly other" in a moral as well as in an ontological sense. Yet he does not remain wholly other but identifies himself with man's guilt and misery in the person of Jesus Christ. God condescends to man in the incarnation of his Son, and this is why biblical religion is not simply theocentric (as in Islam) but theanthropocentric, since its focus is on the God-Man who gave his life on the cross for sinners.

The Bible affirms the infinite-personal God who relates himself to man not only in the act of creation but also in the act of redemption. He is the being who acts, not simply being itself (as in Tillich). He is the one who loves and not simply love itself. He is the ruler and redeemer of the world process rather than subject to the process (as in neo-naturalism). The true God is not a passive being silently contemplating himself but an aggressive, vibrant God actively seeking his people and calling them to obedience.

The true God is both transcendent and immanent, but he is basically transcendent, whereas his immanence is a gift of grace to a fallen humanity. Though essentially beyond suffering, he enters into our travail and affliction out of gratuitous love. What makes evangelical Christianity distinctive is that it sees the living, omnipotent God as the Savior of the world. And this salvation is understood not only in terms of the incarnation but also and preeminently in terms of the atoning sacrifice on Golgotha. Evangelicalism upholds not simply the God who acts in history but the God who reconciles and redeems, and this means that even in the doctrine of God the cross is still central.

THE RADICAL PERVASIVENESS OF SIN

Another doctrine that sets evangelicalism apart from other perspectives on life and the world is the radical sinfulness of man. While acknowledging that man is created in the image of God and that this image is reflected in man's fallen state, it contends that sin distorts and impairs man's reasoning powers as well as utterly perverts his volitional capacity. The human heart is not operatively good or morally neutral but desperately wicked (Jer. 17:9; Eph. 4:18; Rom. 7:18). Sin signifies not simply outward acts but a restless egoism that moves in the secret, hidden depths of the personality. Man is both good and evil, but the good within him is poisoned by the evil. The sinner can choose the natural good but not the spiritual good. Man sins inevitably but not from natural causality or ontological necessity.

Roman Catholicism has been accused by Reformation Protestantism of underplaying the gravity of man's predicament, and much of this criticism is justified.[25] Yet it can be shown that in that tradition, too, the sinful proclivity within man is taken into due account. It was Augustine who contended that through the fall man was robbed of the gifts of grace and wounded in his natural powers. For Augustine man is totally unable to come to God by means of his free will, but once grace invades the human personality, man is empowered to believe and obey. "Grace," he said, "does not nullify free will but rather establishes it, and the law is not fulfilled unless it is freely willed."[26]

The Augustinian view reappeared in Jansenism in the seventeenth century. The Jansenists maintained that "because of sin, man's actual nature was radically different from human nature 'in its integrity'."[27] Pascal referred to "the great change," after which man's present nature impels him irresistibly to seek pleasure in the things of the world. "How hollow," said Pascal, "is the heart of man, how full of filth."

Protestant liberalism lost sight of this realistic appraisal of human nature, upheld by Augustine, the Reformers, and Pascal. For Alois Emanuel Biedermann "Redemption from sin otherwise than by the intrinsic powers of man's own nature is neither necessary or possible."[28] Harnack asserted: "It is by self-conquest that a man is freed from the tyranny of matter."[29] Behind much of neo-Protestantism is the moralistic life- and world-view of Immanuel Kant. To the question, "Where shall we start, i.e., with a faith in what God has done on our behalf, or with what we are to do to become worthy of God's assistance?" he replied, "We cannot hesitate in deciding for the second alternative."[30]

Neo-Catholicism also reflects an Enlightenment perspective, which places it in diametrical opposition to the evangelical and biblical strands in the Catholic tradition itself. Rosemary Ruether exemplifies the new optimism: "We seek to become authentic co-creators with God, upon whose works God can look and declare, at last, that it is indeed 'very good'."[31] This kind of outlook comes under fire from the lay Catholic theologian Ralph Martin: "A completely unfounded, naive view of the human race as consisting of men of immense good will and openness to the truth, completely contradicts the view God's Word gives to us of our condition and the attitude of our hearts toward him and the truth."[32]

In its pessimistic appraisal of the capacity of the human will evangelicalism also stands in contradiction to modern existentialism. This is apparent when we consider the existentialist maxim associated with Sartre and Camus: "Man is free to act, but he must act to be free." In the evangelical view as found in Paul, Augustine, and Calvin man is not free to act, so God must act upon him. True freedom is the ability to fulfill one's destiny in accordance with his nature, to function with regard to his ultimate goal. Man does not have this kind of freedom and is helpless to help himself until he is overwhelmed by the grace of God.

Likewise in its anthropology evangelicalism is arrayed against the moralism endemic to Judaism. The Christian faith teaches that when man commits sin he puts himself in the power of sin. The rabbis on the contrary teach that it is in the power of each wholly to overcome sin and to gain life by study and works. According to Abraham Heschel, "Judaism . . . assumes that man is endowed with the ability to fulfill what God demands, at least to some degree."[33] This viewpoint is certainly evident in A. James Rudin: "It is within the power of every man to redeem himself from sin by resolutely breaking away from it and by repenting or returning . . . to God. . . . Each generation, each person, then, must seek his own repentance and atonement. No intermediaries or vicarious saviors are needed."[34]

Confucianism, too, places the accent on the goodness and innate powers of man and, for the most part, refuses to acknowledge the presence of radical evil within him. Mencius, Confucius' chief disciple, taught that man has innate knowledge of the good and innate ability to do good.[35] Evil is to be attributed not to one's nature but to bad environment, lack of education, and "casting oneself away."

In the Eastern mysticism associated with Hinduism and Buddhism the emphasis is on the natural kinship of man with God, not the infinite qualitative difference between God and man. The Vedantists believe that "if we think of ourselves as sinners and miserable, we forget the Godhead within us and lapse into that mood of doubt, despondence and weakness which is the greatest obstacle of all."[36] In Buddhism "ignorance is at the root of all things that go wrong."[37] What is needed is "enlightenment, neither crucifixion nor resurrection."[38] Zaehner makes this astute observation: "When a Hindu or Buddhist speaks of *moksha,* 'release' or 'salvation', he is not thinking of sin, a concept that is foreign to his religion, he is thinking of release from transmigration."[39]

The core of the Christian faith is a pessimism about man and life and an optimism about God (J. Pelikan). Life itself is under a curse because of the fall, though in its essence life is good because creation is good. Sin is not "the thirst for life" (as in Buddhism) but the abuse of life. Yet even in its abuse and perversion life reflects the goodness of the Creator. And because the whole of creation has been claimed for Jesus Christ, it can look forward to the day of redemption despite the fall into sin (cf. Rom. 8:21, 22). Even in his sin man is under the sign of redemption because God has identified himself with man's guilt and sin in the incarnation of Jesus Christ. In Christ God has taken upon himself the shame and guilt of the world so that all humanity might be set free. Our hope lies not in what man in and of himself is able to do but in what God has done for man in the person of Jesus Christ. Evangelical religion looks beyond man the sinner to Christ the Redeemer, and this is why evangelicalism is essentially a religion of hope. It sees man not just in terms of his present predicament but in light of Jesus Christ, the ideal man. For this reason it can rejoice in humanity and not seek to escape from humanity (as in Gnosticism, Hinduism, and Buddhism).

THE UNIQUENESS OF JESUS CHRIST

Evangelical Christianity insists not only on the deity of Jesus Christ but also on his uniqueness. He is not just God but God in human flesh, and this event happened at only one time and place in human history. Other religions have spoken of the theophanies of divine figures and of the metamorphoses of gods into men. But Christianity affirms that Jesus was not only divine but both true God and true man at the same time; moreover, this union between the Son of God and the man Jesus was unique and incomparable, never to be repeated or duplicated. The early church made belief in the incarnation of the Word the test of the authenticity of the revelation of the Spirit: "By this you know the Spirit of God: every spirit which confesses that Jesus Christ has come in the flesh is of God, and every spirit which does not confess Jesus is not of God" (1 John 4:2, 3).

It is becoming customary in many circles to affirm a "Christology from below," which means starting from the humanity of Jesus and then seeking to relate this to the divine Logos. A Christology from below betrays a subordination of Christology to anthropology and results ultimately in the relativizing of the Christ revelation. Jesus is no longer the Word incarnate but a prophetic figure in history who fully realizes oneness with God.[40] Walter Kasper sharply challenges this approach, contending that Jesus as the Christ can be understood only in light of God's condescension to a broken humanity rather than the spiritual ascent of humanity to God. Against those who assert that Chalcedon represented the accommodation of biblical faith to Greek thought, Kasper powerfully argues that Chalcedon prevented the hellenization of faith by vigorously affirming the paradoxical uniqueness of Christ as truly God and truly man.[41]

The uniqueness of Jesus Christ concerns more than his person: it also has reference to his incomparable work on the cross. Christ is unique not only because he was divine but also because, as divinity, he entered into the human condition, taking upon himself the sin and guilt of the world. He was more than a prophet or holy man: he was a sin-bearer and mediator between God and man. He was not only model or exemplar but Savior of a fallen humanity. As Ambrose put it: "Having become the sin of all men, He washed away the sins of the human race."[42] This evangelical understanding is well expressed by P. T. Forsyth: "It is better to trust Christ and His work than even to imitate Him. He is worth infinitely more to the world as its Saviour than as its model, as God's promise than as man's ideal."[43]

The idea of Jesus as the crucified God is a stumbling block to Jews and folly to Gentiles (1 Cor. 1:23). Maharishi Yogi refuses to consider that "Christ ever suffered or Christ could suffer."[44] Through Transcendental Meditation a sinner "very easily . . . comes out of the field of sin and becomes a virtuous man." Mohammed taught that Jesus was never crucified but that another took his place.

Buddhists too find it difficult to come to terms with the crucified Christ. D. T. Suzuki, the prominent Zen Buddhist scholar, has declared: "Whenever I see a crucified figure of Christ, I cannot help thinking of the gap that lies deep between Christianity and Buddhism."[45] The incontrovertible gulf between Christ and Buddha is pointed out by R. C. Zaehner: "The one conquers suffering and sin by rising high above them as one standing on a peak, sublime, aloof: the other accepts the ultimate disgrace of a felon's death, taking upon himself, absorbing into himself all the wickedness and misery of man."[46]

In the cults of syncretistic mysticism Jesus Christ is simply a supreme manifestation of the World Spirit or the Absolute that is in process of unfolding itself. According to Theosophy Christ is the divine consciousness which indwells all people, and Jesus is one in whom this consciousness becomes palpably visible before the world. In the Unity School of Christianity, "the Christ is the higher self of man." For Carl Jung, a naturalistic mystic, Jesus Christ is but one expression of the universal process of the creativity of the unconscious. Jung's fidelity is to the Christ Archetype, which is exemplified in Jesus.

The faith of the Christian community is not in the teachings of Jesus or in his experience of God but in his person and atoning work. For the Zen Buddhist "our supreme faith . . . is in the Buddha's enlightenment experience,"[47] attainable by anyone through the practice of the holy eightfold path, which entails right conduct and right meditation.

Christianity will not tolerate the view that there are many revelations or various roads to salvation. It cannot agree with Gandhi's asseveration that "the soul of religion is one, but it is encased in a multitude of forms. . . . Truth is the exclusive property of no single scripture."[48] Nor can it share Gerald Heard's appreciation of Hinduism for "teaching the West that since 'All roads lead to God' men have to find that road which suits best their nature. Catholicism helps some, hinders others; Vedanta likewise."[49] In the Christian perspective God has revealed himself fully and definitively in the person of Jesus Christ and has through his work made available to humankind an all-sufficient redemption. The truth of creation is indeed reflected in all world religions, but the saving Gospel of reconciliation and redemption is to be found only in Christianity. There are many roads by which man seeks to come to God, but there is only one road by which God comes to man, namely, Jesus Christ.

In the current ecumenical dialogue between Christian and Jewish theologians, the temptation is very great to surrender that which makes Jesus uniquely distinctive from the prophets of biblical history. The late Will Herberg, renowned Jewish philosopher and theologian, acknowledges that Judaism and Christianity will never perceive Jesus in the same way. For the Jew, Jesus emerges out of Israel and goes forth to the world. The Christian, on the other hand, sees Jesus as coming toward him, in the fullness of divine grace, to judge and to save. Herberg's recommendation to Christians is to take their own messianic faith seriously. Instead of reducing Jesus to a moral teacher, prophet, or holy man, "they should behold him in his splendid uniqueness: the God-appointed and God-incarnate agent through whom the Gentiles are to be brought into the covenant."[50] Herberg wisely recognizes that true ecumenical encounter cannot take place unless both sides remain faithful to their own traditions.

There are some people who acknowledge that Christ made an atonement for sin, but who, nonetheless, argue that we can make reparation for sin by following in his steps. What they need to understand is that Jesus did not simply demonstrate a universal law, nor did he merely bring us a new power; instead he suffered, died, and rose again in our place. His sacrifice is inimitable, though we can testify to this unique sacrifice by lives of outgoing service and self-giving love. We cannot atone for sin, but we can witness to his atonement and thereby be instrumental in the salvation of our fellow human beings.

The current mood is in perceiving Christ as the climax of an evolutionary process within history. He does not enter history from the beyond but instead is history's grandest product. He is the flower or apex of humanity, not a divine Savior who creates a new humanity. P. T. Forsyth's acute analysis of the tensions in the theology of his time seems especially relevant today:

Is Christ in the last resort the eternal Redeemer of a wrecked race or the steady Perfecter of a race merely defective? That will be the difference in principle between the Evangelical and the Catholic type of Christianity in the coming conflict for the lead.[51]

THE FREE GIFT OF SALVATION

At the heart of evangelical religion is the doctrine of *sola gratia,* salvation by grace alone. This indeed is also the essence of the Gospel, since grace is procured for the human race only by the costly sacrifice of Christ, who satisfied and fulfilled the demands of the law by his sinless life and agonizing death. *Sola gratia* consequently entails *solus Christus,* salvation by the work of Christ alone. And this work takes place outside ourselves in the propitiatory sacrifice of Christ, though it is applied to our hearts by the Holy Spirit.

The theme of the Pauline epistles is the righteousness of faith, which is to be contrasted with the righteousness of the law. The righteousness of faith is the alien righteousness of Christ imputed to those who believe. Paul did not claim to have a righteousness of his own, "based on law, but that which is through faith in Christ, the righteousness from God that depends on faith" (Phil. 3:9). Luther described the righteousness of faith as a passive righteousness provided for us by Christ. The fruits of faith or our works of love he called "the righteousness of life," which is an active righteousness, produced in us by the Holy Spirit. This righteousness of life does not justify us, however, since it is mixed with imperfect motivations. In ourselves we remain sinners, though we are now being inwardly cleansed by the Spirit; yet in Christ we are perfect or righteous. Luther used the analogy of the white robe of the righteousness of Christ which covers the believer who remains inwardly a sinner.

The Pauline and Reformation doctrine of justification by the imputed righteousness of Christ is not the whole of the Gospel, but it is the essence of the Gospel and consequently also the central core of evangelical religion. Justification has sometimes been depicted as wholly extrinsic, but this is a misunderstanding, for the Holy Spirit is active also in justification, enabling the sinner to respond and believe. Justification by faith is often considered the antithesis of salvation by works. Yet we should remember that according to the biblical witness faith does not exclude works but gives rise to works. Works of the law as well as of faith are excluded from justification, however, since the ground of our acceptance before God is not our works but Christ's atoning work on the cross. As Warfield puts it: "Justification by faith does not mean . . . salvation by believing things instead of doing right. It means pleading the merits of Christ before the throne of grace instead of our own merits."[52] And in the words of the *Book of Concord,* "In justification before God faith trusts neither in contrition nor in love nor in other virtues, but solely in Christ."[53] Faith itself is an empty vessel, not a meritorious work or virtue, a vessel that holds the alien righteousness of Christ.

In the history of theology the great temptation has been to confuse the alien or imputed righteousness of Christ with the personal holiness of the believer, which is a result or fruit of Christ's righteousness. Then we make the mistake of finding the cause of justification in our own worth or righteousness rather than in the righteousness outside of us in Christ. This is not to deny that Christ makes his dwelling place within us in the moment of faith, but he nevertheless remains distinct from us. Even when he lives within us his righteousness is alien to our being, though it has concrete effects within us through the purifying work of the Holy Spirit. The alien righteousness of Christ might be likened to a spiritual pacemaker applied to the heart of the believer. The pacemaker never becomes an organic part of the believer, but it is the ground of the new life that now directs and molds the believer. The new man is Jesus Christ, who is both our spiritual basis and our future, since in the eschaton we shall be transformed into his likeness and glory.

Justification signifies a change in God, not in his *nature* but in his *relationship* to us. By virtue of the substitutionary, vicarious atonement of Christ on the cross, we are now free from the guilt and penalty of sin, though the salvation that Christ merited and procured for us must be appropriated in faith if we are to benefit. Barth puts it this way: "There is an exchange of status between Him and us: His righteousness and holiness are ours, our sin is His; He is lost for us, and we for His sake are saved. By this exchange . . . revelation stands or falls."[54]

The basic meaning of justification is forensic or juridical, but it also has a mystical dimension, since faith means not only acknowledgement of Christ's righteousness but also being united with him by the work of the Spirit. Justification is the mother of sanctification, for inner renewal begins at the moment of faith. But the basis of our justification is not the inner renewal: this renewal is the result of God's decision to justify us.

James Buchanan shows in his significant study on justification that its forensic meaning was not lost among the church fathers, though it was not until the time of the Reformation that the full understanding of justification became apparent.[55] Justin Martyr proclaimed: "No longer by the blood of goats and of sheep . . . are sins purged; but by faith, through the blood of Christ and His death, who died on this very account."[56] This was Anselm's advice: "Dost thou believe that thou canst not be saved but by the death of Christ? Go to, then, and, whilst thy soul abideth in thee, put all thy confidence in this death alone—place thy trust in no other thing . . . cover thyself wholly with this alone."[57] Bernard of Clairvaux, despite his mystical bent, also perceived that it is the ungodly who are justified: whenever one feels sorrow for his sins and "hungers and thirsts after righteousness, let him believe in Thee, who 'justifiest the ungodly'; and thus, being justified by faith alone, he shall have peace with God."[58] Augustine often employed the term *justification* to denote the whole of the great change wrought in the soul at the time of conversion; yet on other occasions he distinguished between the two effects of divine grace—on the sinner's relation to God and on his spiritual character.

At the same time, we must acknowledge that the forensic character of justification was downplayed among both the patristic fathers and the medieval theologians. Justification came more and more to be conceived as a renewing process in the soul worked within us by the Spirit, to be sure, but always with the cooperation of the believer. It was said that man cannot take the first step, but once assisted by the Spirit, he can then prepare himself for justification. Basil explained: "The grace which comes from above is not given to one who makes no effort. On the contrary, there must be a combination of two things: human effort and the help which by faith comes from above to complete the virtue."[59] And in the words of the author of the mystical tract *The Cloud of Unknowing*: "All men were lost through Adam's sin but all those who by their good will manifest a desire to be saved shall be saved by Christ's redeeming death."[60] In later medieval thought it was claimed that man can turn to God with the aid of prevenient grace and thereby prepare himself for the reception of justifying grace. Once justified, he can merit an increase in his justification by works of love. Since faith itself contains an embryonic love, and is therefore not an empty vessel to be filled only by Christ, the real proximate ground of our justification is our inherent or personal righteousness, and Christ's righteousness is at best only admitted to a partnership with our own. In the traditional Roman view justification is not a creative act which makes man, through grace and in Christ, *totus iustus;* instead it is the culmination of a process in which man himself cooperates with God, which began prior to justification and continues after it. Karl Barth sagaciously observes:

The practical consequence of all this is that the misery of man is not regarded as in any way serious or dangerous either for Christians or non-Christians. The Reformation communions could not reunite with a Church which held this doctrine, and they cannot accept the call to reunion with it today.[61]

Rudolf Ehrlich delineates the salient thrust of the Reformation view against the background of late medieval moralism:

Faith, in the Reformation view, though the source from which love inevitably flows forth, justifies only in the sense that it is the instrument whereby the mercy of God is received. Faith is indeed man's response in love to the love of God. Yet it is not his response to the divine love or even his ability to respond to it that justifies him; it is God's mercy alone which, prior to any human response to it, is received through faith, the work of the Holy Spirit in the heart of man.[62]

In recent years there has been an attempt to reexamine the doctrine of justification as enunciated in the Council of Trent. The most daring reappraisal is Hans Küng's *Justification*, in which he vigorously affirms the forensic and juridical meaning of justification and contends, with the Reformers, that justification goes out to the ungodly and not to those already sanctified by infused grace. Yet by holding that justifying faith nonetheless contains embryonic love, he opens the door again to the medieval doctrine that faith is a *virtus*, which thereby presupposes the cooperation between man's will and God's grace.[63]

Karl Rahner reaffirms the traditional Catholic understanding of justification by seeing it as the act of God in his free grace which gives man a share in the divine nature. It comes not solely from the imputation of Christ's righteousness or solely from the remission of sins but also from the infusion of habitual or sanctifying grace. Rahner's position has been described in this way: "When the human spirit, elevated by the supernatural existential, makes its loving surrender to the Horizon of its world, man receives the justifying grace of Christ."[64]

In the churches that have their source in Protestant revivalism the doctrine of justification by imputed righteousness has been gravely compromised. For the Quaker theologian Robert Barclay the formal cause of justification is the formation of Christ in the soul. While Methodists and Arminians in general ascribe the remission of sins to the suffering and death of Christ, they tend to regard one's own personal obedience as the only ground of future hope.

Among the cults the doctrine of the free gift of salvation, and particularly the idea of the imputation of Christ's righteousness, has been downplayed if not totally rejected. In Mormonism salvation from death is by God's grace only, but salvation understood as entrance into the kingdom of God (exaltation) is dependent on the keeping of laws and ordinances. Mormon scholar Bruce McConkie declares: "There are some serious sins for which the cleansing blood of Christ does not operate, and the law of God is that men must have their own blood shed to atone for their sins."[65] In Spiritualism grace is given only to those who help themselves by exercising moral effort.[66] According to Mary Baker Eddy, founder of Christian Science, "One sacrifice, however great, is insufficient to pay the debt of sin."[67] The Unification Church of Sun Myung Moon teaches the indemnity principle, also called the law of restitution, in which man must fulfill his moral obligations before he wins the favor of God. In the Bahai sect it is only by the practice of the principles laid down by Baha'u'llah and "by making every effort through prayer and personal sacrifice to live in accord with the character of the divine being revealed in him" that we "can arrive at eventual salvation."[68]

As we turn to the great world religions, again we see an unbridgeable gulf between their views and the evangelical doctrine. In Judaism salvation is not a free gift but a prize which one procures with the assistance of God. "Man is an active participant in the redemptive process," says Jewish theologian Byron L. Sherwin, and "with God's help he redeems himself and the Divine presence in the world."[69] When the noted Rabbi Yochanan ben Zakkai heard of the destruction of the temple by the Roman legions in 70 A.D., he consoled Israel with these words: "We have a means of atonement as effective as the Temple: it is doing deeds of loving kindness."[70]

In Hinduism, Buddhism, and Jainism one is saved only by working out one's karma, and grace is the reward for effort well done. Salvation consists not in the forgiveness of sins but in escape from the cycle of rebirth. In Christianity we are justified so long as we have faith in Jesus Christ, even though we cannot undo the wrongs of the past. It is Christ who has reaped what all sinners have sown, and we shall reap what he has sown through the miracle of faith. The law of sowing and reaping still applies even in the new life of the Christian, but the believer reaps beyond what he sows because of the grace of God. In the parable of the laborers in the vineyard (Matt. 20:1–16) the late ones receive the very same wages as the others.

While the idea of divine grace is not absent in Hinduism and Buddhism, it is given a radically different meaning from that of the New Testament. According to Emil Brunner what is meant by grace in the Hindu bhakti religion of India is simply "the expansion of the human self and its submersion in the divine." There is no recognition of the infinite gulf between man and God and nothing about the forgiveness of sin. There is "no redemption from something which lies as an obstacle between God and man. The whole process means merely a supplementing, a perfecting of man's condition."[71]

In Islam, despite the high place accorded to the doctrine of predestination (interpreted in almost fatalistic terms), the essence of religion is seen to be repenting for sin, purging the heart of all but God, and attaining a virtuous character by the exercises of religion. Of priceless value for the ensuring of one's salvation are the "Five Pillars" of faith: the recital of the creed, ritual prayer, fasting, almsgiving, and the religious pilgrimage. Unless one performs these duties and sacrifices from the heart and with the right attitude of mind, he cannot hope to escape punishment on the last day. Along with the demand for faith, understood as unconditional submission to the will of Allah, a works-righteousness looms highly significant in this religion and clearly sets it off from biblical Christianity with its emphasis on grace that goes out to the undeserving.[72]

One danger in the doctrine of free salvation is to conceive of salvation as wholly extrinsic; then we become spectators in a drama that takes place entirely outside our experience. The opposite danger is to regard salvation primarily as an inner process within the soul. Salvation understood as justification is basically extrinsic and forensic, but it must take root in man's being in order to be effective. Its foundation and pivotal center lie outside ourselves in the perfect righteousness of Jesus Christ. Yet salvation must be realized within us by his Holy Spirit if we are to be justified and sanctified de facto.[73]

James Buchanan astutely comments: "The work of the Holy Spirit is as necessary for our Justification as the work of Christ Himself; but it is not necessary for the same reasons, nor is it effectual for the same ends."[74] Christ alone removes the guilt and punishment of sin. The Spirit's task is to persuade us to "receive and rest on Christ alone for salvation as He is freely offered to us in the Gospel."[75] In uniting us with Christ, the Spirit at the same time delivers us from the power and practice of sin.

We can say that salvation takes place in two stages: the doing and dying of Jesus and the sending forth of the Spirit. The latter is more than just the application of the salvation of Christ: it is salvific activity too. Yet the regenerating and sanctifying work of the Spirit is not the basis of the justifying work of God in Christ, but is the result and evidence of our justification and election. At the same time we would

not be effectively justified unless we were engrafted into the righteousness of Christ by the Holy Spirit in faith. Faith is an instrumental cause
of our justification, but not its meritorious condition. It is the means by
which justification is made concrete and effective in our lives.

Salvation is correlative with faith, but faith is not equal to salvation. Salvation has to do first and foremost with what Christ accomplished for us in his sacrificial life and death. Salvation is the remission
of sins procured for us through the atoning death and resurrection of
our Lord. Everything regarding our salvation has been done on our
behalf in Jesus Christ. Yet we must appropriate and receive this if we
are to benefit from it. It has been done *for* us but not yet *in* us. Faith
is necessary to lay hold of the perfect righteousness of Christ.

Because the atoning sacrifice of Christ is complete, our hope is not
something precarious about which we need always be anxious. Indeed,
our glorification has its basis not in the progress of our personal sanctification but in the justification and sanctification accomplished for us
in Christ. By trusting not in our efforts at sanctification but solely in
the merits of Jesus Christ, we attest the reality of our present sanctification as well as our justification. By holding to the faith once delivered
to the saints, we have the assurance that the crown of righteousness
will be granted to us on the last day (2 Tim. 4:8). Those whom he
justified he will also glorify (Rom. 8:30; Phil. 1:6). Moreover, the final
judgment is simply the confirmation and unveiling of our justification
already accomplished and assured through faith in the merits of Jesus
Christ. The thief on the cross was promised glory in paradise simply by
his confession of faith, even though he had not made personal progress
in sanctification. Our sanctification nonetheless prepares us to receive
and appreciate the glory of the eternal future.[76] It is a reflection and
evidence of our justification as well as an anticipation of our glorification.

Though our hope contains the certainty of our future salvation, we
must not become complacent. If we do not continue in the faith, we may
well fall away from it. Fully aware of our weakness, we must endeavor
to trust Christ more fully and serve him more diligently.

It is commonly thought that God is active in our justification and
salvation, and man is passive, since his obligation is only to receive
what has been done for him. Yet this is only part of the truth. Once
grace comes to a person, he is made active in accepting and believing.
Jonathan Edwards perceived the paradox that God's work is accomplished in and through man's activity: "In the Scriptures the same
things are represented as from God and from us. God is said to convert,

and men are said to convert and turn. God makes a new heart, and we are commanded to make us a new heart."[77] Edwards was not returning to the medieval view of basing justification on the infusion of habitual or sanctifying grace in the soul, but he was seeking to recover the biblical truth that justification is effectively applied only in that person who rouses himself from his stupor and lays hold of the fruits of Christ's sacrifice. When grace invades our life, we are not reduced to powerlessness but empowered to believe and obey. We are dead in sin before the incursion of justifying grace, but we are made alive through faith as the Holy Spirit works upon us and in us (Eph. 2:1–8).

INWARD RELIGION

Evangelical religion emphasizes the inward over the outward, though it does not dispense with the latter as does radical mysticism or spiritualism. It is a religion of Gospel, not Law, though it still makes a place for the Law as a guideline for the Christian life. It believes that personal transformation takes priority over social reformation, though it strongly supports efforts toward a more just or equitable society.

Evangelicalism sees the root of man's misery in inward sin, not in external transgressions of known laws. Sin is a contagion that infects every part of man's being; though in itself it is invisible, it has visible fruits and symptoms. No ascetic discipline or human technique can enable one to overcome the sin within. The answer to sin lies in a new birth, not in a new code of behavior.

The new birth itself signifies an inward change, brought about by the invisible work of the Holy Spirit. Evangelical faith resists all attempts to equate the new birth with any external rite such as baptism, though it regards baptism as the sign of the new birth and, when related to the Holy Spirit and the Word of God, a sign with efficacy. Ralph Martin, lay Catholic theologian, manifests a genuinely evangelical concern when he complains:

In the lives of many Christians today, baptism, the new circumcision, functions as the old circumcision did then: as little more than a cultural artifact. Only too often, baptism means nothing in practical terms for the way a person lives his life or for the attitude of his heart and mind towards God. Too many of those who call themselves Christian because of baptism have in fact never experienced the living relationship with Jesus Christ and his Church that baptism is intended to initiate.[78]

While recognizing the place for the cultus and the institution, evangelical religion insists that faith is contingent not on the rites of the church but only on the outpouring of the Spirit, which takes place in the church to be sure but often in spite of the church's ministrations. Forsyth vigorously contends that our faith does not rest on the church, "for Christianity is an absolutely personal faith. That is to say, we are judged and saved eternally—not by our relation to the Church but by our relation to Christ the Redeemer."[79] That the church is nevertheless highly important as an instrument of Jesus Christ in his converting and sanctifying work no evangelical will deny. The church plays a crucial role in our salvation insofar as it witnesses to and directs us to Jesus Christ, the only Savior.

Likewise evangelical religion upholds worship that is done in spirit and in truth (John 4:24). It disdains sacramentalism and ceremonialism, the processions and pageantry associated with ritualistic religion, whether Christian or non-Christian, since true worship is inward and concerns the interior relationship between Christ and the believer.[80] True prayer is the outpouring of the heart before God, not vain repetition of certain prescribed phrases.[81] The temple of God is no longer a building made with hands but wherever two or three are gathered in the name of Christ.

James Packer rightly holds that the true church must not be identified with external forms:

Evangelicals decline to view the Church as either a voluntary human association, like a club which Christians are free to join or not to join, as they wish, or as a divinely accredited institution for dispensing saving sacraments, like an embassy dispensing valid visas. The Church is believing people in fellowship with Christ, and in Christ with each other.[82]

The primary concern of the evangelical church is with the meaning of the Gospel for the situation today, not with the question of the valid ministry and its form. In the Protestant conception it is the word and not the ministry that is "an effective means of salvation." This is not to regard the question of the ministry as inconsequential, but it does mean that the ministry must always be seen as serving the Gospel and not vice versa. It is the Gospel that creates and empowers the ministry; the ministry does not authenticate the Gospel.

Faith itself is something inward, invisible, and must not be reduced to a particular experience or confused with the outward belief in certain historical facts or truths. Rationalistic orthodoxy has often obscured this inward character of faith by emphasizing assent to right doctrine over an interior or personal relationship with Jesus Christ as

Lord and Savior. Luther, in particular, stressed the inward character of faith and the tension between faith, on the one hand, and reason and experience, on the other.

Faith directs itself towards the things that are invisible. Indeed, only when that which is believed on is hidden, can it provide an opportunity for faith. And moreover, those things are most deeply hidden which most clearly contradict the obvious experience of the senses. Therefore, when God makes alive, He kills; when He justifies, He imposes guilt; when He leads us to heaven, He thrusts us down into hell.[83]

Not only the Christian life but theology too must be grounded in the inwardness of faith, even though its object is a divine revelation given in history. Yet this revelation can only be grasped by the inwardness of faith, and apart from this subjective dimension the objective data have little meaning or value. Too often theology focuses upon eternal or objective truths such as predestination or justification without seeing how these are related to the decision and life of faith. Calvin himself vigorously affirmed predestination, but he understood this doctrine primarily in the light of faith in Jesus Christ. One interpreter observes that Calvin's orientation "definitely was from faith to predestination."[84] But in later Reformed orthodoxy, "this was reversed. One moved from predestination to other problems, including that of faith. Whereas faith had once been the foundation of predestination, now predestination was the basis of faith."[85]

The cruciality of faith in the knowledge of salvation was staunchly upheld by Wesley: "None can love God, unless he believe in Christ; unless he have redemption through His blood, and the Spirit of God bearing witness with his spirit that he is a child of God. Faith, therefore, is still the root of all, of present as well as future salvation."[86]

We must avoid both a sterile objectivism and an anarchic subjectivism. We must affirm the objectivity of both revelation and salvation while at the same time recognizing that both of these have a subjective pole or dimension. The stress in evangelicalism on inward religion does not mean a flight from objectivity, but it does mean an awareness that objective truth has no efficacy or power unless it takes root in the heart of man, unless it is grasped in the passion of inwardness (Kierkegaard). The authority of the Gospel is not simply external but internal as well, since it creates within the subject a willingness to believe and obey. Word and Spirit go together, and whenever we lose sight of their inseparable unity, we lapse into either moralism and rationalism on the one hand, or mysticism and spiritualism on the other.

NOTES

1. See Geoffrey J. Paxton, *The Shaking of Adventism* (Wilmington, Del.: Zenith Publishers, 1977). An in-depth appraisal of Paxton's position is given in the avant garde Adventist magazine *Spectrum* Vol. 9, No. 3 (July, 1978). For a stalwart defense of the Reformation understanding of justification by a Seventh-day Adventist scholar see Raoul Dederen, "What Does God's Grace Do?," *Ministry*, vol. 51, no. 3 (March 1978) pp. 4–7.

2. Karl Barth, *Church Dogmatics* II, 2, pp. 16, 17.

3. *Ibid.*, pp. 60 ff.

4. *Ibid.*, p. 534.

5. James W. Woelfel, "Life After Death: Faith or Knowledge,?" *The Christian Century*, vol. 93, no. 23 (July 7–14, 1976), [pp. 632–633], p. 632.

6. Evangelical piety is discernible in such luminaries of Orthodoxy as Archbishop Lucaris (seventeenth century) and Russian Orthodox bishop Tikhon of Zadonsk, who had a marked influence on Dostoevsky. One interpreter comments: "St. Tikhon was quite alien to post-Tridentine Catholicism. . . . The Hesychast spirituality of St. Nilus of Sora is equally absent from his works. St. Tikhon's spirituality may be best termed evangelical. It is exclusively based on the Scriptures. References to the Fathers and mystics are rare. The evangelicalism of St. Tikhon is not Protestant but there was in him, nevertheless, some warm sympathy for German pietists and English evangelicals." Sergius Bolshakoff, *Russian Mystics* (Kalamazoo, Mich.: Cistercian Publications, 1977), p. 69.

7. Adolf Harnack, *What Is Christianity?*, trans. Thomas Bailey Saunders (New York: Harper & Row, 1957).

8. Cited in *Christianity Today*, vol. 20, no. 6 (December 19, 1975), p. 21.

9. In this respect evangelicalism excludes unitarian Pentecostals, Christadelphians, the Children of God, and Jehovah's Witnesses, as well as all deists.

10. G. C. Berkouwer, *Holy Scripture*, trans. Jack Rogers (Grand Rapids: Eerdmans, 1975), p. 180.

11. Eberhard Busch, *Karl Barth*, p. 100.

12. Carl Rogers, *On Becoming a Person* (Boston: Houghton Mifflin, 1961), p. 23.

13. Langdon Gilkey, "Dissolution and Reconstruction in Theology," *The Christian Century*, vol. 82, no. 5 (February 3, 1965), [pp. 135–139] p. 137.

14. John Calvin, *Golden Booklet of the True Christian Life*, p. 22.

15. Quoted in Wilhelm Niesel, *The Gospel and the Churches*, trans. David Lewis (Philadelphia: Westminster Press, 1962), p. 124.

16. Quoted in Rudolf Ehrlich, *Rome Opponent or Partner?* (Philadelphia: Westminster Press, 1965), p. 285.

17. Kilian McDonnell contends that the Word "does not receive its authority from the church" and that the church "is no more free to tamper with the truth or the proclamation of the Word than she is free to tamper with the realities of the sacraments." In his *John Calvin, the Church, and the Eucharist* (Princeton, N.J.: Princeton University Press, 1967), p. 360.

18. S. Radhakrishnan, *Eastern Religions and Western Thought*, 2nd ed. (London: Oxford University Press, 1940), p. 21. It should be noted that Rad-

hakrishnan does not urge Christian missionaries to cease preaching that Jesus is the way to salvation, since they would then not be true to the ruling norm of their own tradition, the Bible. He does ask missionaries to preach their message in a spirit of love.

19. Reinhold Niebuhr, *Beyond Tragedy,* p. 44.

20. John Meyendorff, *St. Gregory Palamas and Orthodox Spirituality* (Tuckahoe, N.Y.: St. Vladimir's Seminary Press, 1974), p. 126.

21. John Macquarrie, *Thinking About God* (New York: Harper & Row, 1975), p. 106.

22. Karl Jaspers, *Anaximander, Heraclitus, Parmenides, Plotinus, Lao-Tzu, Nagarjuna,* ed. Hannah Arendt (New York: Harcourt Brace Jovanovich, Harvest Books, 1974), p. 92.

23. Alan Watts, *Behold the Spirit* (New York: Vintage Books, 1971), p. xviii.

24. *National Catholic Reporter,* vol. 11, no. 139 (September 5, 1975), p. 6.

25. See Donald Bloesch, *Essentials of Evangelical Theology,* vol. I, pp. 94, 102, 103.

26. Cited in Eugene TeSelle, *Augustine the Theologian* (New York: Herder & Herder, 1970), p. 286.

27. R. R. Palmer, *Catholics and Unbelievers in Eighteenth Century France* (New York: Cooper Square Publishers, 1961), p. 36.

28. Cited in H. R. Mackintosh, *Types of Modern Theology,* reprinted. (London: Nisbet & Co, 1949), p. 132.

29. Adolf Harnack, *What Is Christianity?,* p. 150.

30. Immanuel Kant, *Religion Within the Limits of Reason Alone,* trans. Theodore M. Greene and Hoyt H. Hudson (New York: Harper & Row, 1960), p. 108.

31. Rosemary Ruether, *Liberation Theology* (New York: Paulist Press, 1972), p. 22.

32. Ralph Martin, *Unless the Lord build the house. . . .* (Notre Dame, Indiana: Ave Maria Press, 1972), p. 43.

33. Abraham Heschel, in Charles Kegley and Robert Bretall, eds., *Reinhold Niebuhr: His Religious, Social, and Political Thought* (New York: Macmillan, 1956), p. 408.

34. A. James Rudin, "A Jewish View of Jesus," *New World Outlook,* vol. 34, no. 11 (July–August 1974), [pp. 30–32], p. 32.

35. See D. Howard Smith, *Chinese Religions* (New York: Holt, Rinehart and Winston, 1968), pp. 48–54. Also see John B. Noss, *Man's Religions* (New York: Macmillan, 1945), pp. 379–383.

36. In Pat Means, *The Mystical Maze* (Campus Crusade for Christ, 1976), p. 232.

37. D. T. Suzuki, *Mysticism: Christian and Buddhist* (New York: Harper & Row, Perennial Library ed., 1971), p. 153.

38. *Ibid,* p. 149.

39. R. C. Zaehner, *Concordant Discord* (Oxford: Clarendon Press, 1970), p. 437.

40. Among those who adhere to a "Christology from below" are Karl Rahner, Schoonenberg, J.A.T. Robinson, Schillebeeckx, Hans Küng and John Hick.

41. Walter Kasper, *Jesus the Christ,* trans. V. Green (New York: Paulist Press, 1976), pp. 237, 238. Interestingly, Kasper censures Karl Rahner for accommodating the faith to an over-optimistic evolutionary world view. Kasper's ontology is a modified version of the Hegelian concept of being as a historical process of coming to be.

42. Roy J. Deferrari, trans., *Saint Ambrose: Theological and Dogmatic Works* (Washington, D.C.: Catholic University of America Press, 1963), p. 233.

43. P. T. Forsyth, *God the Holy Father* (London: Independent Press, 1957), p. 131.

44. *Meditations of Maharishi Mahesh Yogi* (New York: Bantam Books, 1973), p. 123.

45. D. T. Suzuki, *Mysticism: Christian and Buddhist,* p. 145.

46. R. C. Zaehner, *Concordant Discord,* p. 364. We must not deny to Buddhism or other great world religions any valid insights whatsoever into the human condition. What the Reformed tradition has termed the "common grace" of God, or the general working of the Spirit among people of all religions and cultures, must be duly acknowledged. Zaehner's incisive but somewhat harsh critique of Buddhism must be balanced by Moltmann's call to appreciation: "The meditative power of Buddhism, its insight into the self and man's inner freedom brings back to light repressed mystical elements in the Christian faith, and can lead Christians to reexamine their modern activism." Moltmann, *The Church in the Power of the Spirit,* p. 160. We see the Christian revelation not only in terms of the negation of the world religions but also in terms of the fulfillment of the fundamental needs and aspirations that have given rise to these religions.

A helpful book that pinpoints areas of tension between Buddhism and Christianity from a biblical perspective is Douglas A. Fox, *Buddhism, Christianity, and the Future of Man* (Philadelphia: Westminster Press, 1972). The life and significance of Gautama Buddha are treated with sensitivity and qualified appreciation in B. H. Streeter, *The Buddha and the Christ* (London: Macmillan, 1932). For an equally erudite and still more sympathetic study see Richard Drummond, *Gautama the Buddha* (Grand Rapids: Eerdmans, 1974). A more cautious appraisal is given by Russell Aldwinckle, who underlines the points of contrast between Buddhism and biblical Christianity in *More Than Man* (Grand Rapids: Eerdmans, 1976), pp. 211–246. We encourage evangelicals to acquaint themselves with various perspectives on the world religions without surrendering the distinctive claims of the Christian faith.

47. Philip Kapleau, *The Three Pillars of Zen* (New York: Harper & Row, 1966), p. 59. The quotation is from the Zen Buddhist scholar Yasutani-Roshi.

48. See Nirmal Kumar Bose, *Selections From Gandhi* (Ahmedabad, India: Navajivan Press, 1968), pp. 254 ff. Similarly, Gandhi declares: "I believe in the Bible as I believe in the Gītā. I regard all the great faiths of the world as equally true with my own." Cited in Radhakrishnan, *Eastern Religions and Western Thought,* p. 313. For a positive but not uncritical appraisal of Gandhi's life and thought by a scholar whose evangelical credentials are unassailable, see E. Stanley Jones, *Mahatma Gandhi* (Nashville: Abingdon, 1948).

49. Gerald Heard, in Christopher Isherwood, ed., *Vedanta For the Western World* (New York: Viking Press, 1945), p. 297.

50. Cited by Bernhard W. Anderson in "Herberg as Theologian of Christianity," *The National Review* vol. 29, no. 30 (August 5, 1977), [pp. 884, 885], p. 884.

51. P. T. Forsyth, *Congregationalism and Reunion* (London: Independent Press, 1952), p. 20.

52. Benjamin B. Warfield, "Justification by Faith—Out of Date?," *Present Truth*, vol. 4, no. 4 (August 1975), p. 9.

53. Theodore G. Tappert, ed. and trans., *The Book of Concord* (Philadelphia: Fortress Press, 1959), p. 544.

54. Karl Barth, *Church Dogmatics* I, 2, p. 308.

55. James Buchanan, *The Doctrine of Justification* (Grand Rapids: Baker Book House, 1955).

56. In *Ibid.*, p. 85.

57. In *Ibid.*, p. 96.

58. In *Ibid.*, p. 97.

59. In Wilhelm Niesel, *The Gospel and the Churches*, p. 141.

60. William Johnston, ed., *The Cloud of Unknowing and the Book of Privy Counseling* (Garden City, N.Y.: Doubleday, 1973), p. 82.

61. Karl Barth, *Church Dogmatics* IV, 2, p. 498.

62. Rudolf Ehrlich, *Rome—Opponent or Partner?*, p. 88.

63. On Ehrlich's criticisms of Küng's position see *Ibid.*, pp. 187, 188.

64. Gerald A. McCool, ed., *A Rahner Reader* (New York: Seabury Press, 1975), p. 211. Note that for Rahner faith must be fulfilled in "justifying and sanctifying love." K. Rahner, *Foundations of Christian Faith*, trans. William V. Dych (New York: Seabury, 1978), p. 361.

65. Bruce McConkie, *Mormon Doctrine* (Bookcraft, 1958), p. 87.

66. Ruth Mattson Taylor records this message transmitted through a medium: "The old teachings that 'as you strive, so you'll be helped' are right. The Lord helps those who help themselves." In her *Witness From Beyond* (New York: Hawthorn Books, 1975), p. 54.

67. Mary Baker Eddy, *Science and Health with Key to the Scriptures* (Boston: First Church of Christ Scientist, 1932), p. 473.

68. "An Interview with a Bahai Teacher." In Walter R. Martin, *The Kingdom of the Cults* (Grand Rapids: Zondervan, 1965), p. 256.

69. Byron L. Sherwin, "A Jewish Perspective: Individual and Community in Stress," *The Chicago Theological Seminary Register*, vol. 64, no. 3 (Fall 1974), [pp. 3–19], p. 18.

70. Cited in Richard L. Rubenstein, *Power Struggle* (New York: Charles Scribner's Sons, 1974), p. 172.

71. Emil Brunner, *The Scandal of Christianity* (Philadelphia: Westminster Press, 1951), p. 21.

72. The precise relation of faith and works is not always clear in Islamic writings. A works-righteousness is conspicuous in this statement of Ibn 'Umar's: "There are three [necessary things] of which should a man have two but not have the third [his religion] will not be acceptable. [These three are] prayer, fasting, and the washing oneself pure from that which makes legally impure." Arthur Jeffery, *Islam* (New York: Liberal Arts Press, 1958), p. 83. The strength of the Moslem religion is that it relates the faith to the whole of life and therefore reminds us that faith can never be separated from works.

One danger is that faith itself tends to become a virtuous work, for it is conceived primarily as an act of assent and submission. For a helpful discussion of the Moslem position on faith and works in relationship to salvation see J. Windrow Sweetman, *Islam and Christian Theology*, Part One, vol. 2 (London: Lutterworth Press, 1947), pp. 203–213.

73. Our position is fairly close to that of Mercersburg theologian John Nevin in this regard. While he did not wish to confound justification and sanctification, he nonetheless maintained that justification must take root within us: "This justification, to become ours in fact, must insert us into Christ's life. It reaches us from abroad—the 'act of God's free grace'; but *as* God's act, it is necessarily more than a mere declaration or form of thought. It makes us to be in fact, what it accounts us to be, *in Christ.* The ground of our justification is a righteousness that *was* foreign to us before, but is *now* made to lodge itself in the inmost constitution of our being." John Nevin, *The Mystical Presence* (Philadelphia: United Church Press, 1966), p. 179. We would argue that justifying righteousness even when it takes root within us is still the alien righteousness of Christ—the ground of our personal holiness but not identical with it.

74. James Buchanan, *The Doctrine of Justification*, p. 392.

75. *Ibid.*, p. 398.

76. Another way to phrase this is that the cross we bear does not procure the crown of salvation; only the cross of Christ does that. But our cross prepares us to accept and cherish the crown.

77. Jonathan Edwards, *Works*, vol. 2, ed. Edward Hickman, 2 vols. (London: 1879), p. 557.

78. Ralph Martin, *Fire on the Earth*, (Ann Arbor, Mich.: Word of Life, 1975), p. 15.

79. P. T. Forsyth, *The Principle of Authority* (London: Independent Press, 1952), p. 317.

80. Cf. Moltmann: "This fullness of the Spirit ought not to be smothered by established and regimented forms of worship." Moltmann, *The Church in the Power of the Spirit*, p. 112. Moltmann goes too far when he denies any significant place for office and structure in the New Testament church.

81. The mantras of Hinduism as well as the strictly prescribed ritual of stances, genuflexions, and prostrations in Islam are alien to evangelical, biblical spirituality.

82. In John C. King, ed., *Evangelicals Today* (London: Lutterworth, 1973), p. 23.

83. Cited in Karl Barth, *The Epistle to the Romans*, trans. Edwyn C. Hoskyns, 6th ed. (London: Oxford University Press, 1933), p. 39.

84. John Dillenberger and Claude Welch, *Protestant Christianity* (New York: Charles Scribner's Sons, 1954), p. 91.

85. *Ibid.*

86. *John Wesley's Forty-Four Sermons*, 12th ed. (London: Epworth Press, 1975), p. 350.

XI.
TOWARD THE RECOVERY
OF BIBLICAL FAITH

And he said to me, "Son of man, can these bones live?" And I answered,
"O Lord God, thou knowest."

Ezekiel 37:3

A childish orthodoxy, a pusillanimous Bible interpretation, a foolish and
unchristian defense of Christianity, a bad conscience on the part of the
defenders with respect to their own relation to it, all this has in our
time its share in occasioning passionate and frantic attacks upon
Christianity.

Søren Kierkegaard

I think a great many of us would be agreed that part of the poverty
and weakness of the Church at the present moment is due to the fact
that edification has been pursued to the neglect of instruction. We have
been a little too prone to dwell upon the simple side of the gospel.

P. T. Forsyth

How has the Christian world been divided and its peace destroyed by
the adoption of the names and tenets of particular ministers as the
badges of different parties in the Church: I am of Calvin, and I of
Arminius, and I of Luther. Would to God that it had been always
remembered that Christians are of Christ alone.

John Venn

What we need is . . . a spiritual Reformation and thus a conversion
of Christians and of the Christian churches themselves—a conversion to
the truth of their own message.

Karl Barth

THE OUTLOOK FOR EVANGELICALISM

That there is a renewed interest in evangelicalism today no compe-
tent observer would deny. Whether we are actually entering upon an
evangelical renaissance is another question. My position is that the
present situation holds much promise for evangelicalism, but at the

same time there are accumulating shadows on the horizon that bode ill for genuine biblical revival.

One of the continuing banes of modern evangelicalism is a biblical literalism and obscurantism which effectively nullify the solid gains in biblical-historical research over the past several decades. The first eleven chapters of Genesis, for example, are integrally related to objective history, but most scholars agree that the literary genre of this material reveals that large sections of it are mythopoetic. Though we can say that the event of the fall happened in objective space and time, many of the details of the story are indubitably symbolic. This does not imply that it is any less inspired than those sections of the Bible that give us exact history, but it does mean that unless we become somewhat more sophisticated in our exegesis, we will be erecting for our contemporaries false stumbling blocks to faith. If we take the genealogies in the Old Testament as literal chronologies, we will have to opt for a recent date for the creation of the world and man (5000–4000 B.C.?), and we will then have to resort to spurious science to support our allegations. This is not to say that current science supplies the norm for settling these issues, for this would make scientific rationality the criterion for truth. It does mean that if we use science, we must do so honestly, and much of contemporary evangelical apologetics in this area is dishonest.

Again, we must be alert to the worldliness within evangelicalism, especially when it comes in the guise of religiosity.[1] Notwithstanding the allurements of the positive thinking cult, we should not seek to use the Gospel to gain the goods of life or to find self-fulfillment. We must be cognizant of the incontrovertible chasm between the values of the world and the transcendent Word of God. To equate happiness as the world knows it and the blessedness of the kingdom is inadmissible. We must not lose sight of the tragic dimension of life even though Christianity transcends tragedy. The ineradicable gulf between Christian faith and culture-religion is underlined by Luther: "For that is the highest thing that men want, to have joy and happiness and to be without trouble. Now Christ turns the page and says exactly the opposite; He calls 'blessed' those who sorrow and mourn."[2]

Another pitfall that evangelicals must strive to avoid is parochialism, which can be just as damaging as eclecticism. This refers to the inveterate tendency to interpret God and the world through the lens of one's own cultural and religious background and to reject insights that seem to call into question the particular tradition in which one stands. Parochialism is manifest in those persons who seek to be more Calvinistic than Calvin or more Lutheran than Luther or more Wesleyan than Wesley. It is evident too in conservative Christianity's current fascination with the details of biblical prophecy. "Such activity," one critic aptly observes, "is part of a defensive, separationist mentality that removes itself from modern life culturally (by its blue laws) and temporally (by its prophetic mania)."[3] Parochialism is associated with a hyperorthodoxy and sectarianism that exclude from Christian fellowship those who do not subscribe to the particular tenets of the party in question. It is well to remember that the luminaries of evangelical history have almost unanimously sought to transcend a narrow parochialism for an ecumenical vision, and this includes Calvin, Zinzendorf, Wesley, Spener, and Edwards.

Experientialism is another temptation to which evangelicals seem particularly vulnerable in our time. The search for extraordinary signs of the gift of the Spirit is one obvious example, but in the less charismatic churches there is also a yearning for transforming experiences, and the objective work of Christ on the cross recedes into the background. One reason why modern evangelicalism has produced so little systematic theology is that experience is valued more highly than theology, and soul-winning is regarded more laudable than intellectual endeavor. Theology must not be rejected in favor of either practical piety or devout mysticism (Gordon Rupp).

Finally, we need again to call into question the bent toward rationalism in current evangelicalism. Carl Henry argues that the truth of revelation can be known prior to commitment to Christ, otherwise people would not be culpable for its rejection.[4] In John Warwick Montgomery's schema Christianity can be objectively validated by the historical method alone.[5] Norman Geisler, in his *Philosophy of Religion,* seeks to state the case for belief in God without ever once appealing to divine revelation. For him, it seems, rational verification is the presupposition of faith as well as its necessary preparation.[6] Francis Schaeffer contends that one does not believe until one examines the evidence and is satisfied intellectually that the claims of faith are true.[7]

Many evangelicals are currently attracted to Pannenberg's theology, which gives reason a creative role prior to faith. According to Pannenberg the Spirit enables one to believe what reason can already know. The meaning of revelation can be comprehended by reason alone, but the commitment to revelation is not possible apart from the work of the Spirit. By contrast, we hold that the Spirit must give to man the divinely-intended meaning of Scripture so that he can make an intelligent commitment.

Our position is that revelation is not at the disposal of reason and is never a logical conclusion of human thought. The outsider can arrive at a limited understanding of the biblical proposition by examining its literary and historical context. But he invariably misunderstands the divine intent of this proposition. Historical understanding and perception of theological significance are two different things. While reason can grasp the historical side of revelation, only faith can perceive the revelatory side of history (Paul Althaus).

In the tradition emanating from Protestant scholastic orthodoxy and the Princeton School of theology, systematic theology is simply the coordinating and harmonizing of the axioms of Scripture, which are self-evident as well as clear and distinct (cf. Descartes). The method of Gordon Clark and Carl Henry is deductive, deriving conclusions from given rational principles. The method of Charles Hodge is inductive, arriving at general principles by systematizing the historical data in the Bible. In this general tradition a high confidence is placed in the capacity of reason to judge the truth of revelation.[8]

In our view the concrete reality from which theological concepts are derived is the irreversible and incomparable act of God in Jesus Christ. Insofar as Scripture participates in this act, Scripture too is a primary and indispensable source for theological work. The task of theology is to ascertain how the text of Scripture is related to the material norm, the revelation of God's love and judgment in Jesus Christ. Our goal is not to think the right thoughts and statements (as in Gordon Clark) but to think realities through thoughts and statements. Because the reality of Jesus Christ is more than rational, we can only approximate this transcendent truth in our conceptualization and verbalization. The judgments and operations of God are "inscrutable" and "mysterious" even to the believer (Rom. 11:33), and therefore our theological systems will forever be imperfect and rudimentary, as Thomas Aquinas also recognized. This does not mean that some theologies are not superior to others, but it does mean that even the most ingenious theological system falls drastically short of the existential system which is in the mind of God. We *intend* the truth in our theological statements, but we do not *possess* the truth, since reason is always the servant and never the master or determiner of revelation.

The knowledge of faith is not an empirical objectifying knowledge but a knowledge in which we are lifted above reason and sense into communion with the living God (Luther). Faith must believe against human thought, feeling, and perception, since reason admits the validity only of that which can be perceived or conceived.[9] We do not discount the salutary role of historical investigation and criticism, but the positiveness of historical knowledge is illusory. Historical research can show the historical probability of certain events happening, but it can give only approximate, not final, certainty. The ground of certainty is not what reason can show or prove but what faith grasps and knows as the human subject is acted upon by the Holy Spirit in conjunction with the reading or hearing of the biblical word. Yet a living faith is not possible apart from hard thinking concerning the promises and claims of Scripture.

In seeking understanding, faith must be on guard against making its cardinal doctrines too clear and distinct (à la Descartes), since this serves to undercut or deny the mystery in revelation. Richard Hooker has aptly remarked: "Heresy is more plain than true whereas right belief is more true than plain." Heresy tries to overcome the tensions and paradoxes in Christian faith by overemphasizing one side of the Gospel or reducing the Gospel to what is logically explicable. Orthodoxy, on the other hand, feels the pull of the opposites, but keeps them from flying apart and thereby keeps them true (G. K. Chesterton).

THE NEED TO REAPPRAISE BIBLICAL AUTHORITY

Biblical faith cannot be recovered until we recognize anew the divine authority and inspiration of the Bible. This authority has been eroded both by higher critics who read into Scripture a naturalistic philosophy, which a priori rules out the supernatural, and by its uncritical devotees, who absolutize the outmoded world view reflected in the Bible and thereby render the biblical witness incredible.[10]

The crisis in biblical authority has recently come to a head with the concerted attempts of liberal spokesmen in the mainline denominations to reconceive homosexuality as a viable alternative life style and to approve the ordination of avowed, practicing homosexuals despite the clear witness of Holy Scripture that sexual perversion is morally reprehensible in the sight of God. Proponents of a more relaxed position on this question argue that the biblical strictures against homosexuality are a product of the mores of the culture of that time and cannot be considered binding upon man in the twentieth century. It is also asserted that through the knowledge gained in the social sciences God is speaking a new word in our time that fulfills and even supersedes his revelation to peoples in another era and in a supposedly more primitive culture. This, in effect, denies the divine authority and normativeness of biblical teaching.

As we seek to reaffirm biblical authority, however, there is a need to reinterpret this authority, particularly in light of the present-day impasse in evangelicalism on this question. Rightly understood, infallibility and inerrancy can indeed be posited of the Bible, but wrongly understood, these ideas can create division and confusion. Unfortunately, a great number of inerrancy advocates today want a rationally guaranteed authority, but this makes reason, not revelation, the final criterion. Paul Holmer astutely comments: "Inerrant Scripture gets to be an epistemic crutch, a pseudo-certainty, which while it purports to push doubt away, also inserts a humanly devised conceptual scheme by which to get the Scriptures to disclose the Almighty."[11]

We go astray if we base the authority of Scripture on the inerrancy of the writing and then try to demonstrate this according to the canons of scientific rationality. The authority of the Bible is based on the One whom it attests and the One who speaks through it in every age with the word of regenerating power. We here concur with Calvin: "The highest proof of Scripture derives in general from the fact that God in person speaks in it."[12] This by no means implies that the biblical witness is fallible or untrustworthy. Instead, we hold that this witness does not carry the force of infallible authority apart from the Holy Spirit who acts in and through it. Whenever the Bible functions as the sword of the Spirit in the community of believers, it wields indisputable divine authority in all areas pertaining to faith and practice.

It is possible to discern three basic approaches to Scripture in the history of the church. The first is the sacramental, which sees revelation essentially as God in action and regards Scripture as the primary channel or medium of revelation. Here Scripture is thought to have two sides, the divine and the human, and the human is the instrumentality of the divine. In this category we include Augustine, Calvin, Luther, Spener, Francke, Edwards, Pascal, Forsyth, and such noted representatives of Protestant orthodoxy as Flacius, Voetius, Gerhard, Bavinck, Kuyper, and more recently Geoffrey Bromiley and G. C. Berkouwer.[13] The second position is the scholastic, which understands revelation as the disclosure of a higher truth that nonetheless stands in continuity with rational or natural truth. The Bible becomes a book of revealed propositions which are directly accessible to reason and which contain no errors in any respect. The humanity of the Bible is regarded as an aspect of its divinity. Here we can list Protestant scholastics such as Quenstedt, Wolff, Turretin, and Warfield, as well as contemporaries such as Gordon Clark, Francis Schaeffer, Carl Henry, and John Warwick Montgomery. Finally, in the liberal-modernist approach revelation is understood as inner enlightenment or self-discovery; the Bible is treated as a record of the religious experience of a particular people in history. In this category are to be placed Schleiermacher, Herrmann, Troeltsch, Harry Emerson Fosdick, Tillich, Gilkey, Bernard Meland, Gregory Baum, J. A. T. Robinson, and Rudolf Bultmann.[14]

Karl Barth succeeded, at least in part, in recovering the sacramental character of the Bible and revelation in his middle period (when he wrote the first several volumes of his *Church Dogmatics*), but he was unable to maintain this position because of certain overriding concerns in his theology. In this middle period he conceived revelation as the divine content of Scripture, a content that can only be apprehended by the interior witness of the Holy Spirit. Here he stood very close to Calvin and Luther. Yet later, in Volume IV, 3 of his *Church Dogmatics,* he began to refer to Jesus Christ alone as the Word of God and to the Bible and the sermon, as well as baptism and the Lord's Supper, as signs and witnesses of this Word. The old Reformed principle that the finite cannot bear the infinite *(finitum non capax infiniti)* was undoubtedly at work, together with the growing concern to safeguard the freedom of God in the face of a theology of repristination and a revival of confessionalism. Barth still referred to the Bible as the primary witness of revelation and the church as a secondary witness. He even allowed for true words about God in the secular world, but neither these words nor the words of the Bible or church could be equated with the Word of God itself, the transcendent Gospel concerning Jesus Christ and his reconciliation.[15] Revelation was now seen as a direct word from God spoken to the soul, and the biblical word as only a human witness and pointer to revelation. Barth could no longer speak of the Bible as the Word of God, nor could he consistently affirm the threefold unity of the revealed Word (Christ), the written word, and the proclaimed word, as he did in his middle period. Arthur Cochrane has astutely observed that, in his last years, Barth returned to his much earlier position enunciated at Barmen that Jesus Christ is the one and only Word of God.[16]

To uphold a sacramental approach to Scripture in no way rules out cognitive revelation. Revelation is truly given in and through the words of Scripture, and this means intelligible content as well as spiritual presence (cf. Rom. 16:25, 26; Col. 1:25–28). The action of God in disclosing his will and purpose to man not only entails revelation *through* Scripture but also revelation *as* Scripture. Yet this is not to say that the words of Scripture are directly revealed (as in the scholastic approach) but that Scripture embodies the truth that God desires us to hear. The unity between the revealed Word, Jesus Christ, and the written word lies both in the inspiration of the Spirit, whereby he guarantees a trustworthy witness to Christ, and in his revelatory action, in which he speaks through this witness to people of every age (cf. 1 Cor. 2:10–13).

Luther recognized the sacramental role of Scripture when he described the Word as the carriage of the Spirit. Ragnar Bring perceptively shows the similarity between Luther's understanding of Scripture and his understanding of the Lord's Supper: "Just as Christ's body and blood are given under the elements even though the bread and wine are not transformed, so also the divine Word is given through the temporally and historically conditioned Scriptures."[17]

Some neo-fundamentalists object to speaking of culturally conditioned words and concepts in Scripture, but we contend that if justice is to be done to the true humanity of Scripture, we must fully acknowledge the human element. This in no way detracts from its divine authority but instead establishes Scripture as an authentic witness to a real revelation in history. Inscripturation signifies that the Word of God takes on human dress and imagery as it relates itself to humankind. The Holy Spirit accommodated himself to the thought patterns and language of the peoples of biblical times and so entered into their cultural and historical limitations.[18] Yet because inspiration also means that the Spirit guided and directed the writers not only in their ideas but also in their selection of words, we can affirm that the Bible is a divine as well as a human product. Moreover, we must likewise contend that, because of the superintendence of the Spirit, the Bible is a fully reliable and trustworthy witness to the truth revealed in the history that it records. It gives us an accurate reflection of the mind and purpose of God though not an exact duplication of the very thoughts of God.[19] Its message or teaching transcends human culture and history, though it is mediated only through human language and imagery. Because there is one Divine Author within and behind the many human authors, the Bible has an underlying doctrinal and theological unity, despite significant variations in stress and style.

The Bible's authority is functional in that it is a signpost to Jesus Christ. But it is not simply functional. There is an integral and organic relation between Christ's promises and the written word. The word not only points to Christ, but it was brought into being by the Spirit of Christ acting upon the prophets and apostles.[20] It not only conveys the truth of Christ but also embodies this truth. When we say that the Bible is the Word of God we mean two things: that all the words are selected by the Spirit of God through his guidance of the human authors; and that the truth of God is enshrined in and mediated through these words. The Bible is the Word of God in all that it teaches, though this teaching is not immediately self-evident but must be unveiled by the Spirit.

The Bible is neither the direct, unmediated speech of God (as we sometimes find in Warfield) nor simply an indirect historical witness to divine revelation (as in Barth). It is the Word of God in human clothing, the revelation of God transmitted through human concepts and imagery. Yet the human concepts do not capture the full impact and significance of what is given in revelation, as Augustine makes clear in his comments on John the apostle: "Because he was inspired he was able to say something; but because he who was inspired remained a man, he could not present the full reality, but only what a man could say about it."[21] At the same time we can know this reality when the Spirit of God acts in and through the written witness. "The word of God indeed is sharp as a two-edged sword," says Jonathan Edwards, "but it is so only through the cooperation of that Spirit that gave the word. The word alone, however managed, explained, confirmed and applied, is nothing but a dead letter without the Spirit."[22] A similar sentiment is expressed by Robert Preus, who here presents the view of Lutheran orthodoxy at its best: "The efficacy of the Word of God does not inhere in the letters and syllables and words as they are written. These are merely symbols, the vehicle *(vehiculum)* of the divine content, the *forma,* of the Word, which alone is the Word of God, properly speaking."[23]

In left-wing neo-orthodoxy revelation is dissolved in an existential encounter. In right-wing scholastic orthodoxy revelation is frozen into a propositional formula. In biblical evangelicalism revelation refers to the whole movement of God into biblical history, culminating not only in the prophetic and apostolic witness but also in the act of faith and surrender on the part of those who are caught up in this movement. Thus the reader does not possess the truth, which would be the case if it were merely the writing of Scripture, but instead is possessed by the truth, which is the living, dynamic Word of God.[24]

What is infallible and inerrant is the Word within the words, the divine meaning given in and through the human testimony.[25] Our ultimate norm is not simply what the human author intends but what God intends through the witness of the author (cf. 1 Pet. 1:10–12), though there is always a certain congruity between the latter and the former. It follows that not everything reported in Scripture should be accepted at face value. To hear the eternal, living Word means to have to search the Scriptures, to try to see every text in the light of the divine center, Jesus Christ. It means to distinguish the shell and the kernel, form and content.[26] The evangelist Dwight L. Moody referred to the need for "digging out" the divine truth of Scripture, since this truth is not directly available to the "uncircumcised eye."[27] Johann Christian Konrad von Hofmann remarks that to regard statements about world history or the cosmos as infallible simply because they are reported in Scripture is "the evil consequence of a merely rational doctrine of Inspiration, and creates many conflicts with the actual world."[28] Bavinck is helpful here in his distinction between the historical and normative authority of Scripture. Only in the second sense can we regard Scripture as absolutely binding and therefore supremely authoritative.

While fundamentalists are prone to stress the infallibility of the original manuscripts[29] and liberals the infallibility of conscience, our emphasis is on the infallibility of Word and Spirit, one of the salient themes of the Reformation. The written word partakes of divine infallibility because it is grounded in the incarnate or revealed Word, Jesus Christ. Moreover, it is an effectual sign of the revealed Word in that it serves to communicate the significance of this revelation through the power of the Spirit. There is a union, but not a fusion, between the written word of Scripture and the divine word of revelation.[30]

The present impasse in evangelical circles concerning the authority of Scripture could be overcome if we would but return to a sacramental understanding of revelation: that Scripture is a divinely-appointed means of grace and not simply an earthly, historical witness or sign of grace; and that Scripture is inseparable from the revelation which produced it and which flows through it but that the words of Scripture in and of themselves are not divine revelation. We should also probably substitute what George Eldon Ladd calls historical-theological criticism for the historical-critical method, which has been too often associated with naturalistic presuppositions.[31] Or perhaps it is better to speak of historical-critical methods than of one single critical method, for criticism varies according to the theological outlook of the critic. We need to be free to examine the Scriptures as human literature; yet we must not stop there but go on to find and hear the Word of God in and through the words of the human authors. Historical and critical studies may help to cleanse the lens of Scripture so that it is not simply an opaque medium of the Word of God. Yet "what really makes Scripture a transparent medium is the divine light that shines through it from the face of Jesus Christ into our hearts."[32]

It is important to recover the dynamic and divine character of revelation without separating it from the earthen vessel of the Scriptural writings. We need to recognize anew the element of mystery in revelation, which was generally acknowledged by the church fathers and Reformers. We need to affirm with Pascal that God hides himself in the measure that he discloses himself. This means that our language about God can be at the most analogical, not univocal, for there can be no direct or exact correspondence between human ideas and the veritable Word of God. It is also imperative for us to reaffirm the mystery of the accommodation of the Holy Spirit to the deficiencies and limitations of human language, an insight fully acknowledged by the great teachers of the church, including Origen, Augustine, John Chrysostom, and Calvin. It must never be forgotten that the Bible is time-bound and time-related even as it is timeless. Finally, we would do well to abandon a rationalistic epistemology (whether of the inductive or deductive type) in determining the truth-content of Scripture and confess anew that God can be known only through God.[33] Scripture is authoritative by virtue of its relation to the living Word, not by virtue of its truthfulness as such. This is because its truth is only rightly understood in relation to Christ by the work of the Holy Spirit; it cannot be grasped by any rational hermeneutic.

THE NEED TO RECOVER EVANGELICAL DISTINCTIVES

Part of the current dilemma of evangelicalism is that the crucial doctrines of the historic faith are being underplayed, while peripheral or sectarian tenets occupy the center of attention. This has been aptly described as majoring in minors. It is sad but true that in many evangelical circles today epistemological and eschatological concerns take precedence over the salient themes of the Reformation, and that various of these themes have become foreign to the modern church (including the conservative branch). A pronounced preoccupation with apologetics, in which rationalistic unbelief is challenged on its own ground, has prevented many evangelicals from seeing that the great problem of the church is not with the hearer, not with modern man, but with the authenticity of the church's own message.

In calling for a rediscovery of evangelical distinctives, we need to be aware of heresies on the right: perfectionism, dispensationalism, religious enthusiasm, and hyperfundamentalism. The great evangelical doctrines of *sola Scriptura, solus Christus,* and *sola gratia* contradict the synergism and anthropocentrism in conservative Christianity as well as in liberalism. Even the doctrine of *sola Scriptura,* understood in the Reformation sense, exists in tension with the current evangelical stress on personal religious experience as well as the fundamentalist appeal to arguments from reason and science in support of total biblical reliability.

This is not the place to enumerate the evangelical distinctives, since this entire work is devoted to their explication, but we would like to give special attention to the doctrine of salvation by grace, for it is the heart and soul of evangelicalism. This tenet lies at the basis of the meaning of the cross as well as of the new birth. In it are involved the themes of predestination, justification, reconciliation, and sanctification. It means basically that man the sinner is elected for salvation without regard to his intrinsic merit or worthiness. We cannot affirm with Schleiermacher that election "is grounded in the faith of the elect, foreseen by God."[34] Election means grace going out to the faithless and thereby creating faith where there had previously been only unbelief. The decision of faith itself is a gift of God, and this truth is too readily lost sight of in current revivalism.

The evangelical distinctive of *sola gratia* has its roots in the tradition of the whole church, not just the Reformation. It was Anselm who declared: "Whatsoever our heart rightly willeth, it is of Thy gift."[35] And in Augustine's words, "Men are not saved by good works, nor by the free determination of their own will, but by the grace of God through faith."[36] Grace moreover is not merely an ontological energy instilled into man, but primarily the personal favor of God toward man. "Grace is the royal and sovereign power of God," said Karl Barth, "the existential presentation of men to God for His disposal, the real freedom of the will of God in men."[37]

Besides being the work of God *for us* in Jesus Christ, grace is also the work of God *in us* through the gift of the Holy Spirit. Yet our trust should not be in our own inner renewal, in the presence of grace in our hearts, but only in Christ's perfect work of redemption, the objective reconciliation effected by him (John T. Mueller).

As we have seen, the emphasis in the later Luther and Barth was decidedly on the work of Christ outside us, the perfect or finished work of redemption on the cross. Luther referred to the "alien righteousness" of Christ, by which we are justified while still in our sins. Barth placed the accent on the accomplished reconciliation realized objectively in God's becoming man in Jesus and subjectively in the obedience of Jesus to God. Sometimes Barth spoke of Jesus believing in our place, but this undercuts the urgency of faith and the call to decision.[38]

Evangelicalism is seriously deficient if the interior dimension of salvation is downplayed or denied. Thielicke seeks to correct the objectivism in Lutheranism when he says: "The alien righteousness of Christ is not something that lies in a remote 'outside me.' It is imparted to me. It is also my righteousness. It includes me."[39] Luther himself made a real place for the mystical or inward dimension of faith, even describing his conversion in this way: "Then I suddenly felt that I was born again and entered through open doors into paradise."[40]

As we strive to recover evangelical distinctives, we would do well to qualify and reformulate traditional slogans in the light of Scripture and with an ecumenical sensitivity. The sovereignty of God must not be construed as the unlimited power of an arbitrary God but as the sovereignty of grace, of the God who acts in love. Likewise total depravity must be redefined to allow a place for the remnant of goodness even in the most hardened sinner. The doctrine of the substitutionary atonement must be rethought so as to meet the valid criticism that it portrays a wrathful God who would not otherwise forgive except for the offering of an innocent victim. Thielicke presents this corrective: "Christ does not simply offer himself to God in the name of man, so that God is the object of atonement (as in Anselm). He also offers himself to man in the name of God and as God's sacrifice."[41]

Certainly every reform in the church must spring out of obedience to the Word of God as given in sacred Scripture. Even reforms pertaining to the external life of the church must emanate from an existential encounter with the Scriptures. John Stott expresses it well:

Evangelicals . . . regard as the only possible road to the reunion of churches the road of biblical reformation. In their view the only solid hope for churches which desire to unite is a common willingness to sit down together under the authority of God's Word, in order to be judged and reformed by it.[42]

In the quest for evangelical renewal and church unity we must be cautious in our use of slogans and phrases that are unduly polemical. Instead of always speaking of *irresistible grace,* we should probably employ such terms as *effectual* or *efficacious* grace, which are less offensive to our Arminian brethren. Instead of *limited atonement,* one of the hallmarks of Reformed orthodoxy, it would be biblically more appropriate to speak of *particular redemption* or of a redemption that is both universal and particular. It is universal in its scope and intention and particular in its implementation. Instead of *total depravity* we might more often refer to the *radicality of sin.* We should seek words that have an ecumenical as well as a biblical ring. This does not mean that in academic discourse the older words cannot be used, but they need always to be clarified and redefined.

The call to recover evangelical distinctives is not necessarily an invitation to doctrinal conflict, though it will often entail this, since wherever theology is taken seriously, controversy abounds. Yet doctrinal conflicts may also be a sign of acculturization. Doctrine can be a tool in the struggle for technocratic power, and some observers see this in the recent uproar in the Missouri Synod Lutheran church. Yet if a particular charge of heresy has little basis, this does not mean that real heresy does not exist. In view of the drift of the mainline churches into unitarianism and universalism, the need to reaffirm evangelical distinctives will indubitably create tensions and perhaps division in the church. But a true church can only exist on the basis of doctrine and biblical truth, and where this truth is diluted or ignored we have a false church.

THE NEED TO RECOVER CATHOLIC SUBSTANCE

In addition to upholding evangelical distinctives, we need to regain catholic substance, which means continuity with the tradition of the whole church, including its sacramental side. It is incumbent on us to recover the doctrine of the church, particularly with regard to its indispensable role in the communication of salvation. The church is not a mediator between God and man, but it is a veritable means of grace to man. It cannot dispense grace as though it were in control, but it can function as an instrument of the Holy Spirit who does convey the grace of Christ to a sinful world. The church is not simply an earthen vessel in which faith shines (as in Barth) but our spiritual mother through whom faith comes (as in Calvin and Luther). A rampant individualism that is prominent in both evangelical and liberal Protestantism has obscured the crucial role of the church in our salvation and sanctification.

In catholic tradition the four marks of the true church are holiness, apostolicity, catholicity, and oneness (or unity). The Reformers added the two practical signs of the scriptural preaching of the Gospel and the right administration of the sacraments. These signs were intended not to preempt the traditional marks but instead to complement them. Only an apostolic and catholic church will preach the pure Gospel and faithfully administer the sacraments.

Apostolicity has often been associated with the ministry of the church. In Roman Catholicism the ministry is seen in terms of the sacrament of holy orders, which gives one the spiritual authorization to celebrate the sacraments and function as a pastor. This sacrament is administered by the laying on of hands by bishops who supposedly stand in historical succession to the apostles. We contend that the true apostolic succession is one of doctrine rather than ministry as such. It lies not in the office of the ministry but in the proclamation of the ministry, and this conception too has roots in the pre-Reformation tradition. Moltmann rightly declares: "The apostolic succession is, in fact and in truth, the evangelical succession, the continuing and unadulterated proclamation of the gospel of the risen Christ."[43]

The quest for sacramental integrity (one of the affirmations of the Chicago Call[44]) certainly reflects the growing concern for catholic substance in evangelical circles. The two dominical sacraments are the Lord's Supper and holy baptism, but other rites (e.g., confirmation) can be spoken of as sacramental in that, when they are united with the Word of God and apprehended in faith, they too serve as signs or channels of God's grace. In Roman Catholic theology the sacramental grace of baptism preempted the irresistible grace of predestination (stressed by Augustine), and a sacramentalism obscured the personalistic element in Christian faith. We need to recover the objective reality of grace in the sacraments without succumbing to the error that this grace is automatically effective regardless of personal faith. Hugh of St. Victor conceived the sacraments as works of reparation *(opera reparationis)*. We see them as visible testimonies or signs of what God has done for us in Christ, signs in which the Holy Spirit is active in applying the benefits of Christ's death and resurrection.[45]

Just as Jesus Christ and Holy Scripture have two sides, the divine and the human, so the sacraments have two sides. Conservative evangelical Christianity has lost sight of the divine side in the sacraments, while certain strands in Roman Catholicism underplay, if not virtually deny, the human side. We affirm that Christ is really present in the reception of the elements of bread and wine, not as localized in them but as reaching out through them. Christ meets us in, through, and with these elements so that his words "This is my body" are not merely symbolic (as in Zwingli's conception). In Lutheran orthodoxy it was sometimes said that Christ is in the Eucharistic bread as heat is in a red-hot iron, and while this metaphor must not be pressed unduly,[46] it conveys the truth that there is an inseparable and organic relationship between the sacramental elements and the sacramental presence of our Lord.

Certainly we need also to recover the salutary role of tradition in the interpretation and understanding of Scripture. Scripture interprets itself, to be sure, but tradition can aid us in discerning how Scripture interprets itself. We agree with the Roman Catholic theologian Geiselmann that the role of tradition is not to supplement Scripture but to help us to understand it correctly. Tradition must always remain subordinate to Scripture, but its light can serve to clarify obscure portions of Scripture. Many evangelical Protestants consider any appeal to church tradition, and especially to the pre-Reformation tradition, as heretical, but it can be shown that, when we throw overboard the catholic tradition (which the Reformers never did), we are then led to embrace sectarian traditions, such as the Scofield Reference Bible of dispensationalism.

Whereas the message of Holy Scripture is the ultimate authority for faith, church tradition can be regarded as a proximate or penultimate authority.[47] Moreover, since the Bible is transmitted only through the church tradition, the church plays a crucial, though instrumental, role in bringing people the Word of God. While we affirm the church *under* the Bible, at the same time we affirm the Bible *in* the church insofar as biblical teaching and doctrine carry power and authority only in the community of faith.

At this point it is appropriate to consider the importance of creedal identity within evangelicalism today. On the one hand, we have creedal churches that merely recite creeds handed down from tradition, and, on the other, there are creedless churches that languish in a doctrinal vacuum (see Section 3 in *The Chicago Call*). Our need is for a confessing church that will boldly confront a secularized world with the claims of the Gospel. Confessions should not be straitjackets; yet at the same time they should be more than just general guides. An authentic confession, one that derives its inspiration from Scripture, is a norm for faith, though not an absolute norm. It is a test as well as a testimony of faith, but it does not base the case for the faith on human formulation alone but on fidelity to a living Lord. This subject will be explored at greater length in the last section of this chapter.

In the history of the church Protestantism has laid emphasis on the atonement of Christ, while Catholicism has underlined the centrality of the incarnation of Christ. The reconciling work of Christ has often in Protestant history been restricted to the passion and death of Christ at Calvary, whereas we need to see this work beginning already in his incarnation. If we have the atonement without the incarnation we are still vulnerable to the heresies of Arianism and subordinationism, which accepted the cross but not the full deity of Christ. On the other hand, if we have the incarnation without the atonement, we may very well see Christ as only a transforming leaven in a sinful world rather than a vicarious sin-bearer and mediator. Conservative Protestantism is strong on the atonement but not as strong as it could be in its conception of the incarnation. We here agree with Professor Torrance: "What is supremely needed . . . in all the Churches today, is a far profounder understanding of the Incarnation, the coming of God himself into the structures of creaturely and human being, in order to restore the creation to its unity and harmony in himself."[48] An incarnational Christianity will always stand in contradiction to a gnostic Christianity which separates Christ and salvation from the materiality of the creation and the ambiguity of history. Many conservative evangelicals maintain a docetic view of both Christ and the Scriptures because they are unwilling to affirm that the Word of God really and fully entered into the stream of human history, thereby making itself vulnerable to relativity and temporality.

Again, we as evangelicals need to reappropriate the mystical side of faith. An evangelicalism that denies this element becomes incurably rationalistic, and this is what we find in much of Protestantism today. We would do well to remember with Rudolf Otto that faith contains nonrational elements as well—feeling and will. These are directed by reason but are not wholly subservient to reason. It is important to be alive to the dangers and temptations inherent in mysticism, but this does not mean that we cannot learn positively from the contributions of the great mystics of catholic Christianity. We need always to penetrate through the neo-Platonic framework in which many of the mystics thought and wrote in order to discern their abiding insights that have a biblical foundation. Luther himself drew upon the Rhineland mystics in his effort to come to an evangelical, biblical understanding of God and salvation.[49] From Tauler he perceived that God is hidden and incomprehensible (deus absconditus et incomprehensibilis); this did not mean that God is unknowable (as in radical mysticism) but that he cannot be fully understood conceptually. Luther's spirituality, which combines mystical and evangelical elements, could serve as a welcome antidote to the rationalism that pervades conservative Protestantism today.[50]

We must, of course, avoid the temptation of the neo-Platonic type of mysticism where God is so far beyond the categories of the understanding that he can be described only in terms of negation (as in pseudo-Dionysius). Though he does, of course, transcend human understanding, he does not totally elude rationality but instead embodies it. Because of the illumination of faith there can be a partial conformity of our ideas to the mind of God; this is an analogical, not univocal, knowledge, yet a true knowledge.[51] It is knowledge based not on the light of God in nature, which is obscured by sin, but on the light given to man in faith. Thomas Aquinas, who also can be numbered among the mystics, rightly perceived the analogical character of the knowledge of God, though he arrived at this from a study of the being of man and did not derive it exclusively from the self-revelation of God in Jesus Christ.

Evelyn Underhill is an example of one courageous spirit in Protestantism who sought to recover the treasures of the mystical heritage of the church in the light of the Gospel. In her early years she was in danger of confusing biblical Christianity with an ahistorical mystical religion, but as she progressed in her faith, more and more she came to see the tremendous importance of the incarnation for spirituality.[52] She moved from an early adulation of mysticism in general to a Christocentric orientation in which she sharply distinguished between Christian and non-Christian mysticism. She saw that the Christian mystic cannot "contract out of existence with its tensions and demands. . . . Union with God means self-giving to the purposes of the divine energy and love."[53]

Finally, we need to appreciate the Catholic emphasis on works and Christian life which are a complement to the evangelical stress on grace and faith. While we must always vigorously affirm the sovereignty of grace, we should at the same time make a place for human responsibility and accountability if we are to do justice to the total biblical witness. Puritanism sought to restore this catholic balance that was lost in the controversies following the Reformation. Richard Sibbes reflects the Puritan and also Pietist concern to hold together the gift of grace and human decision: "As soon as God's grace hath seized on us, presently it puts us on doing; what God worketh in thee, thou must work thyself."[54]

Catholic traditionalism and eclecticism are not to be confused with catholic tradition and breadth of vision. We must repudiate what detracts from the evangelical doctrines of the primacy and infallibility of Scripture, the substitutionary atonement, and salvation by grace, but we must not be too hasty in discarding elements within the ancient tradition that may be salutary and helpful in spiritual life and growth, even though they may not be directly rooted in the Scriptures. Church tradition needs to be incorporated into a new and fresh understanding of the Gospel for our time. We should remember that Calvin and Luther drew upon the church fathers as well as the doctors of the medieval church in their exposition of the abiding truths of Holy Scripture. This is what we need to do for our time if we are to achieve a church that is truly catholic, truly reformed, and truly evangelical.

TOWARD A CATHOLIC EVANGELICALISM

In constructing a fresh theology for our day, we need to regain continuity with the historical roots of the faith as well as renew our fidelity to the biblical and evangelical witness. This means an opening to Roman Catholicism and Eastern Orthodoxy as well as a new appreciation of the Reformation and the post-Reformation movements of spiritual purification, Pietism and Puritanism. Barth reminds us that "the meaning of Protestantism (both Lutheran and Reformed) was in the beginning not a lessening but a heightening of the force of all the claims which Catholicism makes for the Church."[55] The theological options today are liberalism or modernism (whether in the guise of neo-Protestantism or neo-Catholicism), a reactionary evangelicalism or fundamentalism, and a catholic evangelicalism, which alone is truly evangelical and biblical.

A prime characteristic of a catholic evangelical church would be its confessional basis. We have already alluded to the need for creedal identity, and it is now appropriate to amplify this. There are three kinds of confessions: one that derives its inspiration from Scripture and that addresses itself to the cultural and religious situation of its time for the purpose of renewing and purifying the church; one that seeks to reconcile or pacify disparate factions in the church in order to present to the world the facade of church unity; and one whose aim is to defend or maintain the traditions of a particular church or party within the church for the purpose of a new church alignment. The Barmen Confession and the Lausanne Covenant are examples of the first type;[56] the new creed in the United Church of Christ approximates the second type; and the narrow creedal statements of many hyperconservative churches and seminaries today exemplify the third type.

A genuine confession of faith will arise out of a fresh confrontation with Scripture and will seek to state the truth disclosed by the Spirit even if this contradicts established and cherished beliefs. Such a confession will address itself to the whole church, not just to one segment in it, and will try to redefine the faith for its time in such a way that those who cannot subscribe are excluded, since an authentic confession concerns the very life of the church itself. Abraham Kuyper expressed the wish that a confession would pronounce only "what was settled and sealed with the blood of the martyrs" so that it might be a watchword in life and death, under the animation of the Holy Spirit. Too often we evangelicals have sought to find heresy where there is none, but this does not mean that true heresy does not exist. Yet only where this heresy becomes a public threat to the order and well-being of the church should the church take a public stand for the purpose of excluding from its fellowship those who have fallen prey to it. With keen perception Berkouwer remarks: "Only where this salvation is obscured or limited may she be 'intolerant,' not in the sad sense of prideful discrimination, but as a reference to the 'forbearance' of God, which radiates in the gospel to the whole creation."[57]

The church's confession must also be addressed to live issues in the church, particularly in its relationship to the world, for otherwise theologians will be speaking only to themselves. What is needed is not a parochial confession but an evangelical catholic confession if the church is to regain biblical relevance. "Whoever restricts the Church's confession to an esoteric mystery," says Berkouwer, "has robbed it of its power, paving the way toward the saltlessness that no longer serves anything."[58] The church's confession must speak to the burning issues of the time with such clarity and intelligibility that people are called to make an existential decision.

The confession will be relatively but not absolutely binding, for every confession stands under the judgment of Holy Scripture. Yet confessions can still be truly binding for a particular situation, since we believe that in the confession (if it is grounded in Scripture) we hear the voice of the living God. In the words of Barth: " 'Confessions' exist for us to go through them (not once but continually), not for us to return to them, take up our abode in them, and conduct our further thinking from their standpoint and in bondage to them."[59]

Similar caution must be exercised in the matter of spirituality. An evangelical catholic church will seek a renewal of spirituality, but one that is genuinely biblical and personalistic. We must avoid at all costs the kind of spirituality advocated by Schleiermacher: "It matters not what conceptions a man adheres to, he can still be pious."[60] We should remember, too, that Troeltsch spoke positively of piety, defining it as "a definitely earnest, warm and practical religious life."[61] We do not mean to imply that we cannot learn from these two towering figures of neo-Protestantism, but we must recognize that piety as they understand it has affinities with the idea of creativity in Romanticism and is closer to the spirit of that movement than to the Bible. Genuine catholic evangelical spirituality will see its pivotal center in the atoning sacrifice of Christ and the outpouring of the Holy Spirit as opposed to an immanental spiritual force resident in all people. It will be characterized by sacrificial service in the midst of the suffering of the world as opposed to flight from the world.

There are signs of promise in the Catholic charismatic renewal insofar as it is promoting a recovery of a biblical spirituality that stands at variance with the neo-Platonic mysticism that is so all-pervasive in Catholicism. Simon Tugwell frankly acknowledges that Catholic spirituality "has for a very long time been heavily conditioned by a mystical theology centered on God's eternal being, in one form or another."[62] "Some writers," he says, "have even encouraged us to leave behind all consideration of the Incarnate Christ, let alone prayer of petition."[63] He goes on to contend that the prayer of petition, and especially intercession, is a prophetic function of the church that cannot be lightly disregarded and is to be exercised precisely by those endowed with the divine Spirit.

In addition to the emphasis on biblical spirituality, a catholic evangelicalism will affirm the social imperatives of the faith: it will bring the faith to bear upon the whole man, upon his political and economic condition as well as his spiritual state. It will call for repentance of social as well as personal sins. It will emphasize the obligation of the Christian to engage in humanitarian service and social reform as well as evangelism. It will affirm with Irenaeus that the glory of God means not the suppression of the human but instead "man fully alive."[64] At the same time it will confess against all forms of secular humanism that the glory of man is the living God (Amandus Polanus).

Still another vital concern of a catholic evangelical theology will be to recover a theological method that is both biblical and catholic.[65] It will seek to transcend the cleavage between fideism and rationalism in order to apprehend anew the divine basis of both faith and understanding. It will see the point of departure in theology as being neither the leap of faith nor rational verification but instead the divine revelation given in Holy Scripture. This revelation, to be sure, can be perceived only by faith, but once apprehended, it then makes sense of all experience. Faith, moreover, is not simply a commitment of the will but an assent of the understanding. Reason is involved in faith from the very beginning, but it is always reason in the service of revelation, never reason as the springboard for revelation. Reason is not a criterion by which we judge revelation, but revelation is the criterion by which reason is placed on a new foundation. The correct approach is *credo, ut intellegam* (I believe in order to understand), not *credo, quia intellego* (I believe because I understand). We, of course, reject the irrationalist option, "I believe because it is absurd" (Tertullian).[66] It can be shown that our position is in accord with the great theologians of evangelical history, including Irenaeus,[67] Augustine, Anselm, Luther, Calvin, Kuyper, and Forsyth, and in our own time Berkouwer and Barth.

In forging an evangelical catholic theology we need to reappraise the apologetic task, which fell into disfavor with the rise of Barthian theology. Karl Barth was far from denying the legitimate concern to answer the questions of unbelief, but he always insisted that this be done within the framework of church dogmatics, where the faith is explicated to the church. He even regarded dogmatics as "an apologetic, polemic discourse from beginning to end"[68] in that the truth of faith must always be set off from the untruth or partial truths of secular philosophy. Yet he rejected an apologetics that conceived of itself as a preparation for dogmatics, that sought a point of contact with the world of unbelief for the purpose of making the faith credible or palatable to its cultured despisers. For Barth it is not the task of theology "to lighten heaven with earth's searchlights, but rather theology is expected to let the light of heaven be seen and understood on earth."[69]

Basically, we are in agreement with Barth on this question, and yet some of his presuppositions tend to undercut even the apologetic task that he allows. If we concentrate all our attention on the explication of faith, we shall not see the need to overthrow the bastions of unbelief, especially if their challenge to faith is not taken seriously. Barth says that unbelief should not be treated with the utmost seriousness, since the unbeliever is already in the sphere of the kingdom of Christ and is destined to become a believer by divine foreordination. For Barth unbelief has its roots in the unreason of man, and therefore cannot be dislodged by arguments from reason. But surely it can be overthrown by the testimony of the Gospel, and Barth here agrees, though he would say that unbelief, having its basis in nothingness, can no longer exist when exposed to the light of the Gospel.

We hold with Berkouwer that there is need in the church for an apologetics that seeks its basic resources within the Gospel itself (cf. Col. 4:6; 1 Pet. 3:15). While we should never try to make the faith palatable or credible, since the cross of Christ will always be a scandal to unbelief, we can make the faith intelligible and explicable. We should be ready to answer criticisms of faith and also to point out the contradictions within unbelief, though always remembering that our feeble apologetics can, at the most, silence criticism. It cannot of itself positively prepare the outsider to accept Christ, since both faith and the condition for faith come from the Holy Spirit as he acts and speaks through the preaching of the Gospel (cf. John 16:8). Apologetics can be of some benefit to those who are struggling under conviction of the Spirit but who have not broken through to repentance and faith. It can be much more valuable to those already within the sphere of faith in enabling them to understand their faith better, especially in the light of attacks upon it.

The kind of theological enterprise we espouse is that of a theology of confrontation as opposed to one of accommodation or one of correlation.[70] In accommodationist theology an attempt is made to find the underlying unity between secular and religious wisdom. In a theology of correlation nature and culture are seen to have their completion or fulfillment in Christ and his redemption. It is said that the creative aspirations and questions of culture have their ultimate answer in the biblical Gospel. In a theology of confrontation the Gospel sharply calls into question the presuppositions of secular culture. Here the criterion of the Gospel stands at variance with secular philosophical wisdom because human reason is not only limited but also tainted by the lust for power. The goal is neither synthesis nor correlation but the conversion of culture and philosophy to the new values and transcendent perspective of the kingdom of God.

Our chief criticism of the theologies of accommodation and correlation is that they too easily reconcile or harmonize the claims of Christ with natural wisdom and morality. In our view the Gospel is not added to what man already knows but, instead, overturns man's knowledge and calls him to break with his past orientation. Apologetics is no longer a preparation or precondition of dogmatics but becomes a branch of dogmatics proper, with the primary object of enabling the Christian to reflect upon his faith so that he can make a forthright witness before the world. An apologetics in the service of a kerygmatic theology of confrontation will enable the church to regain the offensive and rout the forces of evil.

Finally, catholic evangelicals will be preeminently concerned with church unity, since this was the express will and prayer of our Lord (John 17:20–23), and only a united church can make a lasting impact on a disunited and confused world. John Venn appropriately laments:

How has the Christian world been divided and its peace destroyed by the adoption of the names and tenets of particular ministers as the badges of different parties in the Church: I am of Calvin, and I of Arminius, and I of Luther. Would to God that it had been always remembered that Christians are of Christ alone.[71]

We also concur in the judgment of Greek Orthodox Metropolitan Bartholomaios Archondonis: "Division is not a permanent state for Christians. We need to know each other better and love each other more to find together the way to unity."[72] True Christians already have a spiritual unity, but we must seek visible unity as well, though this does not necessarily entail one great world church, as some ecumenists envision. It would definitely involve pulpit and altar fellowship among the churches.

Church unity, however crucial, must not be placed above the concern for truth. True unity can only be on the basis of truth, but the whole truth can only be perceived and appreciated when Christians are united with one another in love. Erasmus made the unity of the church the highest good, even to the extent of clouding over the differences between the old Catholicism and the Reformation. Luther, on the other hand, strove to maintain the truth above all, even at the risk of disunity. Luther's way was the more biblical, but the Reformation was nonetheless a "tragic necessity" (Pelikan) because it meant that the valid insights on both sides were to be submerged in the interests of new sectarian unities.

There are right and wrong ways toward the realization of evangelical catholic unity in our age. One way that we find unacceptable is that proposed by the nineteenth-century Swedish theologian Nikolai Grundtvig, who placed church tradition on a par with Scripture and emphasized spiritual growth and nurture over personal conversion. Another less than satisfactory way was that of the Oxford movement in England, the Anglo-Catholic party that sought to recover the catholic heritage of the church, including a concern for saints and religious orders. It inspired genuine spiritual renewal in the Anglican church but at the cost of overlooking or denying the Reformation understanding of justification as a forensic declaration of pardon rather than inner renewal. Moreover, the mass came to overshadow the preaching of the Word, which was seen as only a preparation for the real means of grace. Neither can we follow Hans Küng, who substitutes the new *magisterium* of university scholars for the Catholic church's old *magisterium* in determining what should be believed about Jesus and what should be discarded. Nor can we empathize with those who uphold a secular ecumenism and thereby try to base unity on ethics rather than doctrine.

The only genuine spiritual way to true evangelical-catholic unity is a return to the message and teachings of Scripture with the aid of the tradition of the whole church.[73] Yet this return will involve not only an acceptance of right doctrine but also a renewal of personal faith. The Pietists rightly teach us that true theology can only be done by regenerated theologians. The conversion that we call for is a spiritual as well as an intellectual one.

In seeking rapprochement between the churches, we must avoid cheap polemics on the one hand and latitudinarianism on the other. It is not necessary to reconcile Thomas Aquinas and Luther to go forward in ecumenical understanding. Nor should we try to blur the very real differences between the Council of Trent and the Augsburg Confession. We cannot subscribe to the position of some scholars (for example, Küng) that Trent and the Reformation were saying the same thing in different ways.[74] Yet because creeds and theologians are not the final arbiter in determining truth, because the judgments of history must be subordinated to the transcendent Word of God in Scripture, we do not need to reconcile all past differences, but instead by the gift of the Spirit we can lay hold of a new vision that both complements and supersedes the partial truths in our various traditions.

A catholic evangelicalism does not yearn for a return to the supposedly undivided church of the patristic era but strives for the visible actualization of the spiritual unity that already exists within and between the churches. It aims not for the repristination of a past glory but for the dawning of a future glory. It seeks not the creedal conformity of the churches in the past but ethical and spiritual conformity to God's will, which, it is hoped, will characterize the coming great church. Such conformity may very well entail a confession of faith, but it will be a living, vibrant confession, not lip-service to articles of faith devised by man. An evangelical catholicism will wish to avoid both the autonomy of Enlightenment Christianity and the heteronomy of the old Catholicism and fundamentalism. It will espouse the theonomy of a biblical, evangelical faith.[75]

A battle is now looming between the true church and the false church. Enlightenment liberalism is being reborn in the process and experience theologies of our day which relativize all truth and deny the very reality of a transcendent order. We hear such voices as that of Bernard Loomer, who contends that "the emphasis throughout Christianity upon the finality of Jesus Christ is ultimately treason to the human spirit."[76] We see a subtle accommodation to the spirit of the times *(Zeitgeist)* in Langdon Gilkey's attempt to dismantle and reconstruct the historic Christian belief "in the light of the modern historical consciousness."[77] We note the much celebrated book by a number of British theologians, *The Myth of God Incarnate,* which in effect denies the deity of Christ and views Jesus as only a prophetic figure in history who was remarkably transparent to the divine presence within all things.[78] We detect the emergence of a new natural theology whose appeal is to universally lived human experience, a theology that would most certainly meet with Barth's thunderous disapproval.[79]

In confronting this crisis we need to create an evangelical-catholic synthesis that will bring together the forces of biblical faith and renewal in all Christian traditions. The cleavage is no longer between denominations but cuts across denominational lines. On the one hand is biblical supernaturalism, the faith of the holy catholic church; on the other is secularistic humanism that frequently appears in the guise of liberal religion and occasionally even of "the old time religion." An apologetics that is also a kerygmatic dogmatics is necessary to defend the faith against present-day errors and misunderstandings. A confession of faith is needed that will say something definite in terms of dogmatics *and* ethics (Barth). Only a church that is rooted in and informed by Scripture but is also willing to speak to the burning issues of our time will command sufficient respect and loyalty so that it can become an effective sign and parable of the inbreaking of the kingdom of God. Only such a church will be used by the Holy Spirit to vanquish the principalities and powers and to spearhead the advancement of the kingdom in human history.

NOTES

1. See Richard Quebedeaux, *The Worldly Evangelicals* (New York: Harper & Row, 1978).

2. *Luther's Works,* vol. 21, p. 17.

3. John Warwick Montgomery, *Principalities and Powers* (Minneapolis: Bethany Fellowship, 1973), p. 213.

4. Carl Henry, *God, Revelation and Authority,* vol. 1 (Waco, Texas: Word Books, 1976), p. 229.

5. Montgomery testifies that he has chosen the Christian world view because it is "accessible to science and rests upon an objective foundation which

will stand up under the most exacting criticism." John Warwick Montgomery, *The Shape of the Past* (Minneapolis: Bethany Fellowship, 1975), p. 138.

6. See Norman Geisler, *Philosophy of Religion* (Grand Rapids: Zondervan, 1974). His incisive critique of process philosophy and theology can be appreciated by all earnest evangelicals. See his "Process Theology" in Stanley N. Gundry and Alan F. Johnson, eds. *Tensions in Contemporary Theology* (Chicago: Moody Press, 1976), pp. 237–286.

7. For a poignant critique of this kind of rationalism from an evangelical conservative perspective see Robert L. Reymond, *The Justification of Knowledge* (Nutley, New Jersey: Presbyterian & Reformed, 1976). Reymond fails to do justice to Barth's contribution by viewing him as an irrationalist.

8. Not all in the tradition of Protestant orthodoxy are to be classified as rationalists. Among those who have seriously questioned a rationalist methodology are M. Flacius, Ernst Wilhelm Hengstenberg, Abraham Kuyper, Theodore Brakel, and, in our own time, G. C. Berkouwer and G. W. Bromiley. James Barr's critique of evangelicalism is somewhat marred by its failure to take into consideration this particular strand of conservative thought. See his *Fundamentalism* (Philadelphia: Westminster Press, 1978).

9. Cf. Luther: "Faith must believe against reason, against its own feeling and intuition, and against its understanding which grasps and admits the validity only of that which is empirical." Cited in Paul Althaus, *The Theology of Martin Luther,* p. 57. Also: "I believe that I cannot, by my own reason or strength, believe in Jesus Christ my Lord, or come to him; but the Holy Ghost has called me through the Gospel." *Small Catechism* II, 3. In Philip Schaff, *The Creeds of Christendom,* vol. 3 (New York: Harper, 1919), p. 80.

10. While the specific understanding of the cosmos held by the biblical authors is indubitably outdated, this must be distinguished from their metaphysical vision, their interpretation of history, which has its basis in their reflection on revelation and which, in this sense, is normative for the believer. In this sense we can speak of a biblical life- and world-view which forms a part of the Christian vision.

11. Paul L. Holmer, "Contemporary Evangelical Faith: An Assessment and Critique." In *The Evangelicals,* ed. David F. Wells and John D. Woodbridge (Nashville: Abingdon Press, 1975), [pp. 68–95], p. 75.

12. John Calvin, *Institutes of the Christian Religion* I, 7, 4, ed. McNeill. p. 78.

13. Some of the early representatives of Protestant orthodoxy can be placed in both the sacramental and scholastic camps in that, while they practically equated Scripture and revelation, they qualified this by maintaining that what is meant by Scripture, is not the actual writing but the "matter itself" or "the thing signified," namely, "that which is meant and designated by the writing, namely the Word of God which informs us about His essence and will" (Gerhard). See J.K.S. Reid, *The Authority of Scripture* (New York: Harper & Bros., 1957), pp. 72 ff.

14. Cf. Bultmann: *"What, then is revealed?* Nothing at all, in so far as the quest for revelation is a quest for doctrines. . . . But everything, so far as *man has his eyes opened regarding himself and can understand* himself again." *Glauben und Verstehen* III (Tübingen: J.C.B. Mohr, 1965), p. 29.

15. Barth goes so far as to declare that the revealed Word "cannot be coordinated or compared with any human word." In his *Church Dogmatics* IV, 3 a, p. 98.

16. It must not be supposed that Barth wholly abandoned his earlier stance, for there are passages even in his later works where the sacramental character of Scripture as a means of grace is still evident. It does mean that he was moving toward a position that broke with this sacramental conception, a position that might be denominated *Christomonism,* though he steadfastly rejected this appellation.

17. Ragnar Bring, *How God Speaks to Us* (Philadelphia: Muhlenberg Press, 1962), p. 30.

18. This is known in evangelical circles as organic inspiration as opposed to a dictation theory, on the one hand, and, on the other, a purely subjective view whereby the Spirit only assists the human authors who remain the sole or primary authors.

19. We acknowledge that the Bible often depicts God as revealing his very thoughts to the prophets and apostles, but this language must not necessarily be taken literally. The ten commandments, for example, are pictured as being given directly by God to Moses. Yet we contend on the basis of the biblical testimony that the meaning invested in these commandments by God was only dimly perceived by the people of Israel (cf. Deut. 9:10 ff; Ps. 119:18–19). Conscious of his inadequacy in this matter, the Psalmist implored: "Teach me, Lord, the meaning of your laws. . . . Explain your law to me, and I will obey it" (Ps. 119:33, 34 TEV; cf. Ps. 139:6). There is always a certain discontinuity between the thoughts of God and the thoughts of man even in the event of revelation (cf. Is. 55:8, 9).

20. We can say that the Bible is authoritative *primarily* because it proclaims Christ and because Christ speaks to us in and through it. It is authoritative *secondarily* because it is inspired by the Spirit of Christ. The inspiredness of its writing is secondary to its function of conveying the riches of salvation in Christ.

21. Cited in Augustin Bea, *The Study of the Synoptic Gospels,* ed. Joseph A. Fitzmyer (New York: Harper & Row, 1965), p. 59.

22. Jonathan Edwards, "Sermons on John 16:8." Yale MSS, p. 101. Cited in Carl Bogue, *Jonathan Edwards and the Covenant of Grace,* p. 283.

23. Robert Preus, *The Inspiration of Scripture* (London: Oliver & Boyd, 1955), p. 174. This position is also reflected in the older Reformed theology which distinguished between the divine content and the external forms and special modes of writing. See Heinrich Heppe, *Reformed Dogmatics* (London: George Allen & Unwin, Ltd., 1950), pp. 15–16. In this view revelation is *in* the Bible rather than identical with the Bible.

It is not classical orthodoxy but the rationalistic orthodoxy of the late Renaissance and the Enlightenment that identifies the divine Word and the human words of the Scriptures. This same misunderstanding is present in modern cultic fundamentalism, whose spiritual affinity is much more with the Enlightenment than the Reformation. The cultic leader Victor Paul Wierwille states with reference to the Bible: "The Word is as much God as God is God." In his *Power for Abundant Living* (New Knoxville, Ohio: American Christian Press, 1971), p. 100.

24. The Thessalonians were enabled to accept the Word of God because it was already at work within them (1 Thess. 2:13; cf. Rom. 15:13; Col. 3:15, 16).

25. Our position must not be confused with the "limited inerrancy" position of Daniel Fuller and others, which discriminates between revelational and nonrevelational statements in Scripture on the basis of an inductive, empirical methodology. Instead, we hold that revelation is in all of Scripture, but this divine truth is veiled to the empirical eye. Moreover, we contend that whatever Scripture truly teaches is authoritative and binding, not just what it affirms on matters of faith and salvation. Our position is at the same time a qualified inerrancy because we recognize that the human expression in which Scriptural truth comes to us bears the marks of cultural and historical contingency.

26. This kind of distinction was frequently made in early Evangelical Pietism (Spener, Francke) and in Puritanism (Richard Sibbes). It is also to be found in early Protestant Orthodoxy.

27. See Stanley N. Gundry, *Love Them In: The Proclamation Theology of D. L. Moody* (Chicago: Moody Press, 1976), pp. 204, 216.

28. Johann Christian Konrad von Hofmann, *Interpreting the Bible* (Minneapolis: Augsburg, 1959), p. 67.

29. The autographs are certainly the measure of textual accuracy, and this means that the antiquity of the texts plays a role in their normativeness. At the same time, the appeal to the autographs does not solve the problem of cultural and historical limitations on the part of the authors.

30. Revelation might be likened to a song on a sheet of music (cf. Deut. 31:19–22.) For those who cannot read music or who have grave difficulties in this area, the song remains veiled even though they can make out the words. But when they hear the song sung by the author, then they truly know it. The living voice does not contradict what is written, but it gives meaning and impact to what is otherwise a dead letter or empty symbol.

31. Gerhard Maier substitutes a "historical-Biblical method" for higher criticism in his *The End of the Historical-Critical Method*. While we have difficulties with his predilection for speaking of "revealed writings," since this serves to deny the humanity of Scripture, we agree with him that our hermeneutic methodology must be theologically informed.

Edgar Krentz, in his *Historical-Critical Method* (Philadelphia: Fortress Press, 1975), seeks to retain the historical-critical method understood as historical-literary investigation but purged of rationalistic presuppositions. We concur with Krentz that theology cannot simply return to a precritical age.

Similarly, Peter Stuhlmacher endeavors to make a place for historical criticism in the service of faith. In his *Historical Criticism and Theological Interpretation of Scripture*, trans. Roy A. Harrisville (Philadelphia: Fortress Press, 1977). For his rather harsh, but nonetheless sometimes telling, criticisms of Gerhard Maier see pp. 66–71.

32. Thomas F. Torrance, *Space, Time and Resurrection* (Grand Rapids: Eerdmans, 1976), p. 12.

33. We allow for the fact that both induction and deduction will be used both prior to faith and in the service of faith, but the truth of revelation can be apprehended only by faith. Moreover, the processes of reason before faith can

only lead to dead ends, since it is not until reason is turned around by the Spirit that it becomes fruitful in a Christian sense.

34. Friedrich Schleiermacher, *The Christian Faith,* vol. 2, ed. H.R. Mackintosh and J. S. Stewart (New York: Harper & Row, 1963), p. 551.

35. Cited in Donald Baillie, *God Was in Christ* (New York: Charles Scribner's Sons, 1948), p. 115.

36. Whitney Oates, ed., *Basic Writings of Saint Augustine,* vol. 1 (New York: Random House, 1948), p. 675.

37. Karl Barth, *The Epistle to the Romans,* trans. from 6th ed. by Edwyn C. Hoskyns, p. 213.

38. This Barthian note can definitely be discerned in Rudolf Ehrlich, who explains: "Not only redemption but also salvation, not only objective but also subjective justification, has already taken place in Christ, the Elect One in whom all men are elected. . . . It is He who believes, trusts and loves God, and He does so in our humanity, in our name and on our behalf." *Rome—Opponent or Partner?* p. 165.

39. Helmut Thielicke, *The Evangelical Faith,* II, trans. & ed. Geoffrey Bromiley (Grand Rapids: Eerdmans, 1977), p. 402.

40. Cited in Emil Brunner, *The Letter to the Romans,* trans. H. A. Kennedy (Philadelphia: Westminster Press, 1959), p. 16.

41. Thielicke, *The Evangelical Faith,* II, p. 395.

42. John R. W. Stott, *Christ the Controversialist* (Downers Grove, Ill.: Inter-Varsity Press, 1972), p. 32.

43. Jürgen Moltmann, *The Church in the Power of the Spirit,* p. 359.

44. On the Chicago Call conference, held in April, 1977, see Robert E. Webber and Donald G. Bloesch, eds., *The Orthodox Evangelicals* (Nashville: Thomas Nelson, 1978).

45. A high view of the sacraments that acknowledges their vital role in communicating the remission of sins is found in the Lutheran *Book of Concord:* "This righteousness is offered to us by the Holy Spirit through the Gospel and in the sacraments, and is applied, appropriated, and accepted by faith, so that thus believers have reconciliation with God, forgiveness of sins, the grace of God, adoption, and the inheritance of eternal life." Theodore G. Tappert, ed. and trans. (Philadelphia: Fortress Press, 1959), p. 541.

A high view of the sacraments is also reflected in the Scots Confession, the Shorter Westminster Catechism, and Calvin's Geneva Catechism, all of which affirm the sacrament as a means of grace. Zwingli's position, which saw the sacrament as a memorial to grace given in the past, is, for the most part, not represented in the major Reformed confessions. Bullinger's mediating position, which affirmed grace given in conjunction with the sacramental sign (as distinguished from *through* this sign) is mirrored in the Second Helvetic Confession, the Heidelberg Catechism, and perhaps also the Westminster Confession. Parts of this last confession can be understood in a purely Zwinglian sense.

46. Regrettably, it connotes that Christ is somewhat bound up in the elements, whereas in reality the elements are taken up into the body of Christ, though never losing their identity. Christ comes into the hearts of the communicants in and through the elements, but also in and through the whole sacramental celebration.

47. If we contend, as Calvin did, that the church began with Abraham, then the church definitely has chronological priority over the Scriptures. Moreover, it was the fourth-century Catholic church that canonized the books that now comprise Holy Scripture. At the same time, because the message of the Bible comes from God himself, we must assert the ontological priority of Scripture over the church.

48. Thomas F. Torrance, *Theology in Reconciliation* (Grand Rapids: Eerdmans, 1975), p. 283.

49. See Heiko Oberman, *"Simul gemitus et raptus: Luther und die Mystik."* In *The Church, Mysticism, Sanctification and the Natural in Luther's Thought,* ed. Ivar Asheim (Philadelphia: Fortress Press, 1967), pp. 34 ff. Also see Bengt R. Hoffman, *Luther and the Mystics* (Minneapolis: Augsburg, 1976).

50. Emanuel Hirsch maintains that the most faithful interpreters of Luther have not been the Lutheran scholastics but the early Pietists such as Arndt, Spener, and Francke.

51. Again in opposition to much classical mysticism, as well as modern existentialism (Bultmann, Ogden), we maintain that the knowledge we have of God is not only or primarily "nonobjective," but also truly objective, since God makes himself an object to our understanding in his revelation.

52. See Christopher J. R. Armstrong, *Evelyn Underhill* (Grand Rapids: Eerdmans, 1975).

53. Evelyn Underhill, *Collected Papers,* ed. Lucy Menzies (London: Longmans, Green, 1946), p. 115.

54. A. B. Grosart, ed. *The Complete Works of Richard Sibbes,* VII (Edinburgh: James Nichol, 1862–1864) p. 510.

55. Karl Barth, *Theology and Church,* trans. Louise Pettibone Smith (New York: Harper & Row, 1962), p. 313.

56. We also regard the Nicene Creed, the Heidelberg Catechism, the Augsburg Confession, and the Westminster Confession as examples of true confessions of faith. The Presbyterian Confession of 1967 falls short of a genuine confession in our understanding.

57. G. C. Berkouwer, *The Church,* trans. James E. Davison (Grand Rapids: Eerdmans, 1976), p. 389.

58. *Ibid.,* p. 303.

59. Eberhard Busch, *Karl Barth,* p. 375. Barth opposed the Confession of the No Other Gospel movement because he felt that it was not related to *praxis* and that it signified a return to the past more than a breakthrough into the future. He wrote to that movement's Dortmund Assembly: "If your *correct* confession to Jesus Christ crucified and raised again for us according to the Holy Scriptures includes and expresses" a position on the burning issues of the time, "then it is a *genuine,* valuable, and fruitful confession. If not, then for all its correctness, it is a dead, cheap, pharisaical confession which strains out gnats and swallows camels." In George Hunsinger, *Karl Barth and Radical Politics* (Philadelphia: Westminster Press, 1976), p. 123. For Barth the No Other Gospel movement did not effectively challenge the principalities and powers of our time. This contention is debatable, however, since that movement certainly has confronted the powers of the world inside the church.

60. Schleiermacher, *On Religion,* p. 95.

61. Cited in John Powell Clayton, ed., *Ernst Troeltsch and the Future of Theology* (Cambridge: Cambridge University Press, 1976), p. 89.

62. Simon Tugwell, *Did You Receive the Spirit?* (New York: Paulist Press, 1972), p. 60.

63. *Ibid.*

64. Irenaeus, *Against Heresies* IV, 20, 7.

65. See Donald G. Bloesch, *The Ground of Certainty* (Grand Rapids: Eerdmans, 1971).

66. Faith in the Christian sense transcends reason but does not contradict it. Faith opposes the direction of our reasoning but not the created structures of reason.

67. One interpreter of Irenaeus says that his "epistemology proceeds from revelation to reason, from God to humans and the world. For him, there is no other method for theology than depending on the Holy Scriptures, guided by the tradition of the church." In Dai Sil Kim, "Irenaeus of Lyons and Teilhard de Chardin: A Comparative Study of 'Recapitulation' and 'Omega'," *Journal of Ecumenical Studies,* vol. 13, no. 1 (Winter 1976), [pp. 69–93], p. 71.

68. See Karl Barth, *Church Dogmatics* I, 1 (Trans. G. T. Thomson), p. 31.

69. Cited in G. C. Berkouwer, *A Half Century of Theology,* ed. and trans. Lewis Smedes (Grand Rapids: Eerdmans, 1977), p. 38.

70. These three types of theology signify the three options in theological method. The theology of accommodation is reflected in the "Christ of culture" approach of liberal Protestantism, where the highest values of the culture are given Christian significance. It is also apparent in syncretistic mysticism, which presupposes a point of identity between the experiencing subject and the ultimate which appears in religious experience.

The theology of correlation is represented by both the older scholasticism, which sought to build a supranatural structure upon a natural substructure, and the "ecstatic naturalism" of Paul Tillich, who eschews any synthesis between revelation and the wisdom of culture but who acknowledges that cultural insights point beyond themselves to revelation. Tillich insists that the answer is derived not from human existence (as in culture-Protestantism) but from historical revelation.

The theology of confrontation is a theology of the Word of God because it begins with the biblical revelation and not with the mood of the culture. It does not confine itself to the biblical revelation, however, for it brings this Word to bear upon the whole of existence. It has affinities with the "Christ transforming culture" approach of Irenaeus, Augustine, Calvin, the Puritans, Abraham Kuyper, and Karl Barth. Though Augustine's principal motto was "I believe in order to understand," he nonetheless belongs only partially to an evangelical theology of confrontation, for he sees a creative though subordinate role for reason prior to faith.

71. Cited in John R. W. Stott, *Christ the Controversialist,* p. 197.

72. Cited in *National Catholic Reporter,* vol. 13, no. 13 (January 21, 1977), p. 17.

73. Among those in the past and present who approximate the kind of catholic evangelicalism we espouse are Count von Zinzendorf, Wilhelm Löhe, Peter Forsyth, Nathan Söderblom, Daniel Jenkins, and Thomas Torrance.

John Nevin and Philip Schaff of the Mercersburg movement should also be included; Schaff, it should be noted, maintained his warm relationship with the pietistic Evangelical Alliance, even after embarking on the road to an evangelical catholicism. We should also mention in this connection the Reformers Luther and Calvin, though in the heat of the controversies of their time they were compelled to discard more in the Catholic tradition than they might have deemed necessary in a more tranquil period of history.

74. The Dutch Catholic scholar W. F. Dankbaar is more honest and also more courageous when he says that the Tridentine decree of justification needs "not merely a new interpretation, but a genuine revision and if not this, the doctrine of Trent will have to be replaced by a completely new definition." Cited in G. C. Berkouwer, *The Second Vatican Council and the New Catholicism,* trans. Lewis B. Smedes (Grand Rapids: Eerdmans, 1965), p. 48.

75. *Theonomy* is here used to denote authority centered not in an external creed or institution (as in *heteronomy*) nor in the inner light or reason (as in *autonomy*) but in the living Jesus Christ who speaks to us through creed, institution, and conscience, but who infinitely transcends these.

76. Bernard Loomer, "S-I-Z-E," *Criterion,* vol. 13, no. 3 (Spring 1974), [pp. 5–8], p. 8.

77. Langdon Gilkey, *Reaping the Whirlwind* (New York: Seabury Press, 1976), p. 240. See also Gilkey's *Naming the Whirlwind* (New York: Bobbs-Merrill, 1969), where he states the case for a natural theology based on the phenomenology of secular human experience. For an illuminating evangelical critique of Gilkey's theology see Clark H. Pinnock, "Langdon Gilkey: A Guide to His Theology," *TSF News and Reviews* (Madison, Wisc.: Theological Students Fellowship, 1977), pp. 15, 16.

78. John Hick, ed., *The Myth of God Incarnate* (Philadelphia: Westminster Press, 1977).

79. A theology of radical immanence whose appeal is to the authority of the totality of human experience, including sensual experience, is to be found in Tom F. Driver, *Patterns of Grace: Human Experience as Word of God* (New York: Harper & Row, 1978). Driver in effect replaces historical theism with a psychosomatically oriented vitalism.

SUBJECT INDEX

agnosticism, 227
Amana Society, 39, 116
Anabaptists, 9, 36, 66, 115, 141, 190, 192
analogy, 275
anchorites, 33
angels, 97, 131, 132, 133, 135, 136, 148, 152, 174, 180, 183, 205, 217
Anglicanism, 38, 288
Anglo-Catholicism, 24, 25, 288
antinomianism, 61
anxiety, 165
apocalypticism, 174, 175, 177, 196, 204
apokatastasis, 218, 221
apologetics, 4, 33, 83, 237, 266, 275, 286, 287
apologists, 33
apostolic succession, 113, 120, 129, 279
Arianism, 280
Arminianism, 45, 60, 253, 277
asceticism, 33, 37, 43, 48, 54, 153, 257
Assemblies of God, 21, 22
Assumption of Mary, 241
assurance of salvation, 11, 19, 26, 38, 91, 106, 127, 256
Augsburg Confession, 114, 289, 295
Augustinianism, 56, 240

Bahaism, 254, 263
baptism, 6, 11–15, 22, 24, 25, 26, 28, 29, 89, 112, 114, 119, 127, 128, 147, 166, 215, 236, 257, 271, 279
baptism of the Holy Spirit, 7, 11 ff., 16, 17, 21, 22, 115
Barmen Confession, 271, 283
Belgic Confession, 113
Bible, the Holy
  its authority, xii, 1, 2, 3, 268, 269 ff., 280, 284, 291
  its inerrancy, 5, 189, 270, 282, 293
  its inspiration, 272, 274, 280, 292
biblical prophecy, 151, 194, 195, 204, 207, 267
Bishop Hill community, 39
Buddhism, 243, 246, 248, 262

Calvinism, 55, 87, 93, 216, 224, 266
capitalism, 147
Catholic Apostolic church, 116, 121, 190
celibacy, 34, 39, 73

Chalcedon, Council of, 247
charismatic gifts, *See* gifts of the Spirit.
charismatic movement, 27, 236, 285
Chicago Call conference, 279, 280, 294
Children of God, 260
Christadelphians, 194, 219, 236
Christian Catholic church, 116
Christian perfection, 21, 36, 43, 47 ff., 68
Christian Science, 64, 254
Christocracy, 149
Christomonism, 62
church
  its authority, 241, 280
  mission of, 108, 130, 155 ff.
  unity of, 189, 283, 288, 289
Churches of Christ, 236
clericalism, 158
communion of saints, 178
Confessing church, 171
Confession of 1967, 295
confession of sin, 58, 74, 80, 91, 113
confessions of faith, 280, 283, 284, 290, 294
confirmation, 13, 25, 30, 127, 279
Confucianism, 246
conscience, 68, 142, 169, 241, 274
contemplation, 33, 48, 53, 54, 57, 73, 243
conversion, 7, 9, 11, 15, 18, 19, 20, 23, 27, 55, 75, 90, 95, 127, 159, 161, 165, 166, 167, 169, 221, 233, 252, 265, 288
counsels of perfection, 34, 47
creation, 145, 146, 151, 220, 221, 240, 242, 243, 246
culture-religion, 64, 242, 266, 296

damnation, 87, 136, 211, 215, 222, 223, 232, 233, 234
deaconesses, 120
death, 69, 170, 178, 182, 186, 188, 211, 215, 219
deification, 33, 238
deism, 260
demonic powers, 17, 131 ff., 144, 191, 196, 203, 215
discipleship, 9, 18, 23, 32, 34, 40, 53, 97
dispensationalism, 142, 190, 195, 200, 206, 236, 275, 280
divorce, 39
dogmatics, 286, 290